Latinos and the New Immigrant Church

Latinos and the New Immigrant Church

David A. Badillo

The Johns Hopkins University Press   Baltimore

© 2006 The Johns Hopkins University Press
All rights reserved. Published 2006
Printed in the United States of America on acid-free paper
9 8 7 6 5 4 3 2 1

The Johns Hopkins University Press
2715 North Charles Street
Baltimore, Maryland 21218-4363
www.press.jhu.edu

Library of Congress Cataloging-in-Publication Data
Badillo, David A.
Latinos and the new immigrant church / David A. Badillo.
    p.   cm.
Includes bibliographical references (p.) and index.
ISBN 0-8018-8387-3 (hardcover : alk. paper) — ISBN 0-8018-8388-1
(pbk. : alk. paper)
1. Hispanic Americans—Religion.   I. Title.
BR563.H57B33 2006
282'.7308968—dc22   2005027697

A catalog record for this book is available from the British Library.

Contents

Illustrations

Acknowledgments

Many mentors and colleagues have contributed to the completion of this work, as have kind friends and family members. Richard C. Wade first encouraged me to study Latinos from an urban historical perspective. Jay Dolan, as editor of the three-volume *Notre Dame History of Hispanic Catholics*, along with Jaime Vidal, Gilberto Hinojosa, Anthony Stevens-Arroyo, Ana Maria Diaz-Stevens, and others who contributed to the project introduced me to the rigors of studying Latino Catholicism. I am also grateful for the ongoing assistance and encouragement of Stephen Warner, Rafael Nuñez-Cedeño, Gilberto Cardenas, and Timothy Matovina, as well as the members of CEHILA USA. Librarians and archivists at countless locales generously helped procure important data.

The University of Illinois at Chicago provided generous travel and research assistance for the launching of this project and the UIC Great Cities Institute granted me a released-time fellowship which resulted in expansion of the study to include Chicago. The University of Notre Dame's History Department and Institute for Latino Studies warmly received me as, respectively, visiting professor and visiting fellow, for several semesters. A particularly insightful manuscript review by Manuel Vasquez resulted in a much improved final product. Mary Reardon provided very careful, thoughtful, and timely editorial assistance. Herminio Martinez and the staff of the Bronx Institute at Lehman College of the City University of New York have graciously supported my work on the manuscript's final revisions. Most important, however, I owe thanks to my wife, Milagros Benitez, for her constant support.

Portions of some chapters were previously published in other forms, as follows: Chapter 2: "Between Alienation and Ethnicity: Church Structures and Mexican-American Catholicism in San Antonio, 1910–1940," *Journal of American Ethnic History* 16 (September 1997): 62–83. Chapter 6: "Mexicanos and Suburban Parish Communities: Religion, Space, and

Identity in Contemporary Chicago," *Journal of Urban History* 31 (November 2004): 23–46; "Religion and Transnational Migration in Chicago: The Case of the Potosinos," *Journal of the Illinois State Historical Society* 94 (Winter 2002): 420–440.

Introduction

To fully understand Latinos in the United States today, one must understand their unique, complex and ever-evolving relationship with the Catholic Church, the Catholic religion, and the various syncretisms born of Catholic interactions in the Americas. The story of the Latino Church is examined here through the history of Latino Catholicism in four urban locales—San Antonio, New York City, Miami, and Chicago—with particular attention to religious tradition, city, and ethnic identity. A comparative approach seeks integration of the religious histories of the three primary Latino groups—Mexican Americans, Puerto Ricans, and Cubans (and, to a lesser extent, more recent migrants)—highlighting distinctive characteristics of each. As the stories are rich and varied, this study of Latino Catholicism and the Catholic Church in the United States illuminates differences and similarities among peoples of Latin American origin and in Latino Catholicism in different cities and regions.

The evolution of the U.S. Latino "immigrant church" has long needed a carefully nuanced look. The earliest communities that arose in northern Mexico and the Caribbean well before the formation of the United States as a nation are a fruitful place to start. This book also provides a detailed look at developments in Latino Catholicism in the early through the middle twentieth century, preceding the vast ecclesiastical and demographic changes beginning around 1965. It was an era that proved central in the development of Latino urbanization and ethnicity, yet Latino religion in this era has been relatively understudied.

This analysis foregrounds historical, sociological, and theological themes. Likewise, it highlights continuities and contrasts between Latin American and U.S. Latino culture and religion, emphasizing the contours of day-to-day life in the context of institutional and lived Catholicism. This text explores "popular" Catholicism, which truly reflects the faith and practice of the majority of people. Practitioners of this popular religion, in its various forms, do not seek to emulate the educated elites, and they show little awareness of the theological issues disputed in the Protestant and Catholic reformations. Popular Catholicism has embodied the visual, oral, and dramatic aspects of the religious practice of the common people searching for a personal spiritual connection. Professional clergy and religious of all national backgrounds have often played upon this sensibility to promote ritualistic observance, but they have also frequently ignored it to invoke a more formal, and often alien, institutional Catholicism. Latino popular Catholicism was often believed to reflect ignorance, superstition, or paganism.[1]

Roots of the Tradition

Latino Catholicism owes its origins to the contest between Iberian Catholicism, fortified by Indian and African religious strains, and a competing Northern European version. Many religious traditions and customs were common across Latin America, yet problems such as lack of sufficient clergy, isolation from urban religious centers, and anticlerical postindependence governments meant that Iberian popular religion developed and changed at different rates in various regions of Latin America.

Roots of the North American scene lie, of course, in Europe. In the sixteenth century Christian religious traditions diverged as the Protestant Reformation fractured Western Christendom and led to a permanent schism between a single Roman Catholic church and several Protestant ones. Wars of religion pitted Catholics and Protestants against one another in France, Germany, and Ireland and produced rival sects of Protestants vying for ecclesiastical supremacy in England and Scotland.[2]

The Council of Trent, reacting to the challenges posed by the Protestant Reformation, met intermittently from 1545 until 1563 in Trento, Italy. Its reforms solidified parish development for the next four centuries and also strengthened the role of the bishop in his diocese. One of the goals was to regularize Catholic practices and priests' activity, which had in many cases taken on varying, nonstandard forms. The sacraments were defined, under threat of excommunication, as not only baptism, Eucharist, and penance but also confirmation, ordination, marriage, and final unction. At the same time the language of the Mass was standardized. Every parish within a diocese was to have a fixed territory; marriages performed without the pastor's consent were invalid; pastors were to be selected by the bishop and guaranteed an income, though missionary religious orders retained the power to preach and to administer the sacraments without the express authorization of bishops.[3] While decrying superstition, the council did approve the veneration of Mary and other saints.[4]

The Council of Trent reorganization imposed greater bureaucracy, but its rules were less closely adhered to in Latin America than in northern Europe. Inefficient transportation and communication reinforced the isolation of the New World and encouraged a remarkable resiliency of medieval forms of piety, especially processions and mystery plays, despite the council's reforms. Further, the Spanish crown did not allow dissemination of the council's decrees until well after 1570, which had the effect of discouraging liturgical changes in preaching and catechesis for generations. A concern for "orthodoxy" of expression that emerged in the centuries of post-Tridentine Catholicism that developed in northern Europe, filled with anti-Protestantism, tended to suppress dramatic ways of expressing the faith, whereas the Catholicism preserved in Latin America reflected the popular faith lived in rural Spain. Spanish Catholicism—to a greater extent even than Catholicism in Italy and Portugal, and unlike that in northern European countries—was only slightly affected by competition with Protestantism and developed into a monopolistic, imperialistic state Catholicism. The Iberian religion brought to the Americas had survived the seven centuries of the Spanish *reconquista*, during which Christians fought, traded with, and lived alongside Muslims and Jews. The fanaticism accompanying the final stages of conquest of the "infidel" in 1492 was marked by a renaissance of piety and devotion, of monasticism, and of theological learning, a renewed religious fervor felt in the villages.[5]

Tridentine Catholicism in Latin America thus retained many medieval practices and attitudes, though it evolved considerably in other respects. Throughout the colonial period, no pontifical document could be executed in any of Spain's territories without the royal approval, which limited access to papal edicts. The Catholic Reformation in the Americas was in practice reduced to the creation of seminaries and schools, mainly for Spaniards and the white *criollo* (native born, of pure-blooded European ancestry) elite, and to stopping some major clerical abuses. In addition to the many members of religious orders who came to the Americas as missionaries, informal teaching by lay Spaniards along with Amerindian, African, and *mestizo* laity who entered the church helped to propagate the Christian faith.[6]

In Spain during the seventeenth and eighteenth centuries, a constant tension existed between the Roman Church, allied with religious orders, and the local church, identified with nation, town, or village, which tended to rely on locally based devotions. This was the case in Latin America as well. Latin American expressions of fervent piety continue to exist outside the liturgy, including the use of home altars, or *altarcitos*. Other elements of popular worship practices were devotion to the Virgin Mary and to saints, as well as to the suffering Christ, *posadas*, *ex-votos*, and Día de los Muertos. In regions dominated by Amerindians, evangelization often encouraged native traditions of dance, music, and crafts. Pious artistic styles of religious imagery, including crucifixes and *santos de palo* (carved wooden images of saints), echoed those of medieval Spain. Many U.S. Latino communities have preserved versions of these songs, rites, and dramas, and thus they can still be witnessed and heard.[7]

Latino religious tradition resisted the rationalism of the Enlightenment. Later attempts at implanting a more doctrinally oriented and sophisticated post-Tridentine Catholicism tended to remain largely at the level of the colonial elites. Increasingly, however, nationalism weakened medieval tradition. Today's Latin American Catholicism reflects the differing impact of northern versus southern Europe—in simple terms, Ireland versus Spain. After 1760, Jansenist influences in Ireland became particularly strong and came to demarcate northern European and U.S. Catholicism from Spanish and Mediterranean Catholicism. In general, today's Latinos, at the intersection of Spanish-Mexican and the doctrinal and austere northern European Catholicism adopted in the United States, can be seen as a product of a religious synthesis. Unlike northern European Catholicism, Latino Catholicism blends pre- and post-Tridentine influences.

The marginal status imposed on indigenous peoples in the Latin American church is another factor in the development of a distinctive popular Catholicism. Their marginalization helps explain their attitude toward frequent Communion, for example. While most Mexicans absorbed European Jansenism's sense of the laity's unworthiness to receive Communion and accepted that they must confess their sins to a priest each time before receiving it, in general they do not seem personally troubled or guilt ridden about "living in sin" because they have not confessed recently.[8]

Theologian Anthony Stevens-Arroyo argues that Latin American Catholicism is rooted largely in the seventeenth century, characterized by the Baroque emphasis on symbol, ritual, and celebration and on Christian exuberance. Moreover, he believes that Marian devotion emerged not as a medieval or pagan carryover but from the sentimentalism and search for universalism that surfaced in the Baroque era, which was also manifested in the massive cathedrals of Mexican cities built in the era's ornate style. An example of a largely post-Tridentine devotion is the special attention to the passion through *cofradías* (confraternities) and the emphasis on the crucified Christ, a distinctive feature of Latino religiosity. The doctrines and worldview born of Trent were more generally present in late colonial Catholicism.[9]

Anthropologist William Christian Jr. sees continuity before and after the Council of Trent and believes that elements that are supposedly pre-Tridentine could have been brought to the New World not merely in the decades of intensive evangelization prior to the middle of the sixteenth century, when the Council of Trent met, but over the following centuries as well, when devotion came to be expressed through images portraying a vivid "sacred" landscape, through strong brotherhoods, and by reenactment of the nativity and Christ's passion. Moreover, the "concentration on Mary, Christ as Child, and Christ Crucified to the gradual exclusion of local and localized saints" which gained favor during the sixteenth century had roots in Spanish, or "Mediterranean," devotion.[10]

Less concerned with orthodoxy than was the post-Tridentine church, many European missionaries evangelized through nonverbal activities, such as processions, statues, paintings, music, and drama. Whereas the overall message of the missionaries was profoundly Christocentric, they participated in the late colonial process of growing identification of the Virgin Mary, particularly the connection between the Mary of Catholic popular devotions and local manifestation, such as the Virgin of Guadalupe in Mexico, la Virgen de la Caridad del Cobre in Cuba, and la Virgen de Montserrat or la Virgen del Carmen in Puerto Rico. In each area, the masses appeal to Mary for succor amid life's trials and tribulations. Within Latino communities it is often women, mothers, and grandmothers who are the leaders of popular religion. They offer blessings, arrange home altars, say the prayers, provide children and grandchildren with religious instruction, and lead the family in religious song. The strong Marian spirituality among Latinos results from the dominant role of women in popular religion.[11]

Mexican Americans, Puerto Ricans, and Cuban Americans—the migrants and descendants of these three largest of the Latin American groups—even today maintain different customs and adhere to distinct traditions; they are anything but interchangeable. Common denominators in the Latino experience include elements derived from the colonial heritage—especially the Spanish language and Catholicism—as well as long-standing racial intermixture. An important outcome was the increased religious influence of the mestizo, who bridged chasms between cleric and layperson, between conquerors and the conquered, establishing both a religious and a secular cultural identity that remained well after the colonial era. Theologians have come to recognize much of contemporary Latin American and Latino popular Catholicism as "mestizo Catholicism."[12]

Indigenous encounters with the mission communities were marked by cultural clash, harsh treatment, and death from European diseases. Parishes and military chapels have been the homes of Latino Catholic faith communities from colonial times to the present. Included in the mid-eighteenth-century heartland were the Hispanic Caribbean and mission territories now known as New Mexico, Texas, and California.[13]

Parish, City, and Ethnic Identity

Migration has forced the U.S. church, as well as its constituents, to adopt a broad hemispheric consciousness bridging Latino and Latin American worlds. As an indicator of space, boundaries, and community, one of our major facets of study here, the parish—the churches themselves—cannot be ignored; it is the point at which the institutional, hierarchical church and the people encounter one another. Parishes in U.S. cities and suburbs constitute both the ecclesial and the social site of sacraments, such as Communion and confession; they are the sites of religious ritual as well as ethnic group identity. Yet Latinos' link to their parish has been historically weaker than that of immigrants of European origins in terms of Mass attendance, receiving the sacraments, and general participation—financial as well as social—in parish communities in accordance with the expectations of clergy and hierarchy.

Historian Jay Dolan notes that mid-nineteenth-century anti-Catholicism contributed to a "defensive" dependency on parishes and a retreat to separateness, designed to neutralize Protestantism and secularism. Urban nativist violence opened a new chapter in the struggle to define American Catholicism, as the number of Catholic immigrants in the United States surged. In the following decades, efforts expanded to construct a universe of institutions for the temporal and spiritual well-being of Catholics, while a war of words continued over the compatibility of Catholicism and U.S. political culture. With the onset of massive waves of European immigration in the 1800s, the American Catholic parish adopted the model of the national (or language) parish, where the community retained its native language. The national parish formed the basis for the immigrant church, led by clergy (and later bishops) from the homeland, with sermons and confessions conducted in the native tongue. This contrasted with what was known as the "territorial" (or geographic) parish, which utilized English. These parishes served people based exclusively on where they lived, and they did little to help parishioners retain their original language, cultural practices, sense of group identity, or divergent religious aspects of the homeland.[14]

The pattern for Latino migrants has been different since 1930, after which few national parishes have been formed. "Integrated" parishes arose among those national parishes already in existence, which were losing elderly European ethnics and sometimes taking in Latinos. Likewise many territorial parishes, to varying degrees depending on local urban configurations, have served Latinos and non-Latinos, offering them separate language services and distinct parish organizations. In many areas non-Latinos have successfully resisted, or until now avoided, mixing with Latinos. In other cases, parishes have been overwhelmed with Latino newcomers, making for "national parishes" that remain officially unrecognized by Rome and the local diocese. Few Latino churches today are recognized national parishes. The hierarchy successfully gained control of the church's institutional development in the United States while combating nativist anti-Catholic agitation.[15]

The structures and challenges of parish growth have in turn helped redefine the Church's role with both new immigrants from Latin America and Latino "ethnics" (second generation and beyond). The waning of national parishes in the early to mid-twentieth century, brought on by episcopal policies, occurred just as Latinos in the Southwest, Northeast, and Midwest were supplanting ethnics of European origin in urban America. This, in turn, set in motion new ethnic patterns and dilemmas, especially for Latin American immigrants, notably in the areas of language and cultural retention, which are both important factors in adjusting to the larger society. Parishes still reinforce neighborhood and ethnic boundaries, but their role in assimilation and in offering a homogenous religious product has changed.[16]

The function of parishes, territorial, national, and integrated, has much to do with the changing urban landscape. Many churchgoing Latinos do not attend their territorial parish but drive or take the bus to a church in a predominantly Latino area. This happens especially after a person or family who lived in such an area moves out of it to a more "integrated" one; in such cases their new parish often cannot compete with the original one's greater feel for the homeland. Such parishes thus become de facto national parishes. Territorial or geographic parishes predominate, even in urban areas, but the Catholic Church has accepted the concept of an immigrant community's choosing local church affiliation in de facto national parishes, which offer little pieces of the homeland. Such churches often enjoy considerable involvement of parishioners.[17]

Latinos may seek the parish for the support network it provides during hard times and turn to the parish for the celebration of special occasions like baptism, marriage, the feast of the Virgin of Guadalupe or of a local patron saint, and the *quinceañera*—the debut of a girl who has reached her fifteenth birthday (the term *quinceañera* applies to both the girl who is having her birthday and the celebration itself). However, otherwise they often spend their religious lives apart from the parish and its church.

Mexicans celebrate the quinceañera in a special way. The custom probably originated in Spain, though some scholars find roots in Aztec or Toltec cultural rituals. The celebration is generally recognized as the religious and secular celebration of a young girl's rite of passage to maturity, her role in the community, and, in the United States, that community's reassertion of ethnic identity. The ceremony generally begins with a Mass after the quinceañera enters the church in procession with an entourage of female attendants, sometimes with male escorts. After the homily and Communion, the quinceañera offers a prayer and a bouquet of flowers at the altar of Our Lady of Guadalupe.[18]

The presence of Latin Americans in cities has contributed to the reshaping of U.S. urban life in distinct patterns. Immigrants try to carve out "sacred spaces" in their city through pilgrimages, festivals, processions, and other public religious behaviors. There are, of course, no fully representative "Latino" or "Hispanic" cities, though the ones featured in this study—San Antonio, New York, Miami, and Chicago—provide helpful contrasts and comparisons. Other cities could have been included, and they are mentioned and recognized in this book as part of the broad scope of urban Latino Catholicism. San Antonio is examined because there, more than in any other Mexican-American city, one finds clear historical patterns of Catholic settlement from the Spanish colonial era through the present. There you can see Catholic Spain and you can see Mexico, patterns predating twentieth-century Mexican-American developments.

As for Chicago, New York City, and Miami, their choice for study is self-explanatory given demographic and historical patterns. Latino Chicago, relatively unstudied from a historical perspective, is a city where large numbers of virtually all major Latino groups have lived for decades and it has emerged as a Latino mecca of sorts. Here, as elsewhere, large-scale migration of refugees and immigrants from Central America in the late twentieth century arose out of civil strife, economic instability, and religious persecution in the homeland; these factors affected parish communities in Chicago and elsewhere north of the border. In the United States, Mexican-American Catholics are dominant numerically, and they pioneered in the urban Southwest and Midwest. Puerto Ricans and Cubans, meanwhile, have a firm grip in other cities and regions and have distinctive religious institutions and patterns of popular observance reflecting their backgrounds and circumstances.

New ecclesial landscapes emerging among Latinos in the postmodern city circumvent the parish, opening new forms of immigrant Catholicism. The tapestry is rich. Public displays of religion, for example popular and/or Marian devotion expressed in lay organizations such as brotherhoods, or religious movements such as the *cursillos* (retreats for laypeople organized to renew individuals' Catholic faith), and the charismatic renewal movement, all represent different aspects of Latino Catholicism. Some charismatic Catholics—followers of a post-1965 Vatican II movement within the Church that espouses highly personal, emotional methods of prayer, often led by priests from the homeland—may refuse to participate in the feast of the parish's patron saint because they abstain from alcohol and dancing. These examples demonstrate a dynamic and open-ended quality to the concept of the sacred within a wider, increasingly global context.[19]

Issues of identity emerge as people "negotiate" religion in new urban spaces and face new social, economic, and political arrangements, as well as ethnic tensions, in their daily lives and social networks. Latino Catholic identities are being regenerated in cities and parishes, with pastoral theology increasingly a part of the process. New cultural and religious data call for reexamination of contemporary city life as Latino religious needs are expressed and modified in distinctive ways. New immigrants, especially women and youth, have contributed to this reformulation, both within and outside of sanctioned, or official, models of local church organization. Transnational trends, such as migrants' participating in parish activities both in homeland communities and in urban U.S. barrios, will also be examined here.

The Structure of This Book

Chapter One explores the convergence of European, Caribbean, Mexican, and early North American history that forms the background for Latino historical identity. Religion lies at the core of this foundation. The chapter examines the roles of the institutional church and popular religiosity during the formative era of Latino Catholicism on the northern

frontier of New Spain and (later independent) Mexico and in the Hispanic Caribbean. It places Spanish colonial conflicts in the context of
Anglo-American expansion—the beginnings of manifest destiny and
the conquest of Texas, contrasted with the rapid rise and slow decline of
Spanish colonial power. Preoccupied with slavery, the Western frontier
movement, and European immigration, U.S. historians have tended to
overlook many aspects of this history, while Latin American historians
have not yet fully examined migration and urbanization, particularly in
the twentieth-century transnational context.

Chapter Two highlights San Antonio's important connection with
the Catholic Church in Mexico in the early twentieth century amid that
country's revolutionary turmoil. From before the 1910 revolution to
1930, the Church in Mexico faced anticlericalism from the revolutionary government and attracted support from the U.S. hierarchy. Religious
workers fled this persecution, including dozens of Mexican priests and
nuns. The hundreds of thousands of Mexican immigrants who crossed
the border in those two decades brought distinct types of Catholicism
into the mix in hundreds of parishes in the Southwest and Midwest, in
some cases overtaking U.S.-born *Tejanos* (Texas-born Mexican Americans) in terms of influence on religious and secular San Antonio society. The chapter shows how Mexican-American Catholicism has resisted
Americanization.

Puerto Rican migrants are the focus of Chapter Three. Like other
groups from Latin America, they came in waves reaching back to the
nineteenth century. Their numbers in New York City grew precipitously
in the 1920s and 1930s, a time when their reception by both the U.S.-run
colonial church in Puerto Rico and the immigrant church in New York
City crystallized. Puerto Rico's history of unrelieved colonialism under
both Spanish and U.S. rule has played a crucial role in its religious evolution and is examined in this book through urban experiences in the
homeland and the U.S. barrio and through the life of a Puerto Rican
family matriarch. Puerto Ricans' struggle for an urban identity in the
East Harlem and Brooklyn barrios that they have dominated since 1920
involved religious elements that became first sublimated and then transformed in the face of pressing survival needs, cultural conflicts with non-
Latino clergy and laity, and alienation produced by racial discrimination
in the secular world.

Chapter Four considers top-down episcopal leadership, focusing on
San Antonio, Chicago, and New York, roughly between 1940 and 1965,
a time of considerable Latino migration. The major players at that time

were Archbishop Robert E. Lucey in San Antonio, Cardinal Francis Spellman in New York City, and Cardinals Samuel Stritch and Albert Meyer in Chicago. During these years in the Southwest and Midwest, the Bishops Committee for the Spanish-Speaking, a regional bishops' conference, gave Latino Catholicism a social justice emphasis through its service to rural and urban immigrants and even, for a spell, to Mexican contract workers participating in the Bracero program. A renewed and sustained influx of immigrants beginning in the 1940s boosted older settlements and led to the expansion of parish networks. Especially in the Northeast and Midwest, immigrants were allowed to develop their own parishes, and, wherever possible, priests of the same national background were assigned. The relationship between the United States and Puerto Rico—unique in both religious and secular terms—allowed for considerable experimentation on the part of Spellman and those clerics working under his charge in the Archdiocese of New York.

Chapter Five describes the attempts of Cuban refugees in Miami to build a religious community and to reconstruct the society they felt they had lost through the monumental revolution of Fidel Castro. Cubans were fierce cold warriors, and much of their activity in Miami was rooted in their opposition to what was happening in Cuba. But their experience differed from the typical experiences of other Latino immigrants in that their inability to return home stripped their experience of many transnational elements. Cubans in Miami received much help in many aspects of their lives from existing U.S. institutions—both the federal government and the Catholic Church. Given their continuing political passion, even their religious shrines became political. The chapter also notes that Miami's increasing non-Cuban Latino presence has affected contemporary developments in Latino Catholicism there.

The case study of Chicago in Chapter Six incorporates suburbanization, religion, and transnational identity; it takes an ethnographic approach, based on oral history interviews, to set Latino Catholics among European-origin ethnic groups, such as Irish, Czechs, Poles, and Italians, as well as the area's large African-American population. In typical central city parish succession, the formerly Czech-dominated Pilsen neighborhood has become almost exclusively Mexican, and the once Polish/Italian Humboldt Park neighborhood has become largely Puerto Rican. Moreover, the Chicago metropolis since the 1960s has seen inner suburbs, notably Cicero, Berwyn, and Melrose Park, fill up with large populations of Mexican Americans and Mexican-born migrants. Demographic changes have also affected outer suburbs—satellite cities such as Elgin, Aurora, and

Waukegan, which increasingly take in new immigrants both from older Chicago neighborhoods and directly from Mexico, Puerto Rico, and elsewhere. Catholic influence on distinct Latino groups has depended on a host of social, economic, and cultural factors, ranging from the formation of enclaves of suburbanized *rancheros* from rural Mexico and Guatemala to a "brain drain" away from city cores among Puerto Rican professional migrants, generated by technological advances in edge cities. Faced with more and differing types of Latino immigrants, the Church has adopted new survival strategies in Chicago. Mexican and other Latin American immigrants, meanwhile, have found the Church a useful tool for their expressing their changing identities, which increasingly extend to homeland activities, causes, and institutions.

Chapter Seven is mostly a tale of two cities, San Antonio and New York. It highlights similarities and contrasts in the Latino experience in the two cities and in the role of the Church in the lives of Latinos in the two locales. In San Antonio, very capable, even excellent, Mexican Catholic leaders arose. Reaching well beyond the confines of the historic Mexican city, they imaginatively sought alliances and, through activism and working with civil authorities, achieved improvements that made for better conditions in Latino neighborhoods. Yet these leaders also kept a distinct religious agenda. This is a testament to their strength. In New York, urban decay undermined religious collective organizing, so that Anglo intervention became necessary for organizing, funding, and even conceptualizing the Latino group. The Puerto Rican rubric proved unenforceable and, for the archdiocese, undesirable. Much has been accomplished, but religious dynamism alone is insufficient for regenerating Puerto Rican identity as a purely ethnic one, or even as a nexus to a larger Latino one.

The transnational, hemispheric, indeed global, dimension exemplified by Chicago appears as well in both San Antonio and New York. The San Antonio Catholic community has launched numerous watershed movements that reach far beyond the city's local population in seeking to foster Latino religious and social solidarity. In New York, new immigrant groups, particularly Mexicans, have changed the nature of parish communities by broadening them into international networks that embrace a wide range of political and social services rooted in common national identity. Global parishes that depend heavily on lay leadership, on women, and on voluntary organizations such as *comités guadalupanos* have tended to embrace Mexican nationalism over a pan-Latino identity. The work of scholars who have studied the history of Catholic immigrants and their church in New York City is broadened in this chapter to address new manifestations of outward piety.

Chapter Eight covers social movements and related developments both within parish communities and in larger church structures since 1965, when city, region, and ethnicity can be said to have merged into a more coherent U.S. Latino history. Mexican Americans, Puerto Ricans, Cubans, and Central American refugees reacted differently to the stimuli, but by 1965 a common outline of a Latino church-within-a-church began to take shape. Following the conclusion of the Second Vatican Council that year, ecumenism and a convergence of Catholic and Protestant religiosity began to take shape. Chapter Eight also provides insights on the Latino experience in other cities and regions in the United States as Latin American and Latino Catholics formed new immigrant congregations in increasingly transnational urban spaces. Significantly, consideration of Washington, D.C., the Atlanta metropolitan region in the heart of the "Nuevo New South," and other cityscapes makes possible a new historical perspective on Latino urban Catholicism. The incorporation of recent sociological studies of religion and globalization helps in the clarification of analytical frameworks for understanding Latino history, urban life, and religion.

Finally, the epilogue contextualizes Latino ethnic identity, a growing field of study. An integrative approach to the history of Latino Catholicism in the United States illuminates both the more established groups and the more recent immigrants of Central American descent as they live out their religious practice in different urban milieus. The evolution of Latino Catholic practices and institutions is closely intertwined with the changing U.S. urban landscape. Large-scale migration in the twentieth century produced large and stable communities and promises to continue for the foreseeable future. Understanding the connections among city, religion, and a continually regenerated ethnic identity is key for appreciating the range and impact of the Latino experience. For centuries, Mexicans, Puerto Ricans, and Cubans have brought with them into the urban United States their Catholicism, the dominant religious tradition of Latin America. Catholicism has faced, and in turn created, many challenges in the various phases of Latino settlement in urban areas. Latinos need to be understood not only for their reception by the old immigrant church but also for their contributions to its historic evolution.

Latinos and the New Immigrant Church

1 Beginnings: Catholic Religious Tradition in Spain and Latin America

Religion, especially the Catholic religion, has been a primary vehicle in the evolution of the Latino experience. European, Caribbean, Mexican, and early North American history are the major threads in the tapestry of today's Latino identity, and Catholic religious tradition has intertwined with that history. Yet religion's primacy has often been ignored in academic writing and other studies on modern Latinos.[1] Unlike modern voluntary forms of Christianity, religion in the Christendom of the past was not a matter of personal choice but of birth and soil. In Spain, for example, Christians considered Jews and Muslims to be foreigners and aliens even though they lived within common borders and submitted to royal rule.

The story of Latino Christianity begins in Spain, even before the key date of 589, when the Visogothic kingdom of Hispania merged church with state. Several centuries before Christ, Iberian villagers had worshiped fertility and nature gods and goddesses, who they believed controlled their life and surroundings, including the agricultural cycle and natural disasters. Holy mountains, fertility rites, and other peasant rituals helped establish a sense of community and define society. Early in the Christian era, local shrines were set up to honor saints and martyrs, competing with official church parish structures. Popular religion flourished among peasants in the countryside while ecclesiastical structures of the official church governed from cities. Several archbishops promoted the veneration of Mary, in an early foreshadowing of the Marian cults that enliven Latino spirituality today.[2]

In 711, the Moors and Berbers entered the Iberian Peninsula from North Africa and forced many Christians north into the mountains. In 718 the Spaniards began what would become a seven-hundred-year "Reconquest" to win back their lands and their people from Moorish rule. During the 844 Battle of Clavijo in Galicia, in the northwestern part of the Iberian Peninsula, the apostle James, who according to tradition visited Hispania shortly after Christ's death, was said to have intervened as a mounted warrior in favor of the Spanish armies. Thus he was given the victorious title Moorslayer. A tomb reported to be James's was discovered during the ninth century at what would later be known as Santiago de Compostela. There a shrine was established which attracted medieval pilgrims from across the Pyrenees, along a trail that centuries later came to be lined with Christian churches. St. James represented military success, and in later centuries he came to be known as Patron of the Reconquest.[3]

In later centuries of the Reconquest, devotion to the Virgin Mary came to represent another path to Christian unity and victory over the Moors. Many legends of the reconquered territories told of the discovery of hidden, miraculous images of Mary. In the most prevalent such legend, a shepherd was visited by a statue of Mary holding the Divine Child Jesus, which had been buried by priests fleeing north to the Guadalupe River Valley in Cáceres when the Moors first invaded Spain. The area near the river became an important site of devotion to Our Lady of Guadalupe as patroness of the Reconquest. Throughout Spain and its colonies, Catholics came to venerate different manifestations of the Virgin Mary as a major intercessor who protected them from military enemies as well as drought, floods, and sickness.[4]

In Spain as well as in Latin America, the Virgin was known in many different forms, including Guadalupe, Pilar, and Montserrat. These varying manifestations often connoted particular attributes of Mary, such as Immaculate Conception, Our Lady of the Rosary, the Virgin of Remedies (Remedios), and the Virgin of Sorrows (Dolores). Other representations were linked to particular locations of religious or secular importance. Pilgrimage networks connected villages within the region, stimulating political, social, and economic activity. Guadalupe in Mexico eventually became the preeminent pilgrimage destination. Following the conquest of Mexico's indigenous people, Marian devotion was conflated with pre-Spanish religious belief. During Hernán Cortes's conquest of the Aztecs (1519–21), the Spanish placed images of the Virgin Mary (la Virgen de Remedios) in indigenous shrines and temples. From this the cult of the Virgin grew during the sixteenth century, in the midst of societal disintegration and death from disease.[5]

Devotion to the Spanish Virgin Mary took on new life in Mexico (New Spain), beginning to flourish around the time of a legendary sixteenth-century apparition at Tepeyac, the strategic point of entry into the Valley of Mexico. This hillside area near present-day Mexico City served as a sanctuary of Tonantzín, the Aztec Mother of all Gods, who had been immensely popular and revered before the Spanish conquest. In 1648, a *criollo priest* (Latin American–born person of "pure" European blood), Miguel Sánchez, wrote a narrative of the shrine of Our Lady of Guadalupe at Tepeyac. He described an apparition of la Virgen Morena, "the dark virgin," or Guadalupe, to a humble indigenous man named Juan Diego on December 12, 1531. According to this account, despite the winter weather she was said to have given roses to Juan Diego; he wrapped them in his *tilma*, a poncholike garment, and when he unfolded the *tilma* before Bishop Juan de Zumárraga, it bore the image of the Virgin. The Sánchez narrative reports that the bishop then ordered the construction of a church on Mount Tepeyac, sacred ground to the indigenous population and one of the four main sacrificial places of the Aztec civilization.[6] Eventually, belief in Tonantzín was supplanted by devotion to the mestiza Virgin of Guadalupe.

In 1649, another criollo, Luis Lasso de la Vega, vicar of the hermitage of Guadalupe—a local shrine to the Virgin of Extremadura that dated to 1556—published the *Nican mopohua*, an account attributed to Antonio Valeriano, a native scholar at the College of Santa Cruz de Tlaltelolco, arguing that devotion to the Spanish Virgin of Guadalupe originated with the Indians, not the Spaniards. Written in the Nahuatl language, the *Nican mopohua* featured, for the first time in writing, extensive dialogue between Juan Diego and the Virgin; its content fits well with Nahua (Aztec) spirituality.

The Guadalupe devotion, initially concentrated in Mexico City and environs, had spread through many locales in New Spain by the mid-eighteenth century, especially in cities linked to the capital but also extending to distant urban networks on the northern frontier. In 1754 Pope Benedict XIV declared Guadalupe the patroness of New Spain and established December 12 as her feast day.[7]

Other shrines, chapels, and devotions in Latin America also emphasized Marian apparitions, frequently linking local entities with known European Madonnas. The devotion to Our Lady of Montserrat, with origins in Spain as far back as A.D. 932, had begun with a series of hermitages and came to represent to the region of Catalonia what Guadalupe meant to Castile. By the sixteenth century, the legend of discovery of a Mary statue in a mountain cave, where it had been hidden at the start of the eighth-century Moorish invasion, had been accepted, and a chapel was erected on the site. The legend is recounted in Catalan-language songs of praise. In an instance of a transplanted devotion reminiscent of that of Guadalupe, in the New World Our Lady of Montserrat came to be venerated with a hilltop shrine in Hormigueros, Puerto Rico, a small municipality founded in the early seventeenth century in the southwestern portion of that colony. For residents of the Dominican Republic, the legend of the origins of the painting of Our Lady of Altagracia has the same function that the story of Our Lady of Guadalupe has for Mexicans, although the names, geography, and other details are different. In another example, during the early 1600s Castile's Our Lady of Charity had become popular in several Spanish cities, especially in Toledo Province, which housed a pilgrimage site after 1562. This name of the Virgin eventually became that of the patroness of the island of Cuba, based on a seventeenth-century apparition in Cobre, Cuba.[8]

Spain transferred tight links between the church and the state to its transatlantic colonies, as religion and politics shaped Latin American colonial Christianity in the wake of the explorations of Christopher Columbus. Spanish monarchs Fernando and Isabela sought and received papal approval confirming Spanish jurisdiction and creating the famous line of demarcation between their acquisitions and those of the Portuguese;these were further clarified in the Treaty of Tordesillas in 1494, which granted Portugal permanent claim to the eastern area that was colonized as Brazil. The pope charged Spain and Portugal with Christianization of the native peoples of the new lands and issued the *patronato real*, which made the king the head of the New World church except in matters of dogma. The Spanish Crown thus gained papal power in ecclesiastical affairs, including the appointment of bishops, becoming the pope's vicar in the New World. The patronato was a power over the church hierarchy (the archbishops, bishops, members of the ecclesiastical *cabildo*, or council, and priests). The state,in the person of the king, and through the council, viceroys, governors, and the like, had total control of all the mechanisms of the Church.[9]

The class system of modern Latin America has roots in Spanish Catholicism. In the mid-fifteenth century, purity-of-blood laws had been decreed in Spain to keep *conversos* from Judaism and Islam out of positions of power and to keep "Old Christians" from intermarriage so as to "protect" Catholicism. Proof of purity was needed to join the royal service or enter into the professions. Although the purity-of-blood laws were initially applied to distinguish Old Christians from newer converts, the system came to encompass formal racial subcategories that restricted the activities of Jews and Moors in Spain. Largely because of this, a caste system developed throughout Latin America, with legal and social discrimination aimed at enforcing the concept of "purity of blood." These statutes of *limpieza de sangre* took on racial dimensions in colonial Latin

America and came to stigmatize individuals of Indian and African ancestry. Anyone seeking to live in the colonies underwent a background check
on racial origin, genealogy, and religious beliefs. In these colonies, the
native-born Christians, or criollos, were considered second-class Christians. During the colonial centuries, only Spaniards and their criollo sons
were admitted to the ordained ministry.[10]

Urban Conquests in Mexico and the Southwest

The first Catholic church in the New World opened in Hispaniola in
1503. Ecclesiastical rule was retained in Seville until the following year,
when the pope set up the basic structure of an archdiocese on Hispaniola.
In 1511, at the request of King Fernando, Pope Julius II established the
diocese of Puerto Rico. The Diocese of Puerto Rico and those of Santo
Domingo and Concepción de la Vega in Hispaniola were the first three
dioceses of the newly settled territories. In 1517 another was established
in Cuba. Clerics conducted missions among the native Taíno Indians as
part of the Spanish conquest; once the Taíno could repeat simple prayers
and show obedience, they were considered converted.[11]

Santo Domingo, San Juan, and Havana became fortified harbors and
had cathedrals, centers of institutional Catholicism, from the 1500s forward. Smaller towns had parish churches located in central plazas that also
served as gathering places and conduits of news from the wider world. After several failed attempts dating back to 1513, the first permanent (and
still functioning) settlement of Spanish Catholics in North America was
launched at St. Augustine, Florida, on September 8, 1565.

Throughout the colonial period, the Hispanic Caribbean and the inhabitants of its capital cities remained subservient to Spain in religious
and secular matters. By 1608, Havana was home to more than half of
Cuba's twenty thousand inhabitants, and Cuba dominated the entrance
to the Gulf of Mexico and hence the route to and from Veracruz, Mexico, as well as the principal exits from the Caribbean Sea, through which
a sizable percentage of South American trade passed. By 1630 Havana
had largely replaced Santo Domingo as a military center. Meanwhile,
San Juan, whose walled and fortified perimeter withstood assaults on the
harbor by land and sea, permitting outside communication only at several
gates at the foot of the enclosure, descended to third place among capitals
of the Hispanic Caribbean. Puerto Rico, the eastern bastion against attacks by British and other European marauders, was forbidden to trade
even with neutral or friendly ports or to conduct unregulated coastal
traffic.[12]

The "Black Legend" of Spanish cruelty in the New World became known largely through the writings of Father Bartolomé de Las Casas in the Indies and was invoked during Anglo-Spanish conflicts in the late sixteenth century. Imperial justification of Indian enslavement had infuriated Las Casas, who believed that gold mining was deadly labor for the natives and sinful for Europeans. Las Casas believed that war and its evils made Indians despise the Christian religion.[13] While serving as a chaplain during the Spanish conquest of Cuba, Las Casas noted numerous atrocities committed against villagers by the Spaniards, who, "not content with what the Indians freely gave, took their wretched subsistence from them, and some, going further, chased after their wives and daughters."[14] Las Casas wanted the Indians to be converted by the force of the gospel message, not by force of arms. Only when the Church managed to separate itself from Spanish culture, notes Latin American historian Enrique Dussel, did the gospel message make great headway among the Indians.[15]

The conversion of Mexico, meanwhile, was entrusted to three mendicant orders: the Franciscans, the Dominicans, and the Augustinians. By far the largest religious order in rural Spain was the Franciscans. In New Spain that regular order took charge of several towns, including Tlatelolco, Texcoco, and Xochimilco, as well as the Aztec capital of Tenochtitlán, with some 200,000 inhabitants, several times more populous than any Spanish city at the time.[16]

Many of these missionaries, confronted with Aztec beliefs, rituals, and feasts, took these cultural elements as the starting point for evangelization, and some incorporated Aztec customs into the conversion process. In the first great wave of missionary Catholicism in Mexico following Cortes's conquest, Dominicans established themselves south of the capital, around Oaxaca. Subsequently, Franciscan missionaries pushed northward and dominated evangelization throughout New Spain. Missions were conceived as temporary measures to evangelize Indians, who would receive spiritual care from clergy of the religious orders until they could be cared for by diocesan clergy. Missions were often completely self-sufficient units, although they depended on towns for certain supplies. Mission land was distributed among colonists, each of whom also received a dwelling plot inside municipal limits. The vast population of newly ordained priests in the Americas sparked missionary zeal. As part of Spain's tradition of conquest and colonization, regular clerics (those who belonged to orders), led by Franciscans, missionized the Indians, while the seculars (priests under diocesan control) ministered to the Spanish laity of developing colonial towns.[17]

Secularization of the missions—in this case, *secularization* meant turning the missions into parishes under control of the diocesan clergy—was considered a key step in colonial maturity. In theory, the Indians would then assume all the rights and duties of Spanish citizens, the mission church would be converted to a parish church, and the missionaries would be relieved of all powers of direction over the Indians. In reality, this rarely happened.

One distinctly Latin American practice that emerged early on was the formation of the *cofradía*, or confraternity. These lay organizations, rooted in medieval Spain, played a large role in financing parish activities, collaborated on a wide range of activities geared toward popular devotion, and facilitated ties between community and church. Cofradías emerged in northern New Spain, and their legacy lasted into the Mexican and U.S. era in the Southwest, as they often eluded the control and approval of cchurch authorities, fostering religious independence. A cofradía often began when a group of parishioners—and occasionally a local functionary—agreed to donate livestock to cover the basic costs of public worship. Neither parish- nor clergy-centered, the cofradías' religion was rooted in devotion to a saint. The cofradía trend was expressed in the building of many small private chapels, replicas of the large mission churches built by individual families as well as the religious brotherhoods. The seventeenth century witnessed a proliferation of cofradias centered on the Virgin Mary, not surprisingly, given the widespread and fervent veneration of the Holy Mother prominent in both Spain and America.[18]

Missionaries and settlers began penetrating today's U.S. Southwest from Mexico as far back as the 1530s. New Spain came to be characterized by changing territorial frontiers, shifting imperial alignments, and widening commercial relationships. Its northern borderland areas lacked a stationary indigenous population such as existed in the Valley of Mexico before the conquest. In what eventually became New Mexico, Texas, Arizona, and California, missions generally accompanied, and were connected to, military and civilian outposts. Spanish colonial pueblos, more than mere towns, served as self-contained urban units wherein settlers could not sell their lands, as absolute title to these belonged to the Crown. Mission chapels, in addition to tending to Indian converts, provided pastoral care for Spaniards who served the military garrisons or lived in civilian communities.[19]

Spanish priests deliberately built Christian churches on sites where Indians had been accustomed to worship their own gods, such as in Tepeyac. In their evangelization of the Americas, the priests organized *autos*

de fe, dramatizations of biblical scenes performed by the laity, usually in
the atrium in front of a church. In the late 1500s the conquest intensified
in Nuevo Mexico, the largest populated frontier settlement, roughly the
settled core area of the upper Rio Grande Valley (considerably smaller
than the state of New Mexico today). Franciscan friars accompanied Juan
de Oñate to New Mexico in 1598 and immediately began building missions and attempting to Christianize the Indians. By 1629 they had supervised the construction of fifty mission churches in Pueblo Indian villages and had "converted" roughly fifty thousand Indians. Demographic
decline among the Pueblos resulted from the introduction of European
diseases, yet recurring epidemics caused Indians to flock to the missions
for food and protection.[20]

On the eve of a great revolt in 1680, the Spanish population totaled
approximately twenty-eight hundred, while the Pueblo Indians of the region totaled about seventeen thousand. Pueblos, led by the cleric Popé,
rose up against the Spanish colonizers at Taos, killing some two-thirds of
the Franciscan friars, burning San Miguel chapel in the Santa Fe plaza,
and destroying other Christian churches while restoring sacred native
sites. The Pueblo Revolt forced a Spanish retreat to El Paso for more
than a decade, until Spanish nobleman Diego de Vargas recaptured New
Mexico in 1693. Spanish missionaries then reestablished missions at numerous Indian pueblos. The Pueblo Revolt makes vivid the clash of civi-
lizations along the northern Spanish frontier in connection with mission
settlements.[21]

In a subsequent *entrada*, or colonial thrust—this time into the part of
northern Mexico called Tejas, on New Spain's northeastern frontier—the
city of San Antonio served as the key urban nucleus. Founded in 1718,
the city was a mixture of civil, military, and religious settlements that had
begun when Franciscan Father Antonio Olivares, accompanied by Spanish soldiers, established a settlement in a fertile river valley that served
as a base thereafter for missionary activities among the Coahuiltecan Indians and other tribes along the coast of the Gulf of Mexico. Spain had
positioned a *presidio* (garrison) on the site.[22] San Antonio, the major U.S.
city that remains the most Mexican in culture, is a case of a city that grew
up around a mission. Mission San Antonio occupied three different locations before its move in 1718 to the San Antonio River, where it took
a new name, San Antonio de Valero. A year later it relocated to the east
bank of the river, a more suitable site with better ground that was more
easily irrigated.

In 1731 the missionaries gathered at the San Antonio presidio to formally reestablish three missions at new, permanent locations on the San Antonio River. Mission Nuestra Señora de la Purísima Concepción de Acuña had first been established several hundred miles to the east in 1716 and now was relocated to San Antonio along with Mission Espada. Mission San Juan Capistrano was also moved from eastern Tejas and placed halfway between Mission San José (founded in San Antonio in 1720) and Mission Espada.[23]

The settlers' area, known in 1731 as San Fernando de Béjar, consisted of a villa, a presidio, and five missions. After first holding religious services in a makeshift chapel, in 1738 the settlers in San Antonio initiated the construction of a parish church, San Fernando, primarily for recently arrived Canary Islanders. The church was built by soldiers and civilian settlers and opened in 1749. Beginning in 1755, notes theologian Timothy Matovina, diocesan clergy and San Fernando parishioners pledged to celebrate the feast of Guadalupe annually. The church has since served as a site of baptism, marriage, and Mass. Under U.S. rule, in 1874 the Diocese of San Antonio was carved out of the Galveston Diocese, and San Fernando Church became a cathedral.[24]

By 1792 San Antonio was home to Spaniards, Indians, and mestizos; a significant number of mestizos settled on the outskirts of the settlement, southwest of Mission San Antonio de Valero. The San Antonio missions operated sizable farms and ranches that not only provided for the mission communities but also produced surpluses, sending maize, meat, tallow, and livestock to other parts of Tejas and to northern regions. In return, they imported a variety of manufactured goods, including clothing, shoes, knives, and saddles. Under Spanish and later Mexican rule, the pueblos that had grown up alongside the mission system remained small and relatively unimportant settlements. The Spanish missions, however, were only one strategic and temporary facet of a broader and more enduring emergence of resilient local churches on the northern frontier of New Spain. Soon the settler population far surpassed that of the missionized Indians, boosted by immigration from the south and east and reinforced by the military protection of Spanish settlements.[25]

In 1824, the secularization of San Antonio—the transfer of responsibility for religious ministry from missionaries to parish authorities and the distribution of the property and possessions of the mission to its residents—started in the early 1790s, was complete. Ecclesiastical supervision fell to the pastor of San Antonio's parish church, San Fernando, who soon parceled out mission land to local residents. The dismantling of the missions was accompanied by a rapid decrease of Franciscans on the frontier in the 1820s and 1830s. By the 1830s, when a revolution brought about the creation of the independent Republic of Texas, the missions had lost their religious significance and were little more than abandoned ruins. Under the Republic of Texas, Catholics in Texas remained nominally under the jurisdiction of the Diocese of Monterrey in northern Mexico, but this left them for all practical purposes cut off from official ecclesiastical oversight due to the heightened animosity between Texas and Mexico.

Parishes first appeared with the establishment of formal towns and grew as missions became secularized in the last decades of the Spanish colonial period. Parish priests played significant roles in visiting the sick, saying Mass, and coordinating observances of the faithful for feast days and other ceremonies, often in remote locations.[26]

Spain's Power Dwindles: Religion and Anglo-American Occupation

By the 1780s, Spain was losing its influence on the North American continent. Increasingly, Catholic Spanish-Mexican settlers clashed with incoming Anglo Americans on several frontiers. Unable to attract enough colonists from Spain or its American colonies, Spanish officials began in the mid-1780s to allow Protestant immigrants from the United States to settle in Louisiana and Florida, which were under Spanish rule at that time. Believing that many of the inhabitants of U.S. western territories were not strongly attached to the U.S. government, the Spanish hoped to transform them into colonial subjects. To attract them, Spain promised free lands and commercial privileges to those immigrants who took loyalty oaths and agreed to become Catholics. The template for manifest destiny had been created as New Spain's (later Mexico's) northeast border became increasingly vulnerable due to a lack of sufficiently populated settlements and neglect from the distant capital.

Between 1763 and the late eighteenth century, Louisiana and Florida belonged to the Diocese of Santiago, Cuba. Father Luis Peñalver y Cárdenas, born of a prominent Havana criollo family, became the first bishop of the Louisiana Diocese, established in 1793; it was centered in New Orleans and extended to sparsely populated Spanish Florida, southern Alabama and Mississippi, Louisiana, and lands north of central Oklahoma between the Rockies and the Mississippi River. In his almost four years of service, Peñalver y Cárdenas decried the widespread practice of concubinage with slaves and worked with the Ursuline Sisters to expand education. Peñalver also assumed many priestly duties on the frontier, catering to a dispersed Spanish civilian and military population. Beginning in 1802. he served as archbishop of the Archdiocese of Guatemala, and in 1805 he retired to Havana.[27]

In 1800, Napoleon conquered Spain and regained Louisiana for France, only to pass the territory on to the U.S. government, which bought it for $15 million in the Louisiana Purchase of 1803. The western border of the United States was now at the Mississippi, and the U.S. Diocese of New Orleans now fell under the jurisdiction of Baltimore-based bishop John Carroll. Following the U.S. purchase of Spanish Florida in 1819, Texas, partly under Spanish and partly under Mexican rule, emerged as the next significant diplomatic and territorial point of conflict, as the push for manifest destiny was on. Here, as in the Mississippi Valley a generation earlier, mostly Protestant U.S. immigrants were required by Spanish frontier officials to respect Catholicism as a condition of their entry.[28]

Mexico won independence from Spain in 1821. The Mexican Constitution of 1824 recognized Catholicism as the national religion, but the government's lack of vigorous enforcement of a Catholic immigration requirement led to a policy of unofficial religious tolerance that threatened a frontier Catholicism already made tenuous by a lack of clergy. In 1821, Mexico offered Stephen Austin a generous grant of prime Texas farmland in order to populate the northern region. This marked the first step in Mexico's loss of its northern territories to U.S.-born *empresarios*, functionaries of the Mexican government who were licensed to introduce U.S. settlers into the territory. Entry was offficially restricted to "Roman Catholics of good character willing to become citizens of the country," but this prohibition against the entry of Protestants was rarely enforced on the frontier.[29]

During the early 1830s, Mexico's centralist government's unsuccessful attempts to control immigration into Tejas, which was still part of Mexico, spurred an alliance between Anglo Americans and Tejanos in rebellion against Mexico. Tejanos with republican sympathies participated in several battles, including the famous Battle of the Alamo, where several fought and died alongside Anglo Americans. In 1836, in the wake of the establishment of the independent Republic of Texas, San Antonio's Mexican population of fifteen hundred faced a sustained and successful Anglo-American onslaught. The newcomers included white Protestant southerners and sometimes their slaves, as well as northerners and a growing variety of European-born settlers of various Protestant denominations. They began to reshape the city and gain positions of power through force of numbers, political maneuvering, and sometimes intermarriage with wealthy Tejanos. Many Tejanos lost their lands under an unfamiliar justice system: in costly litigation in English-language courts, ownership had to be proved by families that had lived on the land for generations.[30]

Unresolved territorial struggles laid the foundation for the Mexican-American War of 1846–48, which culminated with the transfer of over one-third of Mexico's pre-1936 territory to the United States, adding California, Arizona, and other southwestern border territories while formally ceding Texas. The Treaty of Guadalupe Hidalgo, signed in February 1848, allowed those in the annexed territories to remain and "either retain the title and rights of Mexican citizens, or acquire those of citizens of the United States." Most were incorporated into the United States and granted citizenship; the others were nonetheless guaranteed "the free enjoyment of their liberty and property, and secured in the free exercise of their religion without restriction."[31]

At the outset of the Mexican-American War, San Antonio had had only one thousand inhabitants, with hundreds having fled to throughout Texas and to points further south due to wartime conditions. After the war, French clergy entered San Antonio and established churches, colleges, and seminaries that formed the core of institutional Catholicism. Bishop Jean-Marie Odin came to the Texas-Mexico border and established many rural mission churches for Tejanos as part of the Galveston Diocese, and in 1850 French clergy begin to replace Mexican clergy. Appointed vice prefect apostolic of Texas in 1840, Odin removed two native priests at San Antonio, Fathers Refugio de la Garza and José Antonio Valdez, accusing them of mismanagement of parish coffers and concubinage, and appointed a Spaniard to pastor at San Fernando. After 1851 the Ursuline Academy, staffed by nuns, attracted the daughters of some of the city's older Tejano families as well as more recent Anglo arrivals. The Ursuline Sisters also received many pupils from Mexico, including the daughters of Mexican governors, senators, and generals, despite the perils of distant travel.[32]

By 1861 Bishop Odin had repaired the church at Mission Concepción and turned it over, along with "the ruins of the old monastery and the splendid land which adjoins them," to the Brothers of Mary; Mission San José went to the Benedictines, who established a monastery there and cultivated the fields. Meanwhile, the two missions farther south benefited from the efforts of another French priest, who had arrived in San Antonio in 1855. In 1858, Father Francis Bouchu was named parish priest and was able to rehabilitate several of the dilapidated mission churches so that they could be put back into use. "Padre Francisco" also composed and distributed a Spanish-language catechism that came to be employed widely in Texas and New Mexico; it was adopted in 1896 as the official catechism for Spanish speakers in the Diocese of San Antonio.[33]

San Fernando Parish remained a stronghold of Tejano culture and Catholicism, a cohesive force within a city that had become predominantly Protestant in the 1850s. St. Mary's Church became the mother parish of San Antonio's German- and English-speaking (mainly Irish) Catholics in 1857, and newcomers built their own parishes thereafter, including several modeled as national, or language, parishes. Nine parishes emerged between 1857 and 1910, but San Fernando was the only one for Tejanos, with the dwindling Spanish missions still operating, but only barely. Mexican folk religion survived in some locations, notably in the Chapel of Miracles, a private family chapel built in the 1870s near downtown, which featured a Spanish colonial crucifix on the main altar; reportedly it was a remnant of the old mission church of San Antonio de Valero and exhibited miraculous properties.

Tejano culture continued to permeate religion and other realms of frontier society. Texas had become the Anglo-American gateway to Mexico, while it retained its old identity as a *patria chica*, a minihomeland or country within a country.[34]

Latino Religious Roots in Mexico and the Hispanic Caribbean

At the start of the Spanish enterprise in the Western Hemisphere, the Caribbean was the center of interest and of administration. After explorers entered Mexico and Peru a few decades later, Spain's focus shifted to establishing those regions as new viceroyalties. During the early-nineteenth-century wars of independence, Cuba and Puerto Rico increasingly came to depend economically on the United States. Meanwhile, U.S. expansionists proposed annexation of the Southwest along with other parts of Mexico and Cuba. Cuba and Puerto Rico remained part of the diminished Spanish colonial empire until the Spanish-American War of 1898, when both islands came under U.S. jurisdiction. Cuba became an independent republic in 1902, while Puerto Rico has remained a U.S. territory.

On the islands, mobilization against the Napoleonic invasion of Spain in 1808 strengthened the traditional identification of Catholic faith and Spanish nation. After 1820, however, Caribbean-born criollos evinced sparks of nationalism. In the 1830s, violent anticlericalism broke out in Madrid and in other major cities of Spain, resulting in the expulsion of priests and confiscation of church property. By the mid-nineteenth century, the phenomenon of "the two Spains," a Catholic Hispanic Spain and a liberal Europeanizing one, had appeared. The 1868 "Glorious Revolution" brought a brief religious disestablishment and greater religious tolerance, lasting until 1873 in Spain and to a lesser extent in the colonies. Catholicism did remain the state religion during this time, though anarchist and socialist ideologies spread in spite of clerical opposition.

In both Cuba and Puerto Rico, the increasingly nationalistic elite often opposed the Church's support of Spanish colonialism. Spain's neglect of its Caribbean colonies and growing nationalism within them inspired separate criollo-led revolts in 1868 in Cuba and Puerto Rico, with varying results. While 50,000 Cubans and over 150,000 Spaniards lost their lives during the Cuban Ten Years' War, which developed into an all-out separatist struggle, only a handful died in the Puerto Rican revolt, known as the Grito de Lares, which lasted only a few days and was limited to a small part of the highland region. After the Grito's prompt suppression, Ramón Emeterio Betances, Eugenio María de Hostos, and other Puerto Rican separatists cast their lot with Cuba, hoping in vain for an independent Puerto Rico and an Antillean Union. Beginning in 1868, the Puerto Rican separatist movement increasingly called for the separation of church and state and sought the elimination of ecclesiastical privileges in a colonial regime that denied religious and other freedoms throughout the nineteenth century.[35]

During the Ten Years' War from 1868 to 1878, which began the struggle for political independence of Cuba, most rural clergy on the island were Cuban. Several priests participated in the struggle for independence and were persecuted for it. During the decade of insurrection, many Cuban families migrated to Key West, Tampa, and New York City. The end of the war accelerated the emigration from Havana of workers, mainly from the tobacco industry. They took refuge, sought work, and formed mutual-aid societies, cooperatives, and unions that increasingly linked Cuba and Florida. In 1890 José Martí, architect of the Cuban revolution, founded the Liga de Instrucción to gather support from exiles for independence, and later in Tampa and Key West he recruited supporters and collected donations from Cuban cigar makers. In 1892 Martí founded the Partido Revolucionario Cubano, which sought the independence of Cuba and aided Puerto Rican patriots as well. Martí made New York a vital link in Cuban independence between 1890 and 1895, also drawing support from New York's small but growing Puerto Rican exile and *tabaquero* community. Key West's cigar community conspired against Spain and helped launch the final war of independence in 1895.[36]

Cuba's Forgotten Church

Throughout the nineteenth century, when Cuba became the most wealthy sugar-producing nation in the Caribbean, the Church defended the institution of slavery, as it had done throughout the colonial era. Yet, according to sociologist Lisandro Perez, the sugar revolution in Cuba from the late eighteenth to the middle nineteenth century contributed to religious secularization and relative indifference to official Catholicism. The sugar planters' new technologies allowed for the construction of larger mills, replacing the semipatriarchal social order of slavery under which owners had hired a part-time priest to serve at a small chapel. With the expansion of the mills, competing economic pressures increased to minimize the presence of the Church, or at least prevent it from keeping pace with planters' acquisition of additional land and slaves. Owners became reluctant to grant slaves time to practice the sacraments, to receive religious training, and to observe Sundays and religious holidays. Conflicts with the Church also arose over tithing and the opening of cemeteries on land owned by the mills.[37]

Africans had been brought to Cuba from a vast region in western Africa and from Mozambique on the eastern coast, and thus different dialects developed in distinct geographic areas of Cuba. Cuban slavery was most prevalent among western planters; planters' enterprises were smaller in the east, where a large free mulatto, or mixed-blood, population arose. Afro-Cubans retained much of their language, religion, and musical heritage into the twentieth century, and indeed, much of that heritage remains strong in Cuban culture today.[38]

Church structures withered further with the large numbers of arrivals from Africa, as African religious beliefs began to blend with Catholic practices. The syncretic process that led to Santería developed over three centuries. *Cabildos de nación* were institutions that stimulated syncretism and provided the context in which the new Afro-Cuban religions were nurtured. African "nations" were organized into *cabildos*—religious brotherhoods with origins in medieval Spain that the Cuban Church began organizing in 1598 under the direction of diocesan priests. The cabildos, whose purpose was to fit African customs into the Church's worship, became centers of urban social life. At the end of the eighteenth century, there was rapid growth in the number of cabildos in Havana, and many moved their music and ceremonies outside the city walls. The countryside had no cabildos, but on holidays Catholic authorities permitted blacks to assemble in the *batey*, or alleyways between buildings, to rehearse their sacred dances. The hybrid tradition of Santería evolved from the Lucumí cabildos (Lucumí is a West African linguistic dialect).[39]

The African presence proved a major influence on island religious practices. Cuban blacks used major church feast days as occasions for the celebration of their own rites, syncretized with Catholic rites. Yoruba deities, or guardian spirits, known as *orishas*, became identified with Catholic saints: Oshún became known as the Virgen de la Caridad del Cobre (Our Lady of Charity), Santa Bárbara became conflated with Shangó, and so forth. During Easter week, observance of the death and passion of Christ replaced the mourning for deceased royal ancestors.

Spain had paid little attention to the Church in Cuba, and the island was always understaffed, with priests concentrated in cities, especially the capital. Generally, Cuban society tended to have a more secular character than other Spanish colonies had, although Havana and other large cities remained Catholic strongholds. In Cuba in the middle of the eighteenth century, almost all of the rural clergy were criollos, and there was a Cuban-born bishop from Santiago. Popular Catholicism was generally weak in Cuba, and the impact of the Church was particularly weak in rural areas of the island. The Catholic Church limited its evangelistic activities to the white elite, leaving a wide sector practicing Afro-Cuban religion. In the countryside, many people had not seen a priest since baptism, though religious festivals played a significant part in devotional life, especially celebrations of Good Friday, the Epiphany, and the feast days of Santa Bárbara, San Lázaro, and Nuestra Señora de la Caridad del Cobre.[40]

Cuban devotion to the patroness dates to the early 1600s. According to one narrative, two Indian brothers and a boy slave saw a carved statue of the Virgin Mary floating on a piece of wood on a bay near the copper mines of Cobre, on the northwestern tip of the island. She was brought ashore, and then the statue disappeared; it later reappeared, and a church was built on the spot where she was found. Over time the devotion spread westward throughout Cuba. La Virgen came to take on nationalistic overtones during the nineteenth-century wars for independence from Spain. Some soldiers fighting for independence, *los mambises*, adopted her as their patroness and carried her image with them into battle, which is the reason she came to be referred to as la Virgen Mambisa.[41]

Cuba had been influenced by the same ideological trends that spurred independence movements throughout the Latin American mainland, but Cubans were unable to put that ideology into successful action early in the nineteenth century. The Spanish did face unsuccessful challenges from criollo insurgencies later, in the 1860s and 1870s. Despite the greater

concentration of Spanish military power on Cuba, Cubans found it eas-
ier to combat Spanish colonialism than did Puerto Ricans due to their
island's greater size, topographical diversity, and geography, among other
factors. The 1774 inauguration of the Seminario San Carlos y San Ambrosio, a college and seminary catering to Cuba's elite, had served to open
up awareness of Cuba apart from Spain. Among the leading faculty members was Félix Varela y Morales (1788–1853), Cuba's "first revolutionary," an abolitionist and promoter of Cuban independence. Varela served
briefly in 1822 as representative in the Spanish Cortes, or parliament,
where he presented bills calling for the abolition of slavery and autonomy
from Spain. After being exiled from the colonies, he arrived in the United
States in 1823 and launched *El Habanero*, a paper dedicated to science,
literature, politics, and faith. In the 1830s Varela developed a legendary
reputation for his work among Irish immigrants in New York's dangerous
Five Points District, where he founded Transfiguration Church, created
dozens of schools and social services for the city's poor, and rose to become vicar-general of the New York Archdiocese.[42]

A general perception of the Church as pro-Spanish, an enemy of Cuban independence, contributed to the weakness of the Catholic Church
in Cuba. Protestant denominations received a major push with the growing interest of the United States in Cuba, the Spanish-Cuban-American
War, the U.S. occupation of the island from 1898 to 1902, and the influx
of U.S. capital and influence during the first two decades of the twentieth
century.[43]

Puerto Ricans in the Spanish Colonial Church

Puerto Rican towns developed under royal auspices, with a church located
in each central plaza. In the seventeenth century the towns of Arecibo,
Aguada, and Ponce were visited occasionally by priests from San Juan
in the northeast and San German in the southwest. From their towns
of residence, priests journeyed out to create additional royal towns. In
the eighteenth century over a dozen new towns were founded, including
Mayaguez on the west coast and Santurce, Río Piedras, and Bayamón
near the capital. Many new interior towns were gradually populated by
Spanish colonists, including retired military personnel and former cattle
ranchers. The mountain towns remained isolated from imperial ecclesiastical control, and the highlanders, known as *jíbaros*, resisted attempts by
civil and ecclesiastical authorities to fully integrate them into the larger
colonial system and chose to develop religious practices by innovation.[44]

Popular Catholicism in Puerto Rico, then, evolved independently of the sacramental life of the Church. In the more isolated areas, devotion to saints and the rosary constituted the only doctrinal training, which was anchored to the saintly cycle of the liturgical calendar, the veneration of Mary, and the preservation of certain rites and observances, such as *el echar agua* (the pouring of water for baptism in the absence of a priest). Baptism, according to theologian Jaime Vidal "the most important sacrament in the Puerto Rican popular mind," remained important for bringing a child into the religious community. With the shortage of clergy in the latter part of the nineteenth century, delays in baptizing children became more common, as did emergency lay baptism by midwives. The relationship between godparents and godchild, as well as between godparents and blood parents, who became coparents (*compadres*), became a strong bond comparable to kinship.[45]

In 1645 the Spanish bishop in Puerto Rico mandated the frequency of people's expected attendance at religious services, based on proximity to churches. Those within one or two leagues were to hear Mass every other Sunday, those farther away once a month, others still more removed every other month, while those who lived more than six leagues from the parish church had to attend only on Christmas, Easter, Pentecost, and one of the Sundays of Lent. This ruling remained in force throughout the colonial period. By the early part of the nineteenth century, at least half the priests on the island were Puerto Rican, but in spite of the founding of Puerto Rico's sole institution of secondary education, San Juan's Conciliar Seminary, the proportion of natives to Spaniards in holy orders steadily decreased. Many priests remained within the walled capital, primarily in the cathedral and the two friaries, while the population was scattered across the island.[46]

From 1765 to 1810, Puerto Rico underwent rapid population growth, going from 45,000 to 183,000 inhabitants, but the island was still sparsely populated, and the population was overwhelmingly rural, as ranching and subsistence farming attracted families from the coast. The lifestyle of the independent Puerto Rican peasant changed from that of cattle herder to that of mountain peasant—the jíbaro of the mountains, planter of subsistence crops such as plantains, followed by cash crops such as tobacco and finally coffee. With the rise of coffee production for large-scale export in the mid-1800s, many jíbaros were displaced by *jornaleros* (day laborers) working on coastal *haciendas*. The interior withstood outside forces better than the coast did. Landless criollos were pushed to the interior with the usurpation of coastal lands by sugar interests and by a massive importation of slaves, which enlivened coastal commerce. Then, with population growth and as the land became valuable for coffee cultivation, numerous Spanish and other immigrants arrived and found land and work. The island's society was transformed by Catalans, Mallorcans, Corsicans, and other European immigrants. This era represented a key phase in the development of a collective Puerto Rican identity. By the mid-1800s U.S. interests had begun to affect the strategically located island from afar— first through trade and then by conquest.[47]

During the nineteenth century, the Puerto Rican masses remained isolated from institutions of urban Catholicism. The offspring of Spanish immigrants rarely entered the priesthood, leaving parish leadership to be filled increasingly with foreign clergy. In towns, however, families customarily allocated some funds to churches and to local cofradías, which had taken root in Puerto Rico as they did in Mexico. Makeshift parishes, often served by missionary preachers, dominated the countryside through the late nineteenth century. As in Cuba, the Church and the bishop in Puerto Rico owned land and slaves. Slave owners began to discourage matrimony, as having single slaves was more profitable; Spanish law required that married couples be sold as a unit. A sharp rise in concubinage and unsanctioned marriages occurred among the slaves in the decades leading up to abolition in 1873. At five pesos, the regular fee for a wedding, equaling a laborer's wages for a month, marriage had become prohibitive.[48]

In the decade or so after 1803, Spain tried to create reformist conditions to maintain the loyalty of the colonies. The first bishop born on Puerto Rican soil, and the only native-born one appointed during the four centuries of Spanish dominion over the island, was Juan Alejo Arizmendi y de la Torre, in office from 1804 until his death in 1814. In 1815 came the Cédula de Gracias, a royal decree whose measures accelerated the growth of Puerto Rican agrarian capitalism with an influx of Spanish farmers and foreign Protestants. Run by ministers of the Spanish monarchy and corrupt and sometimes tyrannical military governors, Puerto Rico's colonial administration was awash in nepotism and the use of overseas appointments to export political undesirables. Books and foreign ideas, especially those challenging the Catholic religious monopoly, faced censorship. Beginning in the 1810s, Protestant Bibles and other literature began routinely entering Puerto Rico via the Danish Virgin Islands, but, as in Cuba, they were confiscated and censored.[49]

Missionary priests from the Spanish Vincentian Order arrived in Puerto Rico in the 1860s and 1870s. In 1888 they took charge of the sixteenth-century San José Church in the capital; in 1892 they expanded to Ponce.

In early 1898, Spain had granted a charter of autonomy to Puerto Rico. Yet by the terms of the 1899 Treaty of Paris, Spain was forced to hand over Cuba to the United States in preparation for the island's independence, and Puerto Rico and the Philippines were ceded absolutely as U.S. possessions. Spain stipulated a number of safeguards for its subjects who chose to continue residing in the lost colonies, for the free entrance of Spanish literary and cultural material, and for the protection of the interests of the Catholic Church insofar as this was compatible with the U.S. Constitution. These safeguards were written into the treaty and thus bound the United States to honor Spain's outstanding commitments in its new possessions and to guarantee the freedom of the Catholic Church in them. The United States paid the remnants of the Spanish Church a lump sum, based on the value of its previously confiscated properties, and promised that parish churches, rectories, and other ecclesiastical buildings of island towns would not be seized by any branch of local government for secular use.[50]

The disorganized Puerto Rican Church suffered a shortage of priests as Spanish diocesan and religious order clergy departed from Puerto Rico following the U.S. takeover. On the eve of the change of sovereignty, Juan Perpiña y Pibernat, ecclesiastical governor and vicar of Puerto Rico, betrayed the prevalent feelings of cultural and racial superiority as he criticized the religious apathy of the masses. He noted that although "colored priests" (those with African blood) had been "forbidden by the clerical constitution of Spain," persons with mixed blood passed as white in the priesthood. He considered it undesirable "to see colored men with priestly robes administering the sacraments" and said he would never ordain "a colored man" if he were bishop.[51] Perpiña y Pibernat took a pro-Spanish position, fearing for the island under U.S. rule, given the challenge to Spain's language and religion presented by the new colonial overlords. He saw a devastating 1899 hurricane as divine intervention, writing that anyone not blinded by atheism, materialism, and naturalism could see that the storm was God's punishment for the island's sins, including secularism and rejection of Spanish traditions. In 1900–1901, thousands of Puerto Ricans left declining highland coffee areas, bound for the sugar plantations of Hawaii and elsewhere; most of them never returned home.[52]

Archbishop Placide Chapelle of New Orleans had been sent from Rome to Paris during treaty negotiations and helped reconcile U.S. concepts of separation of church and state with protection of the Church's interests. He served as apostolic delegate for Cuba and Puerto Rico but resigned in the wake of U.S. occupation of the two. Chapelle helped his protégé James H. Blenk become Puerto Rico's new bishop. Favoring missionaries from New York and Philadelphia over local clergy, Blenk launched the Americanization of the Church in Puerto Rico, which included reorganization of the island's Catholic school system (with classes now being conducted in English) and the closing of the Conciliar Seminary, founded in the 1830s. Students were sent to American seminaries instead. Puerto Rico underwent annexation and lost even the semblance of home rule for several generations; as noted earlier, Spanish clergy departed en masse. Yet while the island received an imported U.S. hierarchy, it had not officially become part of the U.S. Catholic Church.[53]

Post-1848 U.S. military conquests, then, introduced religious pluralism to the Latin American Catholic tradition. Together with increasing numbers of former Mexican nationals in the Southwest and German- and Irish-American Catholics, the nation's bishops, clergy, and religious women shared in the tremendous work of building the U.S. Catholic Church. Meanwhile, Latin American Catholics in Cuba and Puerto Rico first confronted Tridentine Catholicism only at the dawn of the twentieth century. The religious pluralism that had emerged from the revolutionary era in the United States; was accelerated as new Protestant, Catholic, Jewish, and Orthodox Christian institutions were formed by and for new immigrant groups. The four-month war with Spain from April to August 1898 signaled the rise of the United States as a world power.[54]

Constituting the U.S. Immigrant Church

After 1790, the rapid growth of the U.S. church, especially in the Northeast and Midwest, came largely as a result of the increase of immigration from Germany, France, and Ireland. Almost all of the early clergy under John Carroll (1735–1815), appointed first archbishop of Baltimore in 1789, were either émigrés fleeing the French Revolution or priests who had voluntarily left Europe to become missionaries. The late eighteenth century witnessed the work of a small group known as Pan-Americans, men and women with extensive ties to Latin America and the Caribbean who helped transform the church in Philadelphia. Some hoped to inject the radically democratic spirit of the age, challenging the episcopacy for control of parish appointments and finances. They boldly questioned the relationship between national communities of believers and the suprana-

tional institution of the Church. Others, meanwhile, embraced an ultra-
montane view of Catholicism, supporting papal supremacy over national
and local Catholic authorities and identities.[55]

Some U.S. bishops shared in the creation of a multiethnic immigrant
church. Philadelphia's Germans became the first ethnic group to form
national parishes, and Carroll permitted the establishment of Holy Trinity Parish in that city in 1789. German national parishes began to spread
to the West in 1833. When German congregations with no pastors built
a church, established a parish, and then sought a suitable priest, in effect
the congregation owned the parish and hired or fired the pastor under
the "trustee" system. Trusteeism was a common organizational structure
for churches in the United States during the eighteenth century; it gave
control of resources and clerical appointments to an elected board, generally consisting of both clergy and laypeople. Supporters of trusteeism
argued that the system fused Catholic and American ideas and methods
of governance. Opponents responded that the church transcended political boundaries and that these decisions should reside with the clerical
hierarchy, usually the local bishop, invested by Rome with the proper
authority.[56]

Historians of U.S. Catholicism call the nineteenth century the era of
the old immigrant church, run by an immigrant clergy that had arrived
virtually simultaneously. Nearly two million Irish came to America during the 1840s and over one million Germans during the 1850s, as improvements in transatlantic shipping made it cheaper to travel to America. Until 1880, most European immigrants came from the northern and
western parts of the continent; by the turn of the century, however, almost 80 percent were from the south and the east. The number of Catholics in the United States grew from six million in 1880 to sixteen million
by 1910. For Catholic immigrants and their children, the neighborhood
parish became the focal point of faith and social life. While some parish
groups were strictly devotional, others strove to meet the intellectual,
social, and recreational needs of their members.[57]

2 Mexico's Revolution Travels to San Antonio

Mexican anticlericalism arose in opposition to the Church's allegiance to the monarchy during the country's independence struggle. Anticlericalism surfaced during the Benito Juárez presidency of 1867–72, which implemented a radical program separating church and state. Juárez nationalized church properties, outlawed monastic orders, restricted public religious processions, and exiled many of the top bishops, the apostolic delegate, and many religious men and women from the country. During the presidency of Sebastián Lerdo de Tejada, anticlerical Reform Laws were incorporated into the Constitution of 1875. Under President Porfirio Díaz the measure went largely unenforced, and monasteries and convents barely continued to operate with limited personnel. Despite the constitutional provisions, Mexico's 1910 population census indicated that the country's Catholic population stood at over 95 percent, though there were scarcely enough priests to administer the sacraments.[1]

Religious persecution by socialist-leaning revolutionaries in Mexico was a recurring problem in the early twentieth century. The degree of persecution varied from regime to regime. This anticlericalism resulted from the unresolved legal status of the church and centuries of social persecution. Opposition to the Church was strong during the Mexican Revolution of 1910–1917, although that conflict and its lasting aftermath had primarily economic and social roots. The Mexican Constitution that emerged from the Querétaro Congress in 1917, following seven years of civil war, mandated secular education, prohibited foreign priests from practicing in the country, and subsequently allowed state legislatures to limit the number of clergymen within their boundaries. The constitution also banned the Church from participation in political activities, and marriage was declared a civil ceremony.[2]

A violent period of Mexican church-state conflict, the Cristero Revolt of 1926 to 1929, pitted Mexican bishops, who had ordered all churches in the republic closed in an effort to rescind anticlerical legislation, against the regime of President Plutarco Elías Calles. One thread of the origins of this revolt, La Cristiada, had emerged in 1923, when President Álvaro

Obregón, fearing a clerical resurgence, expelled the Vatican's representative in Mexico for participating in an "illegal religious ceremony" after he attended a gathering for a planned monument to the Sacred Heart of Jesus on the peak of Guanajuato's Cubilete mountain. The ceremony was deemed illegal because it violated a prohibition against public meetings of Catholics. More than forty thousand worshipers, including eleven prelates from various parts of the republic, were present at Cubilete, approximately at the geographic center of the nation, to hear the bishop of San Luis Potosí proclaim Christ the "King of Mexico." The monument to Christ was completed several years later. It had become part of the goal of the hierarchy's "national reconstruction," calling on Mexican believers to defend Catholicism as "the religion that is in the tradition, the history, and in the soul of the Mexican people."[3] In March 1925 the clergy helped found a national organization to challenge the regime, Liga Nacional Defensora de la Libertad Religiosa.

In the mid-1920s in most areas in the country, but especially in the central plateau, the conflict between Catholics and the government was coming to a boiling point. In San Luis Potosí, for example, beginning in early 1926, the governor forced all foreign (mostly Spanish) priests to leave the state, while the state legislature passed a decree reducing the number of clergy. San Luis's popular archbishop, Miguel de la Mora, suspended worship shortly thereafter to avoid confrontations with civil authorities. Police in the capital responded to the escalation of church-state confusion by sealing off El Carmen, La Capilla de Guadalupe, and other churches. Facing a standoff, the archbishop fled the state by the end of the year. Churches in San Luis, meanwhile, remained open so that individuals could worship, and priests held Masses in private houses with little interference. Scars remained from the church-state conflict, with stories of atrocities by government troops passed down to subsequent generations.[4]

President Calles focused on plans for social and economic reforms and called the clergy, because of its coordination of activities with the Vatican, part of the exploiting class that sought to block progress. In early 1926 Calles declared that priests must be subject to government control, and he banned religious schools, public religious ceremonies, and even the wearing of priestly garb in public. In an effort to limit the social influence of the clergy, the provisions of the 1917 Constitution were invoked, highlighting the fact that marriage had been decreed a purely civil contract (though a religious ceremony could follow). To further bring the clergy into conformity with the anticlerical edicts on the books, the revolutionary regime ordered priests to register with the government and empowered state legislatures to reduce the number of clergy. In response, the clergy ordered a suspension of all religious services in Mexico.[5]

The three years of violence involved prochurch Cristero rebels (the anticlerical president-elect Obregón—who had previously held office in 1920–1924—was assassinated by one of their supporters) and government actions to suppress them. The Cristeros, who were mostly rural Catholics with some support from a small urban middle class, wanted to preserve their religion and valued traditional beliefs over revolutionary ideals. They carried banners of Guadalupe inscribed "Viva Cristo Rey!" (Long Live Christ the King!). Both the military efforts of the Cristero Rebellion and the accompanying lengthy clerical "boycott," wherein the Mexican bishops ordered clergy not to perform their religious duties under the revolutionary government's restrictive edicts, ultimately failed. However, the response of the U.S. church hierarchy, as well as that of Mexican-American and Mexican immigrant parishioners, strengthened the Church of the Southwest by providing, at least temporarily, a contingent of trained priests and bishops and by focusing the attention of U.S. Catholics on events in Mexico. Opposing anticlericalism in Mexico, U.S. bishops mediated for the besieged Mexican bishops and garnered the support of U.S. Catholics.[6]

Insurgency, Anticlericalism, and the Mexican Church in the United States

The epic struggles occurring in Mexico had repercussions in Texas, breeding violence and setting in motion new migration flows that boosted the Mexican presence in the Southwest. Many Mexican clerics fled the turmoil and found refuge in San Antonio, a city that by 1914 had become the unofficial capital of revolutionists but that nevertheless maintained a dynamic Mexican religious culture due to the U.S. Catholic presence. San Antonio Catholicism, with its roots in missionary evangelization in the early eighteenth century, was reshaped by the active policies of bishops concerned with the religious neglect of the Mexican-born population in the Southwest, which grew from 100,000 to almost 1.5 million between 1910 and 1930.[7]

As Mexican immigration into the United States progressed in the early twentieth century, the U.S. church hierarchy realized that successful missionary efforts depended upon the establishment of Mexican settlements through church building and that the support of priests was crucial for organizing parishes. In 1911, a new San Antonio bishop, John

William Shaw, rededicated the chapel at Mission Espada. In 1913 a restoration project allowed for the reopening of church services at Mission Concepción, and five years later services resumed at Mission San José. The skeletal mission framework, however, would not serve the huge immigrant influx whose cultural, social, and spatial needs had launched a new phase of urban growth, for which neither the Mexico-centered exile church nor the fledgling U.S. immigrant church of the Southwest had been prepared. The persecution and instability of the Mexican Church amid revolutionary turmoil, along with fears of Protestant proselytizing, greatly worried Catholic bishops and clergy in the Mexican-American heartland of south-central Texas.[8]

"Religious indifference," in the view of San Antonio archbishop Arthur Jerome Drossaerts, made native-born Tejanos "easy marks" for Protestants and Masons.[9] Recent Mexican immigrants, in contrast, valued access to the priest to a much greater extent; one woman in San Antonio lamented that religious conflicts in Mexico had not only disrupted celebrations of Mass but made it impossible even to "kiss the priest's hand."[10]

San Antonio maintained a precarious Protestant-Catholic balance after 1850, with fluctuations depending largely on the volume of Mexican immigration. Protestants sects competed with Mexican-American Catholicism, establishing missionary arms in Texas, led by Southern Methodists in 1874, preparing materials in Spanish, hiring Mexican ministers, and lending financial assistance for the founding of separate Mexican-American congregations. By 1920 several Protestant denominations had established footholds in the Mexican Quarter, on streets once dominated by the Catholic Church. Protestant outreach included the Mexican Christian Institute, which provided a meeting place for Mexican patriotic and mutual aid organizations, while other centers, among them the Baptist Goodwill Center Mission, the Methodist Wesley Community Center, and the Presbyterian House of Neighborly Service, also pioneered in community work.[11]

The Chicago-based Catholic Church Extension Society was entrusted with overseeing missionary work in the United States and its dependencies. Contributions to it were channeled through the American Board of Catholic Missions. The largest donations came from major urban centers in the North and Midwest where Catholics predominated, led by Chicago, New York, Philadelphia, and Pittsburgh. Disbursements went disproportionately to Texas and the South, as well as the Philippine Islands and Puerto Rico. Between 1906 and 1944, most of Extension's early financing went to chapel buildings, including those occupied by religious

Front Façade and Convento of Concepción Mission in San Antonio, ca. 1901 (University of Texas Institute of Texan Cultures at San Antonio, No. 91-338, courtesy of Kitty Lipscomb)

order clergy, and church goods. One effort in 1914, for example, underwrote the transfer of several Oblate fathers to a small community of San Antonio Tejano rock quarry workers and their families in what became Our Lady of Sorrows Church. The adoption of innovative tools such as "chapel cars" and "motor chapels" to reach outlying areas, along with donations collected from the laborers' meager wages and grants from benefactors, especially those reading *Extension* magazine, achieved or were marks of considerable success.[12]

The Extension Society contributed a great deal to the solidifying of parish communities in San Antonio. The Reverend Francis C. Kelley, head of Extension, concluded that fuller religious participation required more church buildings and used the national exposure available to the Extension Society to bring Catholicism to isolated regions. Kelley's plan to found missions and develop them into parishes focused mainly on the Southwest; he saw a great need for establishing schools and training teachers for immigrant populations and hoped, "If we can save the children now they will supply both priests and teachers later on."[13] In 1922

Reverend Kelley noted that although growing numbers of Mexicans lived as far north as Chicago, they remained concentrated in the Southwest. "Whole villages of them," he wrote, "are without schools, and there are still many settlements without churches." He observed, "The worst of their situation is that the largest number of Mexicans go to the poorest of our dioceses, those least equipped to bear additional burdens." Extension assisted in financing churches and schools, which propelled the growth of Catholic institutions in Texas, with Mexican Americans as the primary beneficiaries.

Father Kelley's work also involved alerting U.S. Catholics to violence and instability in Mexico as a means of gaining support for the Mexican church and winning contributions for parish-building projects and for exiled Mexican clergy in Texas, New Orleans, and Cuba. San Antonio parishes received by far the greatest number of exiles and refugees nationally in the period between 1914 and 1920. In light of what he saw as unconscionable depredations, Kelley looked to influence the future of the Mexican church "with a view to insuring future liberty of conscience in Mexico," as he wrote in an article in *Extension* magazine.[14] He voiced support for many bishops who fled Mexico, and they in turn proclaimed in December 1914 that they were placing their affairs in the hands of the Extension Society and appointed Kelley "to represent the [exiled] Mexican church in America."[15] The greatest needs, these bishops contended, lay in continuing the religious training of Mexican seminarians, in resurrecting the Mexican Catholic press, and in preserving the piety of the people.

The Mexican government closed and confiscated property of Mexican seminaries, and their former students were often impressed into the revolutionary army. The Mexican church hierarchy feared the permanent loss of its clergy if they remained too long in the United States and favored continuing to anchor its members in Texas. The exiled bishops begged Extension to open a seminary in the United States after the closing of their seminaries in 1914. Father Kelley responded by establishing St. Philip Neri Seminary in Castroville, near San Antonio, in 1915. It remained open for three years, during which time it ordained more than eighty priests. Most of the clerics returned to Mexico, at least temporarily, after the adoption of the 1917 Mexican Constitution and the cessation of violence that year.[16]

Father Kelley spoke with many exiled bishops and wrote two books seeking to expose the excesses of Venustiano Carranza's regime in Mexico. In 1915 *Extension* published pointed articles that included claims from Mexican nuns that revolutionaries had burned statues of saints and confessionals in public squares, shot church officials, and violated women religious. Kelley's memoirs chronicled a wide range of atrocities in Mexico perpetrated by revolutionaries, including reports of tortured and starving priests, nuns driven out of their convents and mistreated, schools looted, and churches robbed. Not all of these claims were substantiated, but many of them were credible. Kelley recounted Mexican revolutionaries' practice of arresting a bishop and some important pastors in several cities and then demanding ransoms from the Church for their release. Normally lacking funds with which to pay, the prisoners were sent out with soldiers to collect door-to-door contributions. Archbishop Leopoldo Ruiz y Flores of Morelia encountered this fate after his ransom was fixed at 100,000 pesos; he eventually escaped, making his way across the border to Texas disguised as a peon.[17]

In all, hundreds of priests, mostly Spaniards, along with dozens of Mexican-born bishops, often disguised as Mexican peasants to evade government authorities, slipped across the border to El Paso or San Antonio, where they often took menial jobs to survive. Banished priests and nuns believed the Mexican government was essentially enslaving the Church in the revolution and saw the government as upheld by corrupt military power and false elections.

Although not formally assigned to San Fernando Cathedral in San Antonio, many of the exiled bishops, priests, and nuns assisted in enlivening the ritual and devotional life there. Others were more officially involved, such as Eugene Sugranes, an exiled Claretian priest, who was assigned to San Fernando Cathedral from 1917 to 1934. His numerous articles for the diocesan newspaper, the *Southern Messenger*, chronicled Mexican anticlericalism during La Cristiada and afterward, and occasionally he reached a broader Anglo-American Catholic audience nationally through articles in *Extension* magazine. His and others' close coverage of the religious controversy in Mexico was undertaken not only because "outrages" were being perpetrated against fellow Catholics in a neighboring country but because San Antonio served as a refuge for Mexican clerics.

Father Sugranes's bilingualism and journalistic skill gave him a great deal of influence on San Antonio's bishop Drossaerts; he was able to alert Drossaerts, for example, to activities of a schismatic organization branching out in Mexico and San Antonio during the Cristero Revolt.[18] The Mexican government clandestinely supported and encouraged this schismatic organization, known as the Mexican Catholic Apostolic Church, formed in 1925 with the approval of President Calles, who reportedly commissioned an elderly priest in Mexico City, Joaquín Pérez, as "Patriarch of the Mexican Catholic Church." Pérez came to San Antonio along with "three or four self-styled bishops."[19] The schismatic priests were allowed to marry, and for supporters they represented a nationalistic alternative that would, according to one observer, keep money that traditionally had been sent abroad "in Mexico [so] that schools, hospitals and homes may be built and maintained. It is for this reason that they repudiate the Pope as they cannot control their wealth for their own use and recognize the Vatican."[20] Archbishop Drossaerts repeatedly warned of scheming *cismáticos*, "designing proselytizers of the sects supported by Calles and the Mexican government, that archenemy of all Christianity."[21] Although one man purporting to be a bishop from the sect visited a number of Mexicans in Texas, confirming about fifty individuals, most of the schismatic churches soon folded, and by 1930 the schismatic threat diminished in both San Antonio and Mexico. Pérez himself eventually repented and died in the Catholic faith.[22]

The San Antonio exiles' response to the Calles suppression of the Mexican Church reflected both their religious devotion and their nationalistic commitment to cultural traditions. La Cristiada created ripples in San Antonio. A group called the Asociación Nacional de los Vasallos de Cristo Rey (National Association of the Vassals of Christ the King) in San Antonio, in its first major initiative of any kind, raised funds for the monument to Jesus at Cubilete. Devotees in San Antonio, as in Mexico, believed that the monument would help Mexicans become more aware of the "true rulers of Mexico," the Sacred Heart of Jesus and Our Lady of Guadalupe. The Vasallos, moreover, asserted that religious devotion was the best way to save their native land from violence, religious persecution, and political corruption.[23]

An émigré representing the bishop of León presided over the association's early meetings, while the cathedral's rector blessed each meeting on behalf of the archbishop. Monthly dues of ten cents went to special Masses, and a board of directors oversaw separate male and female groups. The San Fernando parish newsletter advertised its local activities, including fiestas as well as pilgrimages to Mexico. Significantly, nationalism, piety, and ethnic cohesion sprang from cooperation among lay leaders, cathedral priests, and the archbishop in these endeavors. The frequent prominence of the Vasallos de Cristo Rey in Guadalupe celebrations thus reflected a new focus on the homeland and a uniquely Mexican expression of Marian piety. Claretians, who had often perceived

Mexicans and Mexican Americans as lax Catholics, tried to seize the opportunity to mold a new Catholic identity marked by greater participation in the Church's sacramental life. Claretians contributed to homeland causes, supported exiled clergy, and sustained the parish community, easing alienation through religious solidarity.[24]

For a wide variety of social, economic, cultural, and political reasons, the years of the Cristero Revolt (1926–29) witnessed an exodus of some 500,000 people to the interior of Mexico; a similar number crossed the U.S. border. As good Catholics, many rancheros participated actively in the Cristiada, engaging in chronic fighting and guerrilla warfare against government troops. The property of some Catholic rancheros was destroyed, and they were obliged to flee deeper into the mountains or to the north. Many defeated Cristeros and others caught in the struggle fled to the larger Mexican cities or other places not torn by war, for the sake of physical security or employment.

A diplomatic rather than military solution to the conflict emerged: churches were opened again in 1929 after Father John Burke, executive secretary of the National Catholic Welfare Conference, and Dwight Morrow, U.S. ambassador to Mexico, worked out a partial solution to religious conflict between church and state. Through this mediation, incoming president Emilio Portes Gil reached a settlement with the clergy, promising that nonregistered priests would be allowed to exercise their ministry.[25]

After 1931, however, under the Obregón regime, government persecution of the Church resumed. Half of the states of Mexico forbade priests to exercise their religious functions. Seminaries, which had been allowed under the Constitution of 1917, were expressly forbidden. Sporadic violence continued, particularly in the more proclerical states such as Michoacán. In 1934 Portes, now the attorney general in Mexico's unstable government, called the actions of the Catholic clergy "open sedition" and "rebellion" based on fanaticism and greed: "[The clergy] tried to exploit the people by means of education and to that end it founded rural schools in the Indian villages, as well as primary, superior and preparatory schools in various centers, in the capitals of the States and in the Federal District." Portes sought to minimize clerical influence and thereby elevate "the poor and downtrodden [with] nothing to expect in this world." He saw the clergy as sinister opponents of the regime.[26]

Active anticlerical persecution was followed by looser enforcement of anticlerical statutes on the books. President Lázaro Cárdenas (1934–40), anxious to undertake far-reaching economic and social reforms,

viewed anticlerical conflict as divisive and in 1936 guided the government into renewed reconciliation with the Roman Catholic Church.
Nevertheless, from his exile post in San Antonio, Archbishop Leopoldo Ruiz continued his attacks against Cárdenas and his socialistic
educational policy. In a pastoral letter, he directed priests and bishops
to forbid Catholic parents in Mexico to send their children to government or public schools. Those who did would be excommunicated. He
also ordered the clergy to continue religious instruction of students to
counteract inroads made by government schools. Ruiz prohibited
members of the sole Mexican political party at the time, the Partido Nacional Revolucionario, from receiving the sacraments or otherwise participating in religious ceremonies. The Mexican bishops sponsored demonstrations and published articles critical of the Mexican government,
hoping to inspire U.S. citizens to demand U.S. intervention against the
Cárdenas administration. The movement also received strong approval
from U.S. Catholic bishops, who asked fellow Americans, Catholic or
otherwise, to join in protesting against Mexico's regime.[27]

Friction over new attempts to implement land reform led to further
divisions within revolutionary governments well into the 1940s. In 1940
Manuel Ávila Camacho, upon his inauguration as president, publicly professed his Catholicism. He modified article 3 of the Constitution, remov-
ing the socialist orientation, but the state's monopoly in the early grades
of schooling was maintained. Prohibitions against the clergy survived,
but tolerance along the Porfirian mode returned. Most religious men and
women in Mexico were Mexican born, with a decreasing number from
Spain, Italy, and the United States. Now, with anticlerical laws were no
longer enforced, the religious order clergy returned to Mexico, and private Catholic schools reopened. The government maintained the policy
of tolerating certain open religious ceremonies and permitting officials to
engage in private religious practices.

Despite this cooling of tensions, Mexico's church-state controversy,
which had dragged on for decades and sparked significant immigration,
colored the religious outlook of the revolutionary generation in Mexico
and Texas for years to come.[28]

San Antonio's Immigrant Church

Throughout San Antonio's history as a defensive outpost on the northern periphery of New Spain, and then briefly Mexico, the Church had
assumed a dominant role in creating and maintaining ethnic cohesion
among Mexicans and Mexican Americans. Parish development programs

of Anglo bishops and clergy and the response of Tejanos and Mexican immigrants synthesized Mexican Catholicism, and the church in San Antonio became increasingly dependent on immigrant participation and support. San Fernando Cathedral blended Tejano and immigrant culture and Catholicism and became a force for secular community cohesion through the several mutual aid societies that it housed. San Fernando was the place for Tejanos, as the Spanish missions became artifacts of a bygone era. Germans, Poles, and other Catholic immigrant groups developed national parishes in the city, making for a somewhat cosmopolitan turn-of-the-century Catholic mix.[29]

In 1911, San Antonio bishop John Shaw noted the staggering dimensions of the task of ministering to new immigrants: "We have at least 20,000 Mexicans in the City yet we have only 8 Fathers and of these some are always absent on the Country Missions."[30] Mexicans and Mexican Americans did not yet have much say in assigning priests and overseeing pastoral work, despite having at least the beginnings of an immigrant clergy that might attempt to bridge the gap between parishioners and the episcopacy.[31]

Bishop Shaw oversaw the creation of seven new parishes from 1911 to 1915 (including several for Mexicans run by diocesan and religious order clergy). "I know of no greater charity than to build a church or a school for them," wrote Shaw of the Mexicans in his community, particularly those of "the humbler classes."[32] Shaw demonstrated how racial and cultural differences influenced the religious equation at this time: "We have at a very conservative count [of] at least seventy thousand . . . Mexican Indians. They are of course all baptized but owing in the past to the inability of providing priests, churches and schools for them, large numbers of them are very poorly instructed in our Holy Faith."[33] Viewing Mexicans as "humble, docile, and worthy of charity," the prelate in 1917 sought to dispel rumors, created by German propaganda and appearing in some Spanish-language papers, that Mexican immigrants faced conscription into the U.S. armed forces during World War I. To correct this "erroneous impression" and prevent a southbound exodus of those fearing conscription, Shaw instructed his pastors to make announcements at their Sunday services persuading Mexican nationals, especially storekeepers and other proprietors who were making valuable economic contributions in the midst of the wartime labor shortage, to remain in his diocese.

The Claretian Missionary Fathers, a Spanish order expelled from Mexico, arrived in San Antonio in 1902. In time, they would have an enormous presence in the city. From their base in San Fernando Cathedral they gradually organized Tejanos and Mexican immigrants into Spanish-speaking missions, chapels, and parishes throughout the diocese. Their urban missionary work filled a vacuum and marked the beginning of a sustained Texas Mexican ministry. The Claretians also branched out to serve Mexicans in California, the Midwest, and other locations. In 1911, Claretians established the parish of Our Lady of Guadalupe, followed by Immaculate Heart of Mary in 1912, Our Lady of Sorrows in 1915, and Christ the King in 1927. Some forty mission churches or chapels outside the city of San Antonio were either erected or taken care of by the Claretians at one time or another.[34]

The Redemptorist Fathers, a group who had served during the nineteenth century in parishes on the East Coast and Midwest, started preaching missions and offering retreats in Texas as early as 1876, but their first permanent foundation was made in San Antonio at the invitation of Bishop Shaw in 1911, when they opened St. Gerard's Parish. Two years later they opened a parish for the Spanish-speaking on the East Side—Our Lady of Perpetual Help—after the diocese acquired some land originally granted by a nineteenth-century Mexican immigrant. Father John Muehlsiepen used the parish as a base for itinerant priests, including some of Spanish birth exiled from Mexico. They ran missionary programs in outlying areas of the diocese, including missions for Mexicans. Redemptorists ministered to communities clustered near San Antonio's once-abandoned downriver missions as well as to immigrants on the West Side after they established St. Alfonsus Church in 1925, where they remained active for five years.[35]

Our Lady of Perpetual Help Church, run by Redemptorists, adopted the tactic of putting the names of families on small portable shrines honoring different saints, to which parishioners deposited contributions in a sealed drawer. At month's end the last family on the list would bring the shrine to the priest, who unlocked the drawer and removed the offerings.[36] Other parish endeavors were pursued to achieve traditional ecclesiastical goals, such as Father Lopez's series of outdoor missions in the late 1930s offering "fix-up" marriages to validate common-law unions. Passersby heard music being played on loudspeakers and came to witness impromptu marriage ceremonies in front of private homes and businesses. These mobile sessions offered Spanish sermons with short talks in English, with confessions sometimes heard through the open window of an automobile parked in someone's backyard as the parishioner knelt on the running board.[37] Some well-organized dramatic programs at St. Gerard's, also run by Redemptorist Fathers, drew volunteer actors from all over the city. Smaller events were not always as lively, as indicated by an entry in one Redemptorist's journal describing a four-hour Christmas performance at Our Lady of Perpetual Help as "a long, dreary, lifeless drama."[38]

Archbishop Drossaerts, who served from 1918 to 1940, approved fourteen new parishes in all, including five specifically catering to Mexican Catholics, keeping pace with territorial expansion, numerical growth, and rising rates of home ownership. By 1940 about one-third of San Antonio's parishes primarily served people of Mexican origin. By then the city's population had risen to 254,000, with persons of Mexican ancestry numbering about 103,000, constituting 40 percent of the total.[39] Catholic churches attempted to ward off Protestants even in the surrounding hinterland, where a church was built in an area that had until recently contained "only mesquite and sage brush growing and no Mexicans at all."[40]

Archbishop Drossaerts believed that the cultural background of the Mexican immigrants, especially because of their time spent on Mexican or Texas ranches, left them inadequately trained, "strangers amongst a strange people," totally unfamiliar with catechism, priests, schools, and churches. This background obviously separated them from Anglo society. Drossaerts viewed educational institutions as agents of assimilation and hoped to keep Mexican Americans in parochial schools. He feared that "the result of their going to the public schools is only too evident in the religious indifference and very loose morals of our Mexican youth. If things are left to drift as in the past we will lose half of our Mexican population for the faith." Through Americanization and the promotion of parochial schools with instruction in English, the Church made the image of the Mexican less threatening and more acceptable to the dominant Anglo society. Public schools, too, presented immigrants with opportunities to "acquire some knowledge of our English language . . . and perhaps even some thin veneer of American ways and manners," according to Drossaerts.[41]

The celebration of All Saints' Day began in the first centuries of the church to commemorate martyrs. Later the feast came to honor all of the deceased who were united with God but unmentioned in the official church calendar. In the eleventh century, the Day of the Dead (Día de los Muertos), or All Souls' Day, as it is known outside of Latin America, was established as an annual feast celebrated on November 2 to pray for the dead who are being purified before entering heaven. When the Spanish brought All Souls' Day to the Americas, they incorporated indigenous beliefs and customs about death. Later in San Antonio, *colonia* residents branched out to participate in a wide range of community-building activities, from baptisms and other rituals to the observance of Mexican holidays, such as the Día de los Muertos, that constitute popular religiosity outside of structures of institutional Catholicism. For the traditional Día de los Muertos, thousands of people "visited" their ancestors at one of the various church cemeteries located at the colonia's western fringes. At San Fernando Church, the archbishop held a Mass, after which priests moved among the graves reciting special prayers for the families, who walked about the grounds in a picniclike atmosphere, carrying flowers purchased from makeshift markets near the entrances. Religion and ethnicity blended in these religious celebrations.[42] Drossaerts tolerated Mexican devotional practices, but he regarded them as fundamentally inadequate since they did not promote "religious instruction and good example."[43]

Throughout the seventeenth and eighteenth centuries, *los pastores* and other forms of popular religious drama had been utilized throughout rural Mexico, including what is now the Southwestern United States, as a means of self-evangelization for local communities. *Los pastores*, which literally means "the shepherds," are plays or performances telling of shepherds' coming to see the baby Jesus as he lay in the manger and to bring him gifts. The Wise Men also make an appearance in these performances. Los pastores were performed in the backyards and driveways of homes in San Antonio barrios and at local churches. Another important focal point of religious faith in the barrio, as elsewhere in Mexican-American life, was the family chapel altar. Mexican-American families adapted customs from rural Mexico, where people expressed religiosity at home. According to one account, a typical Mexican household in the 1920s contained a room with three altars adorned with framed pictures of the Virgin of Guadalupe and other Catholic figures. Portraits or statues set on altar cloths on tables or bedroom chests displayed the image of La Morenita, along with collections of crucifixes, flowers, family photographs, and personal items. Our Lady of Guadalupe symbolized, more than others, the need for protection, whether for journeys, health, jobs, or the like. Each altar thus defined the family's spiritual life, existing separately from the institutional church, as the faithful directed their prayers to various saints or to the deceased. The formation of Guadalupe societies and other parish associations, often involving the performance of special devotions, reinforced ethnic bonds while reflecting the importance of popular religion, especially among women.[44]

The popularity of San Antonio's unofficial shrine, El Señor de los

Milagros, believed by many to be responsible for divine healing, exemplified the involvement of clergy with popular, noninstitutional elements of Mexican-American Catholicism. Legend had it that a saint appeared one day in the early nineteenth century on the outskirts of colonial San Antonio, calling upon a young Tejano to promise to build a chapel at that spot. Within the one-room Chapel of the Miracles, as it became known, worshipers prayed to a crucifix hanging alone on the main altar, reputedly the source of miracles. During the 1920s, donkey-drawn carts and wagons and "pack burros, heavily burdened," brought immigrants and migrants to the chapel from distant points. The setting attracted more assimilated persons as well; one observer noted in 1926 that "girls already '*flapperizadas*' [flapperized]" knelt in the chapel "with their lighted candles [in] an atmosphere of great reverence and faith."[45]

San Fernando Cathedral's fervent Guadalupe celebrations drew huge crowds and on several occasions attracted groups of pilgrims who walked as far as thirty miles to the cathedral from nearby towns (during this era most Texas Mexicans lived in small towns and ranches). In the early 1930s, San Fernando parishioners led processions through the plazas and streets for celebrations like Cristo Rey (Christ the King), Our Lady of Guadalupe, and *las posadas* (a reenactment of Mary and Joseph's search for lodging in Bethlehem). Parish societies and associations facilitated interaction between Tejanos and Mexican immigrants at monthly meetings and social gatherings, as well as Sunday Mass. Some societies that had existed in the parish since the nineteenth century, such as Hijas de María (Daughters of Mary), incorporated members from among the immigrants who joined the cathedral congregation.[46]

Another example of the staying power of Mexican popular religion is the traditional Christmas play, *la pastorela*, which demonstrates continuity with publicly performed Spanish medieval religious dramas and the persistence of cultural traditions of the seventeenth and eighteenth centuries transmitted across the northern Mexican frontier. Leandro Granados, an immigrant who fled Mexico in the early 1920s, initiated San Antonio's *pastorela* in 1913. Granados had memorized and then transcribed a version of the text, and he founded a troupe on the West Side that stopped in parishioners' homes as well as at local parishes and outlying missions. In 1949, Father Carmelo Tranchese of Our Lady of Guadalupe Church edited, translated, and published the Granados *pastorela*, which became a vital part of the community's historical memory.[47]

Crowd Watching Procession outside San Fernando Cathedral on Feast of Our Lady of Guadalupe, December 12, 1933 (San Antonio *Light* Collection, University of Texas Institute of Texan Cultures at San Antonio, No. L-0140-F, courtesy of Hearst Corporation)

Social Upheaval and Parish Communities

During the 1880s a rail connection with the border town of Laredo, over 150 miles away, made San Antonio more accessible to immigrants on both sides of the Rio Grande, who increasingly moved north around the turn of the century. The Alamo and Military plazas, the original nuclei of the city, merged into one urban core while tall, modern structures replaced many of the Mexican adobes in the center and the infrastructure expanded in all directions. Meanwhile, the development of northern Mexico accelerated the interdependency of Mexico and the United States as a commercial and industrial boom displaced and transformed traditional peasants and artisans. The railroads facilitated Mexican entry to the Southwest and Midwest.

The Anglo onslaught in San Antonio in the late nineteenth century ultimately brought the old families and other Mexican-origin people disfranchisement, confusion, and anomie; yet San Antonio in that period was certainly not marked only by the unyielding oppression of Tejanos. Familiar signs of the past remained through the century, as Mexican food stands filled the marketplace. Tejanos were far from outcast economically, as shown by a list of approximately twelve Spanish-surnamed citizens in 1887 having property valued at $10,000 or more. Despite increasingly rigid economic stratification, Mexican-American leaders consistently succeeded in getting themselves elected or appointed to a variety of county and city offices in this period, although their representation in local governmental offices fell with their proportion in the general population.

Significantly, however, the influx of Anglos changed the spatial configuration of San Antonio, leading to the development of a booming central business district and channeling Tejano settlement across San Pedro Creek, thus shaping the Mexican *colonia* on the West Side. The *colonia*, close to the International and Great Northern Railway depot, served as the city's main entry point during the Great Migration between the years 1910 and 1930. After 1910, many more Mexican businesses became established in San Antonio, with concentrations of hotels, restaurants, drugstores, and general stores on the Near West Side. The boundaries of San Antonio's Mexican barrio delimited a four-square-mile region of formidable congestion; it was riddled with shacks with dirt floors and no indoor plumbing and houses built around crowded courts, called "corrals" by Anglos (many had been converted from stables) and *vecindades* by the migrants, for which families often paid less than a dollar weekly. During the 1920s new one-room shacks were thrown up to accommodate the newcomers, and the overcrowded Mexican West Side became synonymous with poverty.[48]

Newer subdivisions on the mostly Anglo North Side, as well as in a few other areas, adopted racially restrictive covenants barring Mexicans and blacks in order to preserve the homogeneity of exclusive neighborhoods. This effort redirected the settlement of Mexican Americans and other minorities in San Antonio to available lots on the West Side, until the Supreme Court in 1948 declared the covenants unenforceable. By then Mexican settlement had been already effectively channeled into unrestricted areas, mostly on the western side of town. The Depression froze residence patterns, reduced mobility, and disrupted the social functions of the parishes. The economic crisis of the 1930s also delayed initiatives or programs for training Mexican seminarians. Eventually the middle class and, sometimes, the U.S. native-born joined mixed congregations, and by the mid-1930s some parishes on the North Side, such as Our Lady of Sorrows, featured English as well as Spanish sermons. Catholic churches created havens in the West Side *colonia*, meanwhile, uniting Tejanos and Mexican immigrants through a common language and religion.[49]

Leadership in San Antonio, the secular as well as religious hub for Tejanos, emerged from a mix of upper-middle-class professionals, businesspeople, and former political figures and educators who had fled the homeland for religious and social as well as purely economic reasons. Tejano political reform was primarily undertaken by Mexican Americans in the League of United Latin American Citizens (LULAC), beginning in 1929, though previous organizations dated back a decade earlier. LULAC sought to eradicate discriminatory practices in education and other areas, and its middle-class, largely U.S.-born leaders adopted strategies geared to gains within the U.S. legal system. Culturally they favored Americanization, in contrast to nationalistic Mexico-focused immigrant elites, who traditionally remained outside of the unfamiliar world of urban politics. By 1940, the Mexican-origin population was up to 103,000, and a Mexican-American middle class, along with a political exile class—*los ricos* (the rich ones)—began to enter the economic mainstream by providing services to other members of the *colonia*.[50]

"Mexican work" became a stigmatization, accompanied and reinforced by separate neighborhoods, churches, schools, and businesses, especially in small Texas towns during the 1920s. The worst-paid workers were pecan shellers, whose sole advantage was that their consumption of pecans were not closely supervised. Pecan shelling, the major industry of San Antonio, had become the top winter occupation of Mexican Americans during the Depression, with West Side plants employing up to twenty thousand workers in the peak year of 1934. The industry perpetuated isolation, since pecans were often shelled at home by the entire family as a cottage industry, at wages of pennies a day.[51]

Shellers gained new vitality when the United Cannery, Agricultural, Packing, and Allied Workers of America (UCAPAWA), a federation of labor organizations whose main source of strength lay among the employees of processing industries closely related to farming, emerged as a union of the Congress of Industrial Organizations in 1937. At this time communists, who believed that LULAC's policies caused isolation of the Mexican masses and a split between native and foreign born, organized workers' alliances on the West Side and included the shellers. A violent strike the following year spread to over a hundred pecan workshops in the Mexican Quarter, as declining pecan prices drove some firms out of business and compelled others to cut wages. The strike lost the support of Archbishop Drossaerts, who failed in attempts to broker a settlement with employers over pay cuts and piece-rate payments and had become wary of potentially divisive political controversies.[52]

Carmelo Tranchese, an Italian-born Jesuit priest who had served at Our Lady of Guadalupe since 1932, helped increase Mexican and Mexican-American involvement in both religious and secular affairs during the 1930s. Long before the shellers' strike, the maverick priest had involved himself in a wide array of community struggles, such as endorsing the West Side School Improvement League in its battle to reform the public schools, primarily by building and maintaining better facilities. One political endeavor won Tranchese widespread acclaim—working with Eleanor Roosevelt and lobbying for federally funded public housing projects on the West Side. His activism helped alleviate the dire housing conditions of Mexican Americans and strengthened his support in the parish.

Through the weekly parish newspaper, *La Voz de la Parroquia*, distributed free after all the masses on the West Side, Tranchese became instrumental in implementing the Church's social philosophy. In 1937, the archbishop intervened and took charge of *La Voz*, broadening its audience while forgoing the announcements of weddings and baptisms, thereby shifting its audience and diluting its impact among some member of the *colonia*. Father Tranchese led street parades every December 12 in commemoration of Our Lady of Guadalupe and presided over festivities on Good Friday and other holidays. Tranchese and Redemptorist Father Juan Lopez, the latter being one of very few ordained Mexican Americans at that time, formed the Catholic Relief Association in 1931, just as the Catholic social action movement was dawning, and unions, cooperatives, and charities came to be seen as steps toward democratizing social structures and institutions. Father Tranchese became a hero of poor Mexicans, supporting the pecan shellers, organizing relief and health care, and preaching the social gospel.[53]

Building on Mexican traditions more than his superiors may have liked, Tranchese cultivated accessibility and demonstrated concern, attracting loyal followers, although he believed that his charges often disregarded the rules of Catholic behavior and adhered more to "Mexican traditions" and "holy superstition" than to his concept of a guided faith. Attendance at Mass and collections were especially fitful during the early years of the Depression, although both improved following the construction of a nearby housing project for which Tranchese had lobbied the Roosevelt administration. Fund raising for other projects took the form of dramatic presentations, dances, movies, parish fairs known as *jamaicas*, as well as *novenas* (prayers offered daily for nine successive days to fulfill specific requests). These events brought in only small collections, but they established a prevailing sense of community. Tranchese, moreover, led several huge processions through the West Side leading up to the Chapel of the Miracles near downtown.[54]

By 1930, Mexican-American Catholicism had evolved from its frontier roots into something new, somewhere between the Mexican religion from south of the border and the European immigrant model in style, practices, and beliefs. The Mass and sacraments emphasis of European immigrant Catholicism was very foreign to the Mexican tradition of Catholicism; regular attendance at Sunday Mass was not part of the Mexican tradition. The "public sphere" featured elaborate outdoor neighborhood celebrations of religious feasts with music, processions, and rich symbolism. The evolution and expansion of Mexican-American urban Catholicism also anchored the immigrants in the West Side barrio.

Mexican Barrios and Immigrant Catholicism

The Catholic Church had had previous dealings with "unchurched" Italian immigrants, who, unlike the Irish, often lapsed in their attendance at Mass but engaged wholeheartedly in popular religious traditions, especially those practiced in the larger community. The characteristic demonstrations of piety among southern Italians of the *mezzogiorno* (the primary immigrant sending region) was the annual feast for the Madonna, or patron saint—part carnival, with brass bands, fireworks, and exotic homeland delicacies. Feasts came to be considered an embarrassment to American Catholics and occasioned anxiety among Italian priests, whose leadership skills within the clerical culture and loyalties within the ethnic culture were set against one another and subject to intense scrutiny. Moreover, Italian Americans were slow to enter U.S. seminaries and to rise in the hierarchy, reflecting their anticlerical culture as well as a lack of political clout, both within and outside of the church.[55]

Historians have noted that Italian-American urban neighborhoods have continued many customs from the homeland—especially from isolated Italian peasants' hilltop villages, where peasants shared customs in a common environment. Transatlantic immigration set the stage for regrouping in Little Italies, which usually arose near job sites. Neighborhood enclaves grew as other newcomers followed, and the newcomers came to dominate the urban landscape, while fluid concepts of citizenship presaged later patterns that developed among Mexican and other Latin American–origin migrants and their homelands in the late twentieth century. Fellow nationals abroad, whether permanent residents or merely birds of passage, came to be included by national and local governments as part of broad development strategies.[56]

Examples of the multifaceted relationship between Catholicism and ethnicity among Italians are noticeable, especially as concerns assimilation, in rural areas and small towns where Little Italies, which have largely come to represent Italian-American identity, never really thrived. In Brazos County, Texas, for example, Italian immigrants have assimilated into the dominant southern Anglo-American culture. Feelings of *campanilismo* (localism), distrust of outsiders, negative attitudes toward education, and political apathy largely disappeared among Italians, and ethnic identity became strongly related to membership in the Roman Catholic Church. This contrasted with the generally weak Italian national parishes in cities such as New York, Chicago, and Philadelphia, which only reluctantly supported parochial education while lagging considerably in stewardship when compared, for example, with Polish Americans.[57]

The religious circumstances of Mexicans were quite similar with regard to urban patterns through much of the twentieth century, with one major difference. Italians, over generations, especially after the imposition of national origins quotas in the 1920s, have moved to the suburbs, leaving urban spaces for new immigrant groups in a continuing process of neighborhood invasion and succession. Mexicans, meanwhile, have constituted a continual contingent to both urban and rural America since the 1920s, with the exception of the 1930s. An acute shortage of trained priests and lack of funds delayed ecclesiastical development in these Mexican communities, as they had among Italians.

In San Antonio by 1940, only 90,000 of more than 250,000 residents were Catholic (over two-thirds of these being Mexican). Yet Mexican immigrants transformed their parishes during times of religious crisis in the homeland, cooperating with the religious-order clergy to develop a base for lobbying the U.S. government. This was evident in the work of the Spanish Claretians exiled from Mexico as well as in the support given to refugee priests and bishops, who were taken in at San Fernando Cathedral and other parishes. During the Mexican revolutionary decades, coherent schemes for strengthening the Mexican ministry north of the border became more necessary, as the area became reinterpreted as mission country for the U.S. church. Since Spain appeared the logical source for clergy, in 1924 the Extension Society had funded stipends to educate forty Claretian seminarians in preparation for U.S. missionary work.[58]

In the summer of 1936, more than 270 Claretians in Catalonia—a seat of religious traditionalism during the Spanish Civil War of 1936–39—were executed by partisans of the Spanish Republican armies. The Spanish priests were now victims of persecution by both revolutionary Mexico and Republican Spain. The anticlerical violence of the Spanish Civil War decreased the number of Spanish Claretian priests available for years to come for Mexican-American barrios in the United States. It also contributed to dissension among Mexican immigrants, with both radical and conservative organizations from Mexico having their own leaders and publications; visits from varying factions to Chicago sparked debate and controversy regarding church-state relations in the 1920s and the Spanish Civil War in the 1930s. Significantly, however, Mexican immigrants increasingly involved themselves with local issues—including labor struggles, discrimination at the hands of police and courts, and the development of parish organizations—though they retained an interest in matters in Mexico.[59]

3 Colonial Dilemmas: Puerto Ricans and the U.S. Church

From its founding in the early 1500s until 1898, the Spanish Church in Puerto Rico monopolized educational as well as religious life. But it had left the Puerto Rican church in disarray. Just before the U.S. takeover, there had been consolidations of several churches under a single priest, who often would be under temporary assignment, so that parish care was disrupted. Many pueblos were left virtually unattended. Spanish priests abandoned several parishes, causing a scarcity of personnel, especially in the country districts. Some priests had two or three parishes in their charge, having had to absorb neighboring parishes because of the flight of their confreres.

After the Spanish-American War, church attendance fell by more than half in dozens of towns as Spanish clergy left the island for Spain. The United States now required Spanish nationals, who were in the majority among the clergy, to renounce loyalty to Spain and accept Puerto Rican (not U.S.) citizenship in order to remain in Puerto Rico. Everyone else was forced to return to Spain and reapply for a visa from the United States in order to return to the island.[1]

The vacuum of Catholic leadership invited proselytizing by the continental U.S. Catholic Church, Protestant denominations, and native Puerto Rican Catholics. Protestant leaders in the United States saw the U.S. acquisition of Puerto Rico as a great opportunity to expand their missionary efforts. Rather than engaging in extensive internal competition, in March 1899, missionaries from a wide variety of denominations gathered in Puerto Rico and on a map dissected the island into spheres of influence. Only the largest cities had congregational infighting. This early ecumenical approach led Puerto Ricans to adopt considerable fluidity, shifting their allegiances as they moved to areas dominated by other denominations. Due to a wide variety of political, social, and cultural factors, not the least of which is its strong connection to the United States, Puerto Rico has become among the most Protestant areas of Latin America. Puerto Rican Protestantism has the virtue of joint training of ministers and publication of common "Christian" newspapers and other pub-

lications. Before 1930, Americanization took place both in Protestantism
and Catholicism, but only among Protestants were there significant numbers of native clergy.[2]

After the war, Puerto Rico was given an apparently open-ended and
purposefully ambiguous territorial status. The Treaty of Paris left Puerto
Rico's status unclear, stating merely that all islands "now under Spanish
sovereignty in the West Indies" would be ceded to the United States. Naturally this led to increasing U.S. economic and political involvement with
Latin America. The subsequent reconstitution of Puerto Rico's government through the appointment of colonial officers forestalled any hopes of
autonomy, let alone independence. The island's fledgling government was
controlled by policies initiated in Washington, D.C., and carried out largely
by an appointed ministry of North Americans, with Puerto Ricans embarking on a supposed tutelage in democracy. Meanwhile, the U.S. presence
quickly transformed Puerto Rico economically through the commercialization of agriculture, investments in processing mills, and the introduction
of new communications and transportation technologies. A modern system
of sugar cultivation was established on the island, with new technologies
for grinding cane on increasingly large areas of land. Sugar became an important factor in the island's development, along with tobacco and coffee;
these "after-dinner crops" soon were heavily capitalized and monopolized
by U.S. investors.[3]

The Island Becomes a Missionary Territory

The birth of La Congregación San Juan Evangelista, more commonly
known as Los Hermanos Cheos, can be credited to José de los Santos
Morales, a young farm laborer who in 1902, at the age of sixteen, began
to preach spontaneously in defense of the Roman Catholic faith in the
Arrozales barrio (neighborhood) in the town of Arecibo. Four years earlier, he had heard it said that the *norteamericanos* came to the island with
the goal of propagating their Protestant faith. It was said that these Protestants were attacking the practices of Roman Catholicism, in particular
the praying of the rosary. Morales's response was to form "an army of
peasants and to rise in arms to defend our faith and our devotion to the
virgin" by preaching to *campesinos*. In 1903, apart from Morales, twenty-
one-year-old José Rodríguez Medina experienced a similar calling and
began preaching in towns. The two men met in 1904 and made a covenant, the Pacto de Cheo, agreeing to preach the teachings of the Church
and defend the praying of the rosary and other Marian devotions. When
not working in the fields, they traveled to village chapels and missions,

where they taught catechism and otherwise offered their services. After several decades of their activities, one bishop feared that their overzealous activities might make over the island into an untrained "camp of fanatics" reminiscent of desert monks.[4]

Puerto Rico was not incorporated into the U.S. ecclesiastical province but was made directly subject to the Holy See. So while the island got a U.S. hierarchy, it was not made a part of the U.S. church. Under the leadership of James Blenk, bishop of San Juan, the United States paid $300,000 to the diocese of Puerto Rico to settle old debts for confiscated properties to the diocese, and this helped establish the church on a firm financial footing. The Redemptorist Order of the American Province established its community in Puerto Rico in 1902; by 1905, the Dutch Dominicans, the Spanish Capuchins, and Augustinians joined the mix. All were dedicated to parish work. In 1907 Bishop Blenk invited other U.S. religious orders to put priests in charge of parishes in Puerto Rico. William Ambrose Jones (1907–1921), Blenk's successor, followed suit and became the real builder of the American institutional church in Puerto Rico, inviting religious orders to send priests to Puerto Rico, where they were given charge of parishes. While the orders of priests were primarily brought in to staff the island's parishes, congregations of teaching sisters were invited to staff another pillar of the new system: the network of parochial schools that spread across the whole island, reaching its apogee in the 1950s.[5]

Jones, who was an Augustinian, rebuilt the institutional church in Puerto Rico according to the "American model," strengthening missionary Catholicism. Missionary Christianity was tied to an ethnocentric Western worldview. The missionary emphasis on the parish revitalized official religion and imposed more centralized control, without introducing cultural pluralism into the Church. The imposition of U.S. church structures, considered "more efficient," introduced new rules and patterns of administration, bureaucracy, correspondence, and record keeping. In 1917 new diocesan statutes embodied and gave permanent form to the policies initiated by Blenk and Jones, which freed the new bishops to administer the lone diocese of San Juan as they saw fit. Parish priests became the administrators of parochial finances, with lay involvement kept to a minimum. Bishop Jones moved for the creation of a parochial school system and American-style lay organizations, such as the Holy Name Society and the Knights of Columbus.[6]

Redemptorists, the most numerous among the missionary priests, emphasized personal piety and drew on traditions of popular religion. Their missions, conducted at first out of the western city of Mayaguez, featured preaching that was usually done at night apart from the liturgy of the Mass. Countryside missions often lasted for an entire week and included counseling, confessions, and preparation for the sacraments of baptism, confirmation, and marriage. The Mass was usually celebrated and the sacraments conferred on the last day of the mission.[7]

As late as 1929 Puerto Rico remained a missionary field, with just a few Catholic chapels scattered around the island, so that U.S. and Spanish priests had to gather congregants in private houses or even barns as they traveled from town to town. Religious women, notably the Mission Helpers of the Sacred Heart, were also active. One priest noted that additional funding "helps bring Sisters, as well as chapels."[8] In the late 1920s the San Juan Diocese and the new Ponce Diocese shared a similar problem: a lack of religious personnel and training facilities to provide for future clergy. *Extension* magazine, recognizing a need "to educate a sufficient number of Puerto Ricans to care for their own brothers plus 'some American priests who for a time would direct operations,'" appealed to its readers for three hundred dollars yearly to "pay the expenses of a young man preparing for the missionary priesthood."[9]

In 1931, at a new chapel on the road from Caguas to San Juan that had electric lights, a tile floor, and an organ, several marriages were "fixed up." Among them was a couple that had been living in a civil union (*a lo civil*) for twenty-eight years.[10] Due to the one-dollar fee for a marriage license, many people had avoided church marriages, though "even those who are failing in some of the very essential duties of a Catholic, having been married out of the Church or not even having gone through the ceremony of marriage, insist that they are '*muy católico*' [that is,] 'nothing else but' Catholic."[11] The very steep, corkscrew-curved and twisted mountain roads were also great obstacles to residents and outsiders. The mountainous coffee country was penetrable only on horseback.

In countryside devoted to coffee raising and on small farms (*fincas*) owned by Catholics, however, missionaries were received hospitably. One missionary priest penned an extensive passage on the piety of the mountain dweller, noting that during Holy Week "the passion and death of 'el Crucificado' react on his sensitive soul like the master-touch of an artist. It is during these ceremonies of the Church that we see the 'Jíbaro' at his best. For he then gives vent to his faith in unreserved expressions of fervor and edification."[12]

By 1930, rural priests were responsible for more than twenty thousand people each in their mountainous missions; elusive parish boundaries usually included a town's entire rural and town population as priests conducted widening circuits, or missions, from major towns and cities.[13] Visiting clergy on periodic missions trying to penetrate the rural *campo* lacked familiar comforts. Upon arrival in a village, a priest often had to hold Mass in "little tumble-down huts" or "tobacco sheds." In 1941, on the offshore island of Vieques, too poor to support a permanent priest, an old movie theater was bought and used as a chapel. It later became imperiled when one whole section of that island was taken over by the U.S. Navy in mid-1941, causing families to disperse to a new settlement. On Culebra, a neighboring island with a population of five hundred mostly baptized Catholics, a concrete chapel was built and dedicated to La Virgen de Carmen.[14] With the help of the Chicago-based Extension Society, many rural chapels were built as "home missions" during the late 1920s and 1930s or were repaired after being hit by hurricanes. Appeals to "our good friends in the United States [for funds] to support more missionaries" gave the Diocese of San Juan hope of passing beyond the missionary stage, as an extensive building program contributed to the further Americanization of island Catholicism.[15]

By the late 1930s, San Juan bishop Aloysius Willinger had become concerned with the colonial question and its relationship to religious adherence: "Our relation with the States does not augur much hope for spiritual progress." Willinger feared the more radical secular aspects of Americanization, which sought "to promote social legislation of a very advanced and dangerous type."[16] From the capital similar voices were heard, noting that "besides Communism, [Puerto Ricans] are now beset with legislation just passed that tends to destroy their virtue and their religion. Birth control, sterilization, and the use of contraceptives have all been made legal. . . . Another [piece of legislation demanded] health certificates for all those who wish to get married; and this in a land where so many have some contagious disease." Catholicism unfortified by the sacraments, Willinger warned, could not withstand "these moral ravages."[17]

U.S. missionaries worked in many rural and urban chapels, holding Mass in the morning and conducting Sunday school classes in the afternoon. In some urban barrios, such as San Salvador in the city of Caguas, hundreds of attendees gathered. The clergy considered the *jíbaros* (mountain subsistence farmers) backward in religious matters when compared with their urban counterparts in Puerto Rico and, especially, in the continental United States.[18] Good Friday Mass attendance in 1931 in rural Guayama was said to involve the *jíbaro's* setting out from his mountain shack (*bohío*) for the village "with a chicken in one hand and dozen or so of eggs in the other, wrapped in a bandanna and carried along for barter."

One weeklong mission in 1931 in Carolina, a town with a population of almost five thousand, brought many confirmations, marriages, baptisms, and first communions. According to one priest, that "was the first Mission given here as far as *we know*. . . . Spiritism and Protestantism have made inroads into the [urban] Catholic population."[19] Protestants at that time did not "penetrate the mountain fastness."[20] One interpretation of Catholic laxity among Puerto Ricans held that there was "plenty of goodwill among the country folk, but a woeful ignorance even of the rudiments of Christian Doctrine."[21]

By the 1930s in some towns, however, Protestantism had made considerably headway. Their presence at baptisms, marriages, and burials put them in direct competition with the Church and threatened ingrained patterns of Catholicism by offering an alternative to the Church in a variety of social, religious, and even political respects. Evangelicals generally perceived Puerto Rican Catholicism in a negative light, as superstitious and lax, and they urged prospective converts to relinquish religious rituals and activities centering on the saints as intermediaries, as well as religious festivals.[22]

In Puerto Rico, Protestant proselytism first targeted to the towns and rural areas, rather than San Juan and Ponce, the largest cities. Their converts in those days generally came from among the poor, at first in small towns and later in the countryside as well. During 1920s and 1930s, Pentecostals spread throughout Puerto Rico, led by Spanish-speaking ministers. Evangelicals mostly used the Spanish language in their church literature, publications, and worship services and almost always used Spanish Bibles. One Catholic missionary wrote that Protestant proselytizing, which "[stooped] to distribution of medals and scapulars and other distinctive Catholic sacramental [items,] has enmeshed quite a few. Pentecostal preachers with their highly emotional services have deluded thousands—and there is another [large] group to whom religion as yet means nothing, or very little." He lamented the lack of rigorous religious education "in a land by tradition and all past history Catholic," noting that "there [are] many who bear the name of Jesus, Mary or one of the Saints without ever having been baptized."[23]

More than one hundred saints were venerated in Puerto Rico, including the Infant Jesus, various representations of the Virgin Mary, the Three Kings, and St. John the Baptist. With the separation of church and state that resulted after Puerto Rico came under U.S. sovereignty, celebrations honoring the towns' patron saints (*fiestas patronales*) became more secular, popular, and commercial. However, large devotional celebrations in Puerto Rico continued to be centered on Three Kings' Day (the Epiphany), with the kings representing the European, African, and Indian heritage of islanders. Catholic missionaries from the United States used the public feast days as the first step in restoring a more regular practice.[24]

Flowers, offerings, lighted candles, and statues were used by many Puerto Ricans to make part of the home a private chapel. In outlying districts, the rosary was much more available than the Mass, and because of the isolation, the family altar, rather than the parish, became the center of religious life. The mother was the cornerstone, leading prayers and preserving popular religion. Especially where priests were scarce and parish churches were distant, people set up *altarcitos*, or home altars, "an extension of the sacred space of the church into one's home, just as a procession extended the sacred space into the streets." It became important to bring newly carved *santos* to the church to be blessed and to have a bowl of holy water or some blessed candles, or branches from the Palm Sunday procession, as part of the *altarcito* arrangement.[25]

Protestants of all stripes opposed the figures of saints, as well as the "pseudo-religious" aspects of the fiestas, which one Puerto Rican pastor called "pagan feasts." Protestants also alleged that the celebrations were a breach of the separation of church and state on the part of municipal government officials. There was very little feeling of denominational rivalry between the Spanish-language evangelical churches. During the 1920s several Protestant churches advertised in Puerto Rican periodicals and newspapers both on the continent and on the island. Though Puerto Ricans who moved to the United States may have intended to join a church of their own denomination, if that particular church could not be found in their vicinity, they readily joined another Spanish-speaking Protestant church. People moved easily between Protestant denominations and often returned to Catholic churches after such religious experimentation.

Redemptorists had many schools in urban centers, and they helped in overcoming the perceived overinvolvement of the locals with spiritism, which had become very much a part of Puerto Rican culture. Even people considered good Catholics might attend spiritist meetings. Puerto Ricans had developed a version of Kardecian spiritism. This was based on the writings of a Frenchman and became the classic exposition of the Spiritualist philosophy in the mid-nineteenth century, having traveled from France to the elite of Latin America. It held that spirits progress through various stages before receiving enlightenment. Spiritism, like Protestantism, had been outlawed in Puerto Rico during the Spanish rule, with the practice condemned by the bishop. Often spiritism was taken up as part of a search for an alternative to the established religion, particularly among the educated classes, who had become alienated from both popular Catholicism, which they considered superstitious, and from what was perceived as a stagnant institutional Catholicism. By the middle of the twentieth century, spiritism began to filter down into the less educated popular classes, and with migration it was transplanted to Puerto Rican communities in the United States, especially New York.[26]

Population Growth and Urbanization

The island's population had increased from 953,000 in 1899, to 1,118,000 in 1910, 1,300,000 in 1920, and 1,544,000 in 1930, when two-thirds of Puerto Ricans were still rural dwellers. Economic conditions caused migration within Puerto Rico as well as to the United States. At the time of the American occupation, Puerto Rico's population was about 15 percent urban; by the middle of the twentieth century, urbanization reached 60 percent. The traditional colonial atmosphere of isolated mountain towns diminished, and many of the artisans moved into industrial occupations. Tenement districts arose in Old San Juan as migrants were pushed into squatter neighborhoods with their clusters of shacks, the *arrabales*. The capital bustled with growth in cigar manufacturing, fruit and sugar shipment, banking, and insurance. Displaced laborers in squalid slums, along with a small middle class, formed a surplus labor force subject to migration abroad.[27]

San Juan was becoming a booming metropolis, although even counting its adjoining municipalities of Río Piedras and Bayamón, it boasted a population of fewer than 177,000 inhabitants out of an islandwide total of slightly more than 1,700,000. As noted, by 1930 about two-thirds of Puerto Rico's population still lived in rural settlements of fewer than 2,500 people. Congested urban slums had arisen, yet the time-honored rural imprint was felt even in fairly large towns, where many had migrated after having grown up in the countryside and where the perils of the one-crop economy might be avoided through employment in some of the rising urban sectors. Some internal migrants proceeded to San Juan, while others went north to New York. An economist warned in 1930 that the "export" of workers from the "supersaturated mountainlands" had prompted a pattern that "threatens to involve San Juan and New York in one of the largest slum developments in modern urban history." The forecast presciently described an important dimension of the migration of the immediate post–World War II decades.[28]

Church and Community in New York City

Puerto Rico, the easternmost of the Greater Antilles, originally served as a base for the expansion and protection of Spain. The capital city, San Juan, took on a military more than a commercial importance; it eventually came to be heavily fortified and supported the commerce passing through Cuba, farther west in the archipelago. Spanish commercial legislation forbade Puerto Ricans to trade with any other port cities, even neutral or friendly ones, or to conduct coastwise traffic. During the seventeenth and eighteenth century, rising Atlantic ports such as Boston, Philadelphia, and especially New York became centers for distribution of flour and fish to Puerto Rico. New York merchant shippers fostered a lucrative commerce in surplus commodities with Spaniards in Havana, Puerto Rico, and Santo Domingo, but the island stagnated for centuries as a neglected backwater of the Spanish mercantile system.[29]

By 1850 New York had displaced Philadelphia as the U.S. eastern seaboard's most important center for relations with the Caribbean. Spanish, Cuban, and Puerto Rican merchants, as well as those of other nationalities coming to New York, regularly conducted business and formed small communities. A Spanish-language press and a mutual aid association, the Spanish Benevolent Society, developed to serve a growing community of merchants and an increasing number of political exiles. One Spaniard from Galicia, Manuel Peña Cagiao, was particularly active, editing the newspaper *La Crónica* in New York for many years until his death in 1865. New York City became a haven for exiles, notably Narciso López, a Venezuelan who had held high office in both Spain and Cuba and planned expeditions to Cuba with the aim of annexing it to the United States. Wealthy merchants financed several such unsuccessful attempts in the 1860s. Several meetings in favor of Antillean revolutionary efforts were held in City Hall Park; in 1869 a large gathering assembled at Manhattan's Cooper Institute to listen to addresses favoring Cuban overthrow of the "Spanish yoke."[30]

The first large, permanent settlements of Puerto Ricans and Cubans in New York were composed primarily of *tabaqueros* (cigar makers) and other skilled laborers. In 1890, Cubans predominated among immigrants from the Hispanic Caribbean. After the early 1900s, regularly scheduled steamship lines ran between New York, Puerto Rico, Curaçao, and Venezuela. The year 1917, when the U.S. Congress voted to naturalize Puerto Ricans collectively, is pivotal in the island's history for its meaning for the islanders' identity. Puerto Rican passenger travel to New York increased throughout the 1920s, and the newcomers contributed to New York's economy, which had suffered from restrictions on the entry of European laborers. During that decade Brooklyn became the hub of the modern-day Puerto Rican community of New York City, as its piers were disembarkation points for the Caribbean steamers.

By 1930 Puerto Ricans had become the largest of New York City's Spanish-speaking groups, twice as numerous as Spaniards, three times as numerous as the Cubans, and fifteen times as numerous as the Mexican community. From only about five hundred people of Puerto Rican birth scattered throughout the city in 1910, the population had climbed to seven thousand by 1920 and to some sixty thousand by 1930 (with considerably higher unofficial estimates). Puerto Rican migration to the United States halted, however, between 1930 and 1934, when almost ten thousand migrants returned home. Puerto Rican migrants came from a variety of backgrounds. One individual from a wealthy family arrived in New York City in 1922 from Rio Grande, a small coastal town, at the age of twenty, having previously attended the University of Puerto Rico. His father had owned a small sugar cane plantation, but a drop in sugar prices in the world market put an end to the family enterprise, forcing the young man to migrate to New York, where he found a job at a candy factory.[31]

Catholicism in New York City became marked by the Puerto Rican colonial heritage. At first, national parishes allowed the migrants to use their own language in church. In 1902 a small national parish, Our Lady of Guadalupe on West Fourteenth Street, was founded for Spaniards and native speakers of Spanish from Latin America. Although most of the Spanish-speaking inhabitants of the immediate neighborhood were Spaniards, the name given to the parish was a clear indication that it was intended as a common home for members of the *raza hispana* from both sides of the Atlantic—including the small Puerto Rican *colonia*. Guadalupe was therefore technically a "language parish" rather than a "national" one. The parish was put under the care of the Augustinians of the Assumption, a French congregation with many members who were fluent in Spanish. In 1912 a second Latino parish was founded, Nuestra Señora de la Esperanza in Washington Heights; like Guadalupe, from the beginning it was a church for various Spanish-speaking nationalities. La Esperanza was also placed under the Assumptionists. After Puerto Rican settlement in East Harlem increased in the mid-1920s, Cardinal Patrick Hayes established two specifically Puerto Rican national parishes run by Spanish Vincentian priests, some of whom had staffed churches in Puerto

Rico. They were La Milagrosa, established in 1926, and Santa Agonía, started in 1930, and they served the community well.[32]

Priests from St. Michael, Bay Ridge, operated a "Spanish Chapel" for Puerto Ricans living near the Navy Yard. From 1906 to 1913, Father Jose Rivera, a native of Puerto Rico, was assigned to St. Cecilia's Parish. In 1914, Brooklyn's growing number of Spanish immigrants, including families of merchants disembarking in Brooklyn's waterfront community, prompted the New York Archdiocese to search for a suitable, preferably self-supporting, priest. Bishop Charles E. McDonnell (1892–1921) appealed, without success, to Bishop John William Shaw of San Antonio for suggestions from among the priests exiled from Mexico then residing in San Antonio. The changing neighborhood south of the Brooklyn Bridge had become "the center of operation for Protestant societies and settlements" seeking to attract the "poorer Catholics." In 1916, Bishop McDonnell opened Brooklyn's first parish for Spanish-speaking Catholics, Our Lady of Pilar, on Cumberland Street. Realizing the need for priests who could speak Spanish, McDonnell sent a few diocesan seminarians to study at the University of Salamanca in Spain. The Vincentians continued at the Cumberland Street location until 1934, when demolition projects shifted the parish to nearby St. Peter's, which included larger numbers of English-speaking parishioners.[33]

Pentecostalism, which involved encountering the power of the "liberating" Holy Spirit, came to Puerto Ricans in New York during this period. Having begun with the Azusa Street Revival (1906–9) in Los Angeles, it was a street-corner revival that reached both Mexican Americans and Puerto Ricans. Mexican evangelistic healers of the immediate postrevival decades included Francisco Olazábal and Romanita Carbajal de Valenzuela; originally converted in Los Angeles, Carbajal spread the message in her homeland and helped plant Pentecostal churches in Mexico in 1914. Preacher Juan Lugo took the Pentecostal message to his native Puerto Rico in 1916 and spread it throughout the island. In 1931, he helped pioneer Pentecostal work among migrants in New York City. Meanwhile, "storefront" churches emerged, run by Puerto Rican ministers in a Puerto Rican style.[34]

Meanwhile, following bitter strikes during the 1920s in Puerto Rico's principal cigar factories, which failed to gain concessions from the plants, absentee owners relocated their largest tobacco enterprises to Northeastern cities on the mainland. As noted earlier, in these years migrants were leaving the island in large numbers. Many women from Mayaguez and other urban needlework centers, having learned dressmaking at an

early age, entered the garment industry in New York City. Others went to
work in the factories of New York. Among those remaining on the island,
desperation drove many adults and some children to the streets, trying to
sell trinkets and even begging for food. Puerto Ricans faced the rigors of
the Great Depression with only the flimsiest institutional support. The
number of Puerto Rican women in the labor force increased, and they
became more actively engaged in personal and community betterment, in
part due to a guarantee of suffrage and improved schooling in towns. At
this time most rural children received only about three years of instruction, while more than half of town dwellers finished the seventh grade.
In the early 1930s, widespread economic distress and several short-lived
strikes in Puerto Rico persuaded labor leaders in New York to organize
"seasonal" unions of needle workers on the island. North American labor
activist Rose Pesotta even conducted a brief campaign on the island in the
mid-1930s, which consolidated the needle trades into a single local with
several thousand members.[35]

Puerto Rican migrants were arriving at a time when skilled manual
occupations had begun to overtake common labor. Some Puerto Ricans
received opportunities as factory machinists and mechanics, but professionals and white-collar workers were rare. Unions in the American Federation of Labor generally did not recruit Puerto Rican carpenters, brick-
layers, tailors, or barbers.[36] Many Puerto Ricans, who had traditionally
had been used as replacement workers hired at lower wages, did become
active in the labor movement during the period of the National Recovery
Administration, 1933–35, when total union membership jumped from
24,000 to 200,000. Early in 1933, Dressmakers Local 22's membership
consisted of about 2,500 workers, mostly men and practically all Jews.
After a general strike a few months later, membership increased to nearly
30,000, and thereafter the local became "a veritable United Nations,"
with some 2,000 Puerto Ricans joining.[37]

During the summer of 1926, following several weeks of street fighting between some Jewish and Puerto Rican owners of small businesses,
migrants led in the formation of a new organization, La Liga Puertorriqueña y Hispana, which was to promote "civic defense and the welfare
of United States citizens from Puerto Rico and others of Latin American
or Spanish origin."

By the late 1920s, Spanish Harlem had clearly become "the most
typical Puerto Rican spot in all New York." Along Upper Fifth Avenue,
drugstores, restaurants, barbershops, bars, candy stores, and dress shops
replicated in an urban environment the habits and customs of the home-

land. Migrants were attracted to its liveliness and the camaraderie of being with other Spanish speakers. Civic groups, hometown clubs, brotherhoods, and similar organizations arose in the 1920s and 1930s for a variety of purposes, including sponsoring dances, helping to raise funds for hurricane relief on the island, and assisting the unemployed in New York's neighborhoods.[38]

New York City housed a wide range of ethnic communities that included European ethnics, African Americans, and a conglomeration of Spanish-speaking peoples as well as others from throughout the globe. Especially close ties developed between Puerto Ricans and Cubans in the city; the latter owned many barrio music and record shops, as well as vaudeville and motion picture theaters such the Teatro Cervantes and the Teatro de Variedades on Upper Fifth Avenue. These institutions, along with cafés, dance halls, and a wealth of other local amusements that were publicized in Spanish, helped foment Spanish-speaking cultural unity.

In the late 1930s one Cuban man noted that he felt at home living in Harlem among Cubans and Puerto Ricans; his family ate "strictly tropical food the whole year around," although his children were fed mostly U.S. style. He found that his neighborhood on Eighth Avenue between 110th and 116th streets was becoming the "most prosperous of the whole Spanish speaking community" as thousands of Puerto Ricans moved into the area. Cuban "satellite" colonies emerged downtown in Chelsea and in Brooklyn as well as uptown in East Harlem.[39] In 1918, José Camprubí, an engineer and buyer for the Spanish railways, who was Puerto Rican-born but raised in Barcelona (the sign of an "elite" upbringing), bought the newspaper *La Prensa* and transformed it into one of the several weeklies read by the New York colonia. During the 1920s, Puerto Ricans concerned themselves less with local affairs than with island politics, and this preference was reflected in the pages of contemporary periodicals.

Spain sent many immigrants to New York City from the turn of the century through World War I. Spanish immigrants, whose population in the city stood at twenty-three thousand by 1930, under half of that of Puerto Ricans, always constituted a diverse group. The Spanish tended to base their immigration societies on regional and provincial origins, celebrating fiestas in the Centro Galicia, the Centro Asturiano, and the Centro Andaluz, among others. The Spanish community of Greenwich Village contained a floating population, varying in size and composition as boatloads of sailors came and went. They kept very strictly to themselves, the women never going out except to church and the men associating closely within their own group, largely avoiding external conflict and contact. They had their own cafés, groceries, tailors, and barbers; the primary institution that brought them into contact with others was the school. Spaniards residing in New York celebrated their own version of Columbus Day, or Día de la Raza—also observed by the Cubans, Puerto Ricans, and South Americans—as well as other national holidays. Despite their clannishness, the Spaniards were particularly militant trade unionists and rose to become skilled laborers in greater numbers than did the more recent Caribbean arrivals.[40]

The growing Puerto Rican presence in East Harlem facilitated the subsequent entry of African Americans from the neighborhood's northern and western boundaries. Harlem Renaissance writer Claude McKay noted this role in transitional areas: "When white Puerto Ricans moved into a house, the brown ones followed." Puerto Rican grocery stores, record shops, and other businesses along Upper Fifth Avenue catered to a sizable Spanish-speaking community as well as to West Indian immigrants. McKay saw Puerto Ricans as composing part of a section of the "Negro Quarter" of Harlem, roughly from 116th to 110th streets, between Lenox and Lexington avenues. With access to less expensive quarters, they "wedged themselves into every available space, in basements and front rooms of first floor apartments," and paved the way for blacks as they moved south. These Puerto Ricans were having to deal with a color line unknown in either urban or rural Puerto Rico; their fine-tuned perceptions and classifications of color clashed with the existing binary black-white categories accepted by New Yorkers.[41]

The 1930s saw local attempts to portray the migrants negatively as intellectually inferior, health risks (due to a tuberculosis epidemic on the island), and radicals.[42] Amid the trials of Americanization was an earnest and idealistic, but ultimately untimely, attempt to establish a Caribbean confederation of Puerto Rico, Cuba, and the Dominican Republic. This effort was promoted by José de Diego (1867–1918), an island-born intellectual—essayist, poet, and politician—who headed the independence branch of the Union Party. Whereas de Diego largely abstained from criticism of the United States, the nationalists of the 1930s, led by Pedro Albizu Campos, bitterly opposed colonial rule and began to rally for complete separation. Albizu also advocated a return to Spanish Catholicism as a means of preserving cultural continuity, and he denounced the U.S. church for its policies of Americanization. Spending many years in both Puerto Rican and continental jails as a martyr for the cause of independence, he warned that the island's Spanish and Catholic heritage was threatened by U.S. cultural imperialism.[43]

Puerto Rican nationalists in New York City worked closely with the American Civil Liberties Union, the Committee for Fair Play in Puerto Rico, and other organizations for the release of political prisoners on the island. Significantly, thousands of Harlem Puerto Ricans marched in protest of the murder of nationalists in the infamous Ponce Massacre of 1937, when the island police force brutally attacked a peaceful assembly in 1937 in the island's second largest city, causing numerous deaths. By 1936, despite having a Puerto Rican population of fewer than 20,000, Spanish Harlem had four political clubs, a score of fraternal and social organizations, and a dozen or so radical and leftist organizations. Most Puerto Rican and other Latino barrio organizations supported the Spanish Loyalists against the Franco-led rebels.[44]

One Puerto Rican who served with the Loyalists in Spain returned to New York in 1937 and equated Spain's political struggle with that brewing among Puerto Rican nationalists, arguing that "sooner or later the people of Puerto Rico must determine their own destiny. Self-determination will mean political, economic, [and] social [freedom]."[45] United around the cause of Puerto Rican independence and support of the Loyalists in the Spanish Civil War, entire migrant families were activists. But nationalists and communists eventually began to question each other's positions at barrio meetings, and both sides occasionally took to street fighting. The Puerto Rican Nationalist Junta of New York City was composed mainly of factory, restaurant, and hotel workers as well as some office workers, small business owners, professional people, and students—a cross-section of the migrant community—with subjuntas outside the main center in East Harlem.[46]

A Puerto Rican Family Story

In far greater percentages than the general population, early (pre-1930) Puerto Rican migrants were urban dwellers and largely literate. Although the new citizens still could not vote for the U.S. president and members of Congress, they were guaranteed due process, equal protection under the law, speedy and public trials, and other rights. But their citizenship clearly was a second-class one, involving political and cultural ambiguities that remain to the present. When migrating to New York City, Puerto Ricans brought along the effects of colonialism and ambiguous religious identities. In New York there were additional problems, such as new forms of racial discrimination and de facto residential and employment segregation. During the 1920s and 1930s, Puerto Ricans became involved in ethnic battles with other migrants. The Puerto Rican identity differs

from those arising elsewhere in Latin America, and an already ambiguous
religious identity changes when Puerto Ricans migrate.

My grand-aunt Aurelia Rivera, known within the family as Titi Yeya,
was born on August 26, 1909 (almost a decade before the edict granting
U.S. citizenship), in the highland town of Cayey, Puerto Rico, and raised
in Caguas. She has lived a colorful and fulfilling life despite a grueling
childhood, adolescence, and early adulthood. Her story illustrates urban
and social developments surrounding migration patterns from the Hispanic Caribbean to New York City.

Yeya's family was a product of the dramatic changes that had reached
into all aspects of Puerto Rican culture and society. Women frequently
became primary wage earners who cemented internal family networks,
as well as those with community institutions, and their tenacity and re-
sourcefulness often made them natural leaders. Entire extended families
participated in the Puerto Rican migration.[47]

Yeya suffered a series of family tragedies throughout her childhood and
early adult life. After she lost her mother at the age of six, Yeya and her two
sisters were separated, and each of the siblings grew up in a home with a different religious affiliation. The eldest child, Carmen, lived with Baptists, the
denomination that had been assigned to the area by U.S. missionaries shortly
after U.S. annexation. The youngest, Damari, came to be raised Catholic.
Yeya went to live with her father, who ran a spiritist *centro*. However, Yeya was
baptized a Protestant (*evangélica*) on the island, and she learned to read the
Bible. She married in the town of Caguas in a Baptist church, with a Puerto
Rican minister presiding. Sometimes, however, she went to Mass with her
younger sister, though she never received sufficient training to pray "Catholic style" and admits her inability to "recite the Padre Nuestro [Our Father]
and all that." An increasingly attenuated pattern of religious observance
persisted during her life, and this was passed down through the family.

Participation in organized religion was a weak suit in Yeya's upbringing. Though Yeya's father had taught spiritism and ran an active spiritist
center, but she never participated in those practices. "How can you speak
with the dead?" she inquires incredulously. She remembers that "they
didn't want me [involved] either." That whole period in her life, as she
tells it, remains shrouded in mystery and some embarrassment, especially
among her sisters, who feared she had become a *bruja* (witch). In those
days Yeya liked church for the opportunity it afforded to "read the Bible
and sing hymns," but once she was in New York City she no longer attended regularly, although El Barrio had churches of all denominations,
including Baptist and Catholic ones, as in Caguas.

Her mother came from the mountain town of Barranquitas; thus the family fit closely the demographic profile of increasing internal migration from the highlands to larger cities closer to the coast. The family had a very poor diet, lacking even oatmeal, eggs, and meat. Tuberculosis spread readily in areas where malnutrition was high, and cramped houses along crowded streets became breeding grounds for the bacilli. Like most municipalities, Caguas maintained a public hospital, but it offered inadequate facilities for treating tuberculosis patients. The overwhelming majority of the afflicted had to live with their families. Unlike enteritis and other diseases, tuberculosis usually struck adults in the prime of life, especially in cities, where the contagion spread at rates almost four times as high as in rural areas. The large urban migration of the previously isolated mountain peasantry, especially after World War I, also increased the incidence and mortality of TB.[48]

In the winter of 1928–29, Caguas, a town with just under 20,000 inhabitants, housed some twenty tobacco factories employing almost 2,500 women and 1,000 men with an average yearly wage of $183 per capita. Life in such towns moved at a slower pace than in San Juan, where boats entered the harbor with food products and the raw materials for needlework—hundreds of cases of handkerchiefs, tablecloths, lingerie, and other items destined for embroidery by the roughly 40,000 women working in the island's garment industry. These women were usually paid at a steady weekly rate, which was preferable to the daily rate customary for men.[49]

As a child and young adult, Yeya had visited San Juan occasionally to see relatives and friends. There she saw neighborhoods with elegant houses and new cars, as well as busy streets and large factories—evidence of much more wealth than existed in her hometown. In the Puerto Rico of her youth, Yeya detected "three societies"—rich people, poor people, and *medianos* (the middle class). Remarkably, despite her family's poverty, she considered herself part of the medianos, more for her aspirations to mobility than because of any realistic assessment of earnings or property: "I belonged to the middle, not the lower, class, because I [always] believed in progressing, getting ahead, going forward" (*yo me movía*). Yeya attended high school up to the third year, surpassing most of her contemporaries. She left high school in the third year to marry a local boy; the couple had two sons.

When Yeya's husband divorced her in the mid-1920s, she entered the labor force, working in cigar production curing leaf tobacco. Yeya's job was to gather and dry the crop's green leaves six days a week. The cured tobacco then was shipped to the United States. This provided enough for the family to eat, but soon the entire industry left the island—going to Connecticut, according to Yeya. She had learned to speak a little English, which helped in landing her next job, for which "if you spoke a few words, you qualified." In search of employment, Yeya had written to a distant relative of her deceased brother-in-law in Aguadilla. Consequently, she managed to get an introduction and interview in San Juan for a position in the Puerto Rican Emergency Relief Agency (PRERA, as it came to be known), a branch of the U.S. federal government that distributed New Deal relief funds to the island. At the height of its activities the PRERA was giving direct or indirect relief to about one-third of the island's population.

The self-described "señora de la PRERA" found herself working in the Caguas countryside for the government, venturing into a field where at the time men held the majority of jobs. Her duties included asking people in rural barrios about their diet and giving them food and clothing vouchers redeemable for canned goods, medical supplies, and cash. Inexpensive buses (carros públicos) took Yeya to various places on her appointed rounds, and the fare was frequently waived. Other times she visited homes on horseback, the jíbaro's preferred mode of travel across the treacherous mountainsides, especially following rainstorms. Yeya would spend entire days in outlying settlements such as San Salvador and Turabo before returning to the home office and supply store. The people were poor, lacking even shoes, and the people of the United States, through the PRERA, had helped them considerably. What did the jíbaros think of the yanquis back then? A great deal, but "they had their prejudices," Yeya chuckled, "since the Americans provided them with money." Governor Luis Muñoz Marín later said of the PRERA that it did little more than illuminate and reflect the failings of the existing social system. It did, however, ameliorate harsh conditions. In 1935 the Puerto Rico Recovery Administration, a successor agency, adopted additional stopgap measures to help impoverished farmers, assist rural families, and expand the traditional agricultural system beyond reliance on limited foreign markets.

Through letters received from extended-family members, Yeya had learned of life on the continent; relatives would also send monthly remittances that helped pay household expenses and sustained several households during hard times. Two of her relatives had, through contact with U.S. tobacco merchants, learned of possible opportunities in Chicago, for which they had boldly taken aim. Now they earned good money as chefs in downtown hotels, and they shared some of their earnings with Yeya and the boys. Yeya hardly imagined making such a trip herself. In a culture where women customarily stayed home, it would take extraordinary circumstances to propel her to an unknown land fraught with unknown dangers. Numerous Puerto Rican town dwellers had been migrating to New York City, beginning around 1917. Even those with trades, however, often found their skills of little help in the new overseas environment.

In the early 1930s, Yeya witnessed the devastating effects of a tuberculosis epidemic that took the lives of her sister Carmen and brother-in-law Francisco Badillo and left her to care for their infant son, as well as her own two children. Her surviving sister, Damari, who had married a restaurateur of Italian ancestry, had moved to San Juan. The childless couple, aware of Yeya's plight and wishing to raise a child, arranged to take her younger son, Manolín, and at the age of six the lad went off to live with his adopted kin. Damari took care of Manolín for several years, raising him as a Catholic and affording him ample material benefits. As everyone was coming to learn, "the Sorrentinis had money." Anchored in the family's hotel and restaurant business and anxious to keep her newfound domesticity, yet concerned by Yeya's lack of resources, Damari contributed half of the cost of a ticket for her sister and the boys, Hermán and José Luis, to migrate to New York City. Yeya paid the other half and later recalled her situation somewhat bitterly: "[I] had three children and no father [and was being] sent out to work."

In early 1941 Yeya, José Luis, and Hermán left San Juan Harbor on the U.S.S. *Coamo*, bound for New York City. Yeya had not prepared much for the trip ahead of time, but she quickly responded to the exigencies of the moment. She remembers the five-day voyage as "fine, [at least] the food was good." The boat docked and passengers disembarked in Brooklyn. Yeya and the boys went to stay with a friend in Manhattan, on 105th Street in El Barrio, or Spanish Harlem. Fortunately, at that time rents were relatively low. She discovered, moreover, that due to a temporary glut in the market, apartments were available rent free for two months, so she was able to save a little on expenses at the start.

Yeya liked El Barrio for its familiar sights and sounds. She soon discovered the vast open market under the train tracks on Park Avenue, spanning several books around 116th Street. Not only did *la marqueta* have a wide selection of many Caribbean food items like *plátanos* and *yautía*, but they were affordable. There were many inexpensive Latin American restaurants on 110th Street and Fifth Avenue. Throughout the neighborhood "there were Cubans, Dominicans, *de todo* [all kinds of people]." On the eastern fringes, by contrast, "Italians and Puerto Ricans [were] fighting with each other." Yeya was always gregarious, but she didn't have any Italian friends; all of them were Latino. Few Jews, who had once dominated the area, remained, though many retained businesses in El Barrio. Mostly their families had moved to the Bronx or Brooklyn; others remained downtown on the Lower East Side. Puerto Ricans and other Latinos were located squarely in the center of East Harlem, mainly between Third and Fifth avenues and 105th and 116th streets.

In her middle age, Yeya returned many times to Puerto Rico, but she always gravitated back to her adopted land. Yeya worked for the *unionistas* and was an admirer of one of that political party's founders, Luis Muñoz Rivera, a respected journalist and politician, "a man who did much for Puerto Rico." During the 1950s she remarried and moved to North Hollywood, California, where she lived for fifteen years and worked as a cook in a hospital. Her new life involved little contact with Puerto Ricans, besides a few members of her extended family, whose presence had prompted her to move there in the first place. She lived and worked among mostly Anglos and some "Germans," with few Latinos ("Mexicans lived on the other side of Los Angeles").

After her second husband died, she moved back to Puerto Rico to live with her sister, Damari, and helped care for her when she fell gravely ill. After a few years in San Juan, Yeya moved to a small town in Florida about an hour east of Orlando, where the climate and lifestyle was in some ways "a lot like California." Then, weary with age and unable to maintain a household alone, Yeya relocated to a senior center in the Bronx, where she has lived since the mid-1990s. Her story and reflections illuminate several core issues and dilemmas of Puerto Ricans in the twentieth century, a time that saw tremendous material progress for the island yet fostered continued political, social, and religious ambiguity, both on the island and on the continent.

Many decades later, when asked about her racial ancestry, Yeya reacted with surprise but eventually responded, "We were Italian. My grandfather was an Italian immigrant. . . . There was [also] another relative from Panama." She described the racial composition of Caguas as "white, colored, [and] mixed." Being Puerto Rican means having close relatives with different skin complexions, and this was certainly evident in Yeya's family: her sister Damari was noticeably more *trigueña* (darker-complexioned, "the color of wheat"), Carmen, her other sister, a redhead, had the fairest skin, while Yeya was somewhere in between. In New York City, however, one was defined by nationality or ethnicity—West Indians, Jews, Italians, southern African Americans—more than appearance. Though she could pass for Italian or vaguely Euro-American, Yeya's identity within El Barrio remained unmistakably Puerto Rican, and she retained a strong affinity with other Spanish speakers. According to the 1935 Census of Puerto Rico, under the ambiguous category of race, enumerators found that residents islandwide were 76 percent white and 24 percent black.

A perception of the Puerto Rican as mulatto has persisted throughout the migration process. The Caribbean racial continuum has created confusion for many non–Puerto Rican or non-Latino residents of communities. The "one-drop [of African blood] rule" implies the inferiority of anyone with even remote traces of African ancestry, such as Puerto Ricans and Cubans. Continental society has long valued race over color, but it never became possible to impose a strict color line on the island—especially given its history and extent of racial intermarriage. The growth of shantytowns in major cities such as San Juan, Ponce, and Mayaguez beginning in the mid-1920s attracted a steady stream of migrants from the interior in search of employment. There and elsewhere, racial distinctions became blurred within a dynamic multiracial society.[50]

In New York, by contrast, sharply defined borders had always separated New York's ethnic groups; not surprisingly, frequent violence occurred between Puerto Ricans and Italians in the 1930s along the southern boundary of East Harlem. "Trespassing" in hostile neighborhoods as well as housing competition triggered this street fighting. When Puerto Rican youths crossed the western and southern borders of Italian Harlem, recognized as running along Park Avenue from 107th to 113th streets, skirmishes broke out with Italian youths, resulting in numerous injuries and arrests. This pattern went hand in hand with residential succession.

Puerto Ricans, despite their presence in congested urban immigrant quarters since the 1920s, never developed a purely "ethnic" identity. Their professed religion has also remained elusive. On the one hand, they share in the Latino religious tradition. Yet for most of a century they have been U.S. citizens, whether they lived on the island, in New York, or elsewhere on the continent. They have pursued a wide range of religious options, enjoying constitutional guarantees of religious freedom under the U.S. system. Religion initially offered little attraction for most Puerto Rican migrants, and they were often fully unprepared to navigate the world of urban U.S. Catholicism. Where the opportunity was available, they joined Catholic parishes with mixed ethnic and linguistic groups. Given the generally unstable residential patterns of the working class, especially during the 1930s, these isolated parish communities became temporary anchors; they gave way to a much larger and continuous migrant wave in the decades after World War II.[51]

4 Powers of the Prelates: Urban Hierarchies Contrasted

In the period from 1940 to 1965, Anglo-American bishops in Chicago, New York, and San Antonio took charge of their Latino flocks, often placing themselves at the forefront of both secular and religious leadership. After World War II, several archbishops adopted new, sometimes interdiocesan, approaches to address contemporary religious and social problems. These centralizing prelates had long tenures, political clout, and a great number of the faithful behind them. Before Vatican II, the assumption of unquestioned hierarchical authority was often evidenced in bishops' ignoring parishioners' language, traditions, and cultures. Catholic institutions, moreover, had come to reinforce male superiority based on centuries of church practice.[1]

For Latinos, these three cities and their archbishops were pivotal, despite the restraints of hierarchy and patriarchy, in opening the doors to cultural, if not religious, pluralism. In San Antonio, Archbishop Robert E. Lucey served from 1941 to 1969, a period in which his city remained a regional hub for the dispersal of Latinos on the migrant circuit and included an active Mexican-American community. In New York, Francis Spellman (1939–67) acted to strategically integrate different Latino Catholic ethnic groups with European-origin ethnics, rather than setting them off in "national" parishes as had been done with Europeans or requiring total assimilation within homogenous "territorial" parishes. He also stressed the importance of clergy's becoming fluent in Spanish. Chicago's cardinal, Samuel Stritch (1939–58), pursued similar strategies. In adopting innovative approaches to ethnic change, all three prelates recognized that the key to regenerating parish structures for the future benefit of the Church lay in successfully managing the entry of Latino immigrants.

In the immediate decades after World War II, U.S. bishops gained considerable power over Latino urbanization patterns, as well as ecclesiastical matters. European immigration was restricted, but a significant wave of newcomers continued arriving in urban America from Mexico and the Caribbean, each developing dual loyalties to the United States and the homeland. The powerful archbishops in San Antonio, Chicago, and New York dominated the course of both religious and social developments for dominant Latino groups within their dioceses. A variety of church-based organizations emerged to address Latino groups' social and economic plight. Prelates determined the Church's social and political policies throughout their respective metropolitan areas, and to varying degrees they became involved in redressing inequality and discrimination against the newest arrivals as well as against older communities of African Americans. The Catholicism of Latinos was culturally different from that of other groups of Catholic immigrants. Nationally, as U.S. Catholicism appeared to be losing its foreignness, the Church began to focus on combating the radicalization and secularization of the working class, encouraging their political assimilation, and acting to preserve Catholic faith against what they perceived as secularizing trends, such as the suburbanization of parishes and parochial schools.[2]

Archbishop Lucey Spearheads National Social Justice Programs

Texas Mexican Americans in the mid-twentieth century encountered considerable de facto segregation, although they were considered "white" under Jim Crow–era segregation statutes. The de facto segregation prompted organizational responses. Race relations were somewhat better in urban San Antonio than in rural settings, where ethnic paternalism reigned unfettered, despite some tentative successes of the League of United Latin American Citizens (LULAC), a civil rights organization. LULAC advocated for Mexican-American equality in education, in employment, and in the courts and other institutions where they had little voice. LULAC relied on the Mexican-American press to publicize its efforts and to educate people on citizenship. The fact that half of LULAC's first ten national presidents came from San Antonio helped make that city a nucleus for subsequent civil rights efforts. San Antonio members played a central role in changing the U.S. justice system to better serve Mexican Americans.

Bishops in the United States, led by Lucey, became increasingly concerned about systematic mistreatment of Mexican immigrants. Among other factors, the fact that San Antonio's Mexican-American community was huge while its black population was small and European-origin ethnics were absent led Archbishop Lucey to focus on Mexican Americans nationally as well as locally. With the entry of the United States into World War II, migrants already within Texas increasingly dropped out of agriculture and settled into more stable jobs in cities and towns where possible. San Antonio received both Mexican-American and Anglo newcomers from rural areas throughout the state. After 1945, with a booming defense industry and Sunbelt economy, it attracted new residents from northern regions as well. The 1950 census counted 2,290,000 Spanish-speaking, overwhelmingly Mexican American residents in the southwestern states, 17 percent of whom were foreign born. Texas led with 1,034,000, followed by California with 760,000, New Mexico with 249,000, Arizona with 128,000, and Colorado with 118,000.

The massive influx of undocumented workers from south of the border—sometimes pejoratively called wetbacks, or *mojados*—created labor surpluses in the 1940s and 1950s, however, especially in low-skilled job categories, and this led some Mexican Americans to leave San Antonio and other southwestern cities. Those who continued migrating had to journey farther to find work. As the number of Mexican nationals entering Texas increased, the number of Texas-born Mexican Americans (*Tejanos*) leaving the state for seasonal employment also rose. Both Tejanos and Mexican-born workers fanned out throughout the country for seasonal employment. *Betabeleros* (beet workers) left San Antonio for the Midwest and increasingly the Rocky Mountain region. Each season, from March until May, San Antonio's principal emigrant agent, who recruited workers for the Michigan Beet Growers Employment Committee, sent about six thousand laborers north in trucks, jalopies, and trains. Migrants often boarded up their San Antonio dwelling at the start of the harvest and returned at the end of the season.[3]

Robert Lucey had been drawn to public service as director of Catholic Charities in Los Angeles during the 1920s. He also served on the board of the California State Welfare Department, on the Los Angeles Housing Commission, and on the Committee on Industrial Problems of the American Association of Social Workers. As bishop in Amarillo, he became outspoken in backing the labor movement. In 1935 he joined Chicago cardinal George Mundelein in supporting John L. Lewis and the CIO (Congress of Industrial Organizations); their support helped legitimize that union in Catholic circles. Lucey continued pursuing social justice for Mexican Americans when he arrived in 1941 in San Antonio, an antiunion, segregated, and economically underdeveloped city. Lucey began rebuilding an urban ministry as well as caring for migrant Mexican farm workers, who encountered few Spanish-speaking mission priests and found it difficult to attend local churches, let alone participate in Catholic school education.[4]

A National Catholic Welfare Conference seminar, "Spanish-Speaking People of the Southwest and West," held in San Antonio in July 1943, was followed by similar conferences in Denver, Santa Fe, and Los Angeles. In 1944, at the Annual Meeting of the Catholic Hierarchy in the United States, held in Washington, D.C., Chicago's archbishop Samuel Stritch spoke of the need for a unified and coordinated program of welfare work among Spanish-speaking people in the Southwest and requested a grant from the American Board of Catholic Missions. Out of these meetings, Archbishop Lucey spearheaded the organization of the Bishops' Committee for the Spanish-Speaking (BCSS) on January 10, 1945, in Oklahoma City. The BCCS, composed of the archbishops and bishops of the Southwest, was established to promote the spiritual and social welfare of approximately two million Catholics of Spanish and Mexican ancestry living in the region, with Archbishop Lucey named its executive chair.[5]

In their 1945 meeting, the bishops authorized the establishment of a regional office to coordinate the work of the Bishops' Committee with that of priests, religious, and laity who were working with Spanish-speaking people. The executive board also approved the formation of the Catholic Council for the Spanish-Speaking (CCSS) as a permanent organization of priests, religious, and laity who were leaders in the work of the Church among the Spanish-speaking. The creation of the committee, which Lucey headed for more than twenty years, marked a shift from building chapels for mission work to offset Protestant proselytizing to adopting a more comprehensive, regional, and interdiocesan approach to social justice. The programs of the BCSS, sponsored by the American Board of Catholic Missions through annual grants, varied according to the needs of the dioceses. The committee's early services included the establishment of infant and maternity clinics, hospitals, and orphanages for the Spanish-speaking, primarily Mexican Americans, in the Southwest and Midwest. BCSS national and regional offices were established along the "trails of the migrants, [and] parochial schools in most of the barrio parishes came into being, [along with] church supported clinics, day-care centers, [and] homes for unwed mothers."[6]

By 1947, how to control the flow of undocumented immigrants became the primary policy problem emerging from the Bracero program. This guest-worker arrangement between the United States and Mexico had been originally designed to replace U.S. workers who had been drafted in the armed services during World War II, and it was extended until 1964 to meet the need for agricultural labor. Stable solutions were hard to come by, as evidenced by the signing of three separate bilateral agreements between 1947 and 1949. Mexico's policymakers, who earlier had opposed emigration as against Mexico's national interest, became accustomed to the generation of foreign exchange through *bracero* workers' remittances. In 1950 Lucey focused the BCSS on the plight of agricultural workers after President Harry Truman asked him to serve on a blue-ribbon panel investigating conditions among migratory farm workers and problems created by the importation of foreign workers. Testifying at congressional hearings in 1951, Lucey faulted the U.S. government for continuing to sponsor the program.[7]

The Church defined the Mexican bracero workers as a religiously deprived group coming into already understaffed regions. The Mexican hierarchy, meanwhile, feared that workers returning to Mexico constituted "a serious problem in Mexican cities and towns since they [taught] Protestantism and hatred of religion or indifferentism" to their fellow *campesinos*.[8] After studying the wide dispersal of Spanish-speaking in the Midwest, Lucey and the BCSS in 1952 embarked on a cooperative program of borrowing "*bracero* priests" from Mexico, especially from the Diocese of Guadalajara, who were to provide a mobile ministry for Mexican workers and domestic migrants, who often worked the same areas. In the program's initial year, eleven U.S. bishops accepted twenty-four Mexican missionary priests. Local parish priests near labor camps and concentrations of braceros chauffeured and interpreted for visiting foreign clergy and seminarians at labor camps, reception centers, and bracero barracks; they also provided information about nearby Catholic parishes. Operation Migratory Labor, which placed Mexican priests in large camps in the Midwest, California, and the Pacific Northwest, was a relatively brief experiment requiring considerable financial resources and personnel, as well as international cooperation. It lost momentum after the mid-1950s as the number of bracero contract laborers declined.[9]

Archbishop Lucey focused closely on San Antonio as well, steering bricks-and-mortar and desegregation projects. Lucey's building program raised many new churches, schools, rectories, and convents, especially after 1945. By his departure in 1969, he had presided over the construction of thirty new parishes, including sixteen in the 1950s. Most were in the suburban fringes of the archdiocese. Formerly Anglo churches on the West Side, as well as in the pockets east and south of downtown, were becoming increasingly Mexican American. In 1946 Our Lady of Good Counsel became the first parish in the western Edgewood area, serving a mixed Anglo and Mexican congregation. Five years later, in order to keep up with continued growth in the area, the archbishop created a neighboring parish, St. John Bosco, north of Castroville Road. Further, Lucey's love of the California missions inspired his affection for the colonial missions in San Antonio, and for nearly three decades he oversaw preservation and restoration efforts at the missions in an effort to secure a permanent place for the Catholic Church in the Texas cultural heritage and to make the missions into attractive tourist sites.[10]

The postwar influx of new jobs and housing reshaped San Antonio into a booming Sunbelt metropolis. Despite the city's rapid growth, the Mexican American *colonia* remained isolated. Its Catholic parishes were seldom visited by Anglos, who, in turn, rarely saw Mexicans attending their churches. After 1945, differing Anglo and Mexican-American suburbanization patterns perpetuated parish segregation.[11] San Fernando Cathedral, which divided the downtown section from the *colonia* business district, had acquired the status of a national parish for Mexican Catholics, but priests from the Polish, German, and Belgian national churches refused pastoral services to them. Lucey lamented, meanwhile, that middle-class Mexican Americans wanted to separate themselves in parishes from both the Anglos and "the poor and newly arrived campesinos."[12] To counter those trends, during the 1950s Lucey initiated a diocesan celebration of the Virgin of Guadalupe that included processions from other parishes to San Fernando for an outdoor Mass, with participants numbering in the tens of thousands.[13]

In the early 1940s, Lucey placed the Missionary Catechists of Divine Providence—a religious order of Mexican-American women that had recently arrived under his predecessor, Archbishop Arthur Drossaerts—in the archdiocese's Mexican parishes. The sisters actively engaged Mexicans and Mexican Americans in councils of the Confraternity of Christian Doctrine, which originally had been geared for public school children. These "barrio evangelists" worked on religious education at San Fernando Cathedral, Immaculate Heart of Mary, St. Timothy's, and several other parishes. After 1948 they also staffed Madonna Center on the western outskirts of San Antonio, providing instruction in leisure activities, cooking, sewing, home nursing, and home economics. By 1960, as other religious orders of women organized home Bible classes and helped in the instruction of parents of children making their First Communion and confirmation, more than one hundred full-time "sister catechists" worked in the archdiocese.[14]

Lucey also strongly encouraged his diocesan priests to learn Spanish to better care for Mexican Americans, who constituted the majority of Catholics in San Antonio. In 1961 he mandated fluency in Spanish for every associate pastor in the archdiocese and required language courses with stringent examinations. In a program with far-reaching implications for hemispheric cooperation, Lucey's continued solicitation of grants from the Extension Society and the American Board of Catholic Missions helped furnish transportation for and paid part of the salaries of the numerous male and female religious who labored among Mexican Americans. In the late 1950s and early 1960s Lucey sent some of his priests to work in catechetical institutions in Latin America, and this helped create lasting organizational structures for religious education.

Mexican housing on the West Side, whether in private homes or in *vecindades* (large tenementlike dwellings encircling a courtyard), remained substandard with poor sanitary facilities. In 1961 the Catholic Council for the Spanish-Speaking monitored the Public Housing Authority and the Urban Renewal Agency's efforts to find decent accommodations "for the more than 120,000 persons in the city [who] still reside in substandard housing."[15] Downtown redevelopment resulted in the demolition of dozens of acres of Mexican housing, including some of the dilapidated housing courts and the infamous red-light zone. The CCSS worked with local engineers, builders, and the development agency in the relocation of several hundred families displaced by the redevelopment. CCSS also participated in plans for the development of jobs in industrial warehousing, and its representatives regularly attended meetings regarding slum clearance and public housing initiatives.

Desegregation was another issue that Lucey tackled. In 1953 he implemented a policy of desegregation of archdiocesan parochial schools, and in the early 1960s he sped up the integration of blacks by supporting the work of Father Sherrill Smith, who led successful "stand-in" protests against the "colored balcony" of the Majestic Theater in downtown San Antonio. Lucey also actively supported the passage of the 1964 Civil Rights Bill and sent Father Smith and another priest to participate in the march from Selma to Birmingham. Lucey believed that opposition to racism constituted a just cause worthy of his attention. Episcopal prerogatives proved crucial to broadening the scope of civil rights for Mexican Americans, beyond religious outreach to Mexican braceros.

Lucey continued focusing on the plight of farm workers, and in 1963 he publicly supported grape pickers in central California. He joined a few other bishops in encouraging organizer Cesar Chavez of the National Farm Workers Association and the United Farm Workers' Organizing Committee, which led successful strikes against growers that culminated in several contracts to protect migrant workers. The archbishop maintained a high profile in other national boycott movements of the 1960s as well. Lucey's successors, Archbishops Francis Furey and Patricio Flores, also championed political and social causes. Their leadership made the San Antonio Archdiocese an agent of positive change in Mexican Americans' lives and surpassed the efforts of their counterparts in most other southwestern cities.[16]

Having come of age before Vatican II, Archbishop Lucey ended his career facing the overwhelming opposition of his priests and a considerable portion of the laity due to his authoritarianism and arbitrary transfer of priests. His strong management style worked against his abiding concern for social justice for farm workers in an episode beginning in spring 1966, when a movement paralleling the Chavez-led Delano strike of grape pickers the previous year began in the lower Rio Grande Valley. Father Smith, the social action director of the archdiocese, and Father William Killian, executive editor of the archdiocesan weekly, went to Brownsville, joined the field workers in picketing, attended several rallies, and marched in an eight-mile "pilgrimage." They were arrested by local authorities for trespassing on private property and sent back to San Antonio. When Fathers Smith and Killian returned to the valley in early 1967 in defiance of Lucey's specific orders, Lucey removed Smith as social action director and demoted Killian and several other activist priests for violating protocol. Sixty-eight of Lucey's priests petitioned Rome for his retirement, and almost five thousand lay Catholics signed their names in support of the priests. In 1969, when the furor had died down, the seventy-eight-year-old archbishop announced his resignation.[17]

Cardinal Spellman's Mark on Puerto Rico and New York City

Beginning right after World War II, charters and later commercial flights of airlines offered low fares between San Juan and New York, effectively dooming the earlier mode of travel by ship. Meanwhile Puerto Rico's population shift from the countryside to San Juan and other coastal cities quickened during the 1940s and fed migration through around 1965. The period 1946 to 1965 thus encompassed what is called the Great Puerto Rican Migration. Despite the exodus, economic growth on the island was rapid, particularly in the 1950s, when Puerto Rico's gross national product (GNP) and gross domestic product (GDP) each more than doubled. An industrialization program, Operation Bootstrap, offered generous capital investment incentives. As a direct consequence of Operation Bootstrap, wages rose and a new middle class emerged.[18]

Puerto Rican governor Luis Muñoz Marín also presided over organized urban planning and urban redevelopment, beginning in 1942 with the passage of the Insular Planning Act, which launched changes in the landscape of the San Juan metropolitan area that were felt for decades. Urban renewal programs eliminated some of the worst slums and cleared the way for new residential, commercial, and public construction, while relocating families from shoddy bayside squatter settlements to public housing projects, known as *caseríos*, and other more permanent locations. Great strides were also taken in other areas, including education, as new schools went up even in the countryside, and health care, as the introduction of birth control technology and information offered resources for family planning.[19]

Muñoz Marín guided the island not only economically but also politically and culturally. In 1954 he presided over the adoption of a commonwealth status for the island, wherein residents retained U.S. citizenship but elected all their own local officers, replacing a system under which federal appointees were sent from Washington, D.C. This type of autonomy, which has been retained to the present time, represented a compromise between the numerically weak but politically active proindependence movement and the much larger statehood contingent. Under Marín's Popular Democratic Party (whose members became known as *populares*), the Puerto Rican government, for the first time since the early 1900s, developed a noticeable Protestant element, which increasingly demanded total separation of church and state and decried government aid to any religious denomination. In response to this accelerated trend away from what it considered Puerto Rico's traditional Catholicism, the clergy-led Partido Acción Cristiana (Christian Action Party) emerged as a Catholic party; it even had the rosary as a symbol on its flag.

Church policies on social issues pitted Governor Muñoz Marín himself, neither a regular churchgoer nor particularly observant in other respects (after a divorce he had married his second wife in a civil ceremony), against the island hierarchy. Though birth control and sterilization had become popular among the people, the bishops fervently opposed these practices. Catholics opposed the secularization of education in Puerto Rico throughout the early and mid-twentieth century. A major dispute arose in early 1960 after the bishops and Catholic groups had formed the Partido Acción Cristiana, seeking to repeal existing birth control and other laws that they believed were contrary to Catholic doctrine. In a fateful move, just two weeks before a gubernatorial election, Luis Aponte Martínez, along with Archbishop James Davis of San Juan and Bishop

James McManus of Ponce, issued a pastoral letter forbidding church members to vote for any candidates from the Popular Democratic Party, including the governor himself. North American bishops (including New York's Francis Spellman) rejected the measures of the Puerto Rican bishops as an attack on democracy in the North American tradition.[20]

Muñoz's *populares* won the gubernatorial election with 458,000 votes, followed by the Republican Statehood Party with 252,000, the new Christian Action Party with 52,000, and the Independence Party with 24,000. By late 1962, however, the rift ended between the Catholic Church and the government of Puerto Rico, and by the next election the Christian Action Party was well on its way to extinction. Bishop McManus was transferred to the Archdiocese of New York, and Archbishop Davis soon departed to Santa Fe, New Mexico. McManus later wrote that the Puerto Rican government was trying to enact laws "contrary to Catholic moral principles," attempts that were "doing a disfavor to the majority of its people and should not go unchallenged." He conceded that the governor "had respect for religion" but noted that he was not inclined to practice it in a visible way and "seemed not to be acquainted with [its] basics."[21]

In the early 1960s Cardinal Spellman of New York found himself in the middle of this debate over church and state sovereignty in Puerto Rico, after Governor Muñoz Marín's administration reasserted the separation of church and state in 1960. The conflict coincided with a new era in island Catholicism, characterized by greater influence of native-born clergy and bishops.[22] In October 1960 Spellman publicly stated that he disagreed with Archbishop Davis; he judged that the pastoral letter and subsequent voting in the island's elections were a matter "between a Catholic and his conscience" and asserted that no penalty would be incurred by Catholics who voted for Governor Muñoz. Bishop McManus, in turn, stated that it was not his intention that the Catholic Church be declared the official religion of the island, but he felt that the same benefits offered to the public schools should be given to the Catholic schools. On the campaign trail, Muñoz told the press, "We Puerto Ricans shall fight to defend the traditional religion of the majority of the Puerto Rican people against the grave errors of bishops who are transitory, while our religion is permanent." He claimed that the position taken by the Puerto Rican bishops was "incredible, unusual, obscure and medieval."[23]

The quarrel between Muñoz and the bishops, and especially their founding of a Catholic party and threatening to excommunicate anyone who voted for Muñoz, riled Spellman. Even though like those in the Puerto Rican Catholic hierarchy, he favored Puerto Rican statehood as offering unifying potential, he feared the rise of radicalism. Toward the end of the 1960 presidential campaign, Spellman had traveled to Puerto Rico to attend a ceremony consecrating Luis Aponte Martínez, a promising priest who during the 1950s had served as chancellor of the Pontifical Catholic University of Puerto Rico, as the new auxiliary bishop of Ponce. Aponte Martinez was the first native Puerto Rican bishop ordained since the early nineteenth century. Four years later, in 1964, Aponte Martinez was installed as archbishop of San Juan with a recommendation from Cardinal Spellman.[24]

Meanwhile, contributions from the increasingly prosperous Catholic community of New York permitted Spellman to build schools and hospitals and to fund numerous charities, for which purpose he continually cultivated relationships with politicians and important business leaders. Spellman refinanced the debt that the archdiocese had incurred during under Cardinal Patrick Hayes and thereby placed the archdiocese on a firmer financial footing. He then launched the largest expansion program in diocesan history and increased the number of parishes by forty-five. During his twenty-eight-year tenure, Spellman spent almost $600 million to build and renovate Catholic educational and charitable facilities and also centralized the financial and administrative operations of the archdiocese.[25]

Urban renewal was destroying vibrant Italian-American and Jewish neighborhoods, homes, and businesses in New York City, while making way for improvements in infrastructure, including transportation and downtown buildings, and spurring suburbanization. During much of the 1950s, Robert Moses laid the basis for moving existing slums and creating new ones, constructing twenty-four public housing projects and eleven superhighways. Clearance around the Navy Yard and the Brooklyn Civic Center allowed the construction of numerous plazas, cantilevered highway approaches, and infrastructure repairs, opening space for increased automobile traffic and arteries fortifying the suburban periphery. Older colonias such as those of South Brooklyn and Red Hook greatly declined thereafter. The construction of the Cross Bronx Expressway in the late 1950s ignored established neighborhood patterns and drove out thousands of middle-class Jewish and Italian residents. Wholesale displacement of Puerto Ricans and blacks from Manhattan's Upper West Side was justified as providing an opportunity to create "balanced communities" in the outer boroughs. Municipal officials' approval of these processes exacerbated racial tensions and encouraged further "white flight."[26]

In the 1940s and 1950s, and even beyond, East Harlem's La Mila-

Overflow Crowds at Our Lady of Montserrat Church, Brooklyn, New York, April 21, 1957 (Justo A. Martí Photographic Collection, Archive of the Puerto Rican Diaspora, Centro de Estudios Puertorriqueños, Hunter College, CUNY)

grosa parish remained central to Puerto Rican Catholic life in New York, with parishioners coming not only from all over El Barrio but from other neighborhoods and even from the Bronx, in spite of the fact that their territorial parishes were by then also offering services in Spanish. In one parish that quickly turned Puerto Rican in Manhattan's Upper West Side in the 1950s, St. Rose of Lima Church in Washington Heights, rural Puerto Rican migrants practiced Catholicism largely without a clergy, organizing confraternities and providing catechetical instruction. Soon groups of lay catechists formed, including the Hijas de María (Children of Mary) and the Sociedad del Santo Nombre (Holy Name Society), marking the emergence of an impromptu parish community. Finally parishioners approached the church's Irish-American pastor and requested a Spanish-speaking priest to celebrate Mass so that they would not have to travel to one of the existing Spanish-language chapels. The pastor invited a religious order priest from Spain to provide first a monthly Mass and later a "basement service."[27]

Neighborhoods in East Harlem, the Bronx, and Brooklyn were uprooted in the 1950s, a process that intensified in the 1960s and 1970s. One writer observed that those who were not always longing to return to their *tierra borinqueña* would constantly move back and forth between Puerto Rico and New York. The migration process disrupted linguistic mastery in both languages, while rural values of humility, support, and credulousness were tested in a new context.

Cardinal Spellman played a key role in the development of ministry to Puerto Ricans, financing personnel, institutional changes and other changes, but the archdiocese also recognized the role of all ethnicities in city building. Italians, mostly from southern Italy, brushed elbows with Puerto Ricans in both the secular and religious domains. By the early twentieth century Italian Americans, who had arrived several generations earlier, had gained control over many of East Harlem's neighborhood institutions. Since the late nineteenth century the Church of Mount Carmel had held a yearly festival, or *festa*, celebrating the Madonna extravagantly and vividly and serving to assert a sense of community. The July festival grew to enormous proportions, with thousands flocking to the food and games, bands and dancing, costumes and parades, parading of La Madonna through the neighborhood's streets and parks. Indeed, the festival placed a permanent Italian-American cultural stamp on the streets of New York. When not in the annual weeklong festival, the statue of la Madonna del Carmine stood above the main altar of the church on East 115th Street.

The church on 115th Street was transformed increasingly into an Italian-American parish during the 1940s and 1950s. It remained inaccessible and impenetrable to Puerto Rican newcomers, though both groups were predominantly Catholic. According to one social historian, when Puerto Ricans began arriving in the 1940s and 1950s, the Italian procession and the devotion to la Madonna del Carmine served as means of reclaiming the margins of El Barrio that had been blurred by the newcomers' arrival. Puerto Ricans' and Italians' frequent conflicts with each other, however, mirrored the Italians' experience with other ethnic groups and the archdiocese. East Harlem's Church of Our Lady of Mount Carmel dated from the early 1880s, when it was situated on the border with Irish and German communities. The bulk of the funds for its construction had come from the older immigrants, while Italians were sent to the basement to worship, even though the church was to become an Italian national parish.[28]

In the 1950s, when Catholic office seekers still depended on the Church's political contacts to obtain votes and jobs, the archdiocese became an institutional power partly because of the educational, hospital, and charity services it provided. Spellman retained clout in other secular processes and institutions throughout his tenure, as seen in 1955, when the Jesuit-led Fordham University wanted to open a downtown campus. That brought master planner Robert Moses into the picture. Moses used his sweeping powers as Slum Clearance Committee chair and city construction coordinator to oust hundreds of tenants from six prime acres of real estate adjacent to his Lincoln Center Title I development. Many of the displaced residents at the location where the Fordham campus was placed were themselves Catholic, including Irish Americans and Puerto Ricans. St. Matthew's parish on West 68th Street, deemed expendable, was destroyed in the course of renewal.

Spellman desegregated his archdiocese's charitable and educational institutions and played an important role as emissary between the White House and Rome. He served as ecclesiastical superior of Roman Catholic chaplains in the armed forces and continued to visit armed forces overseas until his death in 1967. In the process he became a strong advocate of containing the expansion of Soviet communism. He also became involved with Latin American issues. While visiting Puerto Rico in 1938 as a Boston pastor, Spellman noted that "less than ten per cent of the people go to Mass and only one per cent of those who go are men." Spellman acknowledged the valuable work of the Redemptorists Fathers on the island, and he credited the "generosity of Americans who in thirty-five years have contributed two million and a half dollars to build churches and schools in Puerto Rico." The following year, shortly after taking charge of his see in New York, the archbishop removed the diocesan priests from a largely Puerto Rican East Harlem parish, St. Cecilia's, and entrusted it to a Redemptorist pastor with fourteen years' worth of experience with Spanish-speaking parishioners in Puerto Rico and three in Tampa. At Spellman's urging, rather than becoming a national parish for Puerto Ricans like nearby La Milagrosa and Santa Agonía under Spanish religious, St. Cecilia's would remain a territorial parish.

English was the official language of sermons and hymns for the main contingent of Catholic ethnics, although Latin remained the only language for the Mass itself until 1965. Jaime Vidal notes that "Puerto Ricans were granted a Sunday 'Spanish Mass,' that is, a Latin Mass with a Spanish sermon and hymns," which was often held in the church basement. Under this arrangement, confessions were held in the native langue. As newcomers gained proficiency in English, their Spanish usage would diminish, resulting in a more linguistically unified parish community. The arrangement introduced at St. Cecilia's was later justified by the urgent circumstances of the Puerto Rican migration; for example, dozens of Protestant storefront churches opened within the limits of St. Cecilia's parish in the early postwar years.[29]

By 1940, six Roman Catholic churches served Puerto Ricans and other Spanish speakers almost exclusively, with at least two others having a Spanish Mass. No new national parishes—for whose founding or discontinuance permission from the Vatican would have been required—were established. The new model of an "integrated" or mixed parish became the accepted method for meeting the needs of Puerto Ricans and, later, other Latinos. Many integrated parishes developed out of informal agreements between neighboring pastors, often without the archbishop's involvement, allowing Spanish-speaking residents to receive the sacraments.[30]

Spellman saw national parishes as reinforcing ethnic identity even to the point of segregation, as had occurred with African Americans, and feared that setting up national parishes for Puerto Ricans would retard their assimilation. In New York, Puerto Ricans were scattered among numerous neighborhoods, many of which were disrupted by the construction of vast low-income high-rise housing projects, as well as urban renewal programs. It became more difficult for Puerto Ricans to create cohesive communities within neighborhoods than it had been for earlier immigrant groups. As they entered new areas, they became minorities in territorial parishes. The Spanish Mass allowed them a minimum of sacred space, though at the cost of keeping them apart from English-speaking parishioners. In practice, Puerto Ricans proved very reluctant to give up their rural customs or abandon their religious tradition, and Cardinal Spellman respected this. But he sought to modify the popular religious practices of Puerto Ricans to increasingly center them on receiving the Mass and sacraments.[31]

In March 1953, Spellman created the Office of Spanish Catholic Action of the Archdiocese of New York to coordinate Puerto Rican ministry. It was headed by Monsignor Joseph F. Connolly, a respected priest. Within a few weeks of his appointment, Connolly began the institution of the Fiesta of St. John the Baptist—the island's patron saint—as a focus for Puerto Rican Catholic identity. To varying degrees, the archdiocese used the fiesta to foster a sense of unity between Puerto Ricans and other Spanish-speaking Catholics, and ultimately between them and all Catholics in New York. In 1953 the fiesta included a pontifical Mass at St. Patrick's Cathedral, celebrated by Bishop McManus of Ponce, with

Cardinal Spellman presiding and the mayor of New York and a number of civic leaders present.[32]

In 1957 Connolly's successor, Father James J. Wilson, rented Randall's Island stadium and park, a location easily accessible from Manhattan's Lower East Side. For the next eight years this remained the fiesta's location. The event featured a procession of lay sodalities and confraternities, who marched behind their respective banners, followed by an outdoor Mass with a Spanish sermon given by a guest preacher and concluding remarks by the cardinal. An accompanying civic ceremony brought the participation of local and island politicians and leaders, which culminated with the awarding of that year's San Juan Medal. There was also a cultural celebration featuring Puerto Rican music, theater, and other forms of entertainment. By the late 1950s, annual attendance at the fiesta averaged more than fifty-five thousand.[33]

The early 1950s also saw the beginning of another of Spellman's initiatives, this one involving sending a number of priests and seminarians to Puerto Rico to learn the language and culture of the island; this proved to be useful and practical training for work in New York's parishes. In view of the general shortage of priests on the island, it was generally agreed that a Puerto Rican priest was needed more on the island than he would be needed on the continent. Several priests and seminarians went to Puerto Rico each year from 1953 to 1955; in 1956 and 1957 the cardinal accelerated the process, sending half of his ordination class for special Spanish-language training, first at Georgetown University and then to Puerto Rico. Under the influence of young priest Ivan Illich, the archdiocese embarked on a vision of integrating Puerto Ricans with priests who were not only bilingual but bicultural and versed in the migrants' religious tradition. Father Illich, only in his late twenties, was temporarily assigned to Ponce to develop an extensive training program at the Catholic University, which was financially underwritten by Cardinal Spellman and geared to training priests for the Archdiocese of New York. In 1959 it took the name Institute of Intercultural Communication; it remained active until 1972.[34]

Many of the younger priests, sisters, brothers, and laypeople trained at the institute became pastors, teachers and important advocates in ministry to the Puerto Ricans. Though under Spellman's control, the institute also contributed to other continental dioceses' ministries for Puerto Ricans and other immigrants from Latin America. The continued postwar Puerto Rican influx prompted the New York Archdiocese and the Brooklyn Diocese to begin registering people for mainland parishes

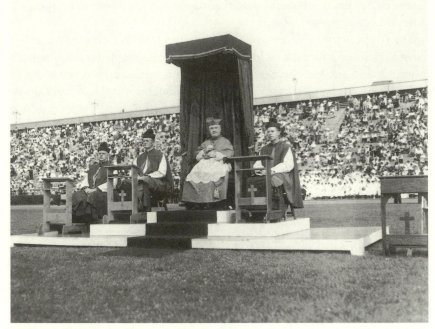

Cardinal Francis Spellman at San Juan Fiesta, June 21, 1959 (The Justo A. Martí Photographic Collection, Archive of the Puerto Rican Diaspora, Centro de Estudios Puertorriqueños, Hunter College, CUNY)

even before they left Puerto Rico. The existing Vincentian and Augustinian parishes in Manhattan (Esperanza and Our Lady of Guadalupe) were staffed by priests from the continental United States, Spain, and a few other European countries, and many of them had never gone to Puerto Rico. Meanwhile, a large number of the Brooklyn clergy came from Spain. There were very few Puerto Rican priests. Several congregations of nuns from the Brooklyn Diocese, who had gone into Puerto Rico early in the twentieth century, continued to render valuable assistance in schools. They directed boarding houses for young women and expanded catechetical work among public school children, while assisting the Redemptorists and other religious orders.[35]

The Spanish Vincentians actively ministered to the needs of many of Brooklyn's Puerto Ricans, while a number of diocesan priests from the Brooklyn Diocese began to study Spanish on their own. In 1958, Bishop Bryan J. McEntegart began assigning newly ordained priests to study Spanish at the Catholic University of Ponce in Puerto Rico, which would also offer an opportunity for cultural immersion. Puerto Rico's religious order clergy—led by the predominantly U.S. Redemptorists, who clustered in larger Puerto Rican cities and towns—outnumbered diocesan priests by more than three to one. By 1960 some two hundred diocesan priests had been trained, and within a decade nearly three hundred additional priests, religious, and laypeople had studied in Ponce's Institute of Intercultural Communication.[36]

In 1961, there were forty-two Catholic parishes in New York City with Spanish-speaking Roman Catholic priests, but only one was Puerto Rican. By contrast, preachers and ministers of Pentecostal churches in New York were almost all Puerto Ricans, which meant that in such churches members could rise rapidly. Pentecostals had been looked upon as most heretical by the more mainline or "ecumenical" Protestant denominations. In Puerto Rico, Pentecostals were not in on the original division of the Protestant pie, and thus they could form congregations anywhere on the island. Protestant leaders of all stripes perceived widespread religious indifference among Puerto Ricans in New York City. Estimates identified almost half of the total New York City population in 1952 as Roman Catholic, but only about one-third were actually affiliated with the Catholic Church. Among Puerto Ricans the figure was much lower, and fully 50 percent of their marriages were being conducted in Protestant churches.[37]

By 1965, Puerto Ricans were further removed from the pan-Latino identity of neighborhoods in the 1920s and 1930s, when they had shared streets and parishes with Cubans, Spaniards, and Latin Americans as part of a larger Spanish-speaking community. The massive migration of the mid-1940s through the mid-1960s had no contemporary counterparts other than the northern migration of southern blacks; the groups competed for jobs, residence, and economic standing. The Puerto Rican color line became increasing confusing and frustrating; reluctant ethnics, they were ambivalent about their perceived standing as nonwhite racial minorities. Puerto Ricans in New York City passively resisted Americanization, however, holding on to their language and culture rather than integrating into parish communities.[38]

Cardinal Stritch in Chicago: Parish Preservation and Community Leadership

With the expansion of agricultural production in the early twentieth century, coinciding with an immigrant influx, the increasingly diverse Tejano population became more mobile within Texas, the region, and the Mid-

west. Many workers and their families joined the migrant stream from
spring to fall, plying the beet fields of Michigan, Minnesota, and elsewhere, then returning to spend the winter in San Antonio. "Luxuries"
like education for migrant children and churches for the families were
easily delayed. Large cities, however, such as Chicago, where stable national parishes had been the norm for succeeding waves of German, Bohemian, Polish, Lithuanian, and Italian Catholics, offered greater ease
of settlement. Since the late nineteenth century, the national parish had
preserved language, faith, and culture while aiding Chicagoans in efforts
at integrating into the larger society. In the 1920s, a reconsideration of
the national parish tradition occurred as Cardinal George Mundelein refused to form national parishes outside ethnic enclaves and instead advocated the Irish-American parish model of English-language or territorial
parishes. Mundelein also developed bureaucratic efficiency, making all
properties of the parishes in the archdiocese fall under the archbishop's
legal ownership. His work as a powerful prelate also involved contesting
the policies of City Hall, and he developed mutually beneficial partner-
ships with both priests and precinct captains.[39]

Also having a great impact on Chicago Catholics was Cardinal Samuel Stritch, who became bishop of Milwaukee in 1930, was installed in
1940 as archbishop of Chicago, and in 1946 became cardinal. Stritch had
visited Texas and seen the poor conditions of Mexican Americans, had
participated in the founding of the BCSS, and had become an ally of
Archbishop Lucey. He had also served as chair of the American Board of
Catholic Missions and president of the Catholic Church Extension Society. He led the Chicago Archdiocese for eighteen years, from 1939 until
his death in 1958; his tenure as cardinal coincided with the rise of neighborhood racial tensions related to suburbanization and urban renewal.

White ethnic Catholics and their priests were among those who offered considerable resistance to open housing and integration in the city.
Chicago Catholics were less likely than Protestants and Jews to leave old
neighborhoods, and they actively resisted encroachment. Jewish syna-
gogues and Protestant churches could sell their buildings both to recover
their equity and to simply relocate away from the expanding African-
American ghetto, but Catholic parishes and their property were registered in the name of the diocese and by definition served the people living within the parish boundaries. Neighborhood and religion remained
intertwined. Catholic churches also routinely sponsored parades and processions through the neighborhood streets, claiming both the parish and
its inhabitants as sacred ground.[40]

During the second large twentieth-century African-American migration to Chicago in the 1940s and especially the 1950s, the housing shortage became acute as an influx of poor, largely non-Catholic blacks threatened to displace ethnics in older neighborhoods. Racial separation was exacerbated by real estate brokers who steered clients toward and away from certain neighbors, and threats of violence sought to prevent blacks from crossing existing residential boundaries. Block organizations frequently met at local parish meeting halls, while some clergymen distributed church newsletters alerting their parishioners to the dangers of "panic selling": a sudden rush to sell homes after a racial incident, they warned, could tip the area's population to a point of no return for Catholic ethnics. Civil rights campaigns were launched not by parish communities but by extraparochial organizations, such as the Catholic Interracial Council, which sought to change attitudes toward racial integration.

Along with other church leaders, Stritch worked to mitigate the publicity generated by the involvement of prominent clergy and lay Catholics in protests and riots against the placement of public and private housing geared toward blacks in predominantly white neighborhoods. In 1956 the cardinal publicly opposed the violent response of working-class Catholics to the entry of blacks in the Trumbull Park neighborhood. Thereafter, however, he adopted a low profile; his stamp was evidenced mainly in his organization of priests throughout the city into parish preservation organizations, designed to ease the trauma of racial change in transitional neighborhoods. Stritch became more engaged in integration in response to Puerto Rican and Mexican Catholics who encountered ethnic friction (though not the violence encountered by African Americans). The U.S. Supreme Court's *Brown v. Board of Education* decision in 1954 served to support the archdiocese's policy of promoting integration and avoiding the construction of new national parishes for Puerto Ricans. The archdiocese hoped to integrate not only Latin American immigrants but also, and more important at that time, the even faster growing African-American community into neighborhood churches.[41]

Chicago's growing Latino presence in the 1940s was fed by Texas Mexican-American and Mexican immigrant farm workers, who formed numerous communities on the metropolitan periphery. They found work as field hands and later in expanding suburban factories. Among the most important developments in the Mexican Catholic community after World War II was the growing number of Mexicans attending parishes not administered by the Claretians. Mexicans entering Chicago during the 1950s had overflowed from the historic barrios but tended to remain on the South Side. Puerto Ricans, meanwhile, found housing mostly on the North Side. The convergence of these two very different Spanish-speaking groups in the Midwest confounded earlier archdiocesan policies.[42]

In 1954 energetic pastors, with Stritch's approval, began organizing Puerto Rican laymen into an organization called Los Caballeros de San Juan. Although by 1955 Chicago housed about twenty thousand Puerto Ricans, they were widely scattered, with never more than a thousand in one parish. They tended to take manufacturing more than heavy industrial jobs and clustered near downtown. Congregationally based institutions often moved with their constituents to new city neighborhoods or the suburbs, draining old neighborhoods of much social capital. On the other hand, parish loyalty resulted in strong resistance to neighborhood change, and it also encouraged opening ministry to newer residents to keep church institutions viable—as long as the change did not involve racial turnover from white to black. Latinos, of course, constituted an intermediate category, and the reception they received varied according to the specific local and neighborhood ethnic mix.[43]

Housing pressures developing in New York City were diverting Puerto Rican migrants elsewhere, and Chicago quickly became another major target. The Commonwealth of Puerto Rico established a second mainland office in Chicago in the late 1950s. The office also served Puerto Ricans in Milwaukee, Wisconsin; Gary, Indiana; and other Midwestern cities, as well as contract farm workers who arrived. By 1955, the influx of Puerto Ricans to Chicago had become quite noticeable, and most families were now arriving directly from the island. The Cardinal's Committee ruled out the establishment of national parishes for ministry to Puerto Ricans, given their lack of priests and wide dispersal in Chicago. The archdiocese instead chose to address the Puerto Rican situation as a social justice problem: Puerto Ricans were often seen as victims of discrimination or, at the very least, as deserving special support as struggling members of the working class.[44]

A year after the foundation of the Caballeros de San Juan, in the fall of 1955, Cardinal Stritch set up the Cardinal's Committee for the Spanish-Speaking in Chicago. In spite of its title, this committee concentrated almost exclusively on Puerto Ricans, because Mexicans, who were at least twice as numerous, had been for decades served by three national parishes under the care of the Claretian Fathers. It was feared that any efforts in this direction would be perceived by the Spanish priests as interference. The committee consisted of twenty-one priests and laypersons. The executive staff consisted of Father Gilbert Carroll as coordinator, Father Leo Mahon as executive assistant, Nicholas Von Hoffman and Lester Hunt as full-time organizers for the Puerto Rican community, and another organizer (a Mexican layman) for work among the Mexican community. Beginning in late 1954, several Spanish Augustinian priests served in the downtown Chicago Cathedral parish to minister to Puerto Ricans—of whom there were almost two thousand.[45]

Given the relatively small numbers of Spanish-speaking in the archdiocese at that time, Stritch decided not to embark on language training for the clergy, as Spellman and Lucey had. Activist Saul Alinsky, organizer of the famous Chicago neighborhood movements Back of the Yards and the Woodlawn Organization, allied with Cardinal Stritch during the 1940s and 1950s and used young priests as community organizers. Since the 1930s Alinsky had trained organizers at the Industrial Areas Foundation (IAF) in Chicago's Back of the Yards neighborhood. He took a particular interest in the archdiocese's budding work with Puerto Ricans and conducted sociological studies and reports, keeping Stritch apprised of migrant dispersal within the city. By the late 1950s Puerto Ricans had also clustered on the Near West Side, next to a large Italian-American contingent, in Woodlawn and other neighborhoods on the South Side, and in East Garfield Park, a neighborhood stretching north toward the heart of Polish Chicago. Alinsky and the IAF helped move Cardinal Stritch and Monsignor John J. Egan, director of the Cardinal's Committee, toward greater advocacy of residential integration.[46]

In 1947, about the time that Puerto Ricans started coming in large numbers to Chicago, the Catholic Youth Organization opened a central office for the newcomers that until the mid-1950s provided most of the archdiocese's early assistance to Puerto Ricans. In 1953 several Puerto Rican men and Father Leo Mahon, a young priest at Holy Cross parish in Woodlawn, started the Woodlawn Latin-American Committee, an association that became the Caballeros de San Juan (Knights of St. John) the following year. When Mahon drove Stritch along Milwaukee Avenue to show him the neighborhood, the cardinal noticed several Protestant storefront churches for Puerto Ricans. Convinced of the need for mission work in Chicago, Stritch paid off the committee's debts and agreed to pay the organizers' salaries. By design the Caballeros accepted men who did not attend Mass regularly or whose marital situation did not meet official Catholic standards. Once under the influence of the Church, they could slowly be attracted to Mass, the sacraments, yearly retreats, and other religious practices. Priests served as chaplains of the councils and provided a further link to parishes. Each club organized its own social events and recreation activities.[47]

A yearly parade, political activity, and a credit union brought the Caballeros public recognition. The association's leaders became the community's political spokesmen. The first parade in 1956 proved a huge success, drawing about six thousand. Cardinal Stritch and Bishop James McManus, of Ponce, Puerto Rico, celebrated Mass before the parade at Holy Name Cathedral. Mayor Richard J. Daley, both U.S. senators from Illinois, and other dignitaries attended, and the city council declared June 19–24, 1956, San Juan Week. The Caballeros organized a parade, later renamed La Parada Puertorriqueña, in East Garfield Park, a neighborhood with a large Puerto Rican population; the event eventually expanded to include other organizations. Tense relations developed between some of the Caballeros' councils and pastors in 1963 at St. Michael's on the Near North Side. Run by Redemptorists, this parish was considered home to one of the more successful councils. In nearby West Town, meanwhile, Polish parishes were also reluctant to welcome Puerto Ricans, as indicated in an archdiocesan report that criticized the Resurrectionists, who ran Holy Trinity, St. Mary of the Angels, and St. Stanislaus Kostka, Chicago's huge North Side Polish national churches.[48]

By 1964 eleven councils of the Caballeros de San Juan existed in Chicago, serving thousands of members. Each council had various social, recreational, and self-help activities, with female auxiliary groups. Several formed credit associations as well. Many Caballeros members saw the organization as a vehicle for preserving Puerto Rican religious practices, ethnic identity, and group cohesion on the mainland. By the mid-1960s, some lay individuals developed a more focused interest in the religious life, and under Father Leo Mahon's direction they formed an offshoot group, Los Hermanos en la Familia de Dios (Brothers in the Family of God), whose principal work consisted of promoting parish catechesis while engaging in frequent reception of the sacraments and daily scriptural reading. By the late 1960s, many of the Hermanos had moved on to become leaders in the permanent diaconate.[49]

For a decade the Caballeros councils were synonymous with Puerto Rican leadership in Chicago. In the mid-1960s, however, a new set of secular leaders arose when Mayor Richard J. Daley appointed Latino community leaders to political posts following the June 1966 Division Street riots. Religious rivals emerged with the ascent of a Protestant social settlement, Casa Central Evangélica. This agency had been founded in 1954 and drew interdenominational support from several organizations in the Humboldt Park and Logan Square barrios. With increasing religious competition during the 1960s, Protestants in Chicago became better organized and gained more adherents from the Puerto Rican migrant community.[50]

The Chicago Archdiocese continued to oppose the formation of additional national parishes. Meanwhile. St. Francis of Assisi, the "Mexican Cathedral" on the Near West Side, served newcomers coming from Mexico, Texas, and elsewhere in the Midwest. It went from offering three of its four Sunday services in English in 1949 to six of seven Masses in Spanish by 1957. In the early 1960s, thousands of people attended Mass at St. Francis, from which Claretians broadcast weekly radio programs. In 1956, a Hull House worker observed regarding St. Francis of Assisi Parish that the parish "should represent the Mexican community but has been reluctant to do so. This church had gone so far as to have pastors of other churches speak directly against other institutions [Hull House] and agencies in the area who had been willing to help the community." The Claretians responded by attacking the settlement house for criticizing the Catholic Church and for holding positions contrary to Catholic moral teachings. Given its predominantly Mexican-origin composition, St. Francis never developed a council of the Los Caballeros de San Juan for its few Puerto Rican members.[51]

As noted, Stritch had started the Chicago Cardinal's Committee for the Spanish-Speaking (CCSS), funded by the American Board of Catholic Missions, in September 1955 to further organize the city's Puerto Rican Catholics. For its first two years the CCSS concentrated on organizing Puerto Ricans, but afterward the committee expanded its operations, starting separate associations for Mexicans, Cubans, and all Latino groups. Few Claretian priests welcomed the changes in the Spanish-speaking apostolate; generally the Claretians perceived them as intrusions on their historic ministry to Chicago's Mexican community. Claretian parishes, meanwhile, sought to incorporate the Mexican community through the Young Catholic Worker and Young Catholic Student movements. Differences of outlook and training also arose between Stritch and diocesan clergy, who dominated the committee. It was in order to placate the Spanish priests that the CCSS avoided Mexican work in its early years. Later the committee tried to unite the city's approximately thirty-five Mexican organizations through the Illinois Federation of Mexican-Americans.[52]

Cardinal Albert G. Meyer headed the Chicago Archdiocese from 1958 until 1965, and like Stritch, he believed in the urgency of improving race relations in Chicago. Meyer continued his predecessor's support of the Catholic Councils for the Spanish-Speaking, and he supported priests working on the city's South Side to desegregate Catholic high schools. In 1960 he issued an order that all Catholic schools accept African-American children. He also was involved in national bodies such as the National Conference on Religion and Race, until he became preoccupied with participating in the Vatican II Council meetings, conducted in Rome from 1962 to 1965, where he emerged as leader of the U.S. bishops.[53]

By the middle of 1960 and the beginning of 1961, the influx of Cuban families to Chicago became very noticeable as a result of their resettlement from Miami. Almost two thousand Cubans had resettled in Chicago by 1964 with the help of the CCSS and Chicago's Resettlement Committee. The Asociación Cubana de Chicago, established under the auspices of the CCSS, secured housing, jobs, and English-language classes and even found foster homes for Cuban children. The Asociación's work with local governmental agencies and Catholic Charities became part of a broad international opposition to communism. This was not surprising, given that many of the Cubans had emigrated to the United States because of Fidel Castro's imposition of communism in Cuba.

The population of Cubans in Chicago exceeded fifteen thousand during the 1960s, and the exiles were dispersed fairly evenly throughout the metropolis, including the suburbs. Within the city proper, a large portion of the Cuban community concentrated in three North Side neighborhoods, Uptown, Edgewater, and Rogers Park, where some parishes started Spanish Masses. In late 1968, a Chicago steering committee established the Association of Our Lady of Charity of El Cobre. Its members put together programs for the social and religious life of the Spanish-speaking families of St. Ita Church and had a shrine to Our Lady of Charity erected in the back of the church. While several ethnically mixed parishes thus took on a distinctly Cuban tinge, however, their numbers never approached those of Mexican and Puerto Rican parishes.[54]

Mexicans, Puerto Ricans, and Cubans were not the only Latinos in Chicago. In 1965, Archbishop John P. Cody took over the Chicago office of the BCSS. One BCSS report highlighted rising immigration of Spanish-speaking people between August 1965 and August 1966, with significant increases reported from Mexico, Colombia, and the Dominican Republic. Neither the Chicago Church nor the Claretian Fathers kept pace with the growing Latino Catholic community. Archbishops ruled with an iron hand and often got similar results. Archbishop Cody's tenure in Chicago lasted from 1965 to 1982, and he decided unilaterally to replace activist priests involved in racial and urban affairs. That led to the formation of the Association of Chicago Priests, a group that challenged his policies and tactics. Despite consistent financial support of Mexican Americans in California and increasing support of the grape pickers' strike, as well as Catholic work in the inner city, Cody's authoritarian manner sparked ongoing internal disputes that alienated him from many of his priests.[55]

The End of an Era

Bishops, as head of institutional networks, engineered the expansion of church structures while priests organized parish communities. Unfortunately, many of the non-Spanish-speaking clergy installed were strangers to the people and their customs. Nevertheless, religion served as a vehicle for cultural transformation, greatly affecting the daily lives of parishioners. Ethnic neighborhoods helped preserve parish cohesion and contributed to maintaining homeland styles of observance amid the homogenizing forces of Americanization. Religion remained the life force of Latin American communities in transformation, energizing communities, disseminating culture, and reflecting growth and urban development. Explosive crises in the homeland, such as wars, persecution, and annexation, were promptly addressed in immigrant communities through parishes.[56]

Latinos had long been left out of the U.S. Roman Catholic immigrant Church, though similarities existed between both Mexican and Puerto Rican Catholics and their European counterparts arriving earlier. Between 1940 and 1965, prelates assumed unprecedented powers in addressing issues brought on by Latin American migration and settlement beyond merely parochial concerns. They expanded their reach, and that of their clergy, both geographically and culturally. The needs of Mexican-American and Puerto Rican regional minorities were given greater attention and sometimes even were considered within a larger national context. Despite obvious limitations, moreover, the clergy and the hierarchy increasingly moved to deal with secular issues affecting Latino immigrant groups. Each group shed its earlier isolation. In both religiosity and identity, however, there was no clear progression for Puerto Ricans. And although considerable strides were made in building the Church, the bishops really failed to bring about lasting institutional change. Nor did they attempt to address larger issues involving human rights, poverty, social justice, or democracy in Latin America. That would await the reforms of Vatican II.[57]

5   Cuban Miami and Exile Catholicism

For European ethnics, immigrant Catholicism that was solidly based in the parish became a base for developing a sense of community from a position of strength. The Cuban pattern that emerged in Miami has been quite different, however, from the European immigrant experience. Cubans' experiences also contrast with the urban Catholicism of Mexican Americans and Puerto Ricans. The most notable difference may be that Cuban clergy accompanied Cuban laity in exile. In just one month, September 1961, more than one hundred priests and some eighty religious sisters from Cuba arrived to give the Church of Miami the critical clerical leadership needed to build the future. Similarities among the groups also exist, including their generally later time of arrival, the presence of a Latin American religious tradition, and other related social factors.[1]

The growth of Catholicism in Miami coincided with the arrival of Cuban exiles in large numbers after the 1959 revolution. In more recent decades there have been additional waves of Cubans who received little Catholic training in the homeland as a consequence of growing up under the Castro regime. Significantly, newcomers from elsewhere in Latin America have changed Miami's ethnic, and thus religious, mix. Their histories have blended into the larger Cuban exile saga in making modern "Latino Miami" a gateway to Latin America in many respects. Consequently the history of Cuba, both secular and religious, and its relationship to south Florida can be seen to have played a crucial role worth detailed examination.

Miami became a magnet for exiles fleeing the Castro revolution, a symbol of resistance to socialism and to numerous forms of repression, including religious discrimination. Because Miami had a long history as a center of opposition to Cuban governments dating back to 1931, when it became a haven for the political opposition led by former president Mario Menocal, it became the most logical destination for exiles. A few Castro-era Cuban exiles gravitated to the late-nineteenth-century centers of Key West and Tampa, where opponents of the Spanish regime, including large numbers of cigar makers, had fled. After Cuba won independence from Spain in 1898, and with the establishment of the Cuban Republic in 1902, the Tampa community in particular grew, but it never gained much significance for the post-Castro wave of exiles over a half-century later. During the first wave of exiles, which happened between 1959 and 1962, most of the 200,000 Cubans who arrived in the United States landed in Miami, which the refugees soon thought of as "Cuba's seventh province."[2] Subsequent waves occurred in the "airlift" from 1965 to 1973 of 261,000 refugees on the Freedom Flights, the 1980 Mariel exodus of 125,000, and, finally, from the mid-1990s to the present, the arrival of more than 40,000 people on rafts and other makeshift vessels.

Historians have noted the importance of churches to urban order and prosperity, as service providers, shapers of civic culture, and urban financiers and developers. They pace the growth of the contemporary metropolis. Catholic churches in particular have served as land consolidators and neighborhood developers, financed home purchases for parishioners, and sponsored building and loan societies and insurance companies that invested in mortgages, while preaching the virtues of home ownership. They also lobbied politicians for city services. While the institutional function of Cuban-American Catholicism in Miami largely followed this pattern, the case of the Cuban exiles became immersed in hemispheric, indeed global, cold war policies of the United States and the Soviet Union, and religion was a major, though neglected, factor in the equation.

The Catholic Church in Cuba and the Revolution

Under Spanish rule, Catholicism was imposed as the official and exclusive religion of Cuba. After independence, in their search for nationhood—at home to some extent, but especially in exile—Cubans virtually abandoned Catholicism and turned to other ideas, including Protestantism, anarchism, and socialism. The Catholic Church remained especially weak in the Cuban countryside and thus had limited reach.[3] Certainly, the Cuban Church's suppression of nationalism in the late nineteenth century made it appear anachronistic to many islanders. A Cuban scholar, Jorge Ramírez Calzadilla, notes that orthodox Catholicism never developed strong roots in Cuban society, because it rejected "leading, foundational ideas [embracing separatism that] were antidogmatic and freethinking, but without being atheistic or antireligious." This line of thought was synthesized by patriot José Martí who sought freedom for Cuba above all.[4]

As Cuba remained longer under the Spanish yoke than all of Spain's other former colonies except Puerto Rico, its brand of imperial Catholicism had a longer tenure on Cuban islands than in colonies in Central and

South America. Yet Catholicism in Cuba remained comparatively weaker. According to sociologist Lisandro Perez, Cuba's relative absence of religiosity and scant observance of Catholic practices owe to a unique set of circumstances: the role of Havana as a secular port city, which flourished while the hinterland languished; the paucity of staff for the Cuban church; the sugar revolution and the secularization of the mills; the prevalence of non-Catholic religions, which brought religious heterogeneity during the last two decades of the nineteenth century; and the perception of a pro-Spanish church, an enemy of Cuban independence.[5]

Under a republican government, the early-twentieth-century Cuban institutional church devoted itself to providing private education, which benefited mostly the country's middle class and elite. Most of the clergy came from Spain, where they had been educated under Francisco Franco's dictatorship. The Cuban revolution occurred and sustained itself with little participation from the institutional church. Fulgencio Batista came to prominence as a brutal military henchman after 1933 and rose to the presidency in a 1952 coup. Condemned to a prison term following a July 26, 1953, attack on the Moncada Army barracks in Santiago, Fidel Castro served only a few months before being given amnesty, with the blessing and support of the archbishop of Santiago, Enrique Pérez Serantes, who had consistently opposed Batista. In the two years before 1959, Father Guillermo Sardiñas, once a parish priest on the Isle of Pines, emerged as a leading guerrilla chaplain in the Sierra Maestra mountains. Promoted to the rank of comandante, Sardiñas became a self-proclaimed Christian revolutionary, anathema to his superiors for his support of Castro's reforms.[6] Castro's revolution changed the history of Cuban society after 1959—socially, politically, and culturally—spawning a massive exile that permanently weakened the island's Catholic leadership.

Whereas in 1959, 84 percent of the Cuban population considered itself Catholic, by 1998 the number had dropped to 43 percent. In addition to this decrease, the Church lost much of its clergy. The numbers dropped from almost 700 priests and 3,500 religious in 1959 to 270 and 577 some forty years later. The general pattern within Latino Catholicism is that clergy do not emigrate with the laity, but Cubans constitute an exception. A significant number of Cuban priests came to the United States as exiles, knowing that return was unlikely.[7]

After 1959, the history of Cuba was the history of a nation divided. Ardent nationalism was expressed by Cubans who stayed and were in favor of, or at least not in overt opposition to, the revolution, while many exiles saw themselves in a struggle for the liberation of Cuba from outside the country. At first Cuba's Catholic hierarchy openly supported the new regime's agrarian reform program. But in 1960–61, as the regime became isolated internationally and radicalized internally, it issued a series of decrees banning public religious practice, seizing churches, expelling foreign priests, and nationalizing education.[8]

Outspoken criticism of the regime, particularly from Havana auxiliary bishop Eduardo Boza Masvidal, who emphasized the alternative role of the Church in an anticommunist pursuit of social justice, led Castro to adopt increasingly harsh anticlerical measures. In early 1961 Castro branded the Church as "the fifth column of the counterrevolution."[9] Meanwhile, the pursuit of a free and independent *Cuba libre* (free Cuba) was undertaken wherever Cuban exiles settled. But Castro's strategic and tactical skill, combined with shortcomings in U.S. policy and the early Soviet decision to provide assistance to Castro's regime, contributed to a lasting divide between the homeland and Cuban communities in Miami and elsewhere in the United States.[10]

By February 1960, Castro was saying that anyone opposed to communism was also opposed to the revolution. The Church began to take a stance of open opposition to the government. This trend culminated in a statement by the Cuban episcopate on August 7, 1960: "Let no one ask us Catholics to silence our opposition . . . out of a false sense of civil loyalty. . . . The vast majority of the Cuban people are Catholic, and only by deceit can they be won over to a communist regime."[11] The failed Bay of Pigs invasion launched by the United States in April 1961 ignited the simmering church-state crisis. Among the prisoners captured when the invasion was crushed were three Catholic priests, all Spanish nationals. Castro attacked the clergy for its predominantly foreign, mostly Spanish, contingent of diocesan and religious-order priests and religious women.[12]

Church leaders believed it wisest to go into exile quietly, then return to Cuba to rebuild the Church. In 1961, Boza Masvidal, who was president of the Catholic Villanueva University, published polemical parish bulletins. His February 1961 pastoral suggested that even the revered patriot-revolutionary Martí would oppose Fidel. In September 1961, some four thousand people celebrating the Virgen de la Caridad outside Boza's church turned into a demonstration when they headed toward the presidential palace shouting slogans critical of the revolutionary government. A passing seventeen-year-old was killed. A week later, more than 130 priests and religious, including Boza, were forced aboard the Spanish ship *Covadonga* in Havana harbor and were expelled from the island. Along with disturbances in Camagüey and other cities, the demonstration thus led to harsh reprisals as Castro's government painted all clergy as harboring counterrevolutionary sentiments. This clerical diaspora served to export religious dissidents, but it did not end their activities. In exile in Venezuela, Boza founded the Unión de Cubanos en el Exilio, which helped organize refugee Cubans; chapters of the organization were formed in Miami, New York, Puerto Rico, and elsewhere. The bishop remained a strong symbol of anti-Castro resistance during the 1960s, visiting exile communities and publishing articles and newsletters.[13]

Despite general religious stigmatization, some congregations in Havana had survived the early years of the revolution by meeting in secret. One Havana resident remembered: "Almost everyone had a Bible hidden in a shoe box in their closet or locked in a chest [and they] hid crucifixes under their mattresses."[14] With a diminished clergy, existing churches in outlying areas fell into disuse and abandonment. It was forbidden by law to build new chapels, so many young people, even in cities, grew up without ever having entered a church. Problems with training clerics, as well as bricks-and-mortar needs, effectively stifled public worship. Cubans were forbidden by law to build new churches, so the Catholic Church focused instead on building new congregations outside of churches. They had to contend with government agents who adopted offensive practices, such as trying to discourage Catholic observance by scheduling loud recreational activities near catechism classes and other religious functions.[15] Father Carlos Manuel de Céspedes, who remained in Cuba to become rector of San Carlos in Havana and of the San Ambrosio Seminary, said that after the clerical expulsions of 1961 the Church "came into a new era, one of reflection and analysis of the de facto situation in which it was called on to carry out its evangelizing within a Marxist revolutionary context—something totally new for the church in Latin America."[16]

By late 1961, the last Catholic periodical in Cuba, La Quinceña, had ceased publication, and obedience to Castroism had become the rule in almost all areas of Cuban life. Journalists and other dissidents choosing to remain after the second year of the revolution faced lengthy periods of imprisonment and forced labor in such infamous Castro prisons as Isla de Pinos, La Fortaleza de la Cabaña, and El Príncipe. There prison authorities routinely confiscated religious books and items during searches, though religious activities did continue in the form of clandestine prayer meetings, pastoral councils, and Sunday Masses. In late 1965, the government launched mass arrests of lay leaders, seminarians, priests, and other "proselytizers" and sent them to UMAP (Unidades Militares de Ayuda a la

Producción) labor camps in Camagüey Province and on sordid island lo-cales. UMAPs, special work camps for "antisocial" elements—who besides religious leaders included homosexuals, criminals, and others not consid-ered suitable for incorporation into the armed forces or Castro's revolution itself—were active between 1962 and 1968. They greatly damaged church-state relations nationally, while giving the regime a black eye internation-ally. Similarly, the 1966 case of Franciscan Father Miguel Loredo, a young Franciscan arrested for allegedly harboring a man who initiated a failed hijacking attempt, gave even sympathizers of the regime cause to view its policies as "heavy-handed."[17]

The revolutionary regime took political prisoners from all sectors of pre-Castro Cuban society—bourgeois figures, labor leaders, Batista mili-tary personnel, and anti-Batista guerrillas, as well as agricultural work-ers. In a 1980 volume published in Venezuela, survivors of Castro's jails brought to light repression that incorporated "the arbitrariness and all the resources of the world of interrogation, and infiltration and terror." They noted that the "ultimate criterion for eliminating real or potential enemies [was] not an ideological question, totally foreign to the dominant group." Rather it was "obedience or lack of it to Fidel Castro."[18] The exiles lamented that the Cuban government presented reforms as inargu-able done deeds, leaving no room for the opposition to maneuver.

Although the regime's policies had an overall withering effect on re-ligiosity in the homeland, former inmates noted that their effect was to increase observance among dissidents. After being transferred from one prison to another, one of the first things many prisoners did was to look for a pastoral council and create one if none existed. This body would customarily hold a Mass or Sunday prayer, with or without a priest, and create nativity scenes for Christmas, such as occurred in the infamous La Cabaña in 1968: in a vivid display of lay participation, one inmate tai-lor made a tunic for a priest, dyed with avocado seed, and tin cans were drummed to accompany the nativity pageant.[19]

According to one prisoner, Oscar Pla, on Christmas in 1965 prisoners celebrated an ecumenical service, or *acto ecuménico*, "for both Baptists and Catholics," led by David Fay, a North American Baptist and former rector of the Baptist Seminary of Matanzas. In Cuba's prisons many post–Vatican II reforms were adopted out of necessity as the secular diaconate or "new priests" performed evangelical duties such as distributing Communion, carrying out baptisms, and hearing group confessions. Meanwhile, pris-oners with ties to the Juventud Obrera Católica (Catholic Youth Work-ers) built up an impressive library of smuggled Catholic materials.[20]

Despite the long odds, numerous dissidents attempted to confront the regime from within. Jorge Valls, a leading activist in the student movement at the University of Havana, had been imprisoned several times under Batista. He challenged the Castro regime soon after it took power, refusing to register for the draft and supporting a friend who was being persecuted. In 1964 he was sentenced to twenty years in prison for "activities against the powers of the state and leading anti-government organizations." Valls's prison memoirs shed valuable light on the dark corners of Cuban society. Many of the most controversial trials were held in secret. Valls belonged to a group of prisoners who were called the *plantados*—the stubborn ones—who refused to participate in the government's various "reeducation" plans. Upon his release he wrote of the brutal actions of the State Security force, or G-2: unwarranted arrests, kidnappings, and executions that terrorized the Cuban citizenry and stifled dissent.[21]

In 1966 Castro contrasted his country's religious situation favorably with that of other Latin American countries, such as Mexico, which legally restricted the right of male and female religious to "walk the streets [in] a [clerical] habit."[22] He required that the Church limit itself to its "ecclesiastical functions," but he allowed churches to remain open for daily Mass, thus presenting the appearance of toleration for religious practices. In pre-Castro Cuba, religious festivals had played a large part in devotional life, especially for the primary public celebrations— Good Friday, Epiphany, and on the feast days of Saint Barbara, Saint Lazarus, and Our Lady of Charity. Between 1961 and 1997, outdoor Catholic services were prohibited in Cuba. In the late 1980s Castro did allow periodic relaxations of restrictions against processions in honor of Cuba's patroness, but the popularity of the parades let to their cancellation. Until relatively recently Christmas and Good Friday were abolished as public national holidays, replaced by mass secular celebrations such as Bay of Pigs Day in April and the commemoration of Castro's attack on the Moncada barracks (July 26).[23]

Two pastoral letters published in 1969 sought to blend the Cuban church with the spirit of Vatican II reforms. In the April document, the Cuban bishops condemned the blockade imposed by the United States as damaging to the Cuban people. A second collective pastoral letter, "On Contemporary Atheism," released in September, urged "openness" in the way Cuban Catholics practiced their faith, allowing alternatives to traditional Catholic practices, assuring Cubans of the validity of living out their Catholic faith by participating in the revolutionary process, and challenging believers to engage in dialogue with nonbelievers.[24]

Cubans in Exile

Before 1959 Cubans had come sporadically to Florida and to New York, New Orleans, and other port cities. Many of the "first wave" refugees, including professionals, managers, entrepreneurs, merchants, and land-owners, arriving in Miami through October 1962 (the time of the Cuban Missile Crisis), had initially favored the revolution, at least to some degree.But they believed that Castro had taken it down the wrong path, and they had come to distrust his specific social, economic, and political measures. By late 1960, when a mass exodus began from Cuba, travel controls and regulations increased, followed by tough decrees prohibiting taking anything of value out of Cuba. All personal possessions, with the exception of three complete changes of clothes, and virtually all cash and accumulated wealth had to be left behind. The failed Bay of Pigs invasion of April 1961 resulted in cancellation of all travel between the two countries and marked the beginning of migration by way of third countries. Dramatic escapes in small, unfit crafts crossing the treacherous Florida Straits indicated the extent of the desperation.

The Diocese of Miami had been established in 1958, one year before the ascent of Castro, and had developed outreach programs for Mexicans and Puerto Ricans in the diocese, primarily migrant farm workers. But it had done little with Cubans prior to the revolutionary-era exile waves. There had been little need to actively incorporate permanent residents in distinct church structures then or even during the mid-1950s, when Miami served as a financial base for supporting Batista. During the mid-1950s, Archbishop Joseph P. Hurley of St. Augustine had sent several U.S. priests to Spain to learn Spanish. Aided by national Catholic organizations, the diocese became a major distributor of social services to exiles after 1959. Established in the first three years after the formation of the Miami diocese were several new parishes, a minor seminary, a center for the elderly, and the Centro Hispano Católico.[25] In March 1959, Bishop Coleman Carroll approved Monsignor Bryan O. Walsh's proposal and announced the opening of the Centro in some vacant classrooms in Gesu School in downtown Miami. It was the only social agency with a bilingual staff when Cuban refugees began to arrive in large numbers in the summer of 1960. The Centro handled some 450,000 exile cases from October 1959 to June 1968. It helped the early group of wealthier exiles during the first year. The U.S. nuns staffing it had all worked in Cuba for many years and knew many of the refugees personally.[26]

Beginning in 1960, the Cuban Refugee Emergency Center (El Refu-

Nun and Two Boys Standing in Front of Centro Hispano Católico, ca. 1961
(*Florida Catholic* / Archdiocese of Miami)

gio), located downtown near what became known as Little Havana, coordinated the voluntary resettlement activities of several religious organizations as well as the disbursement of relief and training funds. Bishop
Carroll sought help in Tallahassee and Washington, which led to the establishment of the federally funded Cuban Refugee Program in March
1961. Through this program the federal government provided financial
support to the exiles and, to a large extent, helped them adjust to life in
Miami by subsidizing housing, distribution of household goods, and employment retraining. It also funded the dispersal, or resettlement, of Cubans throughout the United States. Consequently, by mid-1963 Cubans
had become visible in several other areas across the country. New York
City had the largest number of resettled Cuban refugees (10,000) from
Catholic Relief Services, followed by the Newark area (8,000), Puerto
Rico (3,500), and Los Angeles (2,300).[27]

Monsignor Walsh, who became a major figure in the Miami Archdiocese's Cuban ministry, had through travel and study in the 1950s familiarized himself with Latin American culture and the Spanish language. He applied these skills in the service of Mexican migrant farm workers and Puerto Rican residents of Miami's Wynwood neighborhood, as well as the relatively small number of Cubans arriving prior to 1959. In 1960 Walsh came across a fourteen-year-old boy who had spent a month in Miami being passed from one family to another while his parents remained in Cuba. Many parents in Cuba, including perhaps those of this boy, had become involved in underground or guerrilla activities against Castro and feared for the safety of their family; others decided to send their children to the United States because of rumors that the Cuban government might seek to send youth abroad for indoctrination, perhaps to the Soviet Union. The intervention of Walsh, along with the activities of religious-order priests in Cuba, brought large numbers of children by airplane to Miami, where they came under the care of the diocese until they could be reunited with their families in exile.[28]

The issue of the control of education further solidified exiled Catholics in their fight against the Cuban government, which was creating a series of *escuelas de instrucción revolucionaria* (schools of revolutionary instruction), aimed at reconstituting the ruling elite. In January of 1961, twelve full-time provincial schools were opened, in addition to the national school in Havana. The following year an extensive system of government boarding schools was established. By the end of 1962, some seventy thousand children had attended the boarding schools, and parents sought to protect their children from being sent to the countryside for socialist and atheistic indoctrination programs.[29]

Miami's Cuban exiles, like their archbishop, embraced the idea of "saving" children from communism. Under the aegis of Operación Pedro Pan (Operation Peter Pan), endorsed by the U.S. government but administered by local Catholics, there was a massive migration of some fourteen thousand children between 1960 and 1962. Thereafter the Catholic Church in Cuba continued trying to get children out and successfully reunited many of them with their families. Others tragically went on to live in orphanages, with foster parents, or otherwise apart from their parents.

The Cuban exiles became cold warriors, determined to recapture what they thought was a lost nation resulting from the monumental revolution of Fidel Castro. They received much assistance in religion, as in other realms, from existing U.S. institutions, and they converted religious sentiments into political awareness; even their shrine was politicized. Carroll generally enjoyed the support of the exile community as a whole, and he effectively publicized the exiles' anti-Castroism.

Based on his experience in the Diocese of Pittsburgh, Bishop Carroll believed that newcomers were to be absorbed into existing territorial parishes. Carroll's policies enabled Cubans to worship in their native language with Cuban priests. To encourage the rapid assimilation of Cuban and Spanish priests, Archbishop Carroll assigned every parish at least one Spanish-speaking priest wherever possible. Impromptu arrangements often arose in the early years of the influx; in 1961, for example, the bishop constructed a monastery to house exiled seminarians and brothers awaiting reassignment. With some assistance from the Catholic Church Extension Society, he helped some of the incoming priests "learn the language [so that] within six months or so [they might] be of some service to the Diocese." Other Cuban priests with little or no English were sent to live in rectories with Irish-born or U.S.-born pastors, while Cuban religious women of different orders dispersed throughout the Miami area, most of them "confused and uncertain as to what part of Latin America they [were] destined for."[30]

Moving Belén Jesuit School to Miami was originally proposed as a temporary arrangement, pending the expected return of exiles to the island, and Archbishop Carroll negotiated its transplantation from Havana more than six months before the school in Havana was actually closed. The Miami school was established independent of archdiocesan control, reporting to the Jesuit province of the Antilles, despite the economic hardships that such independence entailed. Jesuits opened their Miami school in 1961 by borrowing space in the building of the elementary school of Gesu Church, a Jesuit parish in downtown Miami. The following year, 1962–63, the school was moved to Southwest Eighth Street (Calle Ocho, a famous and symbolic thoroughfare) and Seventh Avenue. The school was staffed almost exclusively by the priests from Belén, with some help from North American Jesuits. Carroll required that English be used in the teaching of all subjects. Not until 1964 was tuition instituted for those who could pay.[31]

Miami's public schools refused to admit refugee children unless they paid out-of-state tuition. Thus this burden too fell on Catholic schools, but it helped to strengthen the bond between Cuban refugees and the local church. When the Cuban clergy came in the summer of 1961, it became possible to staff every parish with at least one Spanish-speaking priest, and most native English-speaking pastors gained a working knowledge of Spanish. This began the Cubanization of the Miami church. A major seminary, St. Vincent de Paul in Boynton Beach, became bilingual in the early 1970s, and the majority of students and newly ordained priests in recent decades have been Latino.[32]

By 1964, San Juan Bosco Church had become a virtual Cuban national parish, attracting worshipers from well outside its boundaries to its six Sunday Masses, five of which were held in Spanish. To support the construction of a new church building, Father Emilio Vallina organized a parish *tómbola* (festival) in which a Ford Falcon was raffled off. Bishops Carroll and Boza Masvidal presided at the well-publicized dedication ceremony in 1965. Other parishes in Miami, Miami Beach, and Coral Gables drew large numbers of Cubans in the early years, including St. Mary's Cathedral, St. Michael's, Epiphany, and St. Patrick's. Roman Catholics, once a minority group, became by the early 1970s the area's largest religious organization.[33]

The Catholic Church in Florida mobilized rapidly to provide social services and material assistance to those arriving from Cuba. From the start, Archbishop Carroll reinforced the emergent exile ideology and also helped shaped its ethnic identity, arguing that it was a "Christian duty to aid the fugitives from Communism and help the Cuban people recover their liberty" and that "the real task of Miami Catholicism is to save [the] children from Communist indoctrination."[34] Carroll also lobbied for refugee assistance from Washington after local attempts at providing housing had failed. He appealed first to the Eisenhower administration and then, more successfully, to the Kennedy administration. The Church World Service—a consortium of Protestant churches—along with the Hebrew Immigrant Assistance Service, joined forces in mobilizing Cubans of all religious backgrounds to provide material help.

The relative ease of the transplantation of Catholic institutions from Cuba was indicated by the way the devotion to Cuba's national patroness, dating back to the seventeenth century, was carried into exile. Organized public devotions to Our Lady of Charity began shortly after the first waves of migrants arrived from revolutionary Cuba. The first annual Our Lady of Charity Mass was celebrated at Miami's Saints Peter and Paul Church on September 8, 1960. One of the events seen as crucial by Cubans fleeing Castro was the 1961 smuggling of an image of the patroness from a Havana parish church to Miami. There she was displayed in a stadium as twenty-five thousand Cuban exiles celebrated her feast day.[35]

At the 1966 celebration, Archbishop Carroll called on Cuban-American Catholics to construct a shrine to la Virgen de la Caridad del Cobre on a plot bordering Biscayne Bay, partly as a means of reaching out to nominal Catholics. Cubans immediately began raising funds, organizing the devotions, and constructing the building for the shrine, and in December 1967, Father Agustín Román, a native of Matanzas who had arrived a year earlier, began organizing the Ermita. The new chapel was finally dedicated at the end of 1973.[36]

The Ermita reflects what historian Thomas Tweed has called "diasporic nationalism," a nostalgic bridging of faith, nationalism, and popular culture. Miami Cubans gradually inscribed nationalistic aspects of Catholicism in yard shrines, cemeteries, and churches, and exiles reported that their devotion to the patroness of Cuba had increased in exile. Exiled Cuban nationalism includes an abiding concern for democracy, capitalism, and various components of Cuban culture, including music. Religion is constantly being constructed and reconstructed as new sacred spaces and religious sites form. The Cuban community used La Ermita to create an imaginary homeland more than to restore the old one; in this construction, relations with the divine become secondary to the search for nationhood. A mural inside the shrine features the Virgin of Charity and her child along with José Martí, the father of Cuban independence. Scenes of the Cuban landscape occupy the background, and at the bottom of the mural, the Virgin's statue is pictured in a canoe with her reputed discoverers, a slave and two Indians.[37]

Román, the son of Cuban peasants, had been ordained in Cuba and had been forced off the island along with 132 other Cuban priests aboard the *Covadonga* in 1961. Román ministered in Chile for four years before coming to Miami in 1966. Appointed auxiliary bishop of the Miami Archdiocese in 1979, Román exhorted fellow exiles to contribute whatever they could afford in order to pay for the construction of the shrine. Subsequently he remained deeply involved in all aspects of devotion to the Cuban patroness—for example, accompanying the image of Our Lady of Charity on its traditional boat ride across Biscayne Bay during her yearly celebration.[38]

Cubans in exile adapted successfully to their adopted setting by emphasizing rather than shunning an exile mentality. Several periodicals that had been published previously in Cuba, such as *Alerta*, *Bohemia*, and *El Avance Criollo*, were relaunched in the United States. The newspaper *Patria*, first published in Miami in 1959, reflected the political agenda of *batistianos* in vehement attacks not only on the new Cuban government but also on any former supporters of Castro. In late 1960, the paper published several scathing articles attacking the display of prorevolutionary signs in the offices of the 26th of July Movement in Tampa, a city it la-

Miami Auxiliary Bishop Agustín Román Accompanies the Image of Our Lady
of Charity on Traditional Boat Ride across Biscayne Bay, September 8, 2000
(*Florida Catholic* / Archdiocese of Miami)

beled "the last bastion of Castro Communism in Florida."[39] Its letterhead
proclaimed it the newspaper "of Martí, without Martí, but for Martí," a
sign that exiles, as well as Castroites, harked back to the nineteenth-century separatist (*mambisa*) legacy of the struggle against Spanish colonialism. Cubans in both worlds held up Martí, as well as Father Félix Varela
and other nineteenth-century patriots, as exemplary Cubans seeking justice, democracy, and equality.[40]

One exile, Gastón Baquero, a supporter of former president Fulgencio Batista, observed in *Patria* in 1967 that attacks on religion tended
to make churches "suppress their philosophical and doctrinal attacks on
communism." In contrast to the pre-Castro Catholic Easter, "holy week"
under Castro had become "dedicated to a great mobilization to cut sugar
cane, pick coffee, anything that would alienate the great masses from the
churches. Those who did not follow mobilization were enemies of the
regime." The commemoration of Bay of Pigs Week (la Semana de Playa
Girón) included youth carnivals in which "pioneer children" were taken
to dance and sing in front of churches. The government offered "free
music, refreshments, toys, and the children were dressed up, some as Viet

Cong or Russian soldiers, or as whatever took the fancy of the director to express communist ideology that is injected drop by drop and day by day into the souls of the children." Baquero believed that the placement of "thousands of children dancing and singing at the door of the church on the day of Christ's death, while their parents and grandparents were inside the church praying," revealed the regime's low regard for religious values.[41]

Another Miami exile, accountant Luis Manrara, though not a *batistiano*, became head of a major anti-Castro organization of the 1960s, the Truth About Cuba Committee (TACC). He was one of a few outspoken lay critics of the proposed construction of the Ermita. While conceding that it was a "beautiful idea" to honor the Virgen de la Caridad del Cobre, he said he would reserve his support until "after the liberation of Cuba from Imperialist Russian Communism." Manrara suggested that the Virgin would be more favorably honored "if all the effort and money that would have been invested in the construction of the monument be utilized instead to liberate her children, persecuted, terrorized, assassinated and starved, trapped on the island enslaved by the barbarous atheists."[42] The Truth About Cuba Committee had emerged in Miami during the spring of 1961, right after the Bay of Pigs invasion and Castro's announcement that the revolution was socialist in nature, abandoning any former pretense to the contrary.

TACC carefully monitored Cuban radio and newspapers and obtained firsthand information from the constant stream of refugees out of Cuba, and Manrara believed that the struggle being waged in Miami to liberate Cuba from Castro's rule had become desperate. He felt the U.S. people— as well as Cubans in exile—had to be educated about it. Manrara disseminated the most current information on a variety of events, such as the summer 1962 landings of Russian ships at the port city of Mariel, where they unloaded munitions and troops. Manrara served for over a decade as TACC's president and saw chapters spread across the United States and to some foreign countries, with correspondents reporting from Europe, Asia, Africa, and Latin America. Sixty percent of the sustaining members of TACC were Cuban exiles; the rest were mostly non-Latinos.[43]

Manrara sought to "mobilize public opinion worldwide and especially in the United States to gather the military support needed for Cubans to liberate our country," although he opposed the "immediate war" advocated by militant groups such as the Representación Cubana en el Exilio and Alpha 66.[44] The most important struggle was the "psychological war" against "imperial communism" that would precede and inevitably lead to a triumphant shooting war.[45] To Manrara, the liberation of Cuba depended on the Cubans themselves and a new breed of leaders. He felt the old guard—including specifically Batista, former president Carlos Prío Socorrás, and labor leader Eusebio Mujal, who operated by "weak and harmful" moral principles—constituted a "a negative factor in the creation of the present Cuban tragedy."[46]

Religious and quasi-religious zeal permeated Manrara's thought as well as his approach to educating the public. He was dismayed by actions of both the Cuban and the U.S. church, noting: "We are constantly called upon to inform and clarify misconceptions expressed orally or in writing by Catholic clergymen regarding the Cuban situation. The pro-communist propaganda is so intense that even our church is sometimes befuddled." He was rankled, too, by clerics who defended their "enemies," such as one excommunicated Colombian priest, Camilo Torres, who joined the guerrilla movement in Colombia and was killed in action.[47]

Exile organizations like the Truth About Cuba Committee, along with many scholars, often disputed claims about the unprecedented success of the revolution's vaunted health care and education programs. They said the statistics were exaggerated, pointed out the undemocratic nature of the regime's methods, and questioned how the exiles as a group could have been so successful had poverty and illiteracy been as rampant during the last years of the republic as had been claimed. The purposeful, singular outlook of Cubans in Miami was prompted by survival needs and was consistent with an irredentist ideology. These included the belief that while it had needed reforms, pre-Castro society was never as bad as the communists claimed. If it had been, argued one university professor in exile, a "Cuban exodus would have taken place before and not after Castro."[48]

Manrara voiced the frustrations of the exile community to U.S. government and media outlets in extensive policy papers, correspondence, and publications and frequently indicated his disapproval of Cubans who accepted honors for their strident anticommunism in exile. He believed any self-congratulatory accolades prematurely distracted exiles from the serious ongoing business of anti-Castroism. He also decried those who spent time and resources on "frivolous entertainment" in Miami; instead he favored "effort, austerity, and sacrifice" in the real job of serving "God, the homeland, and family."[49] He wondered, publicly, "Are [Cuban] immigrants in search of gold and [pleasure], or are we exiles afire with the love of God and our country?"[50] Manrara and most other Cubans of his era specifically renounced the pursuit of U.S. citizenship as destructive of the goal of maintaining an exile consciousness. They called for the unraveling of Cuban communism from without, especially as it became clear that the underground in Cuba had faltered and as invasions and sabotage proved ineffective strategies.

Miami's Variation of Cuban Catholicism

In prerevolutionary Cuba, Catholics had been accustomed to attend early morning Mass when it was cool, as there was no air conditioning. The Mass and the sacraments were celebrated in Latin, with homilies and popular devotions in the vernacular. In the early 1960s, Miami's Saints Peter and Paul parish, somewhat atypically, adopted a scheduled Spanish Mass at 8:30 a.m., and this became one of its most popular services. In other respects, however, Cuban Catholic practices changed considerably in Miami after May 1964, when Vatican II's introduction of the liturgy in the vernacular resulted in a reworking of Sunday Mass schedules to make them more available in both Spanish and English. Most pastors simply switched from Latin to English, with Masses for Spanish-speaking parishioners added after the regular schedule, usually in the early afternoon hours. Pastors responded to the Cuban presence by having a Spanish-speaking priest hear confessions and say a few words in Spanish after the English homily. The introduction of Sunday evening Masses gave Saints Peter and Paul the opportunity to reach older teens and young adults. Another post–Vatican II "reform" was the introduction of hymns.[51]

The laity in Cuba had a long pre-1959 history of working outside of parishes in Catholic Action organizations, universities, and other institutions. Belén's Jesuit fathers helped the Catholic lay organization Agrupación Católica Universitaria reconstitute itself in Miami after the headquarters of this time-honored and influential university student and professional organization was closed down in Havana. The *agrupados* remained active in exile, as they had been in Cuba, creating networks throughout the United States that functioned as ethnic or social organizations bound by common anti-Castro sentiments. Most *agrupados* formed small organizations based on personal friendship. These lay networks were invaluable in spreading information about professional employment opportunities among members.[52]

The organization Acción Católica (Catholic Action) was linked to the Catholic schools and colleges that had educated the largely urban middle-class elite of Havana, and it also had support among the working class. This social justice movement had been active in opposing the Batista regime in Havana in 1958. Significantly, leaders of Catholic Action became involved in regrouping their organization in exile. This pattern of transplantation over accommodation in an alien immigrant church was also evident in the Movimiento Familiar Cristiano, a Cuban branch of the Christian Family Movement formed in 1961 in St. Agnes Church on Key Biscayne, whose leaders for several years remained independent of direct supervision by the diocese. That same year over a dozen lay groups were represented at a diocesan meeting of the Coordinating Committee of Cuban Catholic Organizations. The Cursillos de Cristiandad was brought to Miami in 1962.[53] Cuban-American women, both in lay movements and increasingly in parishes, quickly became active in creating exile social and professional networks.

The growth and influence of these various *movimientos*, lay organizations operating independently of parish communities, owed much to the impulse generated by the Catholic Action movement in Cuba in the 1950s. Each did have a priest chosen by the laity as "spiritual moderator" and confirmed by the archdiocese. The hierarchy, and particularly Anglo pastors, saw these groups as drawing people away from the parish, the backbone of U.S. Catholicism. Over the years, however, pastors became convinced that parish life could be strengthened by the initiatives of laypeople.[54]

As players in U.S. foreign policy during the cold war, Cubans, particularly during the Freedom Flight era, received unprecedented federal assistance. The U.S. Department of Health, Education, and Welfare agreed to underwrite the costs of facilities, supplies, transportation, and other education-related expenses for each new refugee pupil for up to five years. Another program provided higher-education loans for refugees. Educational adaptation took a new turn after the Ford Foundation underwrote a pilot project in several of Miami's primary schools beginning in 1961, leading to the establishment of Coral Way Elementary as a fully bilingual school. Within a decade, federal funds for bilingual education helped launch several other experimental projects throughout Dade County and elsewhere in the nation. Spanish gradually came to be incorporated throughout the Miami area, another component of the extended homeland. Special courses were offered on Cuban history and culture in Miami's eighteen diocesan parochial schools, although English was at first the only language of instruction; all of this helped maintain a shared ideological outlook.[55]

By 1968, the archdiocese had accepted bilingual programs in Miami's parochial schools for both English- and Spanish-speaking students. Cuban and Spanish priests were asked to learn English in six months and afterward put themselves at the service of the diocese. Archbishop Carroll, with the support of most exiles, spoke out in favor of a more generous federal immigration policy toward Cubans in 1973, and he lobbied on behalf of thousands of Cubans in Spain seeking visas to enter the United States. Between 1967 and 1976, 260,000 Cuban refugees took advantage of the Readjustment Act of 1966, which granted them a special "parole" status, waiving the customary five-year waiting period necessary to begin the citizenship process. A 1976 amendment exempted Cubans from the numerical ceiling of immigrants allowed per country, imposed by Congress in 1965. Federal policies that waived some of the requirements of citizenship helped increase the numbers of Cuban Americans to naturalize in the mid-1970s.[56]

A massive exodus from the port of Camarioca led to a December 1965 agreement between Cuba and the United States for the establishment of two daily "Freedom Flights" from Varadero to Miami. That "memorandum of understanding" provided for the exit of relatives of Cubans already in the United States, with the exception of males of draft age. The airlift, which finally terminated in 1973, brought another 300,000 Cubans to the United States. About half of them remained in Miami. Despite encouragement to resettle outside of Miami by representatives of governmental and voluntary agencies, who thought too great a concentration counterproductive for their assimilation, many refugees chose to remain in the Miami metropolis in order to be nearer the homeland, in a favorable climate, and among fellow exiles.[57]

Cuban émigrés in the United States became more ardently Catholic than Cuban society in general, and Catholic religious practice increased among the exiles, many of whom had not been active Catholics while in Cuba. Although local residents' initial reception of the exiles was favorable, due in part to their strong denunciation of the Castro regime, tensions soon arose as the locals began to realize that the exiles would settle into Miami, rather than merely living there temporarily. A barrier to geographic expansion for Cubans in Miami consisted of a large African-American community to its north. Partly because of that, and because of general growth, second and subsequent generations of Cubans Latinized not only urban but also suburban Miami. Better housing was available in suburban Hialeah, to the northwest of Little Havana. By 1970 two parishes, San Lázaro and Santa Bárbara, created in the working-class suburb of Hialeah, had become almost 50 percent Cuban. The parishes reportedly included large numbers of Santería practitioners, even though Hialeah was filled with white Cubans; their presence made it clear that Santería was by no means exclusively an Afro-Cuban practice.[58]

Unlike many of the newer Sunbelt cities in the South and West, which pushed out their municipal boundaries to boost population, the Miami area was fragmented into over two dozen municipalities, with most of the newcomers filling up the suburban areas and the unincorporated fringe. The rapid growth spawned uniformly modern automobile suburbs without transitional urban cores. Moreover, the diversity of Miami's population was not due to an influx of European immigrants but to the migration of people from states in the U.S. North. The presence of Cubans, other Latinos, and African Americans was part of this diversity. Exile entrepreneurs established hundreds of import-export businesses that catered to Latin America, attracting financial institutions and corporations involved in international trade. Networks formed, based on economic, social, and even political ties based on anti-Castro ideology and Cuban nationalism. These networks translated into intense activity among exiles.

Over time, Cubans in Little Havana increasingly moved westward to some of the Miami area's newer housing. Several of the area's dozens of incorporated municipalities, as well as Dade County's large unincorporated suburban region, became areas of second settlement. Cubans entered into many suburban churches—in Westchester, Sweetwater, and even the formerly exclusive Coral Gables. The late 1960s and 1970s coincided with Anglo flight to Broward and Palm Beach counties; Cubans began moving into those counties as well. The Cubans' faith in exile became more pronounced, and their children entered diocesan and parochial schools, not just those of religious orders. In 1980 Belén High School in Miami moved farther west in suburban Dade County. By that time, about 60 percent of metropolitan Miami's Cuban Americans resided in the suburbs, while Little Havana tended to retain the poor, the elderly, renters, and the most recent arrivals.[59]

Old Exiles, Newer Immigrants

According to one study in January 1959, when Fidel Castro came to power only 15 to 20 percent of the total Cuban population was active in either Protestant or Roman Catholic congregations. While in prerevolutionary times 89 percent of the population could have been regarded as nominal Catholics, practicing Catholics in Cuba were estimated to be no more than 10 percent by 1980. Practicing Catholics—those who had regular contact with a parish in Cuba—had left in disproportionate numbers in the earliest waves of migration from Cuba in the 1960s. Further, among the more than 125,000 refugees of the Mariel exodus between April and October 1980, who included many Afro-Cubans, religious practice over time became more regular and important than it had been in Cuba.[60]

The Catholic Church in south Florida immediately welcomed the Mariel refugees, first by providing emergency services. Auxiliary Bishop Román oversaw assistance by clergy, women religious, and the laity. He also immediately adopted a strong stance against Castro's continued persecution of political prisoners on the island and advocated for and brokered on behalf of Marielitos, supporting requests for asylum among detainees while leading the Church in providing temporary housing and jobs. The Shrine of Our Lady of Charity in Miami became a refuge for countless Marielitos. In July 1981, the Office of Lay Ministry of the Archdiocese of Miami began an outreach program to Cubans and other Latinos at Hialeah's St. John the Apostle parish, which had a particularly large Marielito population. A home visitation program soon led to the establishment of the Centro Católico de Evangelización (Catholic Evangelization Center), an improvised storefront church for thousands of Marielitos.[61]

The 1980 Mariel boatlift threatened the image of all Cubans and led to a backlash against foreigners in general, as seen in the passage of a 1980 antibilingualism ordinance in Dade County. The Mariel refugees' experiences in revolutionary Cuba had not prepared them to participate in the hierarchical Cuban-American enclave. Yet despite this,, and even though they were "less Catholic" and more diverse racially, ultimately Cuban Americans accepted the newest entrants.[62] After the early days, the question of resettlement surfaced, as did the problems of detainees in makeshift centers throughout the United States. Román's persistent advocacy, long after the perceived Mariel problem had subsided, no doubt contributed to the Mariel refugees' successful long-term integration. Significantly, Román saw them as eminently worthwhile targets for evangelization, especially those having allegiance to Santería. In 1987 he presented the National Conference of Catholic Bishops with a list of the names of hundreds of Mariel refugees who had completed their sentences but remained in prison. Román pleaded for their release to relatives willing to receive them. According to Román, Mariel was not only the manifestation of a people in search of liberty, but also a demonstration of family and national loyalty. He pointed out, with respect to Miami Cubans, that "upon learning that people from Cuba could leave, to Miami and elsewhere, to join their relatives, spouses, children, grandchildren, uncles, cousins, even *compadres* and friends, they sacrificed everything. They sold their houses and bought boats to bring over the émigrés."[63]

The Freedom Flights, leaving from the city of Varadero twice daily from 1966 until 1973, brought to Miami approximately one thousand new refugees a week. Many of these exiles resumed their Catholic observance in exile; others did not. Since 1973, probably less than 1 percent of Cuban migrants have been practicing Catholics at the time of their arrival. Among the Mariel refugees, most had even lost their religious tradition, or what Father Walsh termed a "folk knowledge of the Church." After 1980, limited migration from Cuba brought over few practicing Catholics. Mass attendance among Cubans and other Latinos by the mid-1980s was 42 percent, compared to 47 percent for Anglos.[64]

The term *Cuban American*, seldom used before 1980, increasingly become the standard self-designation in the 1980s and thereafter, spurred partly by political expediency but more significantly by the coming of age of successive generations of native-born Americans of Cuban ancestry and decreasing ties with the island. By 1983, Hialeah Cubans not only had a majority on their city council but also a refugee mayor. In 1985, Xavier Suarez became the first Cuban mayor of Miami. In 1981 a group of Cuban businessmen in Miami, many of them veterans of the Bay of Pigs invasion, founded the Cuban American National Foundation (CANF), a nonprofit organization that established its principal base in Washington, D.C., where it focused on influencing legislation and executive policy. The foundation was supported by tens of thousands of members, many of them from Miami's business community.

The formation of CANF as an effective lobbying and political action arm in Washington resulted in strong support for the establishment of Radio Martí and TV Martí in the late 1980s. Rather than merely embarking on an anti-Castro crusade, CANF successfully packaged exile ideology in a more favorable image of the Cuban-American community as supporting multiparty democracy in Cuba. The 1992 Cuban Democracy Act imposed severe punishments for anyone dealing with Cuba and incorporated much of the policy advocated by CANF. This embracing of a visibly "secular" approach contrasts with the stridency of Manrara and the Truth About Cuba Committee in the 1960s and early 1970s. In Miami, resistance to the Castro regime involved considerably more than the relatively passive pursuit of ethnic or cultural retention. It sought to mobilize with the intent of overthrowing the status quo in the homeland, rather than waiting for reforms or a counterrevolution to materialize from within. An extraordinary opportunity for Cubans in Miami to demonstrate their connection with the island was the rescue at sea on Thanksgiving Day, 1999, of Elián González, a child saved when other *balseros* (rafters), including his mother, died on a perilous trip from the island to the coast of Florida.[65]

In Miami, more than in any city of comparable size, Cubans became upwardly mobile. As the middle class had left Cuba in large numbers, its church weakened further; correspondingly, it became strong in Miami and remained staunchly anti-Castro. Active church affiliation became part of a middle-class Miami Cuban ambience in the 1960s and 1970s, and by 1980 thirty-three parishes (25%) in the Archdiocese of Miami were predominantly Latino. Cuban Miami increasingly encompassed people from different worlds, but ideology—transmitted in the family, economically, culturally, and politically—remained the underpinning of ethnic identity within the secular realm. Within the religious sphere, ideology tightened bonds with the Church, as Cuban priests, brothers, and sisters had entered the Miami diocese and forged ties with the exiles in parishes and through their work with lay organizations. Miami's church gained strength by becoming a symbol of resistance to reconciliation with the Castro regime and to its repressive policies, including religious discrimination. Cuban exiles, having witnessed in their homeland what they perceived as the ineffectiveness and subversion of the principles of social movements, remained skeptical of emerging Latin American "liberation theology," perceiving it as a misguided procommunist endeavor.[66]

Miami's anti-Castroism and the relatively high social and economic standing of Cubans, while originally creating an extraordinarily unified Cuban community, undermined possibilities for pan-Latino coalitions. Monsignor Walsh, for example, was generally seen as an ardent friend of the exiles and an effective liaison between the archdiocese and the Cuban community, though occasional disagreements arose over differences in ideological perspective. In 1972, Walsh delivered an invocation at a meeting attended by Cesar Chavez, whose advocacy for the United Farm Workers enjoyed broad national support. The Cuban periodical *Alerta* criticized Walsh for his participation and labeled Chavez a "well-known leftist militant."[67] Many exiles had grown to fear the spread of "social Christianity" as a harbinger of communism throughout the Americas.[68]

Cubans in Miami tended to suspect Chicano and Puerto Rican activists of harboring radical, even communist, sympathies, and this clashed with their view of being Cuban, which meant participation in the crusade against both communism and Castro. The struggle in Cuban Miami, unlike the Chicano struggle (*la lucha*) for civil rights, labor organization, and ethnic identity rooted in the Southwest, was focused on Castro, and Cubans were reluctant to adopt the contemporary language of movements against racial and social injustice. While the exiles may have gained some sympathy from non-Cuban Latinos on the issue of political prisoners, their concerns did not make for ready allegiances with Mexican Americans and Puerto Ricans, who focused on integration and access to institutions and services in urban centers. Other elements of historical identity diversity seem to point away from the merging of Cubans into a pan-Latino Catholic coalition, as fervent and distinct nationalisms have persisted among these three Latino groups as well as others.[69]

Father Mario Vizcaíno was one of the first Cubans to engage the larger Latino Catholic world. In 1972 this Cuban-born Catholic Action priest was involved in founding the Cuban National Planning Council, a social service organization. He helped organize a nationwide meeting of Latinos, the Second National Hispanic Encuentro, in 1975. In the South East Pastoral Institute (SEPI), which stresses reconciliation among Cubans, he worked on behalf of Cubans in collaboration with Mexicans, Central Americans, and Puerto Ricans in the Southeast region. His appeals to educated, middle-class exiles invoked the Catholic social justice teachings adopted by Catholic Action groups, of which he had been a part in prerevolutionary Cuba. According to historian Gerald Poyo, SEPI engaged and involved the middle-class Catholics of greater Miami's Cuban exile community with disparate enclaves of Mexican and Central American migrant workers and the working-class Puerto Rican community of Orlando under the guidance of Father Vizcaíno. SEPI created lasting pan-Latino connections, encompassing not only laity training programs for Cuban Americans but also social service work for Puerto Ricans in Orlando and Mexican migrant workers in central Florida.[70]

Miami has boomed as a Latino capital largely because of the massive Cuban exile influx after 1959. In 2000, the Miami-Dade County area, a Cuban-dominated economic, social, and political preserve, had the highest percentage of Latinos of any large county in the United States, at 57 percent. By the early twenty-first century, more than half of the students registered in Archdiocese of Miami schools were Latino Catholics, but the arrival of hundreds of thousands of non-Cuban newcomers from Colombia, Peru, Venezuela, and other Latin American countries has helped reshape Latino Catholicism in the metropolitan area.[71] "Old" Little Havana came to be inhabited mostly by Nicaraguans; one former resident, writer Gustavo Perez Firmat, observed that Calle Ocho lost its Cuban primacy except as the site of the "annual carnival, a multicultural extravaganza for tourist consumption."[72]

Nicaraguan immigrants generally received the support of Miami Cubans, due in large measure to their militant opposition to the Sandinistas. By 1981, within the space of about two years, from having a population of several hundred Nicaraguans, Miami grew to be second to Managua in Nicaraguan population, with estimates ranging as high as 200,000. Expatriates at first fled the Sandinista regime and were composed primarily of physicians, lawyers, accountants, engineers, teachers, and other professionals. From 1982 to 1987, as the Nicaraguan civil war escalated, draft-age young men, middle-class professionals, and skilled workers left Nicaragua in increasing numbers. Many émigrés had been instrumental in the overthrow of General Anastasio Somoza. Most arrived in the United States illegally after making a difficult overland journey. Migration peaked in 1988–89, with many urban laborers leaving because of severe inflation and unemployment in Nicaragua, and began to recede thereafter.[73]

As of the 2000 U.S. Census, Nicaraguan immigrants formed the second largest Miami Latino population and the largest Nicaraguan settlement in the United States, at an estimated 105,000. About three-quarters of the Nicaraguans in Miami are practicing Roman Catholics; another 20 percent are Protestants, mostly belonging to the Moravian denomination. The Nicaraguan community itself developed institutions, such as the Centro Asistencia Nicaragüense, a social service center run by a Jesuit priest. Among local and regional patronal fiestas celebrated throughout Nicaragua, the one dedicated to the Virgen de la Asunción has become the most widely observed in Miami.[74]

With the outward shift of the Cuban center of settlement, newer groups moved into parishes, inherited housing, and replaced Cubans in Little Havana as well as in churches such as San Juan Bosco. Miami-area churches now have special Masses and processions in honor of non-Cuban saints, while Latin American clergy such as Peruvian bishop Lorenzo León have led religious celebrations at St. Catherine of Siena in suburban Kendall. The rise in the number of Latino parishes in Broward County since 2001 has supported calls for more Spanish-speaking priests there.[75]

Castro's Softer Line on Religion

Miami, a global city by virtue of its Latin American trade, became distinctly Cuban, although in 2000 the exiles and the native-born generations made up only about 60 percent of the total population of residents of Latin American origin. Miami still claims the title of Cuban Catholic capital in exile. Among Cuban exiles, especially those in Miami, changing international scenarios have weakened the first-generation exile mentality. There is a weakening consensus and mixed feelings about isolation from Cuba. As among other Latinos, there is an omnipresent sense of struggle, but it is not always clear what the struggle is or how it should be fought. There is debate on whether it is better to engage in tough measures against Cuba in an effort to effect governmental change or to interact directly through travel with estranged family members.[76]

In the 1990s several organizations arose in Miami emphasizing constructive relations with the Cuban government based on a peaceful transition to democracy. A new, broader ideological spectrum challenged the monolithic tenor of exile politics. Newer arrivals less bent on keeping the anti-Castro struggle alive are likely to place priority on communicating with their families still in Cuba, including sending remittances and returning to visit relatives. Dialogue has appeared as an alternative to ousting the dictator. All U.S.-based Cubans no longer see dialogue as surrender to revolutionary ideologies or as a betrayal of the exile; nor do they place much hope for reform in Fidel Castro or his brother and possible successor, Raúl. Renewed concerns over human rights violations, however, have repeatedly undermined dialogue.[77]

Back in Cuba, in 1971, when the first residents began moving into the new Alamar housing project, no church was constructed for the soon-to-be 100,000 residents of the "model socialist community"; they were advised that worship was not allowed. After two years of door-to-door efforts by seminarians and Catholic missionaries, however, emboldened Christians openly expressed their faith and offered their small apartments for weekly Masses and baptisms. Parishes without churches became the norm, symbols of the island's repressed Catholicism. The undersized nature of the Cuban church can be seen in the small number of children baptized in Havana between 1987 (17,000) and 1996 (33,000). The number of Catholic weddings did rise, however, from 138 to 507 between 1989 and 1995.[78]

Though a dialogue began to open between the Cuban government and Cuban priests residing abroad, for most exiles the Cuban church's evolution under Castro has not been a happy one. To rise in public life in Cuba, whether at the university or in the Communist Party, one had to renounce religious beliefs. Many Cuban exiles have sworn not to return to the island until Fidel Castro is no longer in power; until then they equate return with support of his regime. Some seventy-five Cuban dissidents were sentenced in March and April 2003 for sentences up to twenty-eight years. Dozens of mothers and children of jailed dissidents began to attend a special Sunday Mass in Miami's Santa Rita Church. There have also been signs of softening. The Communist Party decided to admit religious "believers" to its ranks and declared Cuba a secular rather than atheist

Thousands Wave Cuban Flags as Pope John Paul II Visits Miami's Tamiami Stadium in September 1987 (*Florida Catholic* / Archdiocese of Miami)

country, amending the Cuban Constitution in 1992 to outlaw discrimination based on religious beliefs. The government permitted home visitations in which volunteers distributed photos of Pope John Paul II in preparation for his impending visit to Cuba from January 21 to 25, 1998. A six-hour speech by Castro, which advised believers and nonbelievers alike that greeting the pope constituted a "patriotic duty," virtually required Cubans to turn out for the visit. Castro believed that rapprochement with the international church might gain an ally in behalf of lifting the trade embargo, and this proved to be the case. The Exhibition Hall of the José Martí Monument (Sala de Exhibiciones del Monumento a José Martí, in the old Civil Plaza) now holds an exhibition in memory of Pope John Paul II.[79]

Oswaldo Payá Sardiñas, a devout Catholic heading Cuba's independent Christian Liberation Movement, emerged as one of the island's most prominent opposition leaders. On a visit to Miami in 2003, Payá delivered a box of Cuban soil to the Shrine of Our Lady of Charity, and there, at the end of evening Mass, he urged hundreds of worshipers to support his movement by using "forgiveness and reconciliation" as an important basis for a process of "peaceful" transition toward democracy in Cuba and seeking reforms prior to the death of Castro. Other dissenters have also seen the Cuban church as a critical bridge between Cubans in the home-land and those in the diaspora.[80] In August 2004, south Florida hosted an *encuentro* between priests and laity from Cuba and those living outside of Cuba. Seventeen Cuban delegates met with thirty delegates from outside Cuba and throughout the United States. They gathered first with priests in Key West in the parish of St. Mary Star of the Sea; then a group of laypeople met with them at Miami's Agrupación Católica Universitaria. These meetings, both religious and academic in nature, continued the quest for creating a "sacred space" for dialogue among "brothers of the faith."[81]

According to Father Walsh, "In 1960, the Church in Miami was bet-ter prepared to host the refugees than most people have recognized. For the Church, the key was the establishment of the new diocese, the num-ber of active laity among the first waves of refugees, and the availability of the exile clergy." Walsh also believed that an unforeseen result of the Cuban revolution was "the Cubanization of the clergy, both in Cuba and in Miami," as during the 1940s and 1950s the number of Cuban-born priests increased. The trend continued in Cuba under the revolution and also continued in Miami. Walsh suspected that "more Cubans have been ordained priests since January 1, 1959, than in the previous 150 years."[82] Yet, he concluded, the number of active Catholics as a percentage of the population had declined over the last twenty years, slowing the trend of the first twenty years of the Cuban migration, as the number of obser-vant Catholics had dropped slightly since 1986. Given the generational change in Miami's Cuban-American population, and with the continued influx of non-Cuban Latinos, Catholicism in that city has been increas-ingly—and perhaps permanently—separated from the exile nationalism of the 1960s and 1970s.

6 Suburbanization and Mobility in Catholic Chicago

In the early twentieth century, Chicago, seat of the Catholic Church Extension Society, had become the center of missionary activity in the United States and gave much attention to Mexicans in the Southwest. After 1917, with the support of George Cardinal Mundelein, Extension increasingly focused on Mexicans in Chicago, the Great Lakes area, and even the Plains States of the Midwest. Catholic officials in the United States have long struggled to identify the dispersed settlement patterns of Mexican immigrants in their efforts to provide them with religious care. Bishops between 1910 and 1930 carefully gauged regional, national, and hemispheric developments, and their attention proved especially important during the Mexican crisis of church and state. The National Catholic Welfare Council's Bureau of Immigration assisted Mexican immigrants on the border beginning in 1923 at the El Paso Immigration Station. One 1928 report pointed to the need to "safeguard the Faith of the Catholic immigrant and also to assist them in becoming desirable residents of this country by helping them to a knowledge of its language, its laws and its ideals, and to aid them in many difficulties which they may encounter."[1]

During the late 1920s, a meeting of the bishops of the West revealed concerns about emerging and transient Mexican settlements. One Nebraska bishop sought financial assistance for his parishes, noting that "the Mexicans are great movers, here today and gone tomorrow," and "it looks as far as any proposition of this kind can be judged, that this [moving around] will be permanent."[2] Despite some tentative attempts at a comprehensive approach, the individual dioceses and parishes became focal points of Mexican-American ministry. Most prelates recognized that Slavic and Italian ethnics in the Midwest were unlikely to incorporate Mexicans into their national parishes, where language and cultural differences would be acute.

By 1927, Illinois ranked fourth nationally among all the states in number of Mexicans. The city of Chicago had emerged as an industrial entry point in the 1920s for Mexican immigrants and has remained so for Latino groups to the present. Many Mexicans and Tejanos migrated from the Southwest, following agricultural work through the Midwest; indeed a majority of Mexicans who came to Chicago had first lived in other parts of the United States. Almost one-half had spent at least two years in the United States before coming to Chicago, while another one-third had lived more than eight years in the United States. A 1928 survey by Chicago's Immigrant's Protective League of more than one thousand of the city's Mexicans found that that almost two-thirds came from Michoacán, Guanajuato, Jalisco, and Zacatecas, central plateau states that offered the strongest support for the Cristero Rebellion.[3]

To deal with local Mexicans, Mundelein enlisted the community of Spanish Claretian priests and brothers, founded with responsibility for outlying boxcar missions, as well as three large Mexican-American parish communities. Although the Catholic Church Extension Society did not customarily fund immigrant missions in urban areas, beginning in the summer of 1925 Chicago's Mexican missions received support because they had been targeted as a missionary group. Chicago's Claretian missionaries diligently served the region's Mexicans—throughout the city, in the railroad camps, and in other outlying settlements. By the late 1920s, Claretian priests ran two national parishes and assisted in outlying missions in the Chicago area.[4]

The widespread policy of establishing national parishes for Catholic immigrant groups began to change by the 1920s, when Cardinal Mundelein reversed this policy. Mundelein contended that such parishes increased nativist anti-Catholic sentiment and that the rise of the second generation among many immigrant groups warranted a greater use of English and a more integrationist approach. Mundelein also served as president of the American Board of Catholic Missions (ABCM), established in 1919 to coordinate the Catholic home mission movement in the United States. ABCM also provided funding to the Catholic Church Extension Society.

Railroad camps in and around Chicago were the first homes of many Mexican immigrants. The first Spanish-language church services in Chicago were held in makeshift railroad chapels in such camps in 1918. More permanent settlements in ensuing decades resulted in the formation of missions and, in the 1920s, parishes. Mexican immigrants, recruited to work on railroads, had begun arriving on Chicago's Near West Side in 1916, a neighborhood that had become the city's melting pot, serving as the entry point for its newest immigrants from Mexico, Texas, and the Midwestern beet fields. By the end of the 1920s, this area counted some seven thousand Mexicans, many of whom settled among Italians.

The neighborhood had also become the best known of all Italian neighbor-hoods in Chicago and one of the city's poorest and most run-down areas.[5]

Catholic work with Near West Side Mexicans began at St. Francis of Assisi, which had first been a German national parish and later served the neighborhood's Italians. St. Francis, in addition to performing its religious functions, hosted a wide variety of community activities, including meetings of youths such as those in the Asociación Católica de Juventud Mexicana, civic and literary groups, and performing arts troupes. The increasing mobility of Near West Side Mexican immigrants, scattered over a large, bustling area, accentuated breaks with practices from the home-land villages.[6]

In another large barrio, located in the neighborhood of South Chicago, the Claretians Missionary Fathers had, at roughly the same time as at St. Francis, established a national parish, Our Lady of Guadalupe, for Mexicans in a makeshift church. In 1926 they began building a new building; to help raise funds, in the summer of 1927 the Claretians appointed as pastor Father James Tort, who had served in Mexico before being exiled to Texas. That same year industrialist Frank J. Lewis, a bene-factor of the parish, furnished funds for the transportation of four Mexican Cordi-Marian nuns from Texas to form the nucleus of the first faculty of the parish school. Six months after their arrival, the sisters had more than a thousand children in attendance at catechetical classes and had opened three grades of the little school beneath their living quarters. To raise funds, Tort organized a committee of prominent Anglo laity, including Protestant and Catholic politicians, bankers, and businessmen. Irish parishioners proved particularly generous in their donations. Above the church's central altar was an image of the Virgin of Guadalupe, and the side altars featured La Dolorosa (the Sorrowful Mother) on the left and St. Joseph on the right.[7]

Ceremonies dedicating South Chicago's Our Lady of Guadalupe Church in 1927–28 demonstrated Chicago Catholicism's ability to unite a variety of nationalities under one religious umbrella and to welcome the Mexican Catholic community as an integral part of the archdiocese. Our Lady of Guadalupe parish had since its inception sponsored sepa-rate Mexican organizations, but it also fostered interethnic solidarity by introducing the national shrine of St. Jude Thaddeus, the patron saint of lost causes, in 1929. St. Jude served as protector of men and women in a wide range of activities, from military service to the workplace. Above the church's central altar was the image of the Virgin of Guadalupe, and the side altars held La Dolorosa (the Sorrowful Mother) on the left and Saint

Joseph on the right. The shrine and the Saint Jude League broadened the spiritual and financial support for the Mexican mission well beyond the boundaries of South Chicago.[8]

The St. Jude shrine at Our Lady of Guadalupe attracted a sizable non-Mexican attendance at the church, and the onset of the Depression further popularized the devotion. During World War II, the primary focus of Guadalupe feast-day celebrations and monthly Guadalupan devotions abruptly shifted from intercessory prayer for Mexico to pleas for "victory, peace and the safety of the men on the battle fronts."[9] Tort, after departing for California and then studying in Washington, D.C., at the Catholic University of America, returned to Chicago in 1944 and led the Mexican community in Chicago's third major Mexican barrio, in the Back of the Yards neighborhood, near Packingtown. Parishioners worked at the stockyards and soon raised money for yet another new chapel, Immaculate Conception. Priests from both St. Francis and Our Lady of Guadalupe served that neighborhood as an outlying mission and regularly held services in storefronts, and occasionally at nearby settlement houses.[10]

Despite the strong sense of community felt by European ethnics in their Chicago parishes and a considerable archdiocesan investment in church structures, notably parochial schools, urban dynamism dictated a steady pace of geographic mobility, both within neighborhoods and to the suburbs. As historians Gerald Gamm, Eileen McMahon, and others have pointed out, Catholic parish communities defended their areas, stood their ground against residential invasion, and won success to a greater extent than their urban Protestant and Jewish counterparts, particularly in relation to incoming African Americans. They demonstrated less interest in inhibiting ethnic change among Chicago's Mexican Americans (or Mexicanos, a term heavily used by Chicago Latinos) throughout barrios in the metropolis.[11]

The Southwest and Northwest sides of Chicago long remained exclusively "white ethnic" Catholic, with close cultural ties among parish members, blue-collar workers and their unions, and public servants such as police, firefighters, and city government officials at the ward level. But in recent decades the area has seen a growing influx of new people. Before 1970 Chicago was a largely white and black city, but it has since added a large Latino, largely Mexican, component, as well as Asian communities. According to the 2000 census, the City of Chicago has the third largest urban Latino population in the United States. The demographic tide swung increasingly toward Mexicanos and other Latinos after 1970. Among major metropolitan regions, Chicago experienced the greatest suburban Latino (mostly Mexican) growth in the 1990s, increasing 133 percent from 284,000 to 663,000 during the decade, and far outpacing the rates of Los Angeles (28%) and San Antonio (35%).[12]

During the 1960s, downtown highway expansion and urban renewal programs displaced the Mexican residents around St. Francis of Assisi Church on the Near West Side to the adjacent southwestern Pilsen neighborhood. Pilsen had been home to a large Catholic population, primarily Czechs and Poles, and their churches straddled 18th Street. Many former St. Francis parishioners, however, including newer residents of the greater Pilsen area, remained loyal to St. Francis. In 1994 a lengthy ordeal began that dramatized the importance of "sacred space," specifically the parish community, for Chicago's Mexican Americans. The archdiocese, in a policy of retrenchment requiring the consolidation of dozens of former national parishes, closed St. Francis. This action brought unexpected and sustained protests in a broad-based community campaign to convince Cardinal Joseph Bernardin to reopen the church. The Mexican faithful occupied the building in the dead of winter in an attempt to forestall demolition. Finally, by Easter Sunday 1996, with sustained community support, the cardinal acquiesced, and Masses were resumed before a packed church. The church not only remained open but flourished thereafter. The archdiocese returned the parish to its earlier status, with some personnel and administrative modifications—specifically the replacement of the Claretians with diocesan clergy.[13]

Nationwide, 54 percent of Latinos lived in suburbs in 2000. Suburbs have increasingly taken on urban characteristics, and continued suburban expansion has helped to narrow demographic differences between them and the central cities. Although segregation and isolation remain more common in the central cities, segregation and isolation patterns persist in the suburbs as well. The history of Chicago's Mexican immigrants—and to some extent other Latinos—after 1980 illuminates enduring immigrant values of neighborhood and place in both inner city and suburb; it also suggests novel trends and valuable areas of inquiry. Numerous transformations have reshaped the geography of the Chicago area's Latino settlements, as Chicago's Latinos have penetrated most aspects of suburban Catholicism.[14]

From Homeland to the Heartland: The Potosinos

Chicago Catholicism emerged directly from the immigrant church, where ethnically homogeneous national parishes served generations of newcomers. Large networks of parishes and personnel were already established by the time Mexicans arrived in the 1920s. Since the 1970s, transnational exchange has accelerated significantly, leading to the Americanization of Mexican Catholicism as practiced on both sides of the border and the Mexicanization of U.S. Catholicism through the introduction and maintenance of homeland religion. The evolution of Church and community in the Chicago region—as seen in the case of the people with roots in the Mexican state of San Luis Potosí, called *potosinos*—has been fed by sustained immigration from Mexico, the need for the archdiocese to embrace Mexicans as pillars of Catholicism, and the adaptability of the migrants and their institutions. Potosinos are of interest and provide a useful case study because of their state's historic importance as a major source of migrants to Chicago.[15]

Contemporary Mexicano parishioners have reshaped Catholicism according to the circumstances of transnational migration and settlement. The strong Mexican regionalism exhibited by potosino migrants and their descendants in the United States has been reinforced by regular visits to the homeland. Other factors that bind them to the homeland include participation in various secular and religious organizations and, significantly, continuing remittances to support their families and to further the social and economic improvement of entire communities. Ongoing relationships with Mexico are channeled through a wide range of networks among *paisanos* and hometown contacts. Mexicans are in the U.S. immigrant church and play an increasingly important part in it, yet they are simultaneously pulled back to their roots. their practices of worship and other forms of religious observance play central roles in metropolitan interaction, cultural maintenance, and the preservation of ancestral ties. Moreover, religion spans borders.

The potosino migration encompasses a wide breadth of experiences and attitudes. About half of Chicago's potosinos come from the capital city, also named San Luis Potosí, and its environs, which has over one-third of the state's population and some 85 percent of its total urban residents. The capital, some 260 miles north of Mexico City on the central plateau, offers a particularly rich colonial heritage, including distinctive religious architecture. Migration from the state's smaller towns and rural areas, however, has also been large, with the percentages ranging from Villa Juárez at about 10 percent to about 3 percent from Cerritos. San Luis Potosí State, adjoined by nine other Mexican states, features a varied landscape and good transportation along north-south and east-west rail and highway linkages.[16]

Socioeconomic developments in San Luis Potosí have long had repercussions in Chicago and the Midwest. The coming of railroad connections to northern Mexico in the 1880s provided new international links and greatly boosted agriculture in San Luis. The state's central location, as well as the beginnings of emigration to the United States, facilitated migration to other states in Mexico. The turbulence of the revolutionary period delayed development. By the mid-twentieth century, however, San Luis Potosí saw job growth and accelerated population growth, despite lags in both its northern areas of desert and semidesert with high plateaus and the fertile semitropical eastern section. In the realm of religion, specific patterns of state intervention, the role of the clergy, and responses to traditional Catholic teachings in Mexico began to be transmitted abroad; in turn, the homeland received new influences.

A 1932 study of Mexicans in the Chicago area provided the first breakdowns of regional origins; at that time potosinos constituted about 4 percent of the city's Mexican immigrant population. Recent estimates put the proportion at 5 percent, with well over fifty thousand potosinos currently living in the Chicago area. Most are found in the working classes—in manufacturing, the service industries, or small businesses—while an increasing proportion, mostly U.S. born, have made impressive inroads into the ranks of the middle class and professionals.

As for previous entrants, who dreamed foremost of upward mobility and economic opportunity, work remains the central focus of contemporary migration. But religion commands considerable attention from many individuals and sustained effort on the part of countless migrant organizations. One potosino migrant noted that in Chicago "work itself absorbs us so much that we don't have time even for church, or to remember God. Many of us who consider ourselves Catholic forget Mass and confession, and [we] hardly think of spiritual values." Another observed, "Work is my religion."[17]

Potosino civic associations and clubs have faced financial and other obstacles in Chicago due largely to the limited resources of their members,. who increasingly confront dilemmas regarding how much of their income should be shared with family back home. Since 1971 the Club San Luis in Chicago has collected resources to support ranches, towns, and municipal districts in the homeland and to buy necessary materials for distributing potable water to the state's less developed areas. In recent years, the Asociación de Clubes y Organizaciones Potosinas de Illinois (ACOPIL) has helped coordinate a wide range of charitable activities that benefit potosinos on both sides of the border. Since 1999 it has organized annual Chicago celebrations reflecting potosino heritage and their pride in San Luis. The weeklong Semana Potosina has featured speakers from Mexico such as the governor and the archbishop, who celebrated Mass in a Pilsen church, as well as the presidents of several municipalities. One recent celebration included exhibitions of traditional and contemporary art, folkloric entertainment, and lectures. Further, ACOPIL, like earlier organizations but on an even larger scale, funds a wide range of charitable endeavors for schools, churches, and other institutions back in San Luis.[18]

The following ethnographic profiles of migrants reveal many key points of potosino identity in Chicago as well as transnational links among all types of regional music, culture, and work. They also point to broader interpretations of the role of religion in migration, allowing us to look beyond purely ecclesiastical concerns into factors such as lay participation in parishes, social service organizations, and migrants' involvement in political and social concerns while coping with the wide range of challenges of life in the North.

Pedro was a leader of Mariachi Real San Luis, a mariachi band, and a retired railway worker. His experience demonstrates the fusion of Mexican music, religion, and culture at home and abroad. Pedro, though in his mid-eighties, had no plans of giving up performing "as long as the public accepts me." He pointed out that mariachi music is related to the Catholic religion because it can be performed during the Sunday Mass as well as for weddings and religious holidays. His groups have traveled throughout the Chicago area and the greater Midwest. Pedro left Cerritos, in the western part of San Luis, in 1943 to look for a better life ("a buscar la vida").[19]

Only after he embarked for Coahuila and other northern states did Pedro begin to pick up the true mariachi musical form originating in Jalisco, drawn from the *son jalisciense*. On a ranch in Coahuila; in Tampico, where he did day work for a spell in the oil industry; and in cantinas in Reynosa and Matamoros, Pedro and his brothers earned a living performing as the Mariachi Potosino de Mexico. In 1954, after acquiring a work permit and borrowing some money from friends, Pedro migrated to the United States—first to Galveston, then to Mission, Texas, where he played on weekends "for thirty or forty dollars, which was a lot of money." After settling his residency papers, he moved to San Antonio, then to Houston, where he met an acquaintance from Cerritos and began a career in railroad work that took him as far as Alaska. Pedro came to Chicago in 1958 and continued railroad work for twenty-five years, rising to the position of road master. In Chicago, Pedro and his group enjoyed instant and continued success as mariachis, often traveling to St. Paul,

Detroit, and St. Louis. When not on the road, they played at receptions in Chicago's downtown hotels, sometimes accompanying famous visiting performers from Mexico. Pedro organized several groups from his base in the Pilsen neighborhood, and he was a frequent performer at nearby parishes, such as St. Francis.

Dolores, a potosina from the capital, had lived in Chicago for more than thirty years. She was raised in the *colonia ferrocarrilera* of San Luis, which housed many of the families of railroad workers and where "in every corner of each neighborhood stood a church." She retained fond memories of childhood weekdays when the family went to El Montecillo Church in the afternoons for catechism and then again on Sundays. El Carmen, however, was the "central church," very traditional and the most beautiful in San Luis, where festivals were held in the plaza. Dolores remembered hearing from her grandmother, who lived in the countryside, of the turbulence of the Mexican revolution and of the help that the church provided to their family, particularly in sheltering the women. "In the countryside you were able to rely on your neighbors, whereas in the city you hid in your home. They were able to hide my aunts from the soldiers, and also whatever they had they were able to hide it in the church." On balance, she viewed the Mexican church positively: "When I was little we used to do all kinds of stuff out on the streets. I remember when my mother dressed me as an angel. We got dressed up on those [stage] platforms and pretended to be in colonial times." Dolores greatly valued the family unity of her childhood and attributed great significance to religion's role in nurturing ancestral bonds.

One major aspect of San Luis, Dolores noted, was that "the people you go to church with are the people you grow up with, or their sons or daughters," unlike in Chicago, where "you may meet someone from the area but you really don't know who is there." In San Luis, as in Chicago, there has arisen in recent decades a growing competition from Protestants (*cristianos*): "Nowadays people can choose, whereas in the old days you would follow what your parents did." In sum, she had found Catholicism more comfortable in the North, as "new ideas tend to criticize the priests and that's how it is. And I think it's going to take a while for the little towns in the [Mexican] countryside to change." Chicago offered greater choices of churches, more flexible and open-minded pastors, and a modern approach to religion.

Having been brought to Chicago with her parents, Dolores now had her own family: husband, daughters, son, and grandson. She did not think it likely that she would return to live in San Luis, although she enjoyed prolonged visits whenever possible. Her neighborhood was almost entirely Mexican, yet Dolores was unaware of any potosino enclave; the participants in organizations representing San Luis she met were "usually into fútbol [soccer]" and lived on the North Side. On Sundays, she observed, people always seemed to return to their old neighborhood church: "You grow up, you marry, [and] you baptize your kids in the same church." The holidays, as in Mexico, were occasions for public processions in both locales, although the staging of Las Posadas, formerly frequent in Chicago, were disappearing "because a lot of people are working and don't have time to organize these things [which also] are very expensive."

Dolores lived in southwestern Chicago, in the Little Village (La Villita) area, an immigrant enclave with a thriving Mexican-American shopping district. Mexicans from "all areas" come to her parish church, St. Pius V. Its one Mass in English and five in Spanish constituted "the reverse of how it was [decades] earlier," Dolores noted, when Mexican immigrants were a minority in Little Village. She adopted Chicago as home for herself and her family but had not lost touch with her Mexican roots and vividly remembered religious observances in San Luis, where festivals were "big events," with processions going down Avenida Carranza and "from El Carmen to all the different churches." Her mother visited periodically and "basically keeps up to old traditions, like the Day of the Dead"; Dolores, however, did not regularly attend any local church. She believed that in the United States priests can involve themselves more in the "immediate community," unlike their Mexican counterparts, who, with the possible exception of some priests in the countryside, are less inclined to "see what is needed and to fight for it." She was aware that activism on the part of parishioners played a part in the archdiocese's keeping parishes open in the face of constant demographic change.

Another potosina, Carmen, in her fifties, was born in one of the capital's downtown barrios, San Miguelito, and attended Catholic school. She spent most of her adult life in Chicago. Coming to Chicago, where she first settled in 1960, was harsh: "[It was] like going from hot water to cold water, a big change." She soon affiliated with Sacred Heart Church on the South Side, where she encountered Mexicans from the families of earlier waves of migration. She remembered "people who looked like Mexicans but who didn't speak Spanish." As she learned English and "began to learn more about Americans and their customs," her circumstances improved.

Carmen remained very involved with fellow potosinos, raising funds at her Pilsen church, St. Procopius, "so that those of us here can do something for those in San Luis," sending everything from food, shampoo, and clothing to wheelchairs. Potosinos carry packages whenever they return to Mexico for visits. She observed that whenever someone from Chicago goes to San Luis, they make a special effort to visit the neighborhoods of La Tlaxcala and San Sebastián because there are "so many poor people there." There they distribute items not just to family members but to everyone. Carmen preferred to raise money at her church, and she also relied on organizations such as ACOPIL and the Club San Luis Rey (the latter is "more for the people from the capital"), rather than Mexican or U.S. governmental institutions. She did not encourage people to move to the United States from San Luis because she feared that they might suffer, but once anyone arrived she spared no effort on their behalf. Her work had extended to helping people back home acquire ambulances, and she had developed ties with Chicago politicians, especially aldermen. Carmen prospered in Chicago; she preferred the Pilsen neighborhood to life in the suburbs.

Verónica, a U.S.-born potosina in her late twenties, was raised on the North Side of Chicago, in the Humboldt Park neighborhood. She still lived with her parents, who came from a small town in northern San Luis. She joined in occasional family trips to Mexico, which she considered something of a vacation, and stayed in the small pueblo of her ancestors about an hour's drive from the capital. She identified with being from San Luis, yet, she conceded, "I'm not from there, and I don't know the history [of the homeland]. I [really] don't know anything about it." Most of her family lived in Mexico, though some extended family members had settled in McAllen, Texas. An undergraduate at the University of Illinois at Chicago, Verónica traced her conception of religiosity to that of her mother, the "religious one in the family" who goes "the extra mile [in support of Catholicism]." In fact, her mother had helped explain some of the sermons and otherwise encouraged the family's continued attendance at their Pilsen-area church. Verónica took pride in the active role of women in the parish, "the backbone of the church." Men were generally uninterested, even on Father's Day, and when priests called upon them to receive special recognition, there was hardly any reply. To her mother's chagrin, Verónica's brother, an adolescent who was going through "a rebellious stage," was uninterested in participating in the religious community.

Verónica attended St. Mark's, a parish in a predominantly Puerto Rican North Side neighborhood with a large number of Mexican parishioners. Most of the priests were Mexicano, while the prominent deacons were Puerto Rican. Two early English Masses on Sundays served mainly

non-Latinos, especially Polish Americans. Verónica and her family became more receptive to Caribbean culture through living in an area that
for several decades remained the nucleus of Puerto Rican Chicago. Her
father had moved the family there just before she was born, as it was close
to the factory where he worked. She enjoyed the diversity of the neighborhood, which was unlike the monolithic, almost entirely Mexico-centered ambience of Pilsen and Little Village. Verónica even participated
in Humboldt Park's San Juan festival; she said that she and her cousin
enjoyed "being around Puerto Ricans, because we've been living [here] so
long." They enjoyed listening to salsa and merengue music and learned
much about the culture of the Hispanic Caribbean.

In the religious setting, a common language and shared minority status provided a bond for transcending historically distinct styles of observance. Verónica believed that her exposure to the church experience
affected the way she viewed the community: "I think we work together
[and] I feel more comfortable being in that environment so I can relate to
what's going on in the church and the community. But if I were in Pilsen
I wouldn't know about the [Puerto Rican] Virgen de Providencia and [the
parish] would just be strictly Mexican. If they strongly enforce the Virgen
de Guadalupe, why shouldn't we [also] do the other?" At least in this case,
integration and familiarity had produced an appreciation for other Latino
subcultures.

Ramón, a successful businessman in his late forties, arrived in Chicago as a teenager from a "small, sleepy" town in San Luis. He lived
and worked in the inner suburbs but kept ties with organizations in the
city. He saw the situation of the Chicago *potosino* as characterized by a
deep religious confusion, not only rooted in conflicts between Catholicism and Protestantism but also in the range of Church power and the
Church's relationship to larger developments. He remembered that in his
hometown, as in most others, "the Church was pretty much involved in
many activities, but I as an individual was not [involved in] one of them."
It was not that he was not interested in religion, but rather he was raised
with the cultural idea that "males were not supposed to be too close to
religion." His mother was heavily involved with catechism and attended
church regularly; one of his sisters attended fairly often, but his father
had entirely forsaken church services.

Ramón found religion to be lacking in intellectual coherence, and he
observed that migrating from a predominantly Catholic country to one
"with a Protestant ethic" forces a reevaluation of values. This has caused
some harm, as "the whole objective of the Catholic Church in Mexico is to

keep total control of the individual. [To do so] they prohibit the individual from being in other, more productive activities." He interpreted Catholicism as the institutional church and little more. Despite his reservations, Ramón believed religion to be "a very important aspect of a human being. It helps the psyche, the spirit, whatever you want to call it, but the responsibility of the Church [and its] priests is to help the spirit, and they should stop there." Ramón, though having broken with Church doctrine, still considered himself a Catholic, but not a closed-minded one. He no longer struggled with questions of religious identity but readily acknowledged their importance to the human condition.

Mexicanos who have been in the United States longer have developed different interests and ideologies than more recent arrivals. Ramón saw as "one of our basic problems" the refusal to assimilate. "It is clear that migrants hold on to patriotic visions of Mexico, yet they often fail to realize that assimilation can enrich one's culture." One must be aware of and maintain Mexican culture, yet assimilate. To cultivate the two cultures, he observed, "some people feel you're moving a glass from spot A to spot B, you're giving up something"; on the contrary, he asserted, "you're getting richer." Many assimilated Mexicans fail to tackle the issue forthrightly because of lingering ethnic pride, and they fear that they will be seen as *malinchistas* (traitors). Ramón warned that the Church, rather than venturing beyond the spiritual realm and risk abusing its power, should instead play a role in quietly promoting positive assimilation and the work ethic. He saw suburbanites as "more daring to go out there and start seeing the world differently." He believed that leaders and persons in the helping professions, especially teachers, should be encouraged to work inside the barrios yet live elsewhere, if they choose, without being accused of selling out their community.

For Ramón, cultural issues have remained integrally tied to religion, although he believes politics lies at the heart of all change. He criticized both Democrats and Republicans for what he saw as their failure to reach out to Latinos, and priests and other authority figures for pigeonholing: "We're being structured into a certain ideology because our parents were like that, and we're told by the priest or the precinct captain we've always been Democrat, we've always been Catholic. Fine, but I [may] want to be Buddhist [or] a Republican." Ramón believed that Mexicans should become more active in affairs of the homeland by formulating agendas and reevaluating the impact of past policies—everything from NAFTA to educational and cultural programs. He concluded that the infusion of billions of dollars into the homeland economy—"a lot more than is collected [in

Mexico] in taxes"—entitled *paisanos* living in the United States a greater voice in the political, economic, and social affairs of the homeland. He believed that the paisanos, not the Mexican or U.S. government, have the solutions for their problems: "We are the users of the system. We know better than any expert that you might find in Harvard, or Cambridge, or UCLA. Ask us."

These migrants have had dramatic, yet not atypical, experiences—arduous odysseys in search of work, frequent and often continued interaction with religious institutions on both sides of the border, and harrowing tales of survival. Once settled in the city, migrants often look to help their compatriots in Chicago as well as those remaining in the homeland. Those migrants who came north as adults have solid bases from which to compare the cultures and have developed the tools to adapt mentally when visiting the homeland or when dealing with older relatives when they visit Chicago. Among those born or raised in the United States, the local community, and especially the parish, dominates and conditions perceptions of nationality. Where migrant families worship in barrio parishes among non-Mexicanos, a sharing of saints, devotions, and holidays occurs, and the Spanish language and Roman Catholicism serve as common denominators.[20]

Immigrant remittances help transform towns throughout San Luis and elsewhere in Mexico. More than $14 billion annually goes to Mexico from the earnings of migrants working in the United States, and over $2 billion of these remittances come from greater Chicago. According to the Mexican consul, at least one hundred hometown clubs in the area, with more than fifty thousand members, fund public works and other projects south of the border, including building plazas, renovating schools, and overhauling health clinics. Many migrants, particularly the undocumented in low-paying jobs in factories, landscaping, and the like, are torn between sending money home and saving to buy a home up north. Despite this ambivalence, residents frequently return to their Mexican hometown to attend annual festivals. Thousands fly home, drive for several days, or take El Conejo (The Rabbit), a bus line with daily departures to Monterrey and San Luis. A suburban point of departure for El Conejo is Rancho Vargas, a successful clothing and accessory store in suburban Elgin owned by a potosino family. Nearby Aurora is another outlying haven, site of a flourishing Mexican community and a suburban entry point for the area's Latinos.[21]

Residential Succession and Religious Space in the Inner Suburbs

According to historian Jay Dolan, in the postwar era the suburban parish replaced the national parish as the key social institution in the U.S. Catholic community. In moving to the suburbs, Latinos not only have changed the character of suburbs and suburban parishes but also have inaugurated a new era of immigrant Catholicism, challenging the postwar notion that the suburbs are secular places of great homogeneity. Suburbanization produced ethnic tensions in suburban parish communities focusing on the use of resources, religious personnel, and different styles of worship, such as the *quinceañera* (debuting of girls on their fifteenth birthday), which many Anglos perceive as lavish and a poor substitute for investment in parochial school education. As residential succession increased, Chicago's inner suburban parish communities have kept pace with immigrants of Latin American origin, and territorial parishes under the charge of Spanish-speaking priests have increasingly come to serve as strong, cooperative community institutions.[22]

The impact of the expansion of urban barrios into the adjacent inner suburbs of Chicago became especially evident after 1980, with continued migration from Mexico and an outward shift of jobs throughout the metropolitan periphery. One result of the expansion is that several suburban Catholic parishes that are among the largest in the archdiocese have become predominantly Latino, and those parishes serve as valuable laboratories for examining and integrating religion within the larger framework of metropolitan life. The western suburbs of Cicero, Berwyn, and Melrose Park and the nearby parishes with which they form religious clusters offer examples of how some parishes adapted to the influx of Mexicanos, and they offer useful contrasts in religion, race, and ethnicity. Parishes resisted racial change with incoming African Americans, but they have proved versatile and flexible community institutions for Mexicanos.

The following suburban parish communities first settled by European Catholic immigrants in the late nineteenth and early twentieth centuries differ from one another in many respects, including proximity to urban ethnic concentrations, the degree of ecclesiastical and social activism among the clergy and laity, the impact of Latin American and U.S. Latino theology, and general spatial, social, and demographic landscapes. Clergy are important in sustaining ritual and devotion, but their success depends on successfully addressing the religious needs, cultures, and distinctive theologies of parishioners. In response to the theological reforms of Vatican Council II (1962–65), many Chicago-area clergy have learned Spanish and sought to identify with the life and struggles of Mexicano parishioners in the areas of liturgy, popular piety and devotion, and even civic activism.

Cicero

Cicero in many ways resembles adjacent neighborhoods in southwest Chicago in its ethnic patterns. The town's first European Catholic settlers were Poles and Irish in the 1880s, followed in the 1890s by Bohemians (Czechs) who had originally settled on Chicago's Near West Side, then moved to what became known as the Pilsen neighborhood (named for the second largest city of their homeland). Later Czechs and their descendants moved to newer, semirural sections on the southwest side of Chicago. Italians and Lithuanians followed, and by 1930 these foreign-stock, mostly blue-collar residents made up almost 80 percent of Cicero's total population of sixty-six thousand. The northwest portion of Cicero became heavily Italian, with the central neighborhoods bordering either side of Cermak Road mostly Czech and Lithuanian. The neighborhood along Cicero Avenue south of Ogden Avenue was heavily Polish. The newer immigrants tired of traveling back to their national churches in the city and focused on establishing parish communities close to home; this led to newfound territorial sensibilities in and around the industrial areas where they worked.[23]

During the late 1940s and 1950s, with the entry of a handful of African Americans, the town's European ethnics joined "housing mobs" that often violently confronted the newcomers. In the summer of 1951, Czech, Polish, and Italian residents of Cicero assaulted a large apartment building that had recently admitted a black family, burning and looting for several nights until hundreds of National Guardsmen finally restored peace. Our Lady of the Mount parish, located within the riot area, had been a center of Bohemian social and cultural traditions, but local clergy did little to ease racism. On the contrary, clergy who feared for the stability of the neighborhood in the face of outside speculators or panic peddlers—many of whom sought to use "blockbusting" to hasten ethnic turnover—often encouraged resistance.[24]

By the 1980s, less than two generations later, Mexican immigrants began entering Cicero. Though the Lawndale area, slightly to the north, was home to a large population of African Americans, blacks had still largely avoided Cicero. Despite their tolerance toward Mexicans relative to their attitudes about African Americans, many long-time residents of Cicero have perceived Mexicano newcomers as lesser, but still real, threats to property values, adequate zoning regulations, schools, and overall quality of life. There was particular fear of rising crime rates.

Mexican migration to Cicero increased markedly after consent decrees following civil rights lawsuits in the late 1980s and early 1990s mandated more open housing policies. The suits were actually designed to remove restrictions against African Americans. In a negotiated settlement in 1986, Cicero accepted a Fair Housing Resolution. The later arrival of tight-knit Mexican families caused rapid increases in population, school-age children, and overcrowding complaints received by the town. So in 1990 Cicero adopted a "no-growth" policy, and the following year the town's Health and Sanitation Code limited the number of people who could occupy a residential dwelling. But in 1992 a court decree permanently enjoined the town and its agents against engaging in discrimination based on family size or national origin.[25]

Despite general reluctance to incorporate any newcomers, the failure to attribute to Mexican nationals and Mexican Americans the distinct, immutable "racial minority" status given Chicago's African Americans owes to the city's industrial configuration, its historic toleration of immigrants, and the fact that the newly arriving Mexicanos, like most residents of Cicero, had a Roman Catholic religious heritage. In Cicero, the influx of Mexicans continued despite significant difficulties, including several cases of discriminatory treatment, such as a town president's unsuccessful attempt to prevent Good Friday processions by Mexicano Catholics by applying local statutes covering "public demonstrations." In the late 1990s, moreover, Cicero passed several zoning and antiloitering ordinances that many observers saw as aimed at limiting Mexican entry, and residency requirements for voting were tightened in what many saw as an effort to dilute potential political empowerment. Still, since the 1980s a blurring of racial boundaries has caused Mexicanos to be seen more as potential allies against African Americans than as economic, political, or social competitors, especially given the numerical decline of Bohemians, Italians, and others through outmigration and death.

According to U.S. Census figures, Cicero's Mexican-origin population exploded from 9 percent in 1980 to 37 percent in 1990 and 77 percent in 2000, while its African-American population remained at around 1 percent. Mexican landlords, like those of European ancestry, have upheld the color line and avoided renting to blacks, forcing them north to the Austin neighborhood within Chicago city limits. Also, middle-class blacks have been moving into the racially integrated suburb of Oak Park.

Thus the Mexican influx created for Cicero a new ethnic identity. That new identity is now reflected in the government of the suburb, which has for decades suffered from a reputation of corruption. The Mexican presence has also brought a proliferation of businesses to Cicero and other inner suburbs. The immigrants have revitalized commercial strip malls in a steady westward advance of seven miles from Eighteenth Street in Chicago's Pilsen neighborhood, through adjoining Little Village, and continuing along Twenty-second Street (Cermak Road) past Cicero and beyond the town of Berwyn, just to the west.

Cicero's St. Anthony of Padua Church is located close to Chicago's western border. It has become the major Mexican parish among the six in Cicero and is one of the largest Spanish-speaking congregations in the Chicago area. An archdiocesan survey in 2001 revealed that it holds seven weekend Masses (five in Spanish), attended by four thousand parishioners. Cicero community groups have stepped into leadership roles, while diocesan clergy struggle to find religious and secular networks to focus the energies of parish newcomers. St. Anthony has become a model for neighboring parishes in dealing with Latinos, especially in the absence of strong archdiocesan leadership.[26]

A national parish for Lithuanians since 1911, St. Anthony parish had grown with a new influx of Lithuanian refugees after World War II, but their numbers have rapidly dwindled in recent years. Today St. Anthony struggles to protect Eastern European ethnic remnants while increasingly functioning as a de facto Mexican "national" parish. Amidst all of its activities, the church retains signs of its diverse European immigrant history. At the entrance to the parish meeting hall, for instance, there is still lettering indicating its origins as a Bohemian *sokol*, even though most of the descendants of Czech immigrants have moved to the outer suburbs and others have clustered in other, smaller Catholic churches in the area. The Lithuanians receive clerical deference in matters of sharing church space and related issues, due to their history of strong support for the parish. Though many Lithuanians speak the language of the homeland, they currently attend the English Mass and still consider their parish a "national parish."

Berwyn

In Berwyn, a more upscale and middle-class suburb than adjacent Cicero, St. Mary of Celle Church houses a large and growing Mexican congregation that also includes many families of European extraction. The parish's Czech population dates back to about 1909. It owes its founding to the influx of hundreds of families following the opening of the Western Electric Works in Cicero in 1903. The 1950s saw the arrival of Irish, Italian, Polish, and German Catholics. In 1990, prior to the suburban Mexican influx, Berwyn had an aging population; it had among the oldest demographic profiles in the metropolitan area. Unlike Cicero, Berwyn is not a significant port of initial entry for Mexican immigrants, so there are no "entry parishes"; most of its Mexicano parishioners have been in the Chicago area for many years—generations, in some cases.

The pastor of St. Mary of Celle, Father Richard Prendergast, noted, "If you don't offer services in Spanish, they will go somewhere else." Indeed, many old-time Mexicano families who arrived before the current wave now attend the Spanish Mass instituted at St. Mary of Celle in 1999. In recent years, however, more of the Spanish congregation has been attending English Mass. Father Rich, a tall and affable man who has served as pastor since 1992, described the parish as a mixture of several congregations, including the old, the young, different ethnic groups, and those who go to church and those who do not. Catholic ethnics and Latinos tended to pursue separate parish activities, and integration requires deliberate efforts on all levels. One of the places where interaction was most obvious was among the "morning Mass crowd, [which] tends to be older, including many widows and widowers, [who] are very involved in the church, which rapidly bridges culture and language gaps."[27]

St. Mary of Celle contains several Latino contingents, including families from Nicaragua, Peru, Colombia, and elsewhere in Latin America. Yet unlike the conditions in several North Side Chicago parishes, where religious practices are melded in joint celebrations of holidays, saints, and subcultures of Mexican, Caribbean, and Central American Catholics, the Mexican aspect continues to dominate. The Feast of Our Lady of Guadalupe on December 12, notes the pastor, is "D-Day, but if you're Central or South American it's [merely] a nice thing." There is not much demand for incorporating other Latino Marian devotions. Many of the parishioners return to Mexico every year, which reinforces cultural ties. Once when a pastor from the state of Zacatecas came, he was greeted by "a whole group from there, who always [lined] up in church before Mass, and they all knew him."

Chain migration patterns have similarly drawn persons born in Michoacán, prompting the pastor to observe, "I don't think that there is anyone left [there] since they're all in Chicagoland." Those in the North send money back home regularly, a practice that tends to sap the earnings of those aspiring to the middle class. In prior generations about half of

Entrance Procession for Mass, Ethnic Culture Celebration at St. Mary of Celle, 2000 (St. Mary of Celle Parish, Berwyn, Illinois)

the Catholic ethnics in the Chicago area sent their children to parochial schools. Now the parish schools in Berwyn are about one-third Latino and are less ethnically diverse, with a mix that underrepresents the Latino population in the surrounding neighborhood. This is not surprising, given Mexican traditions as well as the difficulty of paying an annual tuition of over $3,000 per child.

Archdiocesan resources have failed to keep pace with Mexican migration throughout the metropolis. Father Rich noted candidly that a three-year effort at suburban planning in the late 1990s, which was designed to preserve the parish structure, schools, and convents and to meet the needs of the new Latino population among ten parishes of Cicero, failed because the archdiocese was "not very good at planning and not much help in the ministry, . . . because [either] they don't have the resources or they don't have the vision." In that same period, several pastors in Cicero, Berwyn, and Stickney formed a cooperative to hold monthly meetings and develop a network for providing a broader set of bilingual options for baptisms, Masses, and other important events. A full-time Mexican-born director of ministry coordinates all the Spanish-speaking work in the five parishes, supervising training of liturgical and catechetical ministers, baptism and marriage preparation (many immigrants had not previously had their marriage sanctioned by the Church), and cooperation with laity in all spheres of parish affairs.

Father Rich, a native Chicagoan who attended Catholic grammar school on the South Side, recalled that at the time of his ordination he was aware of the increased needs of the Spanish-speaking in the archdiocese. Only when faced with the influx from Mexico, however, did he seek to broaden his linguistic and cultural skills. Had there been a huge influx of Italians, he "probably would have gone out and learned Italian" instead. In any event, he traveled to central Mexico and attended language school daily for two months to learn the basics of delivering Mass in Spanish (which he accomplished six months later, after further study). He returns several times a year to visit Nuestros Pequeños Hermanos (Our Little Brothers and Sisters), Mexico's largest orphanage, located south of Mexico City in Morelos. Father Rich has always pursued "issues of justice" and sees as part of his work the use of "the power of the institution to serve the people."

For Mexicanos, Father Rich concluded, though women generally participate in church activities more than men do, "Sunday is the day that families stay together [as] it used to be for Anglos thirty years ago." It remains unclear, however, whether American culture will "undermine Latino families," as "each generation is an entirely new reality." He noted the Mexicano population is generally more conservative than others in the parish in terms of faith: "It is more pious, in the traditional sense; there is less concern with church politics and more concern with whether there are [available] devotions, shrines and services." Concerning traditional roles, "the men are the *machos* [while] the women are passive"; this presents challenges in the contemporary metropolis, especially in the "white business world." While some Mexicanos have adopted a social justice orientation, this "only applies in some areas, not always with regard to gender [and] sexual orientation. [We've realized that] the antigay thing is [still] very strong in that culture."

Not surprisingly, Father Rich cites the Virgin of Guadalupe as the religious icon for Mexicans;, he observed that "Mexicans are first of all *guadalupanos*, and then after that they're [Catholics]. I don't know if [the second generation] will become more Christ-centric here, [but] I think it's a great experiment going on right now in this country [as to] what American Catholics will do to Mexican Catholics and vice versa." The pastor recalls that right after Vatican II the bishop of Cuernavaca, a great reformer who introduced the Mariachi Mass, insisted that in any church built or renovated, the image of Christ must always be higher than any other image, especially higher than Guadalupe. "Mostly the women do the organization for the Guadalupe devotion, though the men come, while with the Vía Crucis (Stations of the Cross) [it is] mostly the men [who] do the organizing." As part of a recent church renovation, a shrine to the Virgin of Guadalupe was installed. This legitimacy and extension of Guadalupe into suburban Chicago demonstrates the potential impact of Mexican Catholicism in reshaping contemporary U.S. Catholicism.

Melrose Park

In another western suburb, Melrose Park, active clerical leadership, clearly influenced by post–Vatican II theology, recognizes "universal" components of the Mexicano experience, as well as demographic trends, and increasingly fosters harmony in suburban residential succession. Here the work of the Scalabrini Fathers (Missionaries of St. Charles) has left a strong imprint on care of the Mexican immigrant. The order, founded in 1886 and named after founder John Baptiste Scalabrini, who was born in northern Italy in 1839, derives its mission from Bishop Scalabrini's concern for supporting nineteenth-century Italian immigrants in their new life in America and using Catholicism as a tie to the homeland. The Scalabrinians expanded their work in parishes, schools, and missions to twenty-six countries in the Americas, Africa, Europe, Australia, and Asia. They also run shelters and information centers and publish migration bulletins, newspapers, and magazines. The Scalabrinians have worked to control the cultural religious practices of parishioners, and they have acquired experience with the vitality of Italian religious life in the various village-specific mutual benefit societies and the multiplicity of village feasts under the control of local ethnic leaders.[28]

The beginnings of Our Lady of Mount Carmel parish can be traced to the venerated statue of Our Lady of Mount Carmel and the feast in her honor. It was first celebrated in July 1884 on a farm in Melrose Park. The following year a chapel was built by one Emanuella DiStefano to house a statue of the Madonna, which she commissioned to be brought from her home region in Laurenzana, Italy, in gratitude for her husband's recovery from a physical infirmity. The annual feast of Our Lady of Mount Carmel grew rapidly to attract hundreds of Italians from Chicago's West Side and suburbs. Following Old World customs, visitors walking in the procession carried a candle in one hand and a rosary in the other, passing by parishioners' houses and often being invited in for meals. Given prevailing anti-Italian antagonisms before World War II, the organizers of the feast always had to make sure that the festivalgoers remained within circumscribed neighborhoods. Much of the process is reminiscent of the street life of the East Harlem Italian religious celebration, the Festa della Madonna, that has "sacralized the streets" for over a century among successive generations of Italian Americans in upper Manhattan.[29]

The Scalabrinians reached out to the first Latino parishioners soon after the arrival of Cuban refugees during the 1960s. In those years Father Peter Corbellini became an advocate among his Scalabrini confreres, as well as in the Italian-American community, by initiating the celebration of a special Mass for exiles who had gravitated to Sacred Heart Church in Melrose Park. Sacred Heart was a mixed parish that came to be staffed by clergy of the archdiocese rather than religious orders. But Father Corbellini was unsuccessful in convincing his superiors to support a proposed project honoring the Cuban patroness, Nuestra Señora de la Caridad del Cobre. The project was modeled on a much more elaborate effort in Miami devoted to freedom and liberation of the homeland. Archbishop John Patrick Cody tabled the project as unworkable for a variety of logistical and other reasons, not the least of which were his reservations regarding possible difficulties stemming from nationalistic "ethnic talk."[30]

Mexicano immigration, beginning in the 1970s, boosted Melrose Park's economy, reversing a decline that had begun with the departure of earlier residents to outer suburbs. It revived empty storefronts and made possible the annual HispanoFest that draws tens of thousands of visitors. By the mid-1990s, with Mexicanos constituting more than one-fourth of the total population, Mexican groceries, bakeries (*panaderías*), and a wide range of other businesses and services had been established and indeed came to dominate the commercial landscape. The Melrose Park Mexicano population surged from a few thousand in 1980 to thirteen thousand in 2000 (just over half of the total).

Since the 1970s, Mexicanos have been inclined to attend Our Lady of Mount Carmel Church. A young Mexican associate pastor there now shares duties in the English, Spanish, and bilingual Masses with the Italian-born Scalabrinians. Significantly, the Melrose Park Festa beginning in the early 1970s broadened the composition of the procession to include a *mariachi* band for the benefit of predominantly first-generation Mexican parishioners. The Vía Crucis procession on Good Friday, similarly, reinforces their visible presence, as have Spanish-language baptism and marriage ceremonies in the church. The Scalabrini parish has, characteristically of the order, sought to facilitate the entry of Mexicanos by fostering a cooperative spirit to ease "customary" ethnic tensions, even in the absence of the racial dimension present in Cicero given the immediate proximity large numbers of African Americans. Scalabrini clergy have also reduced tensions through careful rescheduling of the various time slots for the liturgies.

The Mexicano suburban influx produced changes in the scheduling of Masses that, along with tensions resulting from cultural differences, have bifurcated Our Lady of Mount Carmel's congregation. In 1992, 60 percent of the eleven thousand parishioners in Our Lady of Mount Carmel were still English-speaking, consisting mostly of Italian-American families. They continue to dominate the financial contributions, or stewardship, of the parish, despite some gains from Mexicanos, who make up the remainder of the congregation. The vast majority of those attending Spanish Masses came from within the parish boundaries, though recently the church has attracted some suburban Latinos from elsewhere in the western suburbs. According to one priest, "People come from many different towns all around and create traffic and parking problems. Parishioners are . . . willing to accept the people who live in town, but they feel each parish should provide service for the Latinos of their places." Older residents also have resented being "pushed around" in a parish they had built—and one that had long remained Italian. They also feared declining property values. Groups of young people were organized separately for church activities—Mexicanos who came to the United States as children or were born here, those coming from Mexico as teenagers, and the non-Mexicano youth.[31]

The Scalabrinians have extended their Mexican ministry to missions in surrounding suburbs such as Franklin Park. There they focused on evangelization, using Bible groups as "base communities," one of the prime institutions of Latin American-based liberation theology. Significantly, the Catholic Church has suffered some leakage to suburban Protestants, such as in Rolling Meadows. Rolling Meadows was born in the mid-1950s as a picture-book Chicago suburb with ranch-style homes, which by 2000 contained large proportions of evangelicals among its twenty-five hundred Mexicanos (more than 10 percent of the village's residents).[32]

Scalabrinis have for over a decade also served St. Charles Borromeo Church in Melrose Park. Founded in 1942, St. Charles was once solidly Italian but is now overwhelmingly Mexican and is roughly equal in size to Our Lady of Mount Carmel. St. Charles has also celebrated the Stations of the Cross on Good Friday night with an array of homeowners, including Italian Americans, Lithuanians, and Mexicanos, volunteering

Young Girl at Quinceañera Mass at Our Lady of Mount Carmel, 2003 (Our Lady of Mount Carmel Church, Melrose Park, Illinois)

to have one of the stations represented on their lighted lawns. Also important have been Día de los Muertos celebrations (the Day of the Dead, November 2)—held in memory of the deceased and combining Catholic ritual with pre-Columbian beliefs—and *las posadas*, the nine days before Christmas. The latter observance, which involves dramatization of the pilgrimage of Joseph and Mary, has become part of the church's ministry to suburban Latinos.

Most of the parishioners at St. Charles Borromeo reportedly come from the northern Mexican state of Durango. The characteristic colorful, quasi-equestrian *charro* fashion of that state's residents, not surprisingly, is sometimes highlighted at church functions. Very few young non-Mexicanos remain at St. Charles; these parishioners tend to be senior citizens. By contrast, nearby Our Lady of Mount Carmel parish, with its diehard

Italian contingent, lags somewhat in ethnic turnover, with over one-third of the parish remaining non-Latino.

The Scalabrini Fathers have successfully broadened their mission in light of the "international reality of migration." They pioneered new pastoral approaches, rapidly learning to serve Latino immigrants in Spanish and readily assisting in religious retreats (*cursillos*) with emphasis on, and participation by, the laity.

By the mid-twentieth century, Scalabrinians had taken charge of a dozen parishes in the Chicago area, both inner city and suburban. Forced to essentially abandon their original mission focused on Italian immigrants, they turned their missionary focus to the newest Mexican-American, Puerto Rican, and Cuban arrivals while also expanding their work in Latin America, particularly along the Mexico-U.S. border. Since the early 1990s, in addition to annual ceremonies and celebrations, leadership workshops have been offered for Scalabrinians in a half-dozen or so *comunidades de base* (ecclesial base communities), reflecting continued Scalabrini involvement in liberation theology. The Second Vatican Council had allowed parish communities to deal with broad social justice issues and become more active in leadership in church activities and programs, including parish councils and liturgy committees, and these reforms have facilitated Mexicano participation.[33]

The work of the Scalabrini points to similarities between Latino and Italian Catholic populations. These include a pronounced family orientation, a tendency of women to participate more in church, and a heavy involvement in popular devotions. The Scalabrinians' practical experience and adherence to the mission enunciated by the writings of the order's nineteenth-century founder have continually reshaped the post–Vatican II attitudes of their many Chicago-area priests in adopting a social justice orientation. The pastoral strategies and the approaches of Scalabrinians have proved instrumental in facilitating and monitoring the entry of Latinos into church life, helping to overcome the potential resistance of Italian neighbors, many of whom saw Mexicanos as intrusive and somewhat undesirable outsiders. Scalabrini clergy embraced the newcomers as part of the suburban mosaic and have clearly helped Mexicanos gain legitimacy in the eyes of the surrounding community by incorporating much of the immigrant culture into parish administration.[34]

There no longer is any such thing as the typical American suburb. And the stereotypical upper-middle-class Anglo-Saxon suburban family is no more, if it ever was, an accurate reflection of American suburbia. Suburbia now covers a wide range of contexts. And in Chicago, as elsewhere

Scalabrinian Priests and Mexican Congregation in Fiestas Verano 2003, St. Charles Borromeo (St. Charles Borromeo Church, Melrose Park, Illinois)

around the country, one of those contexts is Latino. A continuous Mexican barrio has emerged, stretching from Chicago's inner city through the inner suburbs, from Pilsen on the South Side of Chicago through suburban Berwyn. The suburb of Cicero, once a bastion of European immigrants, is now 77 percent of Mexican origin. The nearby western suburbs of Melrose Park and Berwyn also have significant Mexicano populations, and Latino communities have been established in other parts of Chicago's suburban ring, including Palatine and Elgin to the northwest, Waukegan to the north, West Chicago to the west, and Aurora to the southwest.

The cohesive parish structures of Catholicism show few signs of breakup as Mexicanos move into Chicago's suburbs, where they constitute less of a "religious minority" than one might expect. In 1996, authorities in the outlying cities and suburbs of Cicero, Addison, and Waukegan passed ordinances limiting the number of extended family members living under the same roof, regardless of the size of the home. These ordinances targeted Latinos (mostly Mexicans) and reflected the anti-immigrant sentiment of the time. Mexicanos successfully challenged the ordinances in court as discriminatory, arguing that the definition of family used by the cities directly conflicted with their cultural concept of family.

Latinos in Edge Cities

Some of the oldest Latino suburbs are the half-dozen or so satellite cities—actually towns in their own right—located in the "collar counties." Here Mexicans settled beginning in the 1920s to work on the many railroads entering Chicago, the hub of the Midwestern transportation network, as well as in steel and other heavy industries. The satellite cities along the outer industrial rail beltway form a 130-mile arc at a distance of thirty-five to forty miles from the downtown area. It connects Waukegan to the north with Elgin and Aurora to the west along the Fox River, and then, curving south and east, Joliet and the Gary and East Chicago, Indiana, cluster. Only Waukegan, in Lake County, Illinois, falls within the Chicago Archdiocese. Mexicanos in the outer suburbs attend parishes offering both Spanish- and English-language Masses.[35]

Chicago, along with early and important *colonias* in the Gary, Indiana, area, has become the Mexican-American hub of the Great Lakes region, projecting a regional influence similar to that of San Antonio. During the 1920s, Mexican clergy and working-class Mexican laborers formed parish communities in rail, agricultural, and industrial areas of Kansas, Nebraska, and the more northern Great Plains states, dispensing Catholicism and community cohesion. Boxcar camps had been set up on the outskirts of Aurora, some thirty-five miles from downtown Chicago. Mexican laborers entered the shops in the mid-1920s, accompanying and later replacing Romanians and other Eastern European immigrants and ethnics.[36]

In Aurora, Mexicans created a community with a church serving as the institutional foundation. Most local Mexicans had previously attended the parish church closest to where they lived; many walked out to the Eola boxcar settlement on occasion to attend Mass at a chapel with their compatriots. In 1928 Mexicans finally built their own wooden-framed church in Aurora, using lumber and nails furnished by the railroad. The makeshift parish located a Mexican priest, one Father Valadez, who had been assigned to St. Charles Hospital in Aurora, and he commuted out to one of the boxcar camps on Sundays. Even after Valadez returned to Mexico, the church survived for a while, as American priests from Aurora came out to say Mass. The closing of the camp in the early 1930s due to economic conditions, however, led to the razing of the church and dissolution of the parish. New communities arose in Aurora and nearby Elgin after World War II, however, when Mexicans became more permanently affiliated with local Catholic churches.[37]

The convergence of social, economic, and religious conditions between city and suburb in northwestern Cook County, in the satellite city of Aurora, and within Chicago itself has created some of the conditions necessary for greater residential integration of Mexicans with other groups. A changing spatial pattern of jobs in metropolitan regions is being driven in large part by increasing flexibility in the spatial organization of economic production. In many satellite cities high-tech production takes the place of heavy industry, often in the form of "business parks" housing light manufacturing, warehousing, offices, and retail establishments, as well as riverboat gambling. Machine operators and other laborers concentrate in Elgin, Waukegan, West Chicago, and Aurora, small communities offering single-family housing and more pleasant surroundings.

The emergence of high-tech edge cities since the 1980s has attracted blue-collar Latino workers in many commercial strips and malls, as well as to industrial, warehousing, and retailing districts. These areas do not serve primarily as bedroom communities for the city, though a sense of detachment from Chicago proper has survived among the earlier arrivals. Compared with contemporary immigrants from Europe and Asia, Latinos constitute a weaker presence in edge cities. Yet even in those locations, such as the suburb of Schaumburg near O'Hare International Airport to the northwest of Chicago, which since the 1960s has been a regional center of the electronics industry and one of the largest business centers of the Midwest, blue-collar Latin American and Eastern European immigrants now share workplaces and parishes with professionals. The Church of the Holy Spirit, erected in 1974, for decades has included Mexicanos in an increasingly diverse parish of transferees from out-of-state and European-origin "ethnics" with roots in Chicago.[38]

To a slightly greater degree than residents of the inner suburbs, Chicago's edge city residents have been predominantly white, well educated, and Catholic, but Latinos have played a key role in bridging the Catholic ethnic divide. Suburban priests and others not raised in the "bricks-and-mortar" era of early-twentieth-century U.S. Catholicism place less emphasis on the buildings and more on the community that they are helping to build. Variations in the Mass since Vatican II, and indeed the entire framework of Catholicism, can be found among urban and suburban parishes, and suburban parishes can foster a sense of community across the metropolis. Latino (and other) immigrants in the outer suburbs and edge cities suffer from a lack of nearby residential community amidst the car culture. The Church's role has become even more important given people's relative isolation from each other day to day.

Religious congregations of new immigrants are not often established within the edge cities, but rapidly expanding employment opportunities, particularly for skilled workers and professionals, have attracted new populations from the city of Chicago as well as from throughout the United States and world. Large numbers of Hindu, Buddhist, and Muslim immigrants have come directly to Chicago's suburbs and built temples and mosques near their homes. Catholicism's recent suburban growth, by contrast, based partly on migration from the city neighborhoods—and derived mostly from Latin American immigrants—often involves the expansion of existing parishes rather than the formation of entirely new ones.[39]

Chicago's Suburban Dynamism

The engaging of religious personnel in Mexicano community formation and adaptation to new locales and circumstances depended on blending urban ethnicity with changing theology in a wide range of communities within the archdiocese. Command of resources and the ethnic composition of neighborhoods before Latinos arrived also proved important, as did the size of the community and whether it could staff its own parishes and organizations or was forced to amalgamate with existing parishes and institutions. New suburbanites arriving from Chicago or migrating from elsewhere because of job opportunities found no reason to assume the same religious roles as their neighbors. Booming suburban Mexican-American populations have increasingly attracted the attention of the archdiocese, which has reluctantly (and only passively) embraced the newcomers as pillars of Catholicism, while an active clergy has assisted the migrant-led rejuvenation of declining parishes in both city and suburb.[40]

The Chicago suburban Mexicano reveals crucial linkages between religion and ethnicity, most notably in the continued importance of the parish community, and is an important subject for those engaged in comparative urban studies. The great importance of Mexicanos as consumers, related to the strength of religious institutions, is seen along Cermak Road, a thoroughfare that links city to suburbs. Restaurants, ranchero clothing stores, and *norteño* music shops patronized mostly by Mexicanos stretch well beyond the North Riverside Shopping Mall centered on Harlem Avenue, several miles west of Chicago's city limit. Nearby, in west suburban Forest Park, lies Forest Home Cemetery, where a sign at the entrance advertises a new "Our Lady of Guadalupe" section. These businesses have helped revitalize neighborhoods and churches alike.[41]

Where suburban Latinos are present in smaller numbers, they are more likely to become residentially integrated over time and less likely to develop residential enclaves. In Chicago's northwestern suburbs, for example, small influxes of Latinos have not coincided with the departure of existing residents. The newest wave of Mexicano suburbanites there has pointed up the lack of sufficient archdiocesan resources. That has become particularly apparent at Misión Juan Diego in Palatine, where overflow crowds watch the several Spanish-language Masses on closed-circuit television screens in the basement while a larger church is under construction.[42]

In recent decades the identities, organizational networks, and cultures of Mexican and Puerto Rican migrants have remained strongly linked to the homeland. (This is less the case among Cubans and Colombians, for example, who often assimilate into the dominant culture rather quickly and lose or—due to relatively small numbers—fail to form urban or suburban enclaves.) Chicago serves as an opportune laboratory for a detailed examination of this interrelationship. A transnational perspective on migration focuses on the multiple and ongoing connections forged and maintained by large numbers of immigrants across the borders of two or more nation-states. As transnational migration reaches the outlying regions of the metropolis, Latino parishes are becoming increasing diverse, adding to the older constituencies from Mexico and Puerto Rico. Migration from city to suburbs addressed immediate problems—usually inadequate housing, illness, and children's problems in schools and with gangs. Links have emerged as well with areas of Latin America beyond Mexico and Puerto Rico. One priest, for example, while serving the suburban Waukegan area in 2001, traveled to Honduras, the country of origin of some of the newest parishioners of Holy Family Church in the nearby municipality of North Chicago. There he distributed thousands of dollars in donations as part of a hurricane relief effort. Back home, his parish's many undocumented immigrants, fearing deportation, often have nowhere else to turn, and his church provides clothing, housing, and even employment information. All of these actions gain the respect of parishioners, though they may not represent a conscious effort to keep people coming to church. After Sunday Mass volunteers offer citizenship classes and other training to help in the secular lives of parishioners.

More than with other Latino groups, the Chicago Archdiocese and its local pastors have taken a more hands-off policy with regards to suburban

Puerto Ricans. That is especially true in relation to the latest influx, made up largely of young professionals who choose to launch their career in Chicago's western suburbs rather than deal with a saturated job market in the homeland. These individuals seek the amenities of a suburban lifestyle for their family. Working-class Mexicanos may find that movement to the suburbs since the 1960s has been more of a lateral more than an upward economic choice, since the suburbs the Mexicanos largely inhabit have become more "urbanized," not very different in feeling from Chicago proper. In some areas, such as banking, recent Puerto Rican migrants have targeted a clientele among already established earlier arrivals who followed the stereotypical pattern of work in factories or the garment industry. The nation's largest Puerto Rican (and Latino-owned) bank, San Juan-based Banco Popular, relocated its U.S. headquarters to Chicago in 1998. Bankers reared in the homeland have largely geared their operations toward reaching a greater share of the continental "Latino market," including suburban first-time homebuyers who are often unreached by non-Latino mortgage-lending institutions. They increasingly bypass urban barrios entirely.[43]

Around Naperville, an edge city in DuPage County, many companies located along the Interstate 88 corridor, such as Lucent Technologies, have recruited young professionals directly from the University of Puerto Rico—particularly its Mayaguez campus, the site of a widely acclaimed engineering school. Most of the newcomers arriving in the western suburbs were raised in middle-class families and educated in the island's prestigious Catholic schools. Consequently, they blend smoothly into local, English-speaking parishes for regular worship. On special occasions they might seek Spanish-speaking pastors or, more frequently, wait until they return home on periodic family visits.

With Mexicanos struggling to define sacred space wherever they settle, European ethnic national parishes, both urban and suburban, have become filled with Mexican Americans. Hoping to reach the growing Latin American-origin population, the Archdiocese of Chicago has expanded its suburban infrastructure, including offering Mass in Spanish at more than half of its almost four hundred parishes, including sixteen in northwestern suburban Cook and Lake Counties. Only about a dozen Latino priests, however, actively serve within an archdiocese that is over one-third Latino.[44] The archdiocese has also increased its awareness of transnational elements of religiosity among Mexican immigrants, and Cardinal Francis George, who speaks Spanish, has designed outreach programs to boost ministry to Latinos. The cardinal, who has traveled to Mexico and generally sought to broaden ties with Latin America, has reached out to Latinos from many countries. He recognizes that Latinos, like ethnic groups who came previously, have come to feel like second-class citizens: "That's the history of a church [and of an archdiocese] that is built generation after generation by migrants." George concedes that the Church is often "not very good" at adapting to newcomers. The prospect of losses to other religious communities or to "disillusionment" has required the maintenance of an intricate system of parochial schools that offer alternatives to poorly performing barrio public schools.[45]

Religion, Race, and Ethnicity

A changeover from national parishes of European ethnics under religious clergy into Mexican parishes under diocesan clergy has marked the Mexicano ministry in Chicago in recent decades. Mexicans first gravitated to St. Pius, a territorial parish serving Poles, Bohemians, and Italians, in the 1960s. It encompasses a geographic territory fourteen blocks long and eight blocks wide within which eight Catholic "ethnic parishes" were located. The dwindling number of Polish members became increasingly unable to maintain the extensive church facilities. St. Vitus, another Pilsen church in transition during the late 1960s, maintained two devotional side altars, one for the Infant of Prague and the other for Our Lady of Guadalupe. Many of Pilsen's other parishes welcomed Mexicans only grudgingly. Parish staffs in the neighborhood have also changed from predominantly Euro-American, or Anglo, clergy to lay and Latinos and Latinas, though even today many churches do not employ Spanish-speaking personnel to interpret for Latin American immigrants. Approximately three thousand people attend Mass each Sunday, and many of these parishioners live beyond the official territorial borders. Hundreds are involved in some form of parish ministry. The longtime pastor of St. Pius, Charles Dahm, writes that his parish "is hamstrung by excessive control by central authorities, distant from and unrelated to local life and its challenges." Parish life becomes hobbled by divisions of secular and the sacred and "by a sacral isolation of the priest from the people, or by a characterization of the laity as ignorant, profane, or inactive." On the other hand, increasing parish activities, especially secular ones, infuses life into the parish and serves to build community. St. Pius became the lead parish in the Alinsky-style Pilsen Neighbors Community Council, which organized neighborhood residents in the 1990s to better the quality of community life.[46]

It is too soon to determine whether the present policies of the Catholic Church will demonstrate the same institutional and ethnic resilience and ability to redistribute human and material resources as occurred in the mid-twentieth century. Chicago remains a city of neighborhoods, with close identification with parishes, though explosive growth can overwhelm established mores and institutions. The outward exodus of non-Latino Catholic ethnics from inner-city urban parishes, moreover, no longer constitutes a decisive blow against community or ethnic cohesion, since these ties can readily be reestablished in the suburban periphery, even in edge cities.[47]

Meanwhile, a somewhat speculative pan-Latino or Hispanic identity has made some inroads in the religious sphere, as elsewhere. Leaders of the institutional church conveniently, but not always accurately, treat all Latin American-origin Catholics as one "national" group with a common faith tradition, in light of shared linguistic and cultural bonds. Along these lines, several North Side parishes reflect the melding of religious practices, observing jointly the holidays, saints, and subcultures of Mexican, Caribbean, and Central American coreligionists. Many Mexicanos, however, especially those born in Mexico, relate more closely to the national identity that genuinely embody their homeland culture, and often also to their region or state of origin.

7 New Urban Opportunities: Church Leadership in Texas and New York City

The study of the immigrant experience in two cities seminal to Latinos, San Antonio and New York City, always reveals large contrasts. Those differences were roiled by Vatican II, which brought changes in religious tradition and reforms in the institutions and practices of urban Catholicism. Another force for change and divergence was the urban growth fueled by new immigration from Mexico, Central America, and the Caribbean, which led to adaptations of ethnic identity. An examination of the dual frameworks of Latin American and Latino Catholicism illuminates the interrelatedness of religion and religious tradition, city, and identity.

Pastoral and other innovations begun by San Antonio's religious leaders spread throughout the United States and even made inroads into Latin America. Before 1965, Archbishop Robert Lucey largely controlled the public religious and to some extent the secular activities of Mexican-American Catholics in San Antonio. As Mexican-American clerical and lay leadership began to flourish in San Antonio, cultural and religious self-awareness converged. In San Antonio, unlike the more diverse urban immigrant cities such as Houston or Dallas that included, beginning in the 1980s, large numbers of refugees from Central America, the Latino population remained overwhelmingly native born and mostly of Mexican origin. San Antonio's Mexican-American population consisted largely of stable homeowners who organized in the grassroots parish-based organization COPS, led by laity with the support of clergy and the archbishop. It was widely emulated for its effectiveness in gaining Mexican Americans access to neglected city services during the 1970s and 1980s. San Antonio also served as the setting for a wide range of other social movements predicated on Catholic institutions, customs, and teachings.[1]

New York, by contrast, is an international entry port whose Catholic immigrants have continually reshaped ethnicity in each generation. Its very mobile second- and third-generation Puerto Ricans, as well as newly arriving immigrants from the Dominican Republic and Mexico, constantly move within and across neighborhoods. In the immediate postwar decades New York City had developed a variegated Latino Catholic identity as the archdiocese continued to absorb newcomers, especially Puerto Rican migrants. Latino, Haitian, and other Catholics with distinctive religious beliefs increasingly moved back and forth from their Caribbean homelands. The case of Puerto Ricans from the 1960s through the 1980s proves instructive, since these migrants, who had come over in especially large numbers in the 1950s, were largely apartment renters on short-term leases in marginal neighborhoods in, and on the outskirts of, barrios. Community networks—especially including the impact of the local church (parishes)—were damaged as neighborhoods succumbed to a wide variety of urban problems in the 1960s and 1970s.

As urban decay threatened the vitality of the new immigrant church, Catholic clergy, such as those in the Northwest Bronx Community and Clergy Coalition, worked with Puerto Rican as well as non-Latino parishioners on initiatives that recreated a sense of community. They contributed to the revitalization of large parts of the city, such as the South Bronx, and fomented ethnic revival or regeneration. The influx of Dominicans and Mexicans also forced the church to reevaluate its local role. There was a replication of patterns previously noted in Chicago, with the rapid development of transnational religious, social, and economic ties. Such was the case when the New York Archdiocese actively supported the Tepeyac Association, which organized largely through parishes for a wide range of religious and secular activities.

Contrasts in the roots and styles of leadership in San Antonio and New York reveal distinct approaches to larger developments emerging within U.S. Catholicism as well as the formation of Latino historical identity. Capable, even excellent leaders arose. They reached well beyond the confines of their historic Latino cities and have imaginatively sought alliances, waged fights for identity with secular forces, yet kept a distinct religious agenda. This is a testament to their importance.

Local Activism, Hemispheric Catholicism

During the 1960s the proportion of Mexican Americans in San Antonio grew from 42 percent to 52 percent, with the greatest increases in the northwestern and southwestern quadrants and lesser gains in the northeast and southwest. San Antonio continued to beckon newcomers from Mexico, who concentrated in the West Side barrio's older areas, close to downtown employment and Kelly Field. During the early 1960s, San Antonio's Mexican slums near downtown were torn down as the area underwent redevelopment. Some $300 million was poured into rehabilitation funds, as the city began to remove dirt-floored shacks, buildings

made out of old Coca-Cola signs, and rows of shotgun "corrals" with five
to ten families cooking over kerosene stoves amid unsanitary conditions.
Predatory housing practices continued to plague the West Side, especially the "contracts-of-sale" financing arrangement commonly offered
to low-income prospective buyers by unscrupulous lumberyard companies that built houses.

Beginning in the 1960s, a new generation of Chicanos engaged in social protest in venues ranging from local schools to major national companies. In 1968, some seven hundred students at Lanier High School
and six hundred from Edgewood High School walked out, demanding
Mexican-American teachers and counselors, special courses, and better
facilities. Protests gained some results, but the involvement of radical
groups such as the Mexican American Youth Organization, led by fire-
brand José Angel Gutierrez, threatened the status quo favored by the
Anglo probusiness government. San Antonio's solid Mexican-American
middle class, moreover, did not readily take to radical action, though it
supported United Farm Workers leader Cesar Chavez. In 1971 the Archdiocese of San Antonio, in response to growing Chicano activism, established the Commission for Mexican-American Affairs to mobilize the
Catholic Church in the interests of the larger secular community.[2] The
commission survived until 1977.

Even as a booming Sunbelt city, San Antonio never really lost touch
with its religious roots. In the pastoral arena, in the mid-1960s Lucey appointed a local Mexican-American pastor, Virgilio Elizondo, to head the
San Antonio Confraternity of Christian Doctrine (CCD). Imbued with
the spirit of recent Vatican II reform, Elizondo imaginatively constructed
a far-reaching ministry as a pastoral theologian, eminent lecturer, and
prolific writer on the Latino reality. Father Elizondo's parents owned a
grocery store in San Antonio, where he had spent his childhood. He came
to believe in working outside of, as well as within, the social movements
of the Catholic Church. Elizondo recalls that, in addition to the civil
rights movement led by Dr. Martin Luther King Jr., another great experience was the interracial and ecumenical farm workers movement led
by Cesar Chavez and Dolores Huerta, which had important offshoots in
Texas.[3]

After observing the radical Chicano movement of the 1960s and then
studying in Paris at the Sorbonne, Elizondo decided to use San Antonio
as a base for shaping the emerging Latino church. In San Antonio he
served from 1983 to 1985 as pastor of San Fernando Cathedral, where
he led the *Misa de las Américas*, a live weekly Spanish Mass broadcast over

television throughout the United States and abroad. He has become a leading commentator on the Latino struggles for civil rights and identity in the United States and in recent years has taught theology at the University of Notre Dame. His many thoughtful and innovative writings helped him earn the unofficial title "Father of U.S. Latino Theology."[4]

Elizondo interprets Catholicism in Latin America and the Southwest through the prism of *mestizaje* (race mixture), beginning with the Spanish conquest and colonization of the Americas. This blending not only took physical forms but also incorporated culture in a dialectical process that, according to Elizondo, reflects universal yearnings for social justice, equality, and ethnic regeneration. His writings interpret the annual celebration of the Guadalupe as "central to the observance of Mexican-American Catholicism in the U.S. and to the future of [its] adherents." The devotion to Guadalupe and its *mestizo* spirituality "is the collective affirmation and cultic celebration of life in spite of the multiple threats of death." It remains not only an annual observance but an immanent presence in Mexican-American households. Elizondo views Latino life as a pilgrimage marked by both suffering and celebration.[5]

Both as a pastor and as a writer, Elizondo has helped Mexican Americans overcome negative experiences of the institutional church. Elizondo's theology has evolved out of his "love/disgust relationship with [the] Catholic Church." He discovered as a young priest "that great numbers of our Mexican-American people had a very negative experience of church and had to rely entirely on the popular faith expressions of our tradition, for they could not rely on the services of the institutional Church."[6] Latino theology in the United States had always focused on the strong ethnic dimensions of religiosity. Elizondo's pastoral theology became crucial in defining *mestizaje* as transcending traditional racial and ethnic hierarchies and signifying an evolving hemispheric panethnicity—a commonality among Latin Americans and Latinos—with Marian devotion embodied in the central symbol of the Virgin of Guadalupe. By contrast, Latin American liberation theology usually involved political struggles and placed clergy as spokespersons for opposition movements against oppressive regimes. It offered solidarity with the poor as its mainstay, rather than ethnicity as defined within the context of Mexican Americans and other Latinos in the United States, where religious pluralism and church-state separation were the rule.[7]

Another internationally known and highly regarded Catholic leader, Patricio Flores, was born in Ganado, Texas, to a migrant family. In 1970 he became the first priest of Mexican descent to be ordained a bishop in the

United States; he rose to become San Antonio archbishop in 1976. After studying at St. Mary's Seminary in Houston and later becoming a pastor, Flores worked under Lucey in the Bishops' Committee for the Spanish-Speaking and the cursillo movement. In 1971, as auxiliary bishop, Flores became involved in the farm workers' unionization struggle, and he soon devoted considerable time to the urban struggles of Mexican Americans. Flores played a vital role in secular as well as religious affairs and served as chair of the Texas Advisory Committee of the U.S. Commission on Civil Rights.

Archbishop Flores came to view the Church as a vehicle for making contact across ethnic lines and opening up communication. For instance, Bishop Flores promoted the idea of enriching the liturgy with music and movements clearly identifiable with the local Latino community. In November 1970, Flores met in Miami with members of the Cuban Movimiento Familiar Cristiano. In 1985, he and several other American prelates became the first U.S. archbishops to travel to Cuba since 1959. The group appealed to Castro to release Cuba's political prisoners and to allow foreign priests to conduct ministry on the island.[8]

Archbishop José H. Gomez, born in Monterrey, Mexico, ordained a priest of the Opus Dei Prelature in 1978, was appointed by Pope John Paul II to lead the Archdiocese of San Antonio in December 2004, replacing Flores. He had been serving as the auxiliary bishop of the Archdiocese of Denver. In 1991, Archbishop Gomez had become a regional representative of the National Association of Hispanic Priests (ANSH). He became president of the group in 1995 and was executive director from 1999 to 2001. ANSH seeks to strengthen fraternity among the twenty-four hundred Latino priests in the United States and to communicate the faith effectively among diverse Latino congregations. From 1998 to 2000, Gomez was on the steering committee for Encuentro 2000, a national celebration in Los Angeles that was sponsored by the U.S. Conference of Catholic Bishops.[9]

Padres Asociados para Derechos Religiosos, Educativos y Sociales

While working out of San Antonio in the early 1970s, both Elizondo and Flores worked on behalf of several important organizations that arose to improve conditions in San Antonio, throughout Texas, and well beyond. Prominent among these was PADRES—an acronym for Padres Asociados para Derechos Religiosos, Educativos y Sociales (Priests Associated for Religious, Educational, and Social Rights). PADRES was formed in

October 1969 when Ralph Ruiz, a San Antonio priest who directed the Inner City Apostolate, summoned dozens of Mexican-American priests, mostly from Texas, New Mexico, Arizona, and Colorado, for a meeting in San Antonio.[10] They convened their first national congress several months later, in February 1970, in Tucson, Arizona. The PADRES mission statement indicated a concern for "an effective pastoral ministry among the vast numbers of Mexican Americans, and other Spanish-speaking people, who have heretofore been traditionally Catholic but are now rapidly becoming dissatisfied with the Church and are leaving in large numbers."[11]

The group refrained from challenging basic church doctrines, such as restriction of ordination to males, and adopted instead a reformist mantle more focused on practices and minority representation under Father Ruiz, who was elected the first national chairman.[12] PADRES voted to actively seek the appointment of Mexican-American bishops in Spanish-speaking dioceses, to reevaluate existing educational programs for Mexican Americans, to fight to keep Catholic schools open in the barrios, and to work for church loan funds for the poor. In the wake of the successful founding meeting, Father Henry Casso, the organization's new national press officer, exulted that the Mexican-American people of the United States were "on the move" and that Catholic leaders were "now jet-propelled and [no longer] just slow freight for La Raza." Casso declared, "The Catholic Church can get on or get off the train. All La Raza asks is [not to] get in the way because we are coming through."[13]

Since its inception, its members publicly supported UFW boycotts. In 1973, some of the organization's members got themselves arrested alongside farm workers while picketing in California's San Joaquin Valley. The following year, PADRES extended associate membership to non-Mexican-American priests with limited voting rights, while lay groups denounced the group as representing their interests inadequately. Throughout the 1970s PADRES remained involved in secular issues as well, such as exposing instances of police brutality. PADRES worked hard to groom Mexican-American bishops and rightly took some of the credit for the appointment of Santa Fe archbishop Roberto Sanchez in 1974 and others subsequently. It peaked at about 350 priests, brothers, and deacons working in Latino ministries throughout the nation. Its limited financial base, however, eventually resulted in loss of salaries and personnel, which contributed to its 1989 amalgamation, along with other groups, into a group called Sacerdotes Hispanos.[14]

During the summer of 1970 a woman religious, Sister Gregoria

Ortega, contacted Edmundo Rodriguez, Jesuit pastor of Our Lady of
Guadalupe Church in San Antonio, who had helped to organize PA-
DRES. Rodriguez supported her effort to organize fifty Mexican-American religious women into Las Hermanas (The Sisters) in April 1971. San
Antonio-born Sister Gloria Gallardo, who belonged to a predominantly
Irish-American religious community, the Holy Ghost Sisters, led the development of Las Hermanas as an organization that developed a broader
ethnic base than PADRES, including not only people of Mexican origin but Spaniards, Puerto Ricans, Cubans, and Latin American sisters. In
1975, unlike its male counterpart, Las Hermanas decided to welcome laypeople who wanted to join, and by 1979 laypeople predominated, helping
to replace the many women who chose to leave the religious life during
these years.[15]

The Mexican American Cultural Center (MACC)

In February 1971, participants in a PADRES retreat and workshop in
Santa Fe proposed the formation of a cultural center with a strong pastoral orientation. Within three months, they held a symposium in San
Antonio attended by Latin American thinkers such as theologian Edgar
Beltrán. Gustavo Gutiérrez, known as the intellectual father of liberation
theology, made Elizondo and others aware of the theological category of
"the poor."[16] The idea of a center dedicated to the preparation of personnel, programs, and materials for the Spanish-speaking Catholics in the
United States was not something totally new, having dated back to the
tenure of Archbishop Lucey. The center would not limit itself to religious
activities but would remain concerned "with every aspect of life which
would advance the liberation and development of the Mexican American
people living in the United States." Archbishop Francis Furey, Lucey's
successor, offered facilities on the Assumption Seminary Campus for the
headquarters of the center, whose functions would include research, education, leadership development, and publications.[17]

Elizondo, along with members of PADRES and Las Hermanas, took
the lead in starting the Mexican American Cultural Center (MACC) "to
begin a serious, critical, and creative process of the theological reflection
from within the living faith tradition of our people."[18] Father Elizondo
served as president and was at the helm from 1972 until 1987. In 1972
MACC opened as a national training and research center that combined
the lessons learned from Latin American liberation theology with analysis of the U.S. Latino experience. It built on earlier advocacy for Latino
ministry and concern for Mexican-American civil rights, affiliated with

Archbishop Patricio Flores and Father Virgilio Elizondo at MACC Night with a Mariachi Band, ca. late 1980s (Reverend Virgil Elizondo Research Center, Mexican American Cultural Center)

various universities, and made itself a necessary stopping point for Latin American theologians.

Language learning became an integral component of the total cultural training. There were also informal meetings and lectures, liturgies, films, and visits to places of historical and cultural interest, including the San Antonio missions. MACC sponsored some twelve different programs, ranging from preparation of missionaries to Latin America to community and cultural awareness workshops and lectures throughout the United States and Canada. Some one thousand students participated in courses every year at the center, while resident faculty and mobile teams reached another thirty-five thousand people through workshops across the nation. One four-month program targeted Latinos in the United States, especially Mexican Americans, while another program included field experience in Mexico. Leadership training included weekend seminars designed for parish personnel, team ministry, and youth. Classes in popular religiosity focused on the integration of religion and culture into the life of the people.[19]

MACC became the national Catholic center for the development of liturgy for the Spanish-speaking, for the creation of materials of religious education in Spanish, and for training missionaries to Latin America. Its visiting professors from Latin America reflected prevailing currents in Latin American theology and sought to apply them in the distinctive urban settings of the United States. Intensive ten-day seminars conducted by a team from Latin America focused on *comunidades eclesiales de base* (ecclesial base communities). Based on innovations pioneered at MACC, several pastoral institutes sprouted up elsewhere in the United States, including the Southeast Pastoral Institute (SEPI) in 1979, the Midwest Institute for Hispanic Ministry in 1981, and the Northeast Pastoral Institute in 1983, all of which helped promote innovations in the Latino ministry.[20]

To unify the various Latino groups nationally and foster their participation in the ongoing life of the Church, between 1972 and 2000 the Hispanic Affairs Office of the U.S. Catholic Conference conducted four national meetings. These *encuentros* brought together diverse elements of Latino clerical and lay leadership, laying the groundwork for common understanding, yet also revealing cultural and differences among participants. The *encuentros* helped break down barriers among regional and linguistic subgroups and create a common agenda, which proved to be a task as daunting as it had been in specific locales. The participants acknowledged common problems in grooming leadership, especially as Latin American connections weakened over time. One concrete result of the Tercer Encuentro was the National Pastoral Plan for Hispanic Ministry, calling for the evangelization of U.S. Latinos and training leadership in ministry in several areas. It was written by a committee of bishops in consultation with the National Advisory Committee and was accepted by the body of U.S. bishops at a 1987 meeting.[21]

Carlos Rosas, Mexican by birth, was one of the first Latino composers taken by the spirit of the Southwest. His compositions were first sung in San Antonio in 1973 at a Mass for the Sociedades Guadalupanas with Bishop Patricio Flores presiding and with a thousand-voice choir. Rosas' popular-style music is easily learned and sung. In the early 1970s Carlos and Teresa Rosas introduced a *danza de ofertorio* (for the rite of preparation of the altar and gifts) and created catecheses about dance as prayer for both children and adults. Other Rosas contributions were his "Misa de San Juan" (1975) and "Rosas de Tepeyac" (1976). Virgilio Elizondo remembers Archbishop Furey of San Antonio as the first bishop to interpret *Mexican-based styles of dance* as prayers and affirm that they belonged "inside of the Church."[22]

Father Virgilio Elizondo Presenting Plaque to Composer Carlos Rosas at MACC, ca. late 1980s (Reverend Virgil Elizondo Research Center, Mexican American Cultural Center)

Communities Organized for Public Service

The emergence and growth of the Mexican-American middle class over the course of the twentieth century allowed greater ethnic mobility and suburbanization. Father Edmundo Rodriguez guided organizer Ernesto Cortes in setting Communities Organized for Public Service (COPS) in San Antonio. The birth of COPS dates from the big rains of the summer of 1974, when drainage problems finally became intolerable to West Side residents. The group received funding from the Campaign for Human Development, the Archdiocese of San Antonio, and the dues of participating, largely Mexican-American, parishes and congregations. San Antonio parishes consist largely of homeowners whose ancestors settled in the city generations ago and have since created a stable sense of neighborhood identity. San Antonio's very concentrated Mexican settlement, with the middle-class and poor Mexicans historically living in relatively close proximity, meant that San Antonio leaders could tap into deep roots on the overwhelmingly Mexican-American West Side.[23]

COPS become San Antonio's preeminent minority political organization. It focused on the physical improvement of the West Side. Using Alinsky-style organizing strategies, residents mobilized and negotiated with city officials to improve their neighborhoods. COPS exerted strong influence in gaining use of federal Community Development Grants as well as urban renewal funds. As urban environmental scholars David Johnson, Derral Cheatwood, and Benjamin Bradshaw note, "COPS compiled a series of remarkable successes in drainage and street-improvement projects. . . . Dozens of miles of sewer lines, new schools, and a massive flood-control project did more to improve the quality of life among the West Side residents than anything since the federally funded public housing projects of the 1930s."[24]

The Catholic clergy played a large role in financing COPS, but they are lesser players in determining the organization's strategy and tactics., Encouraged by Archbishop Flores and other Mexican-American Catholic leaders, COPS built on existing parish structures. It has conducted highly successful voter registration drives, challenged the local chamber of commerce, and channeled federal grant money directly to the neighborhoods. COPS improved neighborhood living conditions in the West Side barrio, has helped equalize distribution of government services, and has slowed favoritism toward the predominantly Anglo North Side. COPS gained a place at the economic and political bargaining table while militantly defending traditional cultural values. Community organizers want the Church to support their efforts at economic advancement and defend their cultural integrity, while they find in the Church resources for preserving traditional faith and cultural values. Several Tejanas have been elected president of COPS, which grew to over twenty-five largely parish-based chapters in San Antonio. It has influenced the formation of similar organizations in the Southwest, including the successful efforts of Bishop Arzube in Los Angeles's UNO (United Neighborhoods Organization), which began in 1976.[25]

Cursillos and Puerto Rican Identity in New York City

In New York, the cursillo movement, a Spanish product of the 1950s, provided the nucleus of Latino leadership in the archdiocese. This diocesan-wide, citywide movement provided a framework and community to individual *cursillistas*, who returned from their short course to strengthen lay leadership in parishes. Cursillos were attractive because they were a counterpart to the small groups favored by the evangelicals and Pentecostals that had challenged the large, impersonal Catholic parish, the historic

center of the Church's sacramental life and celebrations. Closely following official church directives, cursillistas orient their spiritual reflections
and practices to areas such as devotions, family, and helping individuals
Christianize their environment. The cursillo first came to Brooklyn in
1962. In 1963, the St. Peter's Cursillo Center opened in what had been
the nursing residence for St. Peter's Hospital. By 1967, nearly five thousand Spanish-speaking Catholics had participated in the cursillo.[26]

Under Bishop Bryan J. McEntegart (1957–68), more than fifty parishes in Brooklyn and Queens had developed a significant Latino outreach. The services they offered included job placement, housing assistance, immigration information, and care for the elderly. While the post-
conciliar era saw a decline in some forms of Marian devotion, the immigrant nature of the Brooklyn diocese ensured that Mary would continue to be honored within its various ethnic traditions. In June 1974, the
nation's first diocesan congress for Spanish-speaking Catholics was held
in Brooklyn. Committees were established to study the various needs of
Brooklyn's Latino Catholics: sacramental, educational, social, and pastoral. By 1979, 99 of the diocese's 223 parishes offered Mass in Spanish.
Some 50 percent of all Catholics in Brooklyn and Queens are Latino.
Brooklyn has the seventh largest Latino population of any American diocese. In Brooklyn and Queens, 113 parishes offer services in Spanish to a
diverse and growing Latino population.[27]

By early 1962 a diocesan secretariat for cursillos had been set up in the
archdiocese along the movement's recommended lines, with Spanish Augustinians in control. The cursillo movement served important functions
among individual Latino immigrants in danger of losing their identity as
Latino and Catholic. Because priests associated with the cursillo tended
to be Spaniards or Latin Americans, the movement became an important element in the religious life of continental Puerto Ricans and helped
them develop leadership skills. Cursillos never came to be as important
among other Catholics as among Latinos. The movement succeeded in
keeping Latinos within the Church, though it also led to the development
of parallel structures divided by language and cultural differences.[28]

Separation of the Sacred and the Profane

By the 1970s, El Barrio's area around La Milagrosa was noticeably changing from Puerto Rican to black American. La Milagrosa began to decline
swiftly and was closed in 1978. Holy Agony, though it had never been as
important to the New York Puerto Rican community, remained more
Latino. Today New York Catholicism is still based on the Italian com-

munity, though most parishes are now mixed Italian and Puerto Rican. Virtually every Italian child is enrolled in parochial school, while Puerto Ricans tend to go to public rather than parochial schools. Catholic priests in East Harlem are almost exclusively Italian, with some Irish. In 1959–60 there were fifty-four Protestant churches in East Harlem with Puerto Rican congregations; in fifty of them Spanish was the primary language of the church. Puerto Ricans who were dissatisfied with an integrated parish would naturally tend to vote with their feet rather than to complain to the priests or to archdiocesan authorities, either individually or as a group. They did not feel an urgent need to fight (as did the Poles, for example) for the kind of parish or institutional church that they might prefer. They could just as easily worship at home or join a storefront church led by a Puerto Rican Protestant minister. Unlike the "mainline" churches, the overwhelming majority of the Protestants with whom Puerto Ricans came in contact with tended to be bitterly anti-Catholic.[29]

Efforts on the part of U.S. priests and other religious leaders to transmit their theology of secular involvement to the Puerto Rican community were on the whole not successful. While most Puerto Ricans like to separate the sacred from the secular, radical groups like the Young Lords, a street group favoring Puerto Rican independence and composed largely of second-generation Puerto Ricans, struggled along with, and sometimes against, barrio Protestant churches. They believed that churches should engage in social action. In 1969 the Young Lords took over the First Spanish Methodist Church in East Harlem, renaming it the People's Church and launching a free lunch program. In 1971, they interrupted the annual Puerto Rican Day Parade, denouncing the views of the island's governor, Luis Ferré, whose election in 1968 marked the ascendance of the Partido Nuevo Progresista (PNP), the island's modern statehood party. The Young Lords opposed a system that they claimed would never offer more than the illusion of change and democracy to colonized peoples such as Puerto Ricans in New York.[30]

Imbued with the spirit of political activism and reform, the new generation of clergy no longer sought to understand and preserve the migrants' religious tradition. The generation of priests and seminarians trained in Ponce tended to understand their vocation in terms of social action and of building a community of the oppressed on the periphery of the official church, a community that would leave behind the trammels and divisions of the past and move on to create a liberated future. This, together with the desire to qualify for funding under the War on Poverty, led to a very

Stations of the Cross Procession, New York City's Lower East Side, 1991
(Martha Cooper/City Lore)

serious downplaying of both the denominational Catholic aspects and
the culturally Puerto Rican aspects of the Spanish apostolate. The new
generation of clergy simply changed the forms of Spanish ministry and
largely failed to connect to Puerto Ricans or to understand their spirituality. The popular piety of the Caribbean region is rurally based. Except
for Christmas, old communal feasts fade away when Puerto Ricans move
to a new urban environment.[31]

Puerto Rican opposition to introducing politics into religion was evident at St. Bridgid's Church on Manhattan's Lower East Side. Priests
brought the Spanish Mass out of the basement into the main church,
added folk instruments and Puerto Rican songs, and made many innovations in parish liturgy and festival life of the parish. Since the early 1960s,
St. Bridgid's had been performing an outdoor Stations of the Cross procession on Good Friday each year, reenacting Christ's journey through
Jerusalem on his way to the crucifixion. Around 1989 participants began
to enact each of the stations in front of problem areas such as a controversial health clinic, a deteriorating public school, a street corner where
drugs were sold, a luxury condominium, and a park associated with danger and vice. Puerto Ricans thereupon lost interest in that parish. They

favored religious solidarity but not, according to one observer, public social transformation. They similarly declined involvement in the Sanctuary
movement that offered church asylum to Central American refugees.[32]

In the wake of Vatican II, Ponce-trained priests and religious became
the vanguard of the archdiocese. Monsignor Robert Fox defined a pan-
Latino constituency partly to avoid having to coordinate separate cel-
ebrations of patron saints for each Catholic ethnic group. He favored a
"Latino" (or "Hispanic") umbrella approach to with a wide array of Latin
American immigrants. This was evident particularly in his alteration of
the San Juan Fiesta, which had been a staple of archdiocesan outreach
since the early 1950s but was beginning to lose the interest of local clergy.
Fox, who in 1962 assumed directorship of the Archdiocesan Office for
Spanish Catholic Action (later renamed the Office of Spanish Community
Action), supplanted what had been a strictly Puerto Rican festival with pan-
Latino events having strong social justice, even liberationist, overtones.[33]

Puerto Ricans, meanwhile, tended to prefer a more nationally cohesive event, and the annual Puerto Rican Day Parade up Fifth Avenue
took on greater importance as an ethnic and purely secular event. By the
late 1950s, Puerto Rican leaders had broken away from the larger Latin
American group and formed their own parade for Puerto Ricans, a decision supported by Governor Luis Muñoz Marín. Island political dignitaries, including mayors of the many municipalities and others, traveled
to New York every June to march in the affair, which became a display
of cultural pride with political overtones as migrants began to offer up
electoral candidates in the 1960s and beyond. The old San Juan fiesta still
survives, attended by about a thousand people every year, but its role as
the premier event in the New York Puerto Rican community has been
supplanted.[34]

The liberal priests of the late 1960s found Puerto Rican religion de-
fective because it was not centered on social action. Efforts on the part
of American priests and religious to transmit their theology of secular
involvement to the Puerto Rican community were on the whole not successful. Unlike Mexicans, Puerto Ricans prefer to pursue secular goals
in a purely secular spirit, keeping religion out of them, and to pursue
religious experience in frankly "sacral" terms. Efforts to combine the two
seem to make them uncomfortable and tend to meet passive resistance.
The theology of liberation is considered especially threatening among
Charismatics.

From the Church's perspective, preventing disillusionment with Catholicism and flight to other religious communities was a critical task.

Fiesta San Juan 2004, Battery Park, New York City (Edmee Quiñones)

Latino ministry became a most attractive alternative ministry for those who found less and less meaning and satisfaction in the traditional setting of the parish or the parochial school. They ended by trying to transform both groups of traditional Latinos—Puerto Rican and Mexican—into a new creation, oriented to the future rather than the past, based on common oppression more than a shared culture.[35]

Notes theologian Jaime Vidal, "Not only do we have a situation of a Catholic elite encountering popular Catholicism, but the elite in question belongs to one culture and the people to another. Thus we have to deal not only with the temptation to condescension and paternalism, but also with feelings of suspicion and unfamiliarity; with facile assumptions that certain expressions of faith are unacceptable although in fact they may be no worse than expressions which we easily accept or tolerate in our own cultural form of Catholicism."[36] In national parishes Italians, Germans, Poles, and other groups went through a gradual process of collective and often unconscious discernment about what to keep, what to discard, and what to modify in their ethnic heritage. So they were able to integrate into the U.S. church and the larger society on terms they found acceptable and at a pace they found comfortable. This contrasts with the experience of Puerto Ricans, who, Vidal points out, "identify with their cultural expressions of Catholicism more than with the Church as an institution."[37]

Within a year after the Constitution on the Sacred Liturgy was published, Father William Loperena, a Puerto Rican, wrote *Misa Jíbara*, the Roman Mass set to the popular musical rhythms of Puerto Rico. The word *jíbara* refers to the people of the *campo*, the rural sections of the island. This Mass found favor within the general community, though Cardinal Francis Spellman opposed it as too ethnocentric and as being influenced by liberation theology. Lower down the hierarchy, as part of the Spanish-speaking Apostolate Office under the more radical Father Fox, a Spaniard named Angel Perez wrote *Misa Hispana*, an attempt to synthesize the musical styles of the various Latino groups of New York City.[38]

The Church, Puerto Ricans, and Housing in New York

Urban redevelopment and slum clearance programs can radically diminish or even destroy the Puerto Rican character of a neighborhood. A small colony of Puerto Ricans began to move from Manhattan to the lower Bronx in the late 1920s. This marked the beginning of a settlement that, within fifty years, would rise to staggering proportions. Like earlier groups, Puerto Ricans first established large footholds in Manhattan, and there Latinos created organizations to represent their general interests and to deflect prejudicial attitudes and actions. The lower Bronx, a favored site among upwardly mobile former Harlem and East Harlem residents through the late 1940s, contained a large concentration of Puerto Ricans in the 1950s and 1960s. In 1959, although exhibiting signs of urban decay, the area still served its historic function as a site of second settlement, attracting more than two hundred Puerto Rican families who bought homes in the Hunts Point section, where there was more recreational space. On the whole, according to one 1959 study, "the Puerto Ricans of the Bronx seem to exemplify progress in assimilation, and the value to a borough of the sharing of activity by varied cultural groups."[39]

About twelve high-rise low-income housing projects were built in the Bronx between 1960 and 1965. Many Puerto Ricans came to live in these projects, but the sense of community in the area began to erode. This was in large part due to the projects' imposing and impersonal physical layout, which lacked streets and often separated parish from parishioners. The projects also concentrated the poor while leaving room for few homeowners. Few stable social networks remained intact, least of all Catholic parishes. An arson epidemic caused a further downward social spiral in the 1970s, making the borough, in academic, political, and other circles, a symbol of urban destruction. Somewhat surprisingly, however, in the following decades it came to signify rebirth, and Catholic churches in the borough played a big role in the resurrection.[40]

Working against greater dispersal of the migrant community, however, was the fact that, unlike the typical immigrants of previous generations, the rising Puerto Rican middle class tended to remain on the island. In the 1960s, the pace of emigration slowed, and return migration increased markedly, especially among the second generation. Migrants who had moved into the middle class during their working career on the continent could more easily return to their island. Many professionals and others who had established themselves in the prewar migration did avail themselves of opportunities to relocate to uptown Manhattan and other upscale surroundings, but for others, education and employment difficulties often dampened prospects for movement out of barrios.[41]

The economic situation in the Bronx took a sharp turn for the worse, and perceptions of Puerto Ricans as a menace to previously stable neighborhoods increased in the late 1960s and 1970s. As the Bronx filled up with troubled neighborhoods during these decades, middle-class Catholic and Jewish residents departed en masse to the suburbs and to other outer boroughs. Rapidly moving slums destroyed whole South Bronx neighborhoods, giving them a "bombed-out" appearance that evoked analogies to war zones. Arson epidemics resulted in a further, massive dispersal of the Puerto Rican population,. who fled as large areas became uninhabitable. Eventually the burning down of housing stock subsided as the available targets became fewer. But instead of the tenement hulks' being left as lasting monuments to the dreadful time, and despite widespread apocalyptic predictions, the area was effectively rebuilt, allowing subsequent generations of New Yorkers, even in the South Bronx, to enjoy a better urban environment with more congenial surroundings and better housing during the 1990s.[42]

Faced with the devastation of the South Bronx, parish networks rose as a means of neighborhood conservation, and these efforts dovetailed with those of clergy assisting Puerto Ricans in the expanding barrios. The Southeast Bronx Community Organization (SEBCO) began in 1968 as part of the South Bronx Model Cities program, led by Hunts Point activist and Catholic priest Louis Gigante. In the fall of 1976, 360 SEBCO apartment house units were completed in nine buildings around the corner from Gigante's St. Athanasius Church. Father Gigante's well-organized renovations proceeded and helped rebuild the South Bronx, and the Catholic Church quietly emerged as the institution most committed to preserving and resurrecting the borough while keeping parishes and schools open. Although most people moved from the ravaged areas of the South Bronx to other parts of the borough or elsewhere, some occupied their abandoned buildings, rehabilitated them, and ended up owning them cooperatively. Gigante played a large part in developing the Tiffany Street houses under a low-interest subsidy program, after which they were sold to families.[43]

Highly professional community groups worked within the system to promote the borough's resurgence. In 1974, twelve tenant and block associations and sixteen Catholic parishes north of the Cross Bronx Expressway founded the Northwest Bronx Community and Clergy Coalition. This group owed its original leadership to the planning of Paul Brant, a Jesuit scholastic studying for the priesthood and working at Fordham University as a philosophy professor. It came to represent about 400,000 residents, or one-quarter of the borough. An unusually diverse middle-class Catholic coalition, it brought Latinos together with Irish and Italians who predominated north of Fordham Road, focusing on preservation of housing stock by stimulating the formation of hundreds of tenant associations, as well as numerous block associations and anticrime patrols, and prodding banks into making community development loans with housing components.[44]

The Archdiocese of New York invested millions of dollars in loans to help low-income residents get mortgages to finance the building and refurbishing of hundreds of housing units in the South Bronx. The whole institutional structure of the Church, including buildings, parochial schools, and social centers, depended on maintenance of a strong economic base for the borough. If the northwest Bronx were to become like the South Bronx, the Archdiocese of New York stood to lose thousands of its solid middle- and working-class members and the contributions they made annually to the Church's operating budget.[45]

Soon after its founding, the Northwest Bronx Community and Clergy Coalition began to concentrate its efforts on the issue of redlining, whereby entire neighborhoods were blacklisted for mortgages regardless of the merit of individual applicants. By 1980 the coalition had signed a formal agreement with four local savings banks and other financial institutions to help finance rehabilitation for hundreds of apartment buildings on which they held mortgages, so as to preserve the northwest Bronx real estate market and reverse the trend toward deterioration that had afflicted the South Bronx. The coalition employed neighborhood associations, each with a full-time youth organizer and other staffers, to oversee some twelve hundred buildings. It organized picketing of the offices and homes of city officials, bank directors, and insurance executives, often forcing them to comply with housing codes, fair lending laws, and "good repair" clauses to allow the renovation of abandoned structures.[46]

In June 1982, Bishop Francis J. Mugavero (1968–90) and several other religious leaders met with Mayor Edward I. Koch to request his support for the Nehemiah Homes Project, a neighborhood revitalization project in the East New York and Brownsville sections of Brooklyn. This project was an interfaith building project sponsored by East Brooklyn churches. Its goal was to build five thousand moderately priced homes with low-interest mortgages for families in what were arguably Brooklyn's most poverty-stricken neighborhoods. Under Mugavero, the Diocese of Brooklyn was the largest contributor, donating $2.5 million to the project. The Nehemiah Project garnered national attention as a model for enabling disadvantaged people to obtain affordable housing for themselves and their families.[47]

Given the almost empty German or Polish or Italian parish churches in the areas where Puerto Ricans were settling, the archdiocese refrained from building new churches for them. The argument for the integrated parish for Puerto Ricans apparently was that as the children and grandchildren of the original immigrants assimilated into U.S. society, they tended to lose their Spanish language and move out of ethnic neighborhoods into the suburbs or other neighborhoods, where they would attend the local territorial parish.[48] Thus Puerto Ricans became the city's first Catholics to be integrated into existing territorial parishes, instead of into national parishes established for them. Their migration was also unique in that they were the first Catholics to arrive directly from a mission territory. The urban parishes were not geared toward a missionary apostolate.[49]

The Dominican Struggle

New York City's Puerto Rican population rose from about 70,000 in 1940 to 246,000 in 1950, including 58,000 mainland-born. By 1960, there were 613,000, with 183,000 born on the continent. Return migration to Puerto Rico, especially among second-generation New Yorkers, increased markedly after 1950. Taken as a whole, the Puerto Rican experience paved the way for New York's further "Latinization," although the experiences of groups arriving in large numbers after 1965 differed greatly in many respects, a fact seized upon by archdiocesan leaders.[50]

Father Robert Stern was appointed to succeed Fox in the fall of 1969.

Stern had been among the newly ordained priests who studied at Puerto Rico's Institute of Intercultural Communication. During the 1970s, Dominicans replaced Cubans as the second most numerous Latino group in the Archdiocese of New York, and they dramatically increased their presence in ensuing decades. Stern sought to give the newest Catholics special attention and to repeat for them what had been previously attempted for the Puerto Ricans. In 1970 he journeyed to the Dominican Republic and met with some of the bishops to discuss possibilities for greater collaboration between the Archdiocese of Santo Domingo and the Archdiocese of New York in the training of seminarians. In January 1973, the first public celebration of the feast of Our Lady of Altagracia, patroness of the Dominican Republic, was held at St. Patrick's Cathedral, It was attended by about four thousand people, including Terence Cardinal Cooke, who had replaced Spellman after his death in 1967. Cooke presided over a special liturgical celebration for the archbishop of Santo Domingo and lower clergy from the homeland.[51]

In New York City, Dominicans found a Catholic Church that had been sensitized to the needs of Spanish speakers by decades of pastoral outreach directed toward the earlier mass migration of Puerto Ricans. Unlike the Puerto Ricans, Dominicans did not have to fight to have Mass celebrated in Spanish, organize parish agencies and church-based associations for their brand of Catholicism, or struggle to gain recognition as a group different from earlier immigrants. As special celebrations were instituted in the early 1970s, the unique character of Dominican Catholicism was confirmed. Early in the 1970s, some elderly Puerto Rican parishioners of Our Lady of Sorrows called for greater attention to the special needs of the Dominican community. Since the Puerto Ricans were respected in the Church, the pastor responded by allowing Dominicans to organize some social and religious activities separately from those of the existing Puerto Rican groups. Puerto Ricans had been the first to organize a youth group at Our Lady of Sorrows Church, but Dominicans were unable to participate due to language barriers. The Dominican youth decided to form Juventud en Acción Cristiana (JAC, Christian Youth in Action), patterned after the movement in the Dominican Republic. The JAC organized weekend retreats, conferences, and seminars and helped to launch the annual celebration citywide of the patroness. The group joined the cursillos and other church movements.[52]

Puerto Ricans had been received into an integrated church often staffed by non-Latino Spanish-speaking priests fostering assimilation into the already established Irish, Italian, or Polish parish. Masses and services were provided in Spanish, but often in a cold basement or a hallway. *Misas cantadas* (sung Masses) and the reenactment of biblical passages inside the main chapel of the church also became important elements of the religious celebration. During the 1980s, a number of churches located in the Dominican neighborhood became the equivalent of national parishes for the Dominican population.[53]

In the case of Dominican immigrants, the transnational training of clergy created social networks extending back to the island, enhancing cultural understanding and improving rapport between clergy and parishioners, both in the homeland and in the United States. As a result, currently several Dominican-based priests regularly visit New York and Boston during "high-demand" periods such as Holy Week, or they may substitute for vacationing or departing clergy. Differences among parish experiences become evident in home-based baptismal practices, known in the rural Dominican Republic as pouring on water (*echando agua*), to protect a newborn until a priest arrives. In the United States, Dominicans choose friends as godparents with an eye toward their enhancing family resources through financial support for the children.[54]

Anglo priests who have visited parishes in the Dominican Republic said that Masses were livelier than those occurring within the more "reserved, private, and more individualistic" religious culture of U.S. parishes. They were more communal, with much music and wider participation, and overflowed with young children, who begin attending church earlier in life than do children in the North. Convergence in religious practices allowed migrants and nonmigrants to participate almost seamlessly (and, increasingly, simultaneously) in the religious life of both settings, making the Church a powerful institutional arena for asserting dual membership. Religious differences among Latin American-origin groups in U.S. cities of course reflect heterogeneity, accentuated by regional variations within the contemporary metropolis.[55]

The Rise of Pan-Latino Religious Identity

An important step toward strengthening the sense of a pan-Latino identity was the 1970 relocation of the Office for the Spanish-Speaking from Texas to Washington, D.C., where it became part of the complex of national Catholic offices now known as the U.S. Conference of Catholic Bishops (USCCB). Conflict emerged, however, over what type of ministry should be encouraged in the Latino community. Since the 1960s, Latino Catholics have gradually created a church within the Church. That development is similar to the German Catholic experience in the United

States in the late nineteenth century, when there emerged greater self-awareness among Germans that not only were they different from the rest of U.S. Catholics but also had special needs and concerns that had to be addressed. In the twentieth century Latinos were the one group that has succeeded in forming a national church within the Church, with national organizations, offices, conventions, and institutes. It is not centrally organized or controlled but is informally held together by a common concern—the welfare of Latino Catholics.[56]

In 1901, two years after the annexation of several of the Bronx's villages into greater New York, St. Jerome's Church in the Bronx's Mott Haven neighborhood, with nine thousand members. was the largest of that area's four German Catholic churches. Over a century later, Mexican parishioners, most of them first-generation immigrants, made up about 80 percent of St. Jerome's members. Like other parishes, it faced ongoing struggles in ministering to new arrivals who are reluctant to attend regularly and participate in parish life and unprepared to assume traditional responsibilities of financial stewardship. The greater New York City region offers a new and revealing model for Mexicanos, despite their relatively recent arrival there.[57]

The first Mexican communities in New York date to the mid to late 1920s, when Mexican immigration brought several thousand mostly industrial workers. Many immigrants had crossed the border into Texas as unskilled workers and then wandered to New York via the Midwest. Such odysseys frequently lasted several years, passing through Ford automobile assembly plants and the Chicago stockyards before stopping in New York's machine shops. The immigrants established an organization, the Mutualista Obrera Mexicana (Mexican Workers Mutual Aid Society), in 1932 in East Harlem. By the mid-1930s some 250 members (out of a city-wide total of close to 3,000) commemorated Mexican national holidays and went on summer country picnics. By 1927, after a sizable local influx of Mexican immigrants, a new marble altar, with a picture of Our Lady of Guadalupe above it, was consecrated at the Lower Manhattan church of the same name. Shortly thereafter a group of Mexican women donated $780 for a stained-glass window of the apparition of Our Lady to Juan Diego, and it was placed over the church's main entrance, marking the "Mexicanization" of Our Lady of Guadalupe Church now that several thousand Mexican industrial workers lived in New York.[58]

New York City's Mexican population more than tripled during the 1990s to 187,000, accounting for approximately 13 percent of the city's Latino population and making Mexicans the third largest Latino group.

Including the larger metropolitan region, their numbers approached half a million. Contemporary Mexican immigration—mostly undocumented—has coincided with economic decline in Mexico. Mexicans have tended to settle in El Barrio and the Upper West Side in Manhattan, in countless locations in the Bronx, Brooklyn, and Queens, and in suburban Long Island and Westchester County. Mexican migrants have settled disproportionately in existing Latino areas but also among a variety of other ethnic groups. Within the New York context, ethnicity has served to set Mexicans apart not only from whites but also from African Americans and Puerto Ricans. Like many other Latin Americans living in New York City, while immigrants almost uniformly reject the Latino label, second-generation Mexican Americans grudgingly expand definitions of their Mexican identity to include the pan-Latino ethnic concept.[59]

By 2000, the 2,161,000 Latinos constituted just over one-fourth of New York City's population. There were large percentages in some of the boroughs, ranging from almost one-half in the Bronx to about a quarter each in Manhattan, Queens, and Brooklyn and 12 percent on Staten Island. Catholic leadership, both non-Latino and Latino, has struggled to keep pace with population growth and dispersal. *Comités guadalupanos*—organizations responsible for the presentation of the annual December Guadalupe celebration—are small groups of Mexican Catholics, often hailing from the same village in the states of Puebla, Guerrero, or Oaxaca, which hold regular meetings at members' homes to plan the festivities.[60]

Brother Joel Magallán Reyes, sent by the Mexican Jesuits in May 1996 to conduct a diagnostic study of Mexicans in New York, began to develop a support network for New York's Mexicans, visiting local parishes and inviting existing groups to collaborate for a common good. Guadalupe committees became so prominent that they prompted local Catholic priests to look for guidance from Cardinal John O'Connor. In November 1997, he granted them permission to open an office in lower Manhattan. With the help of Magallán, forty Guadalupan committees formed the Asociación Tepeyac de Nueva York, a transparish lay network.

Migration from the Mixteca region of southern Mexico started later than migration from other traditional sending areas in Mexico and was directed to New York rather than the West Coast. About 1990, people from a small farming community in the Mixteca region began running an *antorcha* (literally "torch," in this case meaning relay race) and celebrating a feast in a New York church to coincide with the feast of the town's patron saint. By contributing financially and viewing videotapes of events in the homeland, such as the Feast of Padre Jesús, migrants in New York actively participate in the public life of their hometowns.[61]

New York's 2002 Antorcha Guadalupana took this practice to a much higher level. It began in Mexico City's Basilica de Guadalupe in October. When the Carrera Antorcha Guadalupana Mexico–New York arrived in the town of Buena Vista, Guerrero, the group of forty-two runners was received by dozens of faithful. After an early evening Mass and a speech explaining the significance of the antorcha, the city held a festival. The following morning, more than sixty runners set off to cover the eighty kilometers to the next city, where the torch rested in the local parish overnight. Running became an act of devotion to one's hometown as well as to Guadalupe. Runners proceeded to cross the U.S.-Mexico border and wind up the Atlantic coast, passing through thirty-five cities before reaching New York on December 12, the Feast of the Virgin of Guadalupe. Rallies and Masses were held that day at local churches as well as at St. Patrick's Cathedral.[62]

The organizational structure and decision-making process of Asociación Tepeyac were designed to facilitate the development of grassroots leadership while addressing social inequities, particularly among undocumented Mexican immigrants. Cardinal O'Connor provided a former convent on West Fourteenth Street off Eighth Avenue for the group to use, and Catholic Charities provided financing. Tepeyac, which enjoys support from some Protestant evangelical organizations as well, provides English classes and social services for Mexicans and other Latinos. It runs a summer soccer program for children and offers language and computer training workshops for youth and adults alike. Despite Tepeyac's growing fame and popularity, some parish priests regard the association with ambivalence, believing that its secular activities divert focus away from the parish community.[63]

Mexican immigrants buy property, build houses, start businesses, marry, and influence political developments in their home society, yet they remain simultaneously involved in building lives in New York. Today's immigrants arrive more culturally attuned to the United States than were their counterparts a century ago. As in the past, however, some groups are likely to be more transnational than others, with transnational connections and activities that are more extensive, frequent, and wide ranging. Latino newcomers have become increasingly visible on suburban streets, in shopping malls, and as *esquineros* (day laborers), which has created conflicts with longtime residents who prefer to maintain residential exclusivity reminiscent of bygone eras. The massive influx of poor, undereducated, and highly visible immigrants on sidewalks and in shopping malls reflects the transfer of jobs from the cities to the suburbs. Between 1980 and 1990, for example, 660,000 jobs were created in suburban counties while the city's job market increased by only 212,000.[64]

In addition to Tepeyac, Mexican immigrants have made their mark on New York's Catholic landscape in other ways. In 2003, the predominantly Mexican parish of Our Lady of Guadalupe Church, a religious landmark for Manhattan Latinos in Greenwich Village since the early twentieth century, consolidated with St. Bernard's Church a block away. St. Bernard's smaller congregation consisted of Puerto Ricans and Cubans from the Chelsea neighborhood and elderly non-Latino residents. The renamed church, Our Lady of Guadalupe at St. Bernard's, has been remodeled to make it more attractive to Mexican worshipers. A painting of Guadalupe rests in front of a mosaic portrait of St. Bernard, while paintings of angels behind the altar were replaced with murals depicting Juan Diego, an apparition of the Virgin, and the Basilica of Guadalupe in Mexico City.[65]

Latinos now represent 10 percent of the population of Long Island's Nassau County, 11 percent in Long Island's Suffolk County, and 16 percent in suburban Westchester County. Puerto Ricans had begun to move to Long Island in small numbers after World War II. Cubans joined them in the 1960s and 1970s, and in the 1980s Dominicans, Salvadorans, and many others from Latin America made their homes on the metropolitan fringe. Peruvians, Chileans, and Colombians in the region have tended to come from the more educated urban working class. Interestingly, working-class Salvadorans in "ethnic enclaves" on Long Island's North Shore tended to gather in the back of churches, while South Americans were almost indistinguishable from the Italian ethnics, often entering from the front, in full view of the rest of the congregation, and sitting in the front of the sanctuary as well.[66]

The first Latinos to settle in Long Island, working-class Puerto Rican migrants, typically resisted integration into suburban Catholic churches. It remains unclear to what extent newer suburban Latinos, such as the more than 100,000 Salvadorans on Long Island, will develop distinctive parish communities, merge with other suburbanites, or seek interethnic federations within the metropolis and across the nation. The village of Hempstead in central Nassau County witnessed a dramatic influx of Salvadorans in the 1980s and 1990s. In collaboration with CARECEN, a Central American refugee center, Our Lady of Loretto Parish played an active part in assisting Latinos, particularly Sal-

vadorans, who had no documents to appeal for legalization. The church
celebrates the anniversaries of Archbishop Oscar Romero and of others
assassinated in El Salvador. The local Hispanic Ministry, meanwhile, em-
ploys a deacon as vicar for members of all Latino groups.[67]

From Ethnic to Transnational Social Worlds

The new immigrant church in the United States often maintains contacts
with homeland parishes, even in the second generation. As anthropologist Nancy Foner points out, "Modern technology, the new global economy and culture, and new laws and political arrangements combined to
produce transnational connections that differ in fundamental ways from
those maintained by immigrants a century ago." Presently, however, social scientists must guard against overemphasizing transnationalism and
minimizing the extent to which contemporary immigrants "become
American" and undergo changes in behavior and outlook in response to
circumstances in this country.[68]

In her study of the Corona neighborhood in Queens, New York City,
sociologist Milagros Ricourt detected an emerging neighborhood Latino
"pan-ethnicity" based on a common language. Various church activities
served to acknowledge the presence and activities of several ethnic subgroups. Latinos readily interacted, moreover, with non-Spanish-speaking ethnics in cooperative institutional ventures, as lectors, procession
organizers, and program directors. When they dominated their own parishes, Latinos reached out to surrounding parishes, facilitating adaptation
to new neighborhoods. Latino parishioners readily shared their church
with Italian ethnics active in block and civic associations, the community
board, and political endeavors.[69]

Religious contrasts become especially revealing as Catholicism developed not only as a vehicle for urban reform but as part of transnational
economic and cultural survival strategies to benefit both migrants and
their homeland. Local or "congregational" units, particularly the Roman
Catholic parish, became "reterritorialized" and redefined to meet new
contingencies. The pluralism of U.S. society, coupled with constitution-
ally guaranteed religious freedom, provided the framework for social innovations and power shifts. The rapid growth and transnational ties (religious, economic, and other) of Mexican immigrants prompted the New
York Archdiocese to favor them as a sort of convenient homogenizing influence over the complexity of endless Latino immigrants. For example,
the archdiocese supports the Tepeyac organization and likes the idea, also

favored by the late Pope John Paul II, of using the Virgin of Guadalupe as the evangelizer of all the Americas.

New York is an immigrant city that has had Catholic immigrants continually reshaping each generation. The Mexicans are relative newcomers; their transnational religious and social lifestyle introduces a new element with immediately felt reverberations in archdiocesan offices, in neighborhoods, and in the changing identity of those who may be classified—either internally or from outside—as "Latinos."

In San Antonio, as in New York, parishes play a key role in the preservation of community as well as in reaching out to contemporary Latin American religious culture. San Antonio, however, can also reach back to historic Latino religious roots. Largely due to Elizondo's legacy, the San Fernando Cathedral has remained the focal point of many celebrations, which overflow into the streets and main plaza outside the church in what theologian Roberto Goizueta calls "extensions of domestic religious life." A blending of the worlds of home, church, and public square occurs, even in the midst of a large city. Participants in Good Friday processions and other celebrations include Mexican political and business leaders as well as grassroots parishioners. San Fernando, an "axis of U.S. Latino popular Catholicism," serves as an intersection of home and city, dissolving barriers through worship. As Elizondo argues, a new mestizo identity arises among immigrants who have traveled great distances, as in the sacred space of San Fernando theological, sociological, and historical boundaries of religious tradition are transformed and regenerated.[70]

8 Globalization and the New Immigrant Church

The passage of the Immigration and Nationality Act of 1965 repealed the immigration quota system that had been in effect in the United States since the 1920s. The 1965 act allowed for wider categories of entrants from the Western Hemisphere and elsewhere, including extended family members. With the implementation of these new policies, both legal and undocumented migration increased, diversifying the Latino urban presence beyond Mexican Americans, Puerto Ricans, and Cubans. In the migrant stream were people from virtually all professional and social backgrounds. Many came from Guatemala, the Dominican Republic, Colombia, and other countries that previously had contributed much smaller numbers of immigrants. Mexican immigration, meanwhile, continued to escalate throughout all regions of the country, especially in the South and the Northeast.[1]

After 1965 Christianity boomed in Latin America, Africa, and Asia, areas with extremely high rates of population growth that contained more than 60 percent of the world's Christians. Considering the context of global Catholicism and its local, primarily urban, effects allows for particular attention to changes of the impact of popular religious tradition, the dynamism of urban growth, and ethnic identity. The major guideposts of this era were the edicts of the Vatican II Council, which met from 1962 to 1965; the accelerated immigration of Latin Americans from south of the United States border since 1965; and the challenge of Protestantism. The globalization of Catholicism in conjunction with new immigration from Latin America in recent decades uprooted the traditional moorings of the immigrant church in the United States. New immigrants often fled widespread poverty as well as political oppression by nondemocratic regimes. A rising tide of Protestantism accelerated reforms in Catholic religious practice. Ecumenism flourished in the United States, and religious pluralism made inroads in Latin America as well. In response to Protestant gains among Catholics, the Church accepted increasingly "Protestant" practices of worship and theology.[2]

Church Reform and Latino Catholicism

By 1965, the Second Vatican Council had published sixteen documents to refashion the Church's mission, notably the "Dogmatic Constitution on the Church" and the "Pastoral Constitution on the Church in the Modern World." Its ecumenism decree, "Declaration on Religious Freedom," urged recognition of individuals' freedom of conscience and freedom to read the Bible. Shifts like these helped bring Protestants and Roman Catholics closer together. Vatican II specifically acknowledged that all Christians are "people of God" and asserted that the Holy Spirit is present in all Christian churches. The "Declaration on the Relation of the Church to Non-Christian Religions" appealed for greater dialogue and collaboration with other religions. Of particular significance for the spread of Catholicism was the "Constitution of the Sacred Liturgy," which introduced the use of the vernacular in worship and called for translating the Scriptures into the mother tongues of indigenous and other local cultures. This, according to African religion scholar Lamin Sanneh, opened the gates to a "new world Christianity."[3]

Vatican II innovations also included the introduction of parish councils for shared lay leadership and emphasis on the local church as representing "the Church in miniature"; these sparked an explosion of lay ministries. The combined effect of the reforms moved the Church toward greater cultural sensitivity, promoting the acceptance of more varied forms of liturgy and music in Latino parishes, as well as new expressions of popular Catholicism. With the onset of a debate on the nature of the Church's openness, this spirit reached even Spain by the late 1970s. Democratization transformed Spanish Catholic traditionalism, and the Spanish church, in order to survive, dissociated itself from the Franco dictatorship, which had sought to forestall the secularization of society.[4]

Latin American and Latino Catholicism, by contrast, became ever more dynamic. The 1968 meeting of Latin American bishops (CELAM, Consejo Episcopal Latino Americano) in Medellín, Colombia, attempted to apply Vatican II precepts to the problems of societal inequality evident throughout Latin America. Peruvian scholar Gustavo Gutiérrez and other theologians reevaluated the Bible and church doctrine and called grassroots communities to fight for social justice and challenge hierarchical and rigid structures of the Church. These contemporary theologians emphasized a new liturgy and novel approaches to the sacraments and morality. Their base ecclesial, or "basic communities," derived from the pre-1965 Movement for Basic Education in Brazil, sought to transform the "impersonal parish community at Sunday Mass" and reorganize the basis upon which parochial and diocesan life was built while also transforming society at large.[5]

The Medellín documents guided the Latin American church in a new direction of lay involvement and that of small Christian communities in advocating for the radical transformation of unjust socioeconomic as well as political conditions. Historical critiques looking back to the beginning of the Spanish imperial conquest produced intricate theological interpretations that shaped the evolution of Latin American liberation theology. These have included Gutiérrez's elaborate religious narratives of the struggle of the oppressed. Most notable was his interpretation of Bartolomé de Las Casas as an anticolonial liberationist precursor who condemned Spanish greed and false evangelization of the Caribbean Indians. Gutiérrez, using biblical narratives to represent the struggle for justice against evil exploiters, interpreted Las Casas as a Christlike liberator. The 1979 meeting of the Latin American bishops in Puebla, Mexico, particularly the statement "Preferential Action for the Poor," argued for the need for further "conversion" of the Catholic Church along those lines.[6]

New church doctrine encouraged alternate theological approaches toward traditional Catholicism. In 1969 a Spanish-born Jesuit priest working in Puerto Rico, Father Salvador Freixedo of the San Juan Archdiocese, published a best-selling book called *My Church Is Asleep*. Freixedo's critiques reflected the growing sentiments of the time, including a concern for reconciling the medieval "pomp and ceremony of the Catholic Church with contemporary social awareness." Father Freixedo believed, moreover, that the laity was too inactive and out of touch and needed to mobilize apart from the clergy in order to "to humanize the structures and give them the divine sense that they should have."[7] Freixedo, who was later rebuked and removed by the San Juan archbishop for his candor, also faulted the New York Archdiocese, where he had worked among Puerto Rican and other migrants, for not assigning a full-time priest to work with young Latinos. These Latino newcomers very much represented the urban poor and deserved to benefit from more resources, including parochial schools and academies.[8]

Transmission of Popular Catholicism

According to historian Pierre Chaunu, Catholics of the Reformation and Counter-Reformation era viewed prayer and spirituality as gaining "true significance and full efficacy" through devotions founded largely on the "ancient Christian cult of intercession," as well as by reception of the sacraments. Saints were venerated in many ways and valued "for their protection of earthly goods and their healing of the sick." European Marian piety, Chaunu argues, remained faithful to its medieval forms and espoused a public devotion that connected the Virgin with salvation.[9] Other scholars have suggested that this style of Catholic piety developed from Jansenism. This inflexible and rigorous approach, taken up by moralistic and elitist Catholics in Ireland in the seventeenth and eighteenth centuries, was characterized by an "emphasis on damnation" and advocated penitential rigor as a check on the weaknesses of human beings. Jansenists saw Christ as a severe redemptive figure.[10]

Jay Dolan, who wrote a pioneering historical study of the "old immigrant church" in the United States, with particular emphasis on Irish-American and German-American communities in nineteenth-century New York, notes that the Catholicism brought by these immigrants from Europe in the nineteenth century was a religion formed in great part by the Council of Trent. It had taken at least a century for the council's reforms to reach the grassroots, whether in Spain or America. But out of those reforms emerged the immigrant church of much of the nineteenth and twentieth centuries, which was characterized by an emphasis on attendance at Sunday Mass and reception of the sacraments as a measure of religious commitment. The Church in the United States bifurcated into a white, suburban, middle-class church and an urban, lower-class church for Latinos.[11]

Tridentine reform and the baroque were born together and cannot be fully understood in isolation from each other. The Protestant Reformation had faulted the Mass, the papacy, clerical celibacy, and commercialization of religion. In response, after the mid-sixteenth-century Council of Trent, local bishops were expected to eliminate financial abuses and clerical misbehavior, establish educational institutions, and live exemplary lives. The most significant reforms involved the liturgy and the sacraments. Baptisms and marriages could be held only at a church, the Mass could no longer be celebrated at home, and sermons were to be preached every Sunday at church. Trent prohibited celebrating miracle plays or sacred dramas in churches, but this encouraged the multiplication of these *autos sacramentales* outside of church buildings.[12]

Spanish popular religion of the era invoked local patron saints, shrines, and miracles to combat plagues, droughts, and other disasters. Spanish popular Catholicism was transmitted to the Americas over the course of the colonial period. Late-sixteenth-century Spanish Catholicism preserved the clerical centeredness that it had gained during the Middle Ages. In addition to an adequate supply of diocesan clergy, the heartland of New Castile had more than one hundred monasteries and almost as many convents, whose friars (mostly Franciscans) roamed the villages and the countryside preaching and generally supplementing the work of parish priests. Tridentine Catholicism has not been displaced in the Latin American countryside, and Trent's decrees left open possibilities for reconciliation with some Protestants but also spurred subsequent doctrinal conflicts.

According to theologian Anthony Stevens-Arroyo, the roots of Latino popular Catholicism lie in rosaries, passion plays, *pastorelas*, and devotional prayers in "an artistic style [clearly traceable to the era of the seventeenth-century baroque and Trent] that appeals to the emotions. . . . Both in theology and politics, the baroque bestowed the force of law on tradition, symbols, emotional appeals and communitarian sentiment." Local traditions were seldom challenged by the Castilian authorities. The effort of Spanish monarch Carlos III after 1759 to subordinate the ethnic republics to a centralized monarchy brought both legal and religious traditions under attack. In the attempt to privatize religion and make it more individual, Trent limited processions and local devotions, as it was intended to weaken the national identities of such regions as Catalonia and Galicia in favor of a single concept of "Spaniard." The Iberian countryside was targeted because that was the heartland of the ethnic identities.[13]

Urban centers in the Americas, where criollos vastly outnumbered peninsular Spaniards, became a battleground after 1760, with the enlightened despotism of the Bourbon dynasty. Stevens-Arroyo discounts the idea that Marian devotion is merely a relic of medieval Christianity and considers it to be a product of baroque Catholicism. Catholicism reimaged Marian devotion as a bridge to a global expression of Christianity, resonating with the Ibero-Mediterranean polity of the Hapsburgs. In this polity, tradition was an organic force that expressed a regional identity and preserved local legal custom and language. Religious tradition still plays this role in much of Latin American and Latino popular Catholicism. The evolution of Mexican devotion of Our Lady of Guadalupe offers examples of many of these baroque characteristics, as it reinforces criollo identity and Mexican nationalism.[14]

In Mexico, the need for objects of popular devotion was met by sacred images of Christ and the Virgin. Theologian Allan Figueroa Deck notes that Mexican-American Catholicism, "steeped in symbol and ritual, and centered on the Virgin Mary," seems a remnant of an earlier age. He believes that "the ancient, premodern roots of Latin American cultures remain quite vital" in contemporary Latino Catholicism and provide "a sense of being a people, a community, part of something larger than one's individual existence."[15] In feudal Western Europe, Mary as Mother of God was invoked as mediator between Christ as King and believers as vassals. Subsequent Catholicism expanded Marian devotionalism, while much of Protestantism abandoned the thousand-year old Marian legacy.[16]

The Second Vatican Council, however, eliminated many barriers and made it possible for Latino Catholics and Protestants to share and understand each other's traditions. Previously, Mexican-American Protestants had defined themselves largely in opposition to the Roman Catholic Church. In the 1940s and 1950s the Catholic and Protestant worlds remained separate. Among mainline denominations, in particular, the symbol of the "empty cross" connoted opposition to Roman Catholicism, a religion whose crucifix symbolized and glorified suffering for the masses. However, as Catholics embraced the wider Christian community and common concerns emerged, Protestants overcame historical prejudices. Social justice movements in the United States have embraced Catholic-Protestant ecumenism and attribute much of their success to the resulting coalitions, beginning with the farm workers' struggle.

According to fourth-generation Latino Protestant David Maldonado Jr., choosing one religion meant leaving the other behind, which involved losing friends and relationships. Catholics were convinced that to be Protestant was to be anti-Catholic. He was taught "that Catholics indeed worshipped false idols (saints), worshipped Mary as the mother of God, and were loyal to Rome and to the pope above all other authority. All of this was supposedly because the Catholic faith was not biblical and Catholics were ignorant of the Bible. Besides, Catholics lived unholy lives—they smoked, drank alcohol, and danced." He never felt that he had betrayed the Catholic Church or his parents or grandparents, all of whom were Protestant as well. Catholics, it was believed, used confession "as an easy way to sin, be forgiven, and sin again." By contrast, "to be Protestant was to be [truly] Christian."[17]

The Chicano movement of the 1960s and 1970s provided a shared vision and cause in the Mexican-American community, drawing together clergy and laity who attempted to make ministry relevant to concerns in both the fields and in urban barrios.[18] Many Protestant leaders marched with Cesar Chavez, offered their churches as sanctuaries, and increasingly adopted social justice agendas. Meanwhile Chavez, a prominent *cursillista*, took the parish of Our Lady of Guadalupe, established in 1962, as a meeting place for launching the farm workers' union.[19] It also became a local headquarters of the cursillo movement,

Chavez had received his theological education in the older papal encyclical tradition, not liberation theologians. He was a Catholic by birth and tradition. After joining the Filipino-led Agricultural Workers Organizing Committee (AWOC) strike in September 1965, he observed that many strikers stopped attending Mass in response to the Church's reticence to commit its support. Later more clergy and laity became actively involved in *la causa*, but it took a while for perceptions to change. By August 1966, the National Farm Workers Association (NFWA) had joined with AWOC to form the United Farm Workers Organizing Committee (UFWOC), and soon UFWOC organized a nationwide boycott campaign against table grapes. As part of his labor activism, Chavez organized religious pilgrimages on highways and city streets and prayer vigils at homemade altars in parked vehicles and in union hiring halls. These were often more effective than institutional Catholic intervention, as seen in 1969, when the California bishops denied his request for official support for the boycott. The bishops instead took a more neutral path by appointing a mediating committee to negotiate a labor contract between grape growers and the United Farm Workers during the nationwide boycott.[20]

Traditions transmitted through migration have increasingly become revitalized by individuals and families in the urban United States. Many self-described Chicano artists have improvised and revived the Mesoamerican Día de los Muertos tradition, and several predominantly Mexican parishes in the Archdiocese of Los Angeles have incorporated it into their liturgical calendar. Near downtown Los Angeles's La Placita square, following evening Mass, clergy lead a procession through Olvera Street, blessing altars constructed in businesses and restaurants. East Los Angeles parishes construct *ofrendas* in their worship space. Latinos in the United States retain a religious emphasis on family, children, and immediate community. Home altars (*altarcitos*) create sacred space for prayer. Such forms of religious expression have been transplanted to suburbs, where a *rezadora* may offer religious guidance at weddings, baptisms, and *quinceañeras* and adorn front and back yards. This contrasts with the pre-1965 Anglo emphasis on suburbs as steps on the road to status, privacy, and anonymity.[21]

Some aspects of rural and small-town Catholicism have gained international appeal, such as the *ermitas*, or shrines, long neglected by the institutional church, which have become centers of devotion in the town of San Juan in the lower Rio Grande Valley of Texas. The Virgen de San

Juan de los Lagos has been especially important among migrants from western Mexico into the United States, a wave that began during the Mexican Revolution (1910–17). The original, smaller San Juan shrine was dedicated in 1954 in honor of la Virgen de San Juan de los Lagos in the state of Jalisco, Mexico, in a region that beginning early in the twentieth century was a center of migration to the United States. In 1949 a Spanish priest named Joseph Azpiazú brought to his parish a replica of Our Lady of San Juan, a statue about three feet high. Great enthusiasm prompted him to construct a new chapel dedicated to the Virgin of San Juan del Valle. The shrine was partially destroyed in 1970, after a crazed pilot intentionally crashed a small plane into it. It was rebuilt a decade later to include a sanctuary seating some four thousand people, and it now weekly attracts more than ten thousand pilgrims from across the United States to its Spanish Masses, given throughout the day and night.[22]

In the legacy of *abuelita* (grandmotherly or, broadly construed, female) theology among Latino Catholics, grandmothers and mothers played significant roles in the passing on of religious traditions in the home and community. Newer aspects of women's participation in home religion have expanded the "matriarchal core" of Latino Catholicism, based on rural traditions that evolved throughout Latin America over centuries, largely in the absence of clergy, and updated the roles of respected *rezadoras*, elderly women in the community known for piety in leading communal rituals and prayers. Women frequently have had a better understanding of local culture than did local priests, who played relatively minor roles outside of large cities.[23]

New female religious roles have been adopted by *mujeristas*, or Latina "liberationists," proponents of liberation theology who emphasize the study of women in the struggle for justice. They incorporate pastoral tools to deal with gender oppression, including some from divergent traditions such as those of the Aztecs and Yoruba with those of Christians. New lines of religious and social inquiry emerging in the Church question all manner of power structures. Another particularly strong and largely post–Vatican II focus of Latino religious identity has emerged in the theological paradigm of *mestizaje*. Originally proposed by theologian Virgilio Elizondo as applicable to the Mexican-American experience, it also applies to those of Caribbean origin. The experience of the *mulato* ("both black and white, and neither black nor white," according to theologian Justo Gonzalez) has begun to play a similar role. Mestizaje accompanies a vision for global cultural transformation and salvation from a Latina theological perspective, going beyond the liberationist perspective.[24]

Base ecclesial communities, the grassroots religious groups that became testing grounds for liberation theology, first formed out of the Catholic Action Movement (CAM), which was brought by European missionaries to Latin America after World War I. CAM promoted lay involvement in small groups, or cells, which operated within various sectors of society, such as education, industry, labor, commerce, health, and agriculture, to live as apostles in their daily work. It focused attention primarily on their personal experiences rather than on church doctrine, and and cells developed along geographic lines. Many base communities existed without a priest or even frequent visits from local clergy or the bishop, and they overwhelmingly attracted the working-class poor. That subsequently led to the involvement of the Church in the political and economic affairs of countries whose governments brutally repressed progressive church leaders. It also awakened a sense of social justice toward Latinos.[25]

Though liberation theology has been primarily a south-of-the-border phenomenon, its offshoots have worked their way into the United States. The Valley Missionary Program begun in 1973 by the Congregation of the Holy Cross in California's Coachella Valley, about sixty miles north of the Mexican border, adopted the Latin American model of creating hundreds of base communities among immigrants to pave the way for religious and social activities. Similarly, in the 1970s Sister Rosa Martha Zarate organized dozens of Christian base communities, as well as youth organizations and ministry schools, to provide grassroots theological training throughout the San Diego Diocese. Later in San Bernardino, along with Father Patricio Guillen, Zarate and teams of laity coordinated numerous economic cooperatives and other religious projects. She was forced to leave, however, because of episcopal and clerical opposition to her allegedly Marxist work.[26]

New transportation technology, the electronic media, and other previously unforeseen advances have blended with centuries-old traditions of popular religion that remain very much alive throughout Latin America and among U.S. Latinos. These have traditionally centered on the performance of public religious customs, the celebration of certain feasts, and adherence to a culturally defined value system patterned on a rural past. For example, to Mexican Americans in the Southwest, the term *religión ranchera* (religion emerging from the countryside) denoted a strong relationship with the field, farm, and ranch life that was cherished even after arrival in a city. Expressions of popular Catholicism remain complex and cannot be reduced to mere "devotionalism"; nor can they be relegated to a backward religiosity, syncretism, or response to conditions of poverty. Various "maternal" and "familial" forms of Latino popular religion have existed for almost five centuries in North America and have weathered attempts by non-Latino clergy to alter or adapt them. The synthesis of such traditions with demographic changes brought by new urban immigrants, unprecedented changes in liturgy, and a greater democratization of Catholicism has led to the inauguration, since 1965, of a new immigrant church in the global era.[27]

Mexican Americans in particular and Latinos in general have developed and reinforced their own cultural symbols and faith communities, sometimes parallel to parishes and at other times outside of them. Latino popular Catholicism represents an interface of domestic and public life and continually moves between them; it is impassioned and in no sense "automatic" or routinized. Latino cities have become sites of multiple "sacred spaces" and pluralistic "mini-publics," which promote ethnic regeneration in parish communities. Increasingly mobile Catholic migrants engage in religious choices that go far beyond whether or not to attend Mass. Popular religion can include political activism, as in some observances of the Vía Crucis in Chicago's Pilsen neighborhood, where social justice campaigns for undocumented workers play a part in constructing ethnic identity.[28]

Until recently many clergy in Mexico stressed the need to always confess to a priest before receiving Communion; according to one Chicago priest, this has instilled an exaggerated sense of sinfulness, discouraging people from frequent Communion. Latinos tend to live a traditional, nostalgic, and conservative faith in order to preserve their identity and cultural roots and pass them on to their children. At times they are more conservative in the United States than in their native country because here they do not have as many possibilities to express and live their popular religiosity. The immanence of Latin American religious attitudes and practices can be seen in contemporary urban Sunday Masses, which remain family events filled with children "who not only raise the noise level but at times wander down the aisles exploring unfamiliar terrain, looking for ways to entertain themselves." Many Mexican men attend Masses and adhere to Marian devotions, though they are less inclined to assume active parish leadership roles than are women.[29]

The homeland circumstances of immigrants continue to contribute to the reshaping of landscapes north of the border. Throughout Mexico, *mayordomos*, or sponsors of feasts for local patron saints, frequently look to migrant communities in the United States for funding of these town

fiestas. Following general indifference before 1980, beginning in the
early 1990s the Mexican government started to pay great attention to its
northern diaspora and implemented various programs to assist Mexican
migrants organized as hometown or home-province organizations in the
United States. Municipal authorities seeking support abroad to preserve
social and economic ties to Mexico help orient migrants toward both the
home and host countries simultaneously. Mexican migrants in the United
States financially support their hometown churches in Mexico, which now
serve not only the village population but also the migrants who return for
annual winter fiestas, primarily those honoring their town's patron saint.[30]

Consumerism and the Changing of Religious Tradition

The emergence of new constituencies and new orientations toward Catholicism among clergy and bishops has allowed greater popular participation. Sociologist Stephen Warner has found that, generally speaking,
U.S. religious pluralism has led not to religion's "retreat from public life"
but rather to its becoming a central feature of the identity struggles of
new immigrants. Latinos effectively use religion as a "vehicle for recreat-
ing identities, stabilizing families, adapting to neighborhoods, even participating in the lives of the homeland in absentia, especially while facing
socioeconomic crises and urban anomie," he writes.[31]

Churches continue in their role of identity transmission across generations. Contemporary immigrants have merged religion with economic,
political, and social activities across urban, regional, and international
borders. Sociologists Anna Peterson, Manuel Vasquez, and Philip Williams point out that the Church as an institution has become better suited
to easing "dislocation and fragmentation," both locally and in larger, ever
changing transnational contexts.[32]

They note that global Christianity is a result of social and economic
developments that have "caused lay Catholics to expand traditional roles
and question acceptable boundaries of authority, sometimes adopting a
stronger emphasis on the sacraments and personal spiritual renewal."[33]

Throughout Latin America, a wide range of both imported and indigenous Christian religious movements that view healing and trances as
manifestations of the Holy Spirit, including Pentecostal Protestants and
charismatic Catholics, have arisen in recent decades. Pentecostal pastors
are similar in culture, socioeconomic position, education, occupation,
and marital status to their congregants.

Protestants throughout Latin America increasingly call for an end to
financial subsidies to Catholic schools and other vestiges of special status

and privilege. The growth of pluralistic religious practices has prompted religious, lay, and political leaders to call for greater religious tolerance and full separation of church and state, particularly in countries with large and growing Protestant populations. An example is Guatemala, where in 2000 Protestants made up 25 percent of the population and have had particular success among that country's Mayan Indians and urban working class. Protestants in El Salvador constitute 22 percent of the population, and in Mexico over one hundred Pentecostal denominations serve more than four million people.[34]

Within the United States, a major source of Latino Protestantism has resulted from "reverse missionization," whereby Latin Americans, having adapted the missionary version of Protestantism to their national and local culture, then migrate north, producing an even more mixed or hybrid religion. The mass marketing of evangelical and Pentecostal Protestantism marks a new phase of global consumerism, with larger auditoriums and a more rapid proliferation of churches since the 1970s. Growing numbers of the major denominational, or mainline, Protestant Latino congregations have become "evangelical" or "charismatic" but remain within the mainline church.[35]

The rise of Pentecostals and Charismatics has spurred a more active religious consumerism. Latino Catholics have long been consumeristic, venturing forth to Protestant evangelical services while simultaneously remaining Catholics and attending Mass periodically. Latino Protestant churches have developed programs in literacy training, immigration counseling, and refugee assistance. Furthermore, many Latino Protestant congregations have formed on the basis of a common language, overcoming cultural distinctions linked to nationality. The proliferation of urban storefront Protestant, especially Pentecostal, churches has suggested to the Catholic hierarchy that a purposeful focus be adopted to counter the trend, with parishes serving as bridges to the wider non-Latino community. Pentecostals, meanwhile, have developed and disseminated a popular lived philosophy of evangelization that emphasizes the quality of the individual's religious experience.[36]

Pentecostal churches, where Spanish is often the lingua franca, can also serve as self-help grassroots organizations. Latino leaders can help community residents access services, sometimes without regard for church affiliation. Ministers learning of new residents conduct routine visits, assess needs, and extend invitations to church. Congregants, who are usually women, also assist newcomers, helping families to access service agencies and become familiar with local institutions such as schools and hospitals.

Ministers reported that generally families wait several weeks after a move before finally attending a local church for the first time. New immigrant groups, poorer than established groups and often rooted in rural experiences, became a new audience for evangelicals and a source of new vitality; this presents a challenge to the Catholic institutions that previously monopolized the provision of a wide range of services.[37]

A more active and diverse global Protestantism has accelerated changes in Latino Catholicism. In the mid-1960s, the heyday of the Catholic ecumenical movement, Pentecostalism began to enter the Catholic Church in the form of the Catholic Charismatic Renewal (CCR). The original founding of the Charismatic movement in the United States occurred at Duquesne University in Pittsburgh and the University of Notre Dame in the mid-1960s among Catholic laity who had been involved in peace and justice issues. The movement grew worldwide from just a handful of U.S. English-speaking followers in 1967 to more than seventy-five million worldwide by 2000. CCR reached Latin America mostly via the work of U.S. missionary priests or because of a Latin American priest's exposure to the movement in the United States. It has varied in different settings, depending on national political, cultural, and socioeconomic factors and the composition of parishes. Its pastoral work stresses personal renewal within the ritual and sacramental life of the Church and emphasizes the belief that the second coming of Christ is at hand.[38]

The CCR in Latin America has extended missionary and pastoral boundaries, helping to create a large "megaparish" network. In downtown San Salvador, one charismatic megaparish reached out to people far beyond parish boundaries, and the church's central location near downtown San Salvador also drew participants from nearby churches. The CCR movement in the United States, as in Latin America, borrows Pentecostalism's intimacy, spontaneity, and spirituality and allows Spanish-language prayer groups to express faith through their own culture. Its grassroots growth has attracted more than five million Latino Catholics.

A large percentage of the movement's leadership is made up of Latin American immigrants who have had contact with the movement in their sending country. Despite its emphasis on meetings outside the parish, its revitalization of U.S. Catholicism has led to support from more than two thousand priests, a hundred bishops, and tens of thousands of lay leaders. A 1969 report from the meeting of the U.S. Catholic bishops in Washington, D.C., marked a turning point, generating positive ecclesiastical evaluations of the renewal movement. Several U.S. bishops became involved in the renewal during the 1980s and 1990s as a way of preventing further defections from the Church in the United States.[39]

Like other lay movements in the Catholic Church, the CCR has a strong diocesan organization that commands allegiance from its members, at times appearing to supersede their commitment to the local parish. The sustained popularity of the CCR among Latino Catholics owes to a need for a more personally appropriated faith through charismatic manifestations, such as prophecy, healings, and tongues, which take place outside the local parish in prayer meetings scheduled on days other than Sunday in order not to compete with parish services. Unlike Latino Pentecostals, Charismatics tend to retain sympathy for the traditional Marian devotions central to Latino popular Catholicism. Moreover, they discourage displays of extreme emotionalism, especially in public. Although they try to maintain a direct connection with Catholic tradition in their small, unstructured prayer groups, they have also formed more structured and somewhat autonomous "covenant communities."[40]

The migration to the continent of Catholic Charismatics, primarily from Puerto Rico but also increasingly from Mexico and Central America, has contributed to the movement's growth among U.S. Latinos. In 1971, a team of American Redemptorist priests gave a retreat in Aguas Buenas, Puerto Rico, where many of the participants received the baptism of the Spirit; after this the movement began to spread rapidly on the island. Having caught on in Puerto Rico, it spread via migration to continental Puerto Rican communities. As it simultaneously surfaced in Mexico, Guatemala, the Dominican Republic, and other southern lands, where in some cases annual national CCR assemblies filled soccer stadiums, the movement spread to Latino communities having large proportions of new immigrants throughout the United States.

For example, many members of Houston's St. Catherine's Church became involved in the city's Catholic Charismatic Center, which has become a site for pursuing alternative modes of physical and psychological healing through prayer. Attendance at the center supplements parish participation, especially for the undocumented, and it allows the celebration of ethnicity and religion without the separatism feared by some bishops and pastors as undermining parish integrity, even though the movement was deemed acceptable by the Vatican. Like the parish, the center caters to a heavily immigrant population from Mexico and Central America, who often meet in private homes.[41]

Pope John Paul II's "new evangelization" approach after 1983 linked

CCR more closely with the institutional church. Having deplored "incorrect interpretations of Medellín" and "rereadings of the gospel," he saw the renewal as a vehicle for combining lay participation with deference to hierarchical authority. In 1992, concerned with the unchecked and rapid expansion of other religions, particularly Protestant "sects" in Latin America, he called for increased participation and issued a "call to conversion" to all Catholics to revitalize the religion.[42] He also downplayed the radical struggle for social justice for the poor as articulated by liberation theology. Vatican support for the Charismatics has made their movement a politically acceptable alternative to perceived leftist ideologies geared toward the pursuit of social justice.[43]

Latino religious practices reflect the religious dynamism not only of contemporary immigrants but of non-Latino practitioners, such as attendees at Protestant "megachurches," which generally have thousands of attendees for Sunday services. These congregations are focused largely in the Sunbelt and share these characteristics: a charismatic, authoritative senior minister, a very active congregational community, a multitude of social and outreach ministries, and, complex organizational structures. The largest megachurches in America average twenty thousand in attendance, and for most of them denominational affiliation has become relatively insignificant, as the church's size, pastor, programs, and reputation attract adherents. As the significance of denominational labels declines, congregants increasingly draw on multiple sources of religious experience to construct a faith. These megachurches, moreover, create a message of their unique identity, and many have come to function like a shopping mall, providing an umbrella for diverse ministries including elementary and secondary private schools, daycare centers, and numerous other activities for young and old alike. Members are highly mobile, transient, and without roots.[44]

Central Americans as Global Migrants

By 2000 Central Americans represented 5 percent of U.S. Latinos, with Salvadorans the largest group (655,000), followed by Guatemalans (372,000) and Hondurans (218,000). Central American migration to the United States coincides with the growth of global Christianity, and the experiences of these migrants are distinct from the experiences of those already groomed in the immigrant church—Mexican Americans, Puerto Ricans, and Cubans. The histories of the Central Americans varied greatly after the ripples throughout the region from the chain of events set in motion by the 1978 Sandinista overthrow of Nicaraguan strongman Anastasio Somoza.

At first the Catholic Church and mainline Protestants generally supported the Nicaraguan revolution. However, once the Sandinistas were firmly in power, this religious consensus deteriorated.

During the 1980s the Catholic Church in Nicaragua became polarized between advocates who supported the redistributive goals of the Sandinistas and traditionalists such as Cardinal Manuel Obando y Bravo, who, along with other bishops, supported Violeta Chamorro in her successful campaign for the presidency in 1990. Ecclesial base communities and liberationists began to lose many of their activists as people joined secular Sandinista organizations or became involved in government-sponsored programs and activities after the 1990 electoral defeat of the Sandinistas.[45]

In 1980 civil war erupted in El Salvador when a military coup overturned the results of a legitimate, democratic election. Later that year, guerrilla groups united to form the Farabundo Martí Liberation Front (FMLN), and after El Salvador's 1982 election, war and guerrilla activity further intensified. From 1981 to 1992, El Salvador underwent a full-scale civil war that claimed the lives of at least eighty thousand people. Among them were four American churchwomen; five national guardsmen were later found guilty and sentenced for their murders.[46]

Central American military regimes attacked religious workers and laypeople alike. At least forty nuns and priests and one archbishop were murdered between 1971 and 1990. More than half of those killings occurred in El Salvador, where Jesuits led literacy campaigns and Bible-reading groups and increasingly carried out labor and peasant organizing in base communities. In March 1980 a gunman assassinated Archbishop Oscar Romero as he said Mass in San Salvador's cathedral.

More than 500,000 Salvadoran refugees, coming from the smallest and most densely populated country of the Central American isthmus, journeyed north during the 1980s into Mexico and especially the United States. At least an equal number were displaced within their own country. By 1990, some Salvadoran refugees began returning to repopulate their villages, where the core of organized religious life became grassroots Christian communities led by laity. After the civil war, however, El Salvador was ravaged by violent crime, and growing membership in adolescent gangs has reached across borders into U.S. immigrant communities.[47]

Political and social instability and its religious consequences have thus contributed to a new stream of Latino migration to the United States. During the 1980s the plight of immigrants fleeing political violence in El Salvador, Guatemala, and other nations of Central America sometimes inspired U.S. clergy to adopt tactics that opposed their government's foreign policy and immigration policies, as the Sanctuary movement shows. The Sanctuary movement was firmly rooted in parishes and a wide range of urban congregations. It was launched in 1982 in Los Angeles in response to reports of deplorable conditions in U.S. Immigration and Naturalization detention centers and dangers facing refugees if they were deported to their homelands. More than forty Los Angeles churches officially declared themselves sanctuaries within the first three years of the movement; nationally, Sanctuary churches doubled from two hundred to four hundred between 1982 and 1986. Sanctuary was both a political movement against U.S. policy in Central America and a humanitarian effort to assist victims. The movement provided refuge in U.S. churches for Salvadorans, Guatemalans, and others fleeing persecution in their homeland. But it had a limited effect on policy, as thousands of Central Americans were deported to their native countries.

The Sanctuary movement, which attempted to extend liberation theology principles to immigration issues, was premised on Judeo-Christian ancestral traditions of offering a sanctuary as both a place for worship and a refuge from avengers, as well as on the early U.S. religious tradition of protecting political refugees and runaway slaves. It provided congregations of several faiths with a way to protect newcomers, both religiously and politically.[48]

Although religious-order clergy and individual bishops took a strong stand in support of Central American refugees, U.S. bishops as a group withheld public endorsement of the Sanctuary movement, primarily because of their traditional reluctance to introduce social justice issues into their council, especially when taking a stand would conflict with U.S. immigration law. In 1988, however, the hierarchy of the U.S. Catholic Church began a much more explicit campaign for social justice, calling for greater refugee access to political asylum and more uniform asylum policies, as well as focusing on immigrants' rights more broadly amid a vigorous debate on federal immigration reform. After the U.S. Immigration and Naturalization Service moved to deport hundreds of thousands of Salvadoran immigrants who had not been in the United States long enough to qualify for amnesty as political refugees, it was criticized at bishops' conferences, along with specific U.S. policies in Central America.[49]

The Central American diaspora of the 1980s was shaped in Mexico as refugees traveled through that country to the United States. Largely in response to demographic growth, U.S. dioceses established administrative offices to advocate for the new immigrants. On the Mexican side of the border, during the 1990s Father Leonardo López directed Casa del

Peregrino (House of the Pilgrim), which assisted and housed the needy in Nuevo Laredo while they prepared for their passage north. He communicated with their families in the United States and advised them to send them money through Western Union's Laredo offices. The bishop of Nuevo Laredo supported this humanitarian work, even though it provoked tensions with civil authorities. While Mexican priests played significant roles in the protection and aid of Central American refugees transiting northern Mexico, the Guatemalan Catholic Church became increasingly identified as the chief institutional voice of opposition to the army's spreading repression in the countryside. The evangelical Protestant churches in Guatemala, meanwhile, were seen as safe havens for those wishing to steer clear of the contest for secular authority.[50]

Immigrant Revitalization and Post–Vatican II Cityscapes

In 1974, the National Secretariat for Hispanic Affairs was formed to define new methods of dealing with immigrants while both lay and clerical representatives of Latino dioceses worked with the U.S. Conference of Catholic Bishops on immigration and global concerns. During the 1980s, U.S. bishops increasingly recognized that strong international Catholic institutional networks could help them to acquire rights, seek protections, and articulate their interests. The U.S. church's increasingly pluralistic structure after 1965 transcends inner-city urban parish communities and, increasingly, borders, serving multiple Latino ethnic identities. The complex Latino configuration of the San Francisco Bay area, for example, has evolved quite differently from that on the East Coast. After 1945, Mexicans and small numbers of Central and South Americans began moving into the Mission District, an area that had long been a point of entry for European immigrants. The early Salvadoran and Nicaraguan cultural presence diluted Mexican dominance somewhat, though most of the city's major Latino fiestas were organized around Mexican patriotic holidays. Churches, too, incorporated more nuanced and varied national saint days and the like.[51]

To take another setting, Washington, D.C., had by 1985 amassed an ← estimated 200,000 Latinos, with Salvadorans the largest group alongside sizable contingents of Guatemalans and other Latin Americans. Despite their diversity, Latinos in the Adams Morgan and Mount Pleasant barrios forged a common identity as a cultural and political group. In the 1990s, a Salvadoran priest coordinated Augustana Lutheran Church's Latino outreach, with programs focused on educational and other social issues. Many Salvadorans have moved to Washington suburbs, such as Takoma Park,

Maryland, where Our Lady of Sorrows, whose nearly half Latino parish also includes African Americans and European-origin ethnics, serves charismatic Catholics and other groups. Of the more than 560,000 Catholics in the Washington archdiocese, about 30 percent are Latino. More than half of the Catholic Diocese of Arlington's fifty-six parishes in northern Virginia, with nearly 400,000 registered Catholics encompassing twenty-one countries of origin, offer a Spanish Mass.[52]

The large U.S. Guatemalan urban refugee community includes the most rural and largest number of indigenous inhabitants, including Quiches, Chujes, Acatecs, and Kanjobales. Their fastest-growing congregations are part of nonmainline Protestant denominations. In 1981, soon after assuming the pastorate of La Placita, a Claretian mission church near downtown Los Angeles, Father Luis Olivares transformed the old plaza church into the city's major base of liberationist social practice, declaring the church grounds a sanctuary for undocumented immigrants. In 1985, Olivares and his pastors dedicated La Placita as the first "sanctuary church" in the archdiocese, declaring it off limits to INS agents. During the 1980s a large, concentrated, and expansive Central American barrio developed in Los Angeles west of downtown in the communities of Westlake and Pico-Union. Refugees from El Salvador, Nicaragua, and Guatemala gave the area a more rebellious and political flavor than most other immigrant enclaves of the decade. These immigrants were used to organizing themselves and often expected churches to be involved in actively confronting societal injustice.[53]

Charismatic Catholic and Protestant evangelical new immigrant congregations throughout the city played an important role in the integration of new Latin American immigrants, particularly Central Americans. Mayan identity appeared fragmented in Los Angeles and other U.S. locales, a sign of the reluctant assimilation characteristic of the new immigrant church and its constituent congregations. One of the earliest Los Mayan groups formed in the Los Angeles area in 1986 with the financial backing of Maryknoll, a Catholic missionary organization with projects in Guatemala and elsewhere in Latin America. Several indigenous Maya hometown associations, referred to as *fraternidades*, also formed in Los Angeles at this time, One was the Fraternidad Eulense Maya Q'anjob'al, founded by predominantly rural people from the region of Santa Eulalia who had faced devastating violence and land loss at home. This fraternidad has helped raise funds to reconstruct the hometown church, build a new hospital, and oversee other projects in that village from the meager earnings of these immigrant men and women, many of whom work in the Los Angeles garment and textile industries.[54]

The Kanjobal population as a whole included traditional and charismatic Catholics as well as participants in evangelical groups, the largest of which claimed two to three hundred members in Los Angeles during the mid-1980s. The Los Angeles highland Maya held a weekly prayer service in private homes, and they preferred their ancestral Indian identity to the acquired Latino identity. Many of these Maya spoke Spanish only as a second language. For this and other reasons they remained relatively untouched by church policies designed to promote Latino "panethnicity" for the sake of administrative and economic efficiency. Somewhat typically, however, the archdiocese preferred not to distinguish them from more urban-based Maya who arrived subsequently. Some parishes did offer special Masses with passages in the native language, along with meeting-room privileges.[55]

Central Americans have also joined Mexican immigrants in suburban Atlanta in the heart of the "Nuevo New South." Metropolitan Atlanta, with 269,000 Latinos in 2000, up from just over 50,000 a decade earlier, offers another example of urban migration patterns, with a surprising amount of integration and a relative lack of immigrant-dominated barrios. Large numbers of Latinos first migrated to Atlanta in the early 1980s. The Atlanta Archdiocese's Office of the Hispanic Apostolate persuaded several parishes to offer a Spanish-language Mass in the early 1980s in an effort to imbue newcomers with appreciation for sacraments and the weekly liturgy as the focus of parish life.[56]

The Misión Católica de Nuestra Señora de las Américas was run by a Cuban-born priest from 1994 to 2000. Latinos in Atlanta are more likely to attend religious services at this Latino church than at suburban parishes with territorial boundaries serving predominantly English-speaking members. Misión Católica has attracted thousands of mostly undocumented Mexican migrants with its annual procession in honor of Our Lady of Guadalupe. More than three thousand Mexican, Central American, and South American immigrants gather at the site of a former warehouse for Mass each weekend, arriving by car, by public transportation, and on foot. Statues and paintings of various Latin American national and regional patron saints have been placed there by migrants from over a dozen countries. Other religious institutions have also helped Latinos established a viable community. The Lutheran church Sagrada Familia has fostered a different brand of incorporation and pluralism through maintenance of parishioners' distinct national identity as Mexicans, Hondurans, and Salvadorans. In both Catholic and Protestant congregations, the newest residents "find in their churches support for the formation and maintenance of transnational, transregional, and translocal ties that shape the ways in which they negotiate the city's often inhospitable landscapes."[57]

Immigrant Revitalization

Early-twentieth-century Catholicism designed the urban parish as a center of worship and the key source of communal identity for ethnic groups. The transition to the new immigrant church has necessarily incorporated immigrants in a struggle to maintain dual identities and to challenge the Church to adapt more broadly to local events and needs. The post-1965 immigrant experience reflects a continued lack of both lay and clerical power in parishes and within U.S. church structures generally, despite increasing numbers. The old immigrant church focused on assimilating a wide variety of newcomers, and, according to historian Jay Dolan, its decline coincided with restrictive immigration in the 1920s and the gradual dissolution of European ethnic residential enclaves, giving way to even more rapid Americanization and assimilation of Catholic ethnics into a single religious entity, distinct from Protestants and Jews.[58]

The incorporation of Vatican II theology, meanwhile, increasingly challenged the idea of the Catholic parish as the normative institution. Religious tradition and urban dynamism occurred apart from church structures and personnel, accelerating changes in identity while promoting ethnic regeneration. Latino parishioners, clergy, and others have increasingly integrated into the new immigrant church and formed novel configurations of hemispheric and global religious movements. Globalization has contributed to the growth of Latino communities, requiring that parishes as well as church bodies adopt a wider range of social resource functions, while suburbanization has hastened ethnic integration within each major metropolis.

Epilogue: Latino Religious Tradition as Metaphor

Spanish popular Catholicism, which emerged from Mediterranean Catholicism and the Reconquest experience, came to be embodied in Latino religious tradition. Throughout Spain's overseas empire in the late fifteenth and early sixteenth centuries, clergy evangelized through conquest and largely by means of symbols and plays. Latino religious tradition has roots in the religion implanted by the early missionaries at Santa Fe—the oldest continuous site of Latino Catholicism in what is now the U.S. Southwest—founded during the winter of 1609–10, a decade before the landing of the Pilgrims at Plymouth Rock. The religious synthesis in Spain's northern New World colonies was patterned on the Spanish colonial mission system in the Valley of Mexico during the sixteenth century. From the late sixteenth to the mid-eighteenth century it spread from New Mexico to California.[1]

The religion preached to the newly conquered peoples was a Castilian brand of Roman Catholicism, centered on village festivals and traditions but also dependent on access to the sacraments. Spanish colonialism—and Latino religious tradition—in Mexico (as elsewhere in Latin America) developed regionally, keeping devotions alive in relative isolation. The Spanish Virgen de los Remedios, for instance, came with Hernán Cortés to Mexico in 1519 and was lost when the Spaniards were driven from Tenochtitlán, but was recovered and decades later came to be known as an aid for military success. Guadalupe, too, became rooted in New Mexican life after the Diego de Vargas *entrada* of 1692; her devotion remains prominent in street names, church names, and village landmarks. To this day many Santa Fe chapels have white altar cloths bearing an image of Guadalupe in the folk art of *paño* (cloth and handkerchief painting).[2]

In the Hispanic Caribbean, Cuban Catholicism served as a base for northward expansion into St. Augustine, Florida, beginning in 1565. Puerto Rico shared the general characteristics of implantation of Spanish Catholicism, mixed with indigenous and African influences. There native-born criollos and mestizos remained largely uninvolved in ecclesiastical activities mandated by a Spanish church administered from Seville.

Nineteenth- and twentieth-century versions of colonialism met with resistance, and some exile movements and nationalist struggles overflowed
into the United States.

Migration to the continental United States in the twentieth century,
in the cases of both Cuba and Puerto Rico, coincided with the decline of
the old immigrant church of the nineteenth and early twentieth centuries
geared largely to Europeans. The national parish model had aimed to
preserve the immigrants' language and ethnic identity, linking them to
their homelands through parish communities and parochial schools in
which culture was transmitted across generations.

Understanding the evolution of the U.S. parish in the twentieth century is crucial to understanding the role of Latino identity in urban Catholicism. The overall process was marked by successive dilemmas of
assimilation: separatism (national parish), total assimilation (territorial
parish), partial (integrated territorial parish), and pluralism (de facto national Latino parish). The current practice of splitting once-cohesive parish communities has resulted in a proliferation of churches offering arrangements for baptisms, *quinceañeras*, and other occasions. Latinos have
more effectively resisted religious assimilation than other ethnic groups,
owing to the timing of their arrival, their extensive Latin American background—including the background of the Southwest and other border
areas that later became part of the United States—and their ability to
hold on to their ancestral religious tradition, both within and outside
parish communities. Latino parishioners, clerical leaders, and others have
increasingly seen integration into the new immigrant church in nontradi-
tional terms, within hemispheric and global religious frameworks.[3]

Regardless of the operative administrative division and parish structure at any given time, Latino theologians emphasize the importance of
the Spanish language for identity and values. Puerto Rican theologian
Jaime Vidal points out that this significance of the Spanish language leads
to "a very deep attachment to it, not only on the part of intellectuals, who
might be able to articulate these feelings, but also on the part of the popular class, who feel them instinctively, but with no less force or clarity."[4]
The challenges of functioning within several cultural worlds simultaneously have led Latinos to pursue different urban strategies according to
their own national background and with respect to the demands of their
immediate environment. Geographic, spatial, social, even civic differences gradually gave way to a collective Catholicism as the homogenizing
forces inherent in the globalization of religion have been expressed in the

rise of the new immigrant church in the United States since 1965, shaped by unprecedented immigration from Europe, Latin America, and Asia.[5]

Catholicism and Urban Dynamism

Anglo-European Catholicism was brought to Maryland by English Catholic settlers and was later reshaped by nineteenth-century Irish and German immigrant clergy and laity. German and Irish immigrant communities developed a brand of parish-centered Tridentine Catholicism that emphasized the sacraments of baptism and confirmation, attendance at Sunday Mass, Communion, and confession. These practices held sway by the time large numbers of Italian and Polish Catholics came to the United States. Thus, pre-1965 church policies required that newcomers adapt to the existing variations of European Catholicism in a changing urban environment. However, the "Mass and sacraments" style of most non-Latino U.S. Catholics, foreign to Mexicans, Puerto Ricans, and Cubans, has since been giving way to a more home- and public-oriented Latino Catholicism, which is maternal in the sense that women take on a disproportionate share of church responsibilities.[6]

Urbanization has tended to produce serious religious upheavals, which have sometimes had a negative impact but other times have produced new devotions that enrich the Christian tradition. Latinos have had to negotiate their urban space and identity with other immigrant groups, as well as with a large African-American population and in some cases Native Americans. After Vatican II, for example, the Church encouraged Pueblo Indians to express their culture in their religious participation, and this has encouraged an "underground spirituality" in whch Pueblo children are baptized in both native and Catholic rituals. For religious festivals, Pueblos perform native dances and ceremonies; they also retain non-Christian religious beliefs pertaining to creation.[7]

San Antonio retains a symbolic primacy due to its leadership in recent decades, as well as its historic importance. The San Antonio missions, four churches established in the eighteenth century, are being preserved by the Church for their structural, historical, and spiritual significance. In 1978, the Catholic Archdiocese of San Antonio and the U.S. Department of the Interior established the San Antonio Missions National Historical Park alongside the active Catholic communities of worship that, in cooperation with federal park rangers, have remained in the mission churches.[8] Parishes at both Mission San José and Mission Concepción have grown accustomed to accommodating requests from couples (including non-Catholics) for weddings. In recent years, about half of Mission San José's three hundred weddings per year have involved couples from the parish, with the rest being "tourist weddings" of proclaimed "friends of the missions." The pastor of Mission San Juan has warned against excessive consumerism, or what he termed the creation of "a religious Las Vegas," in which performance and the sale of memorabilia overwhelm genuine devotion.[9]

San Antonio's San Fernando Cathedral, the oldest cathedral in the United States, contains an image of El Señor de Esquípulas (of Guatemala). Supplicants from all over Texas come to express their thanks to the image through photographs and other offerings. Latino parishes increasingly celebrate the feasts of the patron saints of multiple nations, with processions, novenas, and special Masses to patronesses from the Dominican Republic (Nuestra Señora de la Altagracia) and Colombia (Nuestra Señora de Chiquinquirá) occupying liturgical calendars alongside celebrations for Mexico's Virgen de Guadalupe, Puerto Rico's San Juan Bautista, and Cuba's Nuestra Señora de la Caridad del Cobre. Guatemalan popular Catholicism appears most prominently in *cofradías*, which mix Mayan customs and Catholic rituals.[10]

According to one nonreligious observer, novelist Larry McMurtry, the urban frontier was masculine, not feminine. "The Texas Metropolis swallowed the Frontier like a small snake swallows a large frog: slowly, not without strain, but inexorably. And if something of the Frontier remains alive in the innards of the Metropolis it is because the process of digestion has only just begun." San Antonio's rich Catholic history distinguishes it from other "adolescent" Texas cities.[11] Indeed, twentieth-century metropolitan landscapes fostered "sacred spaces" where religious minorities in suburbia have flourished, propelled by Latinos' movement up the socioeconomic ladder and increasing participation in consumer trends. Despite their distinctiveness, the various nationally based Latino communities in the United States share many structures, functions, and features—and a crucial relationship to urban ethnicity in the institutional church. There has appeared no common narrative of Latinos' transplantation to the urban United States, yet their lived religion allows them to adapt by creating, negotiating, and otherwise participating in new religious movements with considerable significance for parishes, cities, and ethnicity.[12]

In their early-twentieth-century settlements in large metropolises, Latino Catholics endured harsh and discriminatory treatment, especially in parish schools where speaking Spanish was discouraged and often forbidden. The hierarchy in Chicago and New York, along with many Spanish-speaking priests, has long floundered in attempts to adequately serve Puerto Ricans, even though by the end of the 1960s all diocesan and auxiliary bishops on the island itself were native born. The "Great Migration" of 1946–65 put Puerto Ricans in a bad position, and consequently the migrants tended to see the urban parish as an alien institution.

Puerto Rico's mid-twentieth-century economic development had prompted internal migration on the island, which placed new pressures on both rural and urban Catholicism, requiring replacement of an old infrastructure for churches and schools. It also created religious dilemmas. According to the 1950 census, 25 percent of the unions of men and women in Puerto Rico were classified as "consensual" common-law marriages, that is, lacking a civil or religious ceremony; these had been a common feature of Puerto Rican culture for centuries despite church-led opposition. Puerto Rican migration spanned the old and new immigrant church and stood on the brink of a new era in transnational migration, spurred on by airplanes and telephones. It also played an important role in bridging gaps between U.S., Latin American, and Caribbean Protestantism. This is particularly true for Pentecostals, who sent Puerto Rican missionaries throughout much of Latin America.[13]

The Puerto Ricans' arrival in U.S. cities replicated patterns of religious and residential succession similar to those of European immigrants—particularly those from southern Italy. Historian Robert Orsi has written of how Italian Americans in Harlem, including oldtimers visiting the neighborhood, considered the influx of Puerto Ricans a threat, physically as well as racially. Surprisingly, Italian Americans exempted black Haitian immigrants at the summer feast to Our Lady of Mount Carmel in East Harlem. That is, the Italian Americans welcomed Haitians in their processions as they would boost attendance. It helped that they were merely visitors from Brooklyn and therefore less immediately "threatening" to the neighborhood. Puerto Ricans, by contrast, were not welcomed, partly due to fears of being close to neighbors "of color" and partly because of their supposed tendencies toward criminality. After 1965, however, many Catholics and Protestants have come to share a vision of social justice, and both have affirmed that religious values are fundamental in the struggle against discrimination.

Pan-Latino enclaves of early-twentieth-century New York, largely under the care of Spanish priests after 1945, gave way to identifiable Puerto Rican colonias that grew in population and significance. Among new groups, such as Dominicans, religion, national pride, and community intertwined. They began to observe their country's independence with special Masses. Other Latin American groups, such as Guatemalans, brought new religious traditions, such as the use of an *alfombra*, an intricate, multicolored sawdust carpet created by hand, for church display over the Christmas and Easter holidays.[14]

The Cuban case is somewhat exceptional in both its Latin American and U.S. contexts. Under Spain, the Cuban church remained closely tied to the symbolic figure of its bishop. Its power base crumbled in the early 1960s as wealthy and middle-class Cubans fled to Miami; the island also lost the basis of its ecclesiastical leadership and a potential source of internal opposition as approximately two-thirds of the (mostly Spanish) priests on the island departed. After the failed 1961 Bay of Pigs invasion, the revolutionary government seized on the role played by Catholics such as Manuel Artimé, a former leader of the Agrupación Católica Universitaria who headed the invasion by a largely exile force known as Brigade 2506. Also damaging were the presence of three Spanish priests and a Protestant minister and the fact that crosses were prominently featured on the invaders' shoulder patches, which confirmed for the regime "an air of a modern-day religious crusade against the communist infidel."[15]

Latino Urban Identity and Ethnic Regeneration

Useful contrasts within Latino urban Catholicism emerge from examinations of differences in origin, destination, and socioeconomic status, as well as religious and social conditions in city life. Part of this heterogeneity comes from religious innovation and experimentation, which create urban subcultures. As cities have gone through industrial and postindustrial phases, churches have had to adapt their worship and organizational styles. High rates of in-migration create attractive "markets" for religious organizations, as churches located in growing communities (particularly suburbs) have a better chance of growing in membership than those in stable or declining areas. Common experiences at local, metropolitan, national, and global levels create vast, locally rooted communities that reflect global trends toward greater religious pluralism and immigrant revitalization of religion in distinctive styles of worship.[16]

Cities in the United States constitute ideal laboratories for examining new immigrant congregations, as well as their religious components. Transnational migration and urban ethnicity have helped reshape the industrial city into a "post-Fordist" spatial and social configuration. This ongoing process mixes old and new social, economic, and political arrangements. Whereas industrialization and manufacturing created earlier

urban structures, deindustrialization—or service-sector-led global economic expansion—has created new urban structures. As cities have gone
through industrial and postindustrial phases, churches have adapted their
worship and organizational styles. Industrial decentralization accelerated
during the mass production era and, accompanied by suburbanization,
led to the increasing dispersal of factories and blue-collar workers once
concentrated in and around downtown central cities.[17]

Twentieth-century urbanism is rich in religious and social diversity.
The Catholic Church's reforms arising from the Second Vatican Council
resulted in the elimination of some differentiating religious practices that
made the Catholic religion stand out from other Christian faiths. Now
Catholics were no longer set apart by their Latin Mass or their abstinence
from meat on Fridays, and they began to look more like other religious
groups. Previously, the Mass was celebrated in Latin, a language that
was not understood by any parishioners, regardless of birthplace. Latinos
now have access to their own parishes, and the Mass is often completely in
Spanish with distinctive music; the experience can differ considerably from
that of European-origin Catholics within a given integrated parish.[18]

Latino religious needs adjust to contemporary society, as it did to earlier religious worlds. Historian John McGreevy suggests that overcoming barriers to racial integration in the twenty-first century has gone well
beyond struggles for and against "neighborhood conservation" in the face
of incoming African Americans. Catholic-led community organizational
efforts in many cities have supplanted ineffective antipoverty organizations and led to greater acceptance of the Church's secular role in cities.
Meanwhile, the rise of an increasingly Latino Catholic constituency may
result in "either the first [truly] American Church, combining the people
and ideas of the northern and southern halves of the continent, or an
impoverished vehicle." A weakened Church, divided between homeland
and urban parish communities in diaspora, may produce overwhelming,
though not insurmountable, cultural divides.[19]

Too often Latino history is parachuted into U.S. history without any
indication of specific religious continuities and discontinuities. Over
the past two centuries religious identity has increasingly become a matter of voluntary association, though churches still baptize, confirm, and
marry—defining events that circumscribe Catholicism. New identities
materialize as individuals differentiate themselves from their communities of origin. A struggle between individualism and communalism has
persisted in the transition to the new immigrant church, where Latinos
may function with or without native clergy. Transformation into a larger

"ethnic" Latino identity has made some inroads in the religious sphere, as elsewhere.[20]

The identities of Mexican Americans, Puerto Ricans, and Cubans have been regenerated through a wide range of factors, depending on the time of arrival, contacts with the homeland, and the intervention of local institutions. The continuities and discontinuities of Latino religious tradition, which historians and social scientists have not previously examined within a comparative urban framework, along with more studied phenomena such as postmodern cities and identities, constitute the pillars of Latino Catholicism in the new immigrant church. This new body also takes in indigenous and African roots of religiosity in the Latin American and U.S. contexts, offering useful alternatives to outmoded concepts of race, ethnicity, and assimilation.[21]

Notes

Abbreviations Used for Archival Sources

AASA Archives of the Archdiocese of San Antonio, Texas
ACA   Archives of the Chicago Archdiocese
CCES Catholic Church Extension Society Papers, Loyola University of Chicago
RA Redemptorist Fathers Archives, Bay Ridge, Brooklyn, New York
SA Scalabrinian Archives, Western Branch of the Missionaries of St. Charles, Oak Park, Illinois
SB Spanish Book, New York City Municipal Archives and Records Center
TACC Truth About Cuba Committee, Cuban Exile Collection, University of Miami
UNDA Robert E. Lucey Collection, University of Notre Dame, South Bend, Indiana

Introduction

1. Vidal, "Popular Religion among the Hispanics in the General Area of Newark," 238.

2. Toynbee, *An Historian's Approach to Religion*, 171–173; Vidal, "Towards an Understanding of Synthesis in Iberian and Hispanic American Popular Religiosity," 72.

3. Turner and Turner, *Image and Pilgrimage in Christian Culture*, 49, 209.

4. Francis, "The Hispanic Liturgical Year," 130, 131.

5. Espin, "Popular Catholicism among Latinos," 316. See also Sanneh, *Encountering the West*.

6. Espin, "Tradition and Popular Religion," 69, 78.

7. Espin, "Popular Catholicism among Latinos," 323, 331, 332.

8. Ibid., 344; Dahm, *Parish Ministry in a Hispanic Community*, 119.

9. Stevens-Arroyo, "The Evolution of Marian Devotionalism within Christianity and the Ibero-Mediterrean Polity," 53–57.

10. Christian, "Spain in Latino Religiosity," 326–329.

11. Espin, "Popular Catholicism among Latinos," 323, 331.

12. Ibid., 345, 355n63. For a useful and wide-ranging collection of essays on Latino religion, see Avalos, ed., *Introduction to the U.S. Latina and Latino Religious Experience*.

13. See Wright, "Popular Religiosity."

14. Dolan, *The American Catholic Experience*, 162, 189, 203, 204.

15. Dolan, *In Search of an American Catholicism*, 65, 91, 224.

16. Warren, "Displaced 'Pan-Americans' and the Transformation of the Catholic Church in Philadelphia, 1789–1850," 349, 351, 366.

17. Vidal, "Popular Religion among the Hispanics," 333, 334, 346.

18. Dahm, *Parish Ministry in a Hispanic Community*, 197–199; A. Perez, *Popular Catholicism*, 23.

19. Vidal, "Popular Religion among the Hispanics," 308.

Chapter 1. Beginnings

1. On missionary Christianity and culture, see the writings of Sanneh, especially *West African Christianity* and *Translating the Message*.

2. For background see two works by Brown, *The World of Late Antiquity, A.D. 150–750* and *The Rise of Western Christendom*.

3. Salisbury, *Iberian Popular Religion, 600 B.C. to 700 A.D.*, 2, 116, 168. See also Collins, *Early Medieval Spain*; Reilly, *The Contest of Christian and Muslim Spain, 1031–1157*; R. Fletcher, *Moorish Spain*; and Menocal, *The Ornament of the World*.

4. Hall, *Mary, Mother and Warrior*, 24.

5. Ibid., 12.

6. Nebel, *Santa María Tonantzín Virgen de Guadalupe*, 28, 39, 339.

7. Poole, *Our Lady of Guadalupe*, 1–3, 101. See also Ricard, *The Spiritual Conquest of Mexico*; Sylvest, *Nuestra Señora de Guadalupe*; and Christian, *Local Religion in Sixteenth-Century Spain*.

8. On the Guadalupe devotion north of Mexico, see Dunnington, *Guadalupe*. See also Christian, *Apparitions in Late Medieval and Renaissance Spain*.

9. For a background on the foundations of Latin American and Latino Catholicism, see, respectively, Dussel, ed., *Historia general de la iglesia en América Latina*, vol. 1, *Introducción general*, and Diaz-Stevens and Stevens-Arroyo, *Recognizing the Latino Resurgence in U.S. Religion*.

10. Jimenez de Wagenheim, *Puerto Rico*, 48. See also Nirenberg, *Communities of Violence*; Nirenberg, "Conversion, Sex, and Segregation"; Pike, *Linajudos and Conversos in Seville*; and Fernandez-Armesto and Wilson, *Reformations*.

11. See, for example, Caro Costas, "The Organization of an Institutional and Social Life."

12. Segre, Coyula, and Scarpaci, *Havana*, 11–13, 15, 16.

13. Lewis, *Main Currents in Caribbean Thought*, 42. On the oppressive nature of the conquest, see G. Gutiérrez, *Las Casas*, and Rivera, *A Violent Evangelism*.

14. Quoted in "The Conquest of Cuba," in Sanderlin, ed., *Bartolomé de Las Casas*, 63.

15. Dussel, *History and the Theology of Liberation*, 84.

16. Kapitzke, *Religion, Power, and Politics in Colonial St. Augustine*, 133. See also A. Perez, *Popular Catholicism*.

17. Kapitzke, *Religion, Power, and Politics in Colonial St. Augustine*, 132. See also Charles Gibson, *The Aztecs under Spanish Rule*, and Carrasco, *Daily Life of the Aztecs*.

18. Tijerina, *Tejano Empire*, 91–93; Dolan, *The American Catholic Experience*, 13, 281. See also Stevens-Arroyo, "The Inter-Atlantic Paradigm."

19. Reps, *The Forgotten Frontier*, 93; Reps, *Cities of the American West*, 119; Weber, *The Spanish Frontier in North America*, 52–54. See also R. Wright, "Local Church Emergence and Mission Decline."

20. Espin, "Tradition and Popular Religion," 63, 69.

21. Vecsey, "Pueblo Indian Catholicism," 5, 11, 12. See also Chavez, *Our Lady of the Conquest*, and Leal, *"La Conquistadora* as History and Fictitious Autobiography."

22. Simons and Hoyt, *Hispanic Texas*, 32, 108, 109.

23. Bremer, *Blessed with Tourists*, 21.

24. Matovina, "Our Lady of Guadalupe Celebrations in San Antonio, Texas, 1840–41," 116–118. See also Matovina, *Tejano Religion and Ethnicity*.

25. Almaraz, *The San Antonio Missions and Their System of Land Tenure*, 44.

26. Fernando Alanís Enciso, "Los extranjeros en Mexico, la inmigración, y el gobierno," 545, 552, 565; Archdiocese of San Antonio, *Archdiocese of San Antonio, 1874–1974*, 74. See also Weber, *The Mexican Frontier, 1821–1846*, and Poyo, "Immigrants and Integration in Late Eighteenth-Century Bexar." On continuing conflicts in Texas, see Montejano, *Anglos and Mexicans in the Making of Texas, 1836–1986*.

27. Rogelio Zelada, "Nuestro primer obispo: Don Luis Peñalver y Cárdenas," *La Voz Católica* (Miami), May 2005, 18.

28. Griffin, *The United States and the Disruption of the Spanish Empire, 1810–1822*, 77; Brooks, *Diplomacy and the Borderlands*, 94; Manning, *Early Diplomatic Relations between the United States and Mexico*, 212. See also Powell, *Tree of Hate*; Shea, *History of the Catholic Church in the United States*, vol. 3; and R. Wright, "The Hispanic Church in Texas under Spain and Mexico."

29. Quoted in Narrett, "A Choice of Destiny," 55.

30. Crook, "San Antonio, Texas, 1846–1861," 212; Downs, "The History of Mexicans in Texas, 1820–1845," 41. See also two works by De Leon, *The Tejano Community, 1836–1900* and *They Called Them Greasers*.

31. *The Handbook of Texas Online*, www.tsha.utexas.edu/handbook/online/articles/TT/nbt1_print.html.

32. See Matovina, "Tejano Lay Initiatives in Worship, 1830–1860." For the New Mexican perspective, see Romero, *Reluctant Dawn*.

33. Bremer, *Blessed with Tourists*, 66, 69.

34. Fehrenbach, *The San Antonio Story*, 155, 156; Stewart and De Leon, *Not Room Enough*, 44. See also the *Constitución y leyes de la Sociedad Mutualista Mexicana de San Antonio de Béjar, Texas* (San Antonio: T. J. Scott, 1883), Cassiano-Pérez Collection, Daughters of the Republic of Texas Library, San Antonio, 13.

35. See Rivera-Pagan, "Formation of a Hispanic Theology," and Callahan, *Church, Politics, and Society in Spain, 1750–1874*.

36. Juan de Onis, introduction to Martí, *The America of José Martí*, 12–14.

37. Perez, "Cuban Catholics in the United States," 149, 152.

38. Castellanos and Castellanos, *Cultura afrocubana*, vol. 3, *Las religiones y las lenguas*, 11, 22, 23; Martinez-Alier, *Marriage, Class, and Colour in Nineteenth-Century Cuba*, 133.

39. Cros Sandoval, "Afro-Cuban Religion in Perspective," 83–84. See also Bascom, *The Yoruba of Southwestern Nigeria*; Barnet, *Afro-Cuban Religions*; and Howard, *Changing History*.

40. On the Cuban patroness, Our Lady of Charity, see Tweed, *Our Lady of the Exile.*

41. Luis, *Culture and Customs of Cuba,* 19, 22, 23.

42. De la Torre, *The Quest for the Cuban Christ,* 22. See also Estévez, "La contribución social del Padre Varela en los Estados Unidos."

43. See Martinez-Fernandez, *Protestantism and Political Conflict in the Nineteenth-Century Hispanic Caribbean.*

44. Vidal, "Citizens Yet Strangers," 18.

45. Ibid., 23.

46. Ibid., 17, 22.

47. De Hostos, ed., *Diccionario histórico bibliográfico comentado de Puerto Rico,* 588; Picó, *Libertad y servidumbre en el Puerto Rico del siglo XIX,* 143, 159, 161; History Task Force, Centro de Estudios Puertorriqueños, *Labor Migration under Capitalism,* 72–75; Dietz, *Economic History of Puerto Rico,* 154.

48. Vidal, "Citizens Yet Strangers,"23.

49. Silva Gotay, "Historia social de las iglesias en Puerto Rico," 258.

50. Vidal, "Citizens Yet Strangers,"26.

51. Quoted in Carroll, Appendix (Hearing before the United States Commissioner), in *Report on the Island of Porto Rico,* 616–618.

52. S. Schwartz, "The Hurricane of San Ciriaco," 316, 317, 334.

53. For background see Julian de Nieves, *The Catholic Church in Colonial Puerto Rico, 1898–1964,* and Hennesey, *American Catholics.*

54. Sweetser and Holden, *Leadership in a Successful Parish,* 8, 9.

55. Warren, "Displaced 'Pan-Americans' and the Transformation of the Catholic Church in Philadelphia, 1789–1850," 343, 344.

56. Ibid., 349–351.

57. Diocese of Brooklyn, *Diocese of Immigrants,* 18, 19, 37. See also Cohalan, *A Popular History of the Archdiocese of New York.*

Chapter 2. Mexico's Revolution Travels to San Antonio

1. Quirk. *The Mexican Revolution and the Catholic Church, 1910–1929,* 3, 7, 11. See also Bazant, *Alienation of Church Wealth in Mexico.*

2. MacLachlan and Beezley, *El Gran Pueblo,* 90, 93; Crow, *Mexico Today,* 65; Clark, "Mexican Labor in the United States," 112–114; Montejano y Aguinaga, *El clero y la independencia en San Luis Potosí,* 7, 9.

3. Mecham, *Church and State in Latin America,* 390. See also Reich, *Mexico's Hidden Revolution.*

4. Zamudio, "*Huejuquillense* Immigrants in Chicago," 36, 41, 51.

5. Roman, "Church-State Relations and the Mexican Constitutional Congress, 1916–1917," 73, 80. See also Veliz, *The Centralist Tradition of Latin America.*

6. Dulles, *Yesterday in Mexico,* 311–314; Taylor, *A Spanish-Mexican Peasant Community,* 133, 135. See also Meyer, *The Cristero Rebellion.*

7. D. Johnson, "Exiles and Intrigue," 36; Matovina, *Tejano Religion and Ethnicity*, 66.

8. See Bremer, *Blessed with Tourists*, and Deck, introduction to Deck, ed., *Frontiers of Hispanic Theology in the United States*.

9. Arthur Drossaerts, American Board of Catholic Missions (ABCM) *Annual Report to the American Episcopate* (1928–1929), 161, in Catholic Church Extension Society Collection (CCES), Loyola University of Chicago.

10. Sra. Tafolla interview, 1929, Paul S. Taylor Papers, Bancroft Library, University of California, Berkeley.

11. Chappelle, "Local Welfare Work of Religious Organizations in San Antonio, Texas," 150.

12. W. W. Hume, "The Motor Chapel 'St. Peter' in Texas," *Extension*, December 1914, 18–19; F. Montero, "Historical Sketch of Our Lady of Sorrows Church," typesecript, San Antonio, Texas, 1949, Vertical File, San Antonio Churches, Benson Latin American Collection, University of Texas, Austin.

13. Kelley, *The Story of Extension*, 237–239.

14. Kelley to Shaw, November 14, 1914, Extension Society File, Archives of the Archdiocese of San Antonio (AASA).

15. James Quigley, "To All American Bishops," January 25, 1915, Extension Society File, AASA.

16. Kelley to Shaw, January 25, 1915, Extension Society File, AASA. See also Kelley, *The Bishop Jots It Down*, and "Protest of the Mexican Catholic Hierarchy to the February 5, 1917 Constitution" (February 24, 1917), in Colman, ed., *Readings in Church History*.

17. Gaffey, *Francis Clement Kelley and the American Catholic Dream*, 1:7, 8, 26.

18. Hasdorff, "The *Southern Messenger* and the Mexican Church-State Controversy, 1917–1941," 147, 150; Bishop Ledvina to Eugene J. McGuinness, vice-president of the Catholic Church Extension Society, August 13, 1925, San Antonio Archdiocesan Correspondence, CCES.

19. Drossaerts, ABCM Annual Report (1930–1931). See also Schlarman, *Mexico, a Land of Volcanoes*.

20. Annie P. Carlyle, representative, American Friends Service Committee, Mexico City, to Jane Addams, March 14, 1925, Jane Addams Papers, University of Illinois at Chicago.

21. Drossaerts, quoted in ABCM *Annual Report* (1928–1929), 45.

22. Annals of the Redemptorist Community, New Orleans, Our Lady of Perpetual Help Parish, San Antonio, "Selected Passages from the Community Annals of the History of the Vice Province of New Orleans," November 13, 1930, Redemptorist Archives of the Vice-Province of New Orleans.

23. Matovina and Poyo, eds., editors' note for pt. 4, "Exiles, Faith, and the Homeland," in *Presente!* 157.

24. Asociación Nacional de los Vasallos de Cristo Rey, *Libro de Actas*, vol. 1,

August 30, 1925, 1–4, AASA; Asociación Nacional de los Vasallos, "Reglamento de la Asociación Nacional de los Vasallos de Cristo Rey," November 1925, 2, 7, AASA. In the 1930s other Vasallo organizations emerged elsewhere in Texas. However, after the acute phases of the church-state crisis had abated, the Asociación faced dwindling membership.

25. Mecham, *Church and State in Latin America*, 381–384.

26. Portes Gil, *The Conflict between the Civil Power and the Clergy*, 97.

27. Archbishop Leopoldo Ruiz y Flores, apostolic delegate, "Al episcopado, clero, y católicos de Mexico," December 12, 1934, Arthur J. Drossaerts Papers, AASA; Mecham, *Church and State in Latin America*, 405, 408, 410. See also Vinca, "The American Catholic Reaction to the Persecution of the Church in Mexico, 1926–1936."

28. See also Alvear Acevedo, "La iglesia de Mexico en el período 1900–1962."

29. See, for example, *Constitución y leyes de la Sociedad Mutualista Mexicana de San Antonio de Béjar Texas* (San Antonio, 1883), 13, Cassiano-Pérez Collection, Daughters of the Republic of Texas Library, San Antonio.

30. Shaw to Archbishop J. H. Blenk, January 20, 1911, Shaw Papers, AASA.

31. Daries, "Historical Sketch," 8–10, 18; Gabriel Campo Villegas, "The Claretian Martyrs of Barbastro" [trans. Joseph Daries] (Los Angeles: Claretian Mission Fathers, May 1992), 1–5, Claretian Missionary Fathers Archive, Oak Park, Illinois; Kelley to Mundelein, December 18, 1918, Madaj Collection, ACA.

32. Shaw to George R. Holohan, October 9, 1914, Shaw Papers, AASA. See also Drossaerts, ABCM *Annual Report* (1936–1937). On the feared exodus of Mexicans, see Shaw to "Reverendo Padre," May 17, 1917, Shaw Papers, AASA.

33. Shaw to George R. Holohan, October 9, 1914, Shaw Papers.

34. Hinojosa, "Mexican-American Faith Communities in Texas and the Southwest," 115.

35. Father Gerald Bass, "History of the Vice Province of New Orleans," 1994, typescript, 3, 4, Redemptorist Archives of the Vice-Province of New Orleans.

36. *Annals* of Our Lady of Perpetual Help, September 6, 1932.

37. "Outdoor Missions," Fall 1939, typescript, in *Annals* of Our Lady of Perpetual Help.

38. *Annals* of Our Lady of Perpetual Help, January 22, 1933.

39. "Growth of the San Antonio Archdiocese: In Town Parishes by Chronology," May 11, 1989, typescript, AASA; Drossaerts, ABCM *Annual Report* (1934–1935). On Mexican-American identity during the 1930s, see Garcia, *Rise of the Mexican American Middle Class*.

40. Drossaerts to J. M. Preciado, January 15, 1925, Drossaerts Papers.

41. Drossaerts to William O'Brien, July 10, 1937, San Antonio Archdiocesan Correspondence, CCES.

42. Wright, "Religious *Fiestas* in San Antonio," 44–47.

43. Arthur J. Drossaerts, "The Children of Guadalupe," *Extension*, October 1937, 131–132.

44. See Flores, "Para el Niño Dios." On San Antonio's home altars, see, for example, "Capilla de Sr. de los Milagros," October 1926, Field Notes, Manuel Gamio Collection, Bancroft Library.

45. For a description of clubs and societies as well as bazaars and related activities at a West Side Claretian parish, see "A Prospectus Containing the Activities Religious, Educational, and Social for the Parish," January 1, 1926, Immaculate Heart of Mary File, Daughters of the Republic of Texas Library, San Antonio. The National Shrine of the Little Flower under the Spanish Carmelites also drew much attention for its shrine at Our Lady of Mt. Carmel Church.

46. Matovina, "Companion in Exile," 36, 38; Matovina, "Sacred Place and Collective Memory," 43.

47. Flores, "'Los Pastores': Performance, Poetics, and Politics in Folk Drama," 1, 2.

48. Bartholomew and Associates, *A Comprehensive City Plan, San Antonio, Texas*, 109.

49. In 1930, foreign-born Mexicans in the United States numbered 617,000; U.S. Department of Commerce, Bureau of the Census, *Fifteenth Census of the Population of the United States: 1930, Population*, vol. 6, *Supplement, Special Report on Foreign-Born White Families by Country of Birth of Head* (Washington, D.C.: General Printing Office, 1933), 318.

50. See Marquez, *LULAC*.

51. Arreola, *Tejano South Texas*, 141.

52. Greene, *Another Mexico*, 92, 93; "'La Pasionera' Still Speaks Out for Justice," *San Antonio Light*, March 6, 1988, 21, 23; Center for American History, Labor Movement in Texas file, Meyer Perlstein to Ben L. Owens, April 5, 1940; Blackwelder, *Women of the Depression*, 55. See also Vargas, "Tejana Radical."

53. Quezada, "Father Carmelo Tranchese, S.J.," 78–81, 112, 129. The term "social justice" first appeared in Catholic teaching with the 1931 release of Pope Pius XI's encyclical *Quadragesimo Anno*, subtitled *On the Reconstruction of the Social Order*, published to commemorate the fortieth anniversary of *Rerum Novarum*, the Catholic workers' charter; see O'Brien, *Public Catholicism*, and Gremillion and Castelli, *The Emerging Parish*.

54. Tranchese to Robert E. Lucey, April 1941, typescript, Jesuit Order File, AASA.

55. See, for example, Krase, "Italian American Urban Landscapes."

56. For a comparative perspective incorporating aspects of the homeland experiences of Italians with that of Mexicans, see R. Smith, "Los Ausentes Siempre Presentes."

57. Befiglio, "Italians in Small Town and Rural Texas," 35, 37, 38.

58. Rt. Rev. William D. O'Brien, president, Extension Society, to George Cardinal Mundelein, March 8, 1929, Diocesan Correspondence, CCES.

59. Sanchez, *The Spanish Civil War as a Religious Tragedy*, 10.

Chapter 3. Colonial Dilemmas

1. Silva Gotay, "The Ideological Dimensions of Popular Religiosity and Cultural Identity in Puerto Rico," 143, 151. See also Diaz-Stevens and Stevens-Arroyo, *Recognizing the Latino Resurgence in U.S. Religion.*

2. Santaella Rivera, *Historia de los Hermanos Cheos,* 35, 39. See also Lewis, *Puerto Rico,* and D. Moore, "American Religious Influence in Puerto Rico in the Twentieth Century."

3. Dietz, *Economic History of Puerto Rico,* 154; Baralt, *La buena vista, 1833–1904,* 101.

4. A. J. Willinger, "Diocese of Ponce, Puerto Rico," in American Board of Catholic Missions (ABCM), *Annual Report to the American Episcopate* (1928–1929). See also Pulido, "Sacred Expressions of the Popular," and McCormick, "Puerto Rico and the Lay Apostolate."

5. Vidal, "Citizens Yet Strangers," 42–45.

6. Reuter, *Catholic Influence on American Colonial Policies, 1898–1904,* 17, 21.

7. "Bodas de plata de los Padres Redentoristas en Puerto Rico, 1902–1927" (Mayaguez, P.R.: Redemptorist Fathers, 1927), 53, 55, 56.

8. Rev. Mariano Vassallo, "Mission Life in Porto Rico—San Juan Diocese," ABCM *Report* (1928–1929).

9. Rev. J. P. Flanagan, "Diocese of San Juan, Puerto Rico," ABCM *Report* (1928–1929).

10. Eugenio McGillicudy, "'Report' of Country Mission from Punta de Tierra, San Juan, to Country Chapel in Río Cañas, Caguas, Puerto Rico," April 26–May 3, 1931, Redemptorist Fathers Archives, Bay Ridge, Brooklyn, New York (RA).

11. Father Gregory, Report, Country Mission to Barrio Limaní, Adjuntas, Diocese of Ponce, Puerto Rico (February 21–28, 1932), RA.

12. Most Rev. A. J. Willinger, "Diocese of Ponce, P.R.," ABCM *Report* (1934–1935).

13. For background see Diaz-Stevens, "Missionizing the Missionaries."

14. "Provincial Chronicles," Vieques Parish File, 1941, RA.

15. Most Rev. Edwin V. Byrne, "Diocese of San Juan, Puerto Rico," ABCM *Report* (1939–1940).

16. Most Rev. A. J. Willinger, "Diocese of Ponce, P.R.," ABCM *Report* (1936–1937).

17. Rev. M. J. Conley, "Diocese of San Juan, Puerto Rico," ABCM *Report* (1936–1937).

18. Santaella Rivera, *Historia de los Hermanos Cheos,* 35. See also Bram, "Spirits, Mediums, and Believers in Contemporary Puerto Rico."

19. Eugene McGillicuddy and Adam Wolf, "Report from Puerta de Tierra to San Fernando in Carolina" (July 19–26, 1931), RA.

20. "Report, McGillicudy to Barrio Latorre, Lares" (November 29–December 6, 1931), RA.

21. Ibid.

22. Rogler, *Comerio*, 130, 137, 139.

23. Eugene McGillicuddy, "Report, Country Mission to Chapel of St. Anthony, Barrio Mameyes, Utuado" (January 30–February 8, 1932), RA.

24. See Vidal, "Towards an Understanding of Synthesis in Iberian and Hispanic American Popular Religiosity."

25. Ibid., 85.

26. Perez y Mena, *Speaking with the Dead*, 1–3, 237. See also Duany, "La religiosidad popular en Puerto Rico," and Orsi, "Introduction: Crossing the City Line."

27. Puerto Rico Bureau of Labor, *Report on the Housing Conditions of Laborers in Porto Rico*, 40–48, 55, 110.

28. Augelli, "San Lorenzo, a Case Study of Recent Migrations in Interior Puerto Rico," 203, 204.

29. Jordan, *White over Black*, 221.

30. Ernst, *Immigrant Life in New York City*, 181; Eiras Roel and Rey Castelao, *Los Gallegos y América*, 49–51; Albion, *The Rise of New York Port, 1815–1860*, 221.

31. Charles E. McDonnell, bishop of Brooklyn, to Right Rev. John W. Shaw, San Antonio, December 12, 1914, RA; "Facts Regarding Spanish Work," January 21, 1937, Spanish Book (SB); Case History 7, March 13, 1939, SB. For additional background see Sanchez Korrol, *From Colonia to Community*; Andreu Iglesias, ed., *Memoirs of Bernardo Vega*; and James, *Holding Aloft the Banner of Ethiopia*.

32. Nicolás Bagueña, C.M., "La nueva casa e iglesia del Sto. Cristo de la Agonía de Limpias," *Anales de la Congregación de la Misión* (Spanish Vincentians), October 3, 1930, 83; Nicolás Bagueña, C.M., "La nueva casa iglesia del Sto. Cristo de Limpias," *Anales de la Congregación de la Misión*, January 14, 1931, 191. See also Rybolt, "Parish Apostolate."

33. Diocese of Brooklyn, *Diocese of Immigrants*, 61, 65.

34. See Espinosa, "*El Azteca*"; Espinosa, "Borderland Religion"; Justo Gonzalez, "In Quest of a Protestant Hispanic Ecclesiology" and "Postscript: Hanging on an Empty Cross." On race and identity among Puerto Ricans, see Betances, "The Prejudice of Having No Prejudice in Puerto Rico, Part 2"; Seda Bonilla, *Los derechos civiles en la cultura puertorriqueña;* and Rodriguez, *Puerto Ricans.*

35. Leeder, *The Gentle General*, 65, 66.

36. Barney Conal, "Puerto Rican Societies," August 31, 1936, SB.

37. Sanchez Korrol, *From Colonia to Community*, 111.

38. Bayor, *Neighbors in Conflict*, 167.

39. Spanish Speaking Migrants in New York, Life Histories, 1939, SB; Individual Case Study 2, February 21, 1939, SB; Leo Lancier, "Spanish Colony," December 16, 1935, SB; Ware, *Greenwich Village, 1920–1930*, 16.

40. Bayor, "The Neighborhood Invasion Pattern," 34; Gerald Fitzgerald, "Spanish Fiestas, Songs and Dances in New York," August 6, 1936, SB; Louis Masin, "Spaniards in New York: José Camprubí," November 27, 1936, SB.

41. McKay, *Harlem*, 41, 69, 112.

42. Chenault, *The Puerto Rican Migrant in New York City*, 97.

43. See the following studies by Stevens-Arroyo: "The Catholic Ethos as Politics," "Jaime Balmes Redux," and "Catholicism as Civilization: Contemporary Reflections on the Political Philosophy of Pedro Albizu Campos."

44. See Naisson, *Communists in Harlem during the Depression.*

45. Barney Conal and Gerald Fitzgerald, "Spanish-American Societies in New York," Works Progress Administration Federal Writers Project (1936), SB.

46. On the Spanish Civil War, see Sanchez, *Anticlericalism*, and Sanchez, *Reform and Reaction.*

47. For background see Vidal, "Popular Religion among the Hispanics in the General Area of Newark." Some of the material in this section has been published in a different form as David A. Badillo, "Titi Yeya's Memories: A Matriarch of the Puerto Rican Migration," in Jerome Krase and Ray Hutchison, eds., *Race and Ethnicity in New York City*, 137–158, special issue of *Research in Urban Sociology* 7 (2004); and David A. Badillo, "Aurelia Rivera," in Virginia Sanchez Korrol and Vicki Ruiz, eds., *Latinas in the United States: An Historical Encyclopedia* (Bloomington: Indiana University Press, 2005).

48. See Clark, *Porto Rico and Its Problems.*

49. Puerto Rico Reconstruction Administration, *Census of Puerto Rico, 1935*, 52.

50. Williamson, *New People*, 88; Mencke, *Mulattoes and Race Mixture*, 99.

51. Orsi, *The Madonna on 115th Street*, 34, 66; D. Di Pino to L. Covello, October 20, 1938, Leonard Covello Papers, Balch Institute for Ethnic Studies, Philadelphia. See also Leonard Covello, *The Social Background of the Italo-American School Child.*

Chapter 4. Powers of the Prelates

1. For background see Dolores Liptak, "The Incorporation of Immigrants into the American Catholic Community, 1790–1990"; Orsi, *Thank You, St. Jude;* Orsi, "Introduction: Crossing the City Line"; and Morris, *American Catholic.*

2. Kane, *Separatism and Subculture*, 323.

3. Clinchy, *Equality of Opportunity for Latin-Americans in Texas*, 33, 44; Grebler, Moore, and Guzman, *The Mexican-American People*, 123.

4. Burns, "The Mexican Catholic Community in California," 207.

5. Robert E. Lucey, archbishop of San Antonio, to Archbishop Samuel Stritch, June 19, 1945, Box 20, Samuel A. Stritch Papers, Archives of the Archdiocese of Chicago (ACA); "Progress Report," Bishops' Committee for the Spanish Speaking, November 1945, Box 20, Samuel A. Stritch Papers, ACA. See also McWilliams, *North from Mexico.*

6. Most Rev. Patrick Flores, "Role of the Church in Mexican American Affairs Measured by Results," September 25, 1971, Box 53, Joe J. Bernal Papers, University of Texas at San Antonio.

7. See Badillo, "The Catholic Church and the Making of Mexican-American Parish Communities in the Midwest."

8. José Garibay Rivera, Archbishop of Guadalajara, quoted in "Administrative Board, N.C.W.C.," August 30, 1952, 61, University of Notre Dame Archives (UNDA).

9. Privett, *The U.S. Catholic Church and Its Hispanic Members*, 153.

10. Bremer, *Blessed with Tourists*, 84, 86.

11. See Johnson, "Edgewood."

12. Privett, *The U.S. Catholic Church and Its Hispanic Members*, 158.

13. See Matovina, "Our Lady of Guadalupe."

14. Father John A. Wagner, executive secretary, Bishops' Committee for the Spanish Speaking, San Antonio, to Monsignor Arthur F. McDonald, chancellor, Diocese of Ft. Wayne–South Bend, Chancery Office, April 20, 1965, UNDA. See also Hinojosa, "Mexican-American Faith Communities in Texas and the Southwest," and De Luna, *Faith Formation and Popular Religion*.

15. Robert E. Lucey to Bishop Leven, May 2, 1962, UNDA.

16. For a comparison of Los Angeles and San Antonio Mexican Americans, see Skerry, *Mexican Americans*.

17. See Bronder, *Social Justice and Church Authority*.

18. From 1950 to 1960 in Puerto Rico, GNP grew from $755 million to $1.676 billion, and GDP grew from $724 million to $1.691 billion. On religious and cultural repercussions of Operation Bootstrap, see Dohen, "The Background of Consensual Union in Puerto Rico," and Diaz-Stevens, "The Saving Grace."

19. See Maldonado, *Teodoro Moscoso and Puerto Rico's Operation Bootstrap*.

20. "Remarks by Mayor Robert F. Wagner at Afternoon Session of Annual Meeting of Council of Spanish-American Organizations of New York, held at the Benjamin Franklin High School," April 14, 1956, Box 276, Wagner File, NYC-MARC.

21. Alonso, *Muñoz Marin vs. the Bishops*, 173.

22. Ibid., 184.

23. Ibid., 97.

24. See Julian de Nieves, *The Catholic Church in Colonial Puerto Rico, 1898–1964*.

25. Binder and Reimers, *All the Nations under Heaven*, 202.

26. Caro, *The Power Broker*, 740, 741, 845. For the effects of urban renewal on Italian American communities, see Krase, "Italian American Urban Landscapes: Images of Social and Cultural Capital."

27. Diaz-Stevens, *Oxcart Catholicism on Fifth Avenue*, 112.

28. Orsi, *The Madonna on 115th Street*, 102, 182, 183.

29. Vidal, "Citizens Yet Strangers," 73, 75, 78.

30. "Report," March 9–15, 1942, St. Cecilia's Parish File, RA; "St. Cecilia's, New York," typescript, St. Cecilia's General File, January 1940, RA; "St. Cecilia's Church," New York St. Cecilia's File, 1948, RA.

31. Vidal, "Popular Religion among the Hispanics in the General Area of Newark," 72.

32. Vidal, "Citizens Yet Strangers," 94.

33. Ibid., 101.

34. Fitzpatrick, *The Stranger Is Our Own.*

35. Gannon, *Up to the Present,* 272; Cooney, *The American Pope,* 323. See also Fitzpatrick, "The Dilemma of Social Research and Social Policy."

36. Diocese of Brooklyn, *Diocese of Immigrants,* 122.

37. Glazer and Moynihan, *Beyond the Melting Pot,* 106; Wakefield, *Island in the City,* 62, 65, 76. On the connection between immigrant and ethnic Catholicism, see Abramson, "Ethnic Diversity within Catholicism."

38. See Estades, "Symbolic Unity," and Kantrowitz, *Ethnic and Racial Segregation in the New York Metropolis.*

39. Skerrett, "The Irish Parish in Chicago, 1880–1930," 1.

40. Neary, "Black-Belt Catholic Space," 79, 86, 87.

41. Kelliher, "Hispanic Catholics and the Archdiocese of Chicago, 1923–1970," 126, 133.

42. See Valdes, *Barrios Norteños.*

43. Lennon, *A Comparative Study of the Patterns of Acculturation of Selected Puerto Rican Protestant and Roman Catholic Families in an Urban Metropolitan Area,* 36, 37, 119.

44. See Kelliher, "Mexican Catholics and Chicago's Parishes, 1955–1976."

45. See Msgr. Vincent W. Cooke, "Archdiocese of Chicago," in *Spiritual Care of Puerto Rican Migrants,* ed. Ferree, Illich, and Fitzpatrick.

46. Samuel Stritch, "Neighborhood Conservation: Housing as a Pastoral Problem," *Catholic Charities Review* 37 (February 1953): 33–35. See also Ralph, *Northern Protest.*

47. Finks, *The Radical Vision of Saul Alinsky,* 17, 111, 233.

48. Kelliher, "Hispanic Catholics and the Archdiocese of Chicago, 1923–1970," 296.

49. Catechism classes in progress, March 24, 1962; Knights of St. John, Report for 1961, Catholic Charities Extension Society File, AAC. See also Mahon, *La familia de Dios: Un curso para catequistas* (Chicago: Cardinal's Committee for the Spanish-Speaking in Chicago, 1961).

50. Welfare Council of Metropolitan Chicago, May 1956, Box 373, Welfare Council Papers, Chicago Historical Society.

51. Kelliher, "Hispanic Catholics and the Archdiocese of Chicago, 1923–1970," 166.

52. Ibid., 190.

53. See Koenig, ed., *A History of the Parishes of the Archdiocese of Chicago,* vol. 2.

54. U.S. Department of Health, Education, and Welfare (HEW), *Resettlement Recap: A Periodic Report from the Cuban Refugee Center* (Washington, D.C.: HEW, February 1964), 3; Harry C. Koenig, *Caritas Christi Urget Nos,* 2:958, 959.

55. Bishops' Committee for the Spanish-Speaking, "Annual Report 1966" (Washington, D.C.: National Catholic Welfare Conference, 1966).

56. On the origins of the Anglo-Latino bifurcation within the U.S. church, see Dolan, "Conclusion," 442, 453.

57. See McGreevy, *Parish Boundaries.*

Chapter 5. Cuban Miami and Exile Catholicism

1. Portions of this chapter appeared in David A. Badillo, "Catholicism and the Search for Nationhood in Miami's Cuban Community," *U.S. Catholic Historian* 20 (Fall 2002). For comparisons among the religious experiences of urban immigrant groups, see Conzen, "The Place of Religion in Urban and Community Studies," 110–114.

2. McNally, "Presence and Persistence," 74, 76, 78.

3. See Stevens-Arroyo, "Introduction."

4. Ramirez Calzadilla, "Religion in the Work of Fernando Ortiz," 194. See also Crahan, "Salvation through Christ or Marx."

5. L. Perez, "Cuban Catholics in the United States," 5.

6. Lampe, "Las iglesias a la hora de la revolución cubana," 397.

7. See Tweed, "Diasporic Nationalism and Urban Landscape."

8. Kirk, *Between God and the Party,* 96.

9. Gomez Treto, *The Church and Socialism in Cuba,* 30, 35, 39.

10. Poyo, *"With All, and for the Good of All,"* 121; Segre, Coyula, and Scarpaci, *Havana,* 80, 98. See also Poyo, "The Cuban Experience in the United States, 1865–1940."

11. Dussel, *History and the Theology of Liberation.*

12. Alfonso, *Cuba, Castro, y los católicos,* 28. See also Dewart, *Christianity and Revolution.*

13. Kirk, *Between God and the Party,* 100.

14. Quoted in Ginger Thompson, "Eager Cubans Ache for Hope after Four Decades of Atheism," *Chicago Tribune,* January 18, 1998, 8.

15. Ibid. See also Clark, De Fana, and Sánchez, *Human Rights in Cuba,* and Pedraza, "Pope John Paul II's Visit and the Process of Democratic Transition in Cuba."

16. Quoted in Lampe, "Las iglesias a la hora de la revolución cubana," 398.

17. "The Attack on the Church Continues," *Cuba Information Service* (Coral Gables, Fla.), September 23, 1961, 4, Cuban Exile Collection, University of Miami; "Cuban Communist Tactics: The Agrarian Fiasco," *Cuba Information Service,* February 24, 1962, 11, 12; "The Communist Destruction of the Free Press in Cuba," *Cuba Information Service,* July 13, 1963, 9–12.

18. Instituto Cubano de Cooperación y Solidaridad en Venezuela, *El presidio político en Cuba comunista,* 18.

19. Ibid., 466.

20. Ibid., 469.

21. Valls, *Forty Years and Twenty Days*, 86, 112, 141; Martino, *I Was Castro's Prisoner*, 41.

22. Fidel Castro quoted. See also Hageman and Wheaton, eds., *Religion in Cuba Today*.

23. Clark, De Fana, and Sánchez, *Human Rights in Cuba*, 60.

24. Kirk, *Between God and the Party*, 129.

25. Walsh. "Religion in the Cuban Diaspora."

26. Ibid.

27. Howard Kleinberg, "1933: Cuban Exiles in Miami," *Miami Herald*, August 10, 1993, 12B; U.S. Department of Health, Education, and Welfare (HEW), *Resettlement Recap: A Periodic Report from the Cuban Refugee Center* (Washington, D.C.: HEW, February 1964), 3.

28. Triay, *Fleeing Castro*, 34, 43; Walsh, "Cuban Refugee Children," 218.

29. De los Angeles Torres, *The Lost Apple*, 20. See also Diaz, "Díme con Quien Andas y Te Diré Quien Eres."

30. Bishop Coleman O. Carroll, Miami, to Rev. Joseph A. Cusack, director, Order of Martha, Chicago, July 27, 1961, Correspondence File (Miami), Catholic Church Extension Society Archives, Loyola University of Chicago (CCES).

31. L. Perez, "Cuban Catholics in the United States," 200.

32. Walsh, "Religion in the Cuban Diaspora."

33. "El Templo de San Juan Bosco: Monumento a la fe y a la libertad," *Bohemia Libre*, July 18, 1965, 23A. See also McNally, *Catholicism in South Florida, 1868–1968*, and Strong, "Refugees from Castro's Cuba—Of Fish and Freedom."

34. "Respaldo del Catolicismo de Miami al éxodo cubano," *Patria* (Miami), October 22, 1965, 1.

35. Hall, *Mary, Mother and Warrior*, 276, 277.

36. Archdiocese of Miami, Terrenos del Mercy Hospital, Ermita de la Caridad, "Historic Data regarding the Lady of Charity," 1, 2.

37. Tweed, "Diasporic Nationalism and Urban Landscape," 132, 142, 148. See also García, *Havana USA*, and Grenier and Perez, *The Legacy of Exile*.

38. A. Gonzalez, "Pastoral Care of 'los Marielitos,'" 53, 57, 58.

39. "Ybor City: Último bastión del Fidelo-comunismo en Florida," *Avance*, December 23, 1960, 18.

40. On nationalism and U.S.-Cuba relations, see Casanovas, *Bread or Bullets!* See also Zolberg, Suhrke, and Aguayo, *Escape from Violence*.

41. Gastón Baquero, "La iglesia en Cuba antes y después del comunismo," *Patria*, September 29, 1967, 1.

42. Luis V. Manrara, president, Truth About Cuba Committee, "Monumento a la Virgen del Cobre," *Diario las Américas* (Miami), January 13, 1970, 5.

43. "Special Report, the Communist Invasion of Cuba: A Summary of Intelligence Reports Received by Various Cuban Organizations in Exile, Individual Sources, Covering the Landings and Disposition of Soviet and Communist Bloc Troops in Cuba," *Cuba Information Service*, September 15, 1962, 1–3, 6–8.

44. "Conferencia de Manrara en la RECE," *Diario las Américas*, December 20, 1968, 1.

45. Luis V. Manrara, "Plan para la victoria: Un esquema," typescript, September 1968, Box 13, Truth About Cuba Committee, Cuban Exile Collection, University of Miami (TACC).

46. Luis V. Manrara to Hardgrove Norris Jr., M.D., St. Augustine, Florida, March 19, 1964, Box 27, TACC.

47. Luis V. Manrara to Father John J. Kelly, St. Patrick's Rectory, San Diego, August 22, 1967, Box 6, TACC.

48. Ernesto E. Blanco, associate professor, Department of Engineering Graphics and Design, Tufts University, to Erwin D. Canham, editor in chief, *Christian Science Monitor*, Boston, January 12, 1969, Box 91, TACC.

49. Luis V. Manrara to Manuel R. Morales Gómez, Holiday Tours, Miami, September 7, 1966, Box 25, TACC.

50. Luis V. Manrara, "Cubano, no preguntes más en tono de queja: Cuando volvemos a Cuba?" *Comandos "L"* (Miami) 1 (December 1966): 1–2.

51. Walsh, "Religion in the Cuban Diaspora."

52. Herrera, "The Cuban Ecclesial Enclave in Miami," 212, 218, 220. See also Hernandez, "The ACU."

53. Portes and Stepick, *City on the Edge*, 139, 144, 149. See also Clark, *Religious Repression in Cuba*.

54. Walsh, "Religion in the Cuban Diaspora." See also M. Garcia, "Adapting to Exile."

55. Boswell and Curtis, *The Cuban-American Experience*, 82, 154–156; Mackey and Beebe, *Bilingual Schooling and the Miami Experience*, 119–121. See also Masud Piloto, *With Open Arms*; Gonzalez-Pando, *The Cuban Americans*; and University of Miami, *The Cuban Immigration, 1959–1966, and Its Impact on Miami-Dade County, Florida*.

56. Clark et al., *The 1980 Mariel Exodus*, 42.

57. "A Time to Reconsider Value of Cuban Airlift" (editorial), *Miami Herald*, July 31, 1968, 6A; "Time for New Answers to Refugee Dilemmas" (editorial), *Miami Herald*, August 6, 1969, 4A. The origins of the memorandum date to September 1965, when Castro allowed unrestricted departure of all dissatisfied Cubans whose relatives came to pick them up by sea from the port of Camarioca. By early November, 450 boats providing transportation for ten thousand refugees awaited passengers off Cuban shores. Once initial U.S. opposition dissipated, the Coast Guard began escorting the boats and securing those that were not seaworthy. "A Resettlement Plan That Might Work" (editorial), *Miami News*, December 17, 1961, 4B; U.S. Department of Health, Education, and Welfare (HEW), *Resettlement Recap: A Periodic Report from the Cuban Refugee Center* (Washington, D.C.: HEW, December 1963), 1, 3; HEW, *Resettlement Re-cap* (July 1963), 2–5; "Nada disminuirá la asistencia a los cubanos del Centro de Refugiados," *Diario las Américas* (Miami), January 14, 1970, 12; "La obra prodigiosa de los cubanos en Puerto Rico," *Impresiones: Una Revista de Principios* 3 (April-May 1964), 4.

58. University of Miami, *The Cuban Immigration, 1959–1966, and Its Impact on Miami-Dade County, Florida*, 159.

59. See Morrisey, ed., *Miami's Neighborhoods*.

60. See Moore, "Afro-Cubans and the Communist Revolution."

61. A. Gonzalez, "Pastoral Care of 'los Marielitos,'" 58.

62. Espin, "Popular Catholicism among Latinos," 311.

63. Agustín Román, "El Mariel demostró al amor familiar del pueblo cubano," *En Comunión* (Miami), May 2005, 4.

64. Walsh, "Religion in the Cuban Diaspora."

65. See Haney and Vanderbush, "The Role of Ethnic Interest Groups in U.S. Foreign Policy," 347.

66. Mireya Navarro, "One City, Two Cubas," *New York Times*, February 11, 1999, A1, A25. See Kirk, "From Counterrevolution to *Modus Vivendi*, " and Pedraza, "This Too Shall Pass."

67. "Cuban Exiles Denounce Archbishop for Discrimination," *Alerta* (Miami), September 1, 1972, translated and reprinted in Matovina and Poyo, eds., *Presente!* 223.

68. "Comunismo-ateismo y el 'catolicismo,'" *Patria*, February 24, 1967, 10.

69. De la Torre, *La Lucha for Cuba*, 139.

70. A. Perez, "The History of Hispanic Liturgy since 1965," 145. See also Stevens-Arroyo, "Introduction," and Stevens-Arroyo, "The Emergence of a Social Identity among Latino Catholics."

71. Angelique Ruhí-Lopez, "Aumento de estudiantes hispanos enriquece a las escuelas católicas de Broward," *La Voz Católica* (Miami) 52 (August 2004): 2.

72. Perez Firmat, *Next Year in Cuba*, 90. See also his *Life on the Hyphen*.

73. Cruz and Suchlicki, *The Impact of Nicaraguans in Miami*, 4, 5, 24. See also Sommers, "Musical Traditions of Miami's New Managua."

74. Cruz and Suchlicki, *The Impact of Nicaraguans in Miami*, 38, 97.

75. Max Barbosa, "Comunidad peruana celebra con júbilo al Señor de los Milagros," *La Voz Católica* 52 (October 2004): 2; Brenda Tirado Torres, "Hispanos de Broward: 'Por favor, mas misas en español!" *La Voz Católica* 51 (September 2003): 5.

76. Elaine De Valle, "Madres y esposas piden libertad de disidentes presos," *La Voz Católica* 52 (May 2004): 3.

77. Elaine De Valle, "Cuba's Paya Met by Divided Exiles on Visit to Miami," *Miami Herald*, January 13, 2003, 1A; Andrea Elliott and Elaine De Valle, "Cuban Exiles Shifting Hard-Line Position," *Miami Herald*, February 12, 2003, 1A.

78. Pedraza, "Pope John Paul II's Visit and the Process of Democratic Transition in Cuba," 145.

79. Stan Yarbo, "Prisoner of Conscience," *New Times* (Miami) 8 (August 4–10, 1993): 25, 26, 30, 34. See also Jorge Luis Mota, "Even to See Pontiff, Many Cubans in Chicago Opposing Pilgrimages," *Chicago Tribune*, January 18, 1998, 15.

80. Elaine De Valle, "Cuba's Paya Met by Divided Exiles on Visit to Miami," *Miami Herald*, January 13, 2003, 1A.

81. Juan J. Sosa, "La iglesia en diálogo: Un espacio sagrado," *La Voz Católica* 52 (August 2004): 11.

82. Walsh, "Religion in the Cuban Diaspora."

Chapter 6. Suburbanization and Mobility in Catholic Chicago

1. "Immigration," in Bureau of Immigration, National Catholic Welfare Council, *Official Year Book* (Washington, D.C.: National Catholic Welfare Council, 1928), 1.

2. American Board of Catholic Missions, "Minutes of Meetings of May Twelfth and Thirteenth, 1927, with the Bishops of the West" (Chicago: ABCM, 1927), 7, Madaj Collection, ACA. See also Badillo, "The Catholic Church and the Making of Mexican-American Parish Communities in the Midwest."

3. Kelliher, "Hispanic Catholics and the Archdiocese of Chicago, 1923–1970." See also Jones, "Conditions Surrounding Mexicans in Chicago."

4. Dolan, *In Search of an American Catholicism*, 216. See also D'Agostino, *Rome in America*, and D'Agostino, "The Scalabrini Fathers, the Italian Emigrant Church, and Ethnic Nationalism in America."

5. For a comparative perspective, see Vecoli, "Prelates and Peasants."

6. For background see McCarthy, "Which Christ Came to Chicago," and Badillo, "Incorporating Reform and Religion: Americanization and Mexican Immigrants in Chicago." On deed restrictions and Chicago Mexican Americans, who were judged white, see Philpott, *The Slum and the Ghetto*, 146.

7. On non-Mexican devotions at Our Lady of Guadalupe Church, see Orsi, *Thank You, St. Jude*.

8. McCarthy, "Which Christ Came to Chicago," 220; San Antonio Archdiocese, Religious Women, Cordi-Marian Sisters File, 1930–1954, AASA.

9. Matovina, "Our Lady of Guadalupe," 9.

10. See Kerr, "The Chicano Experience in Chicago, 1920–1970."

11. McMahon, *What Parish Are You From?* 2, 19, 189; Gamm, *Urban Exodus*, 15–18. See also McGreevy, *Parish Boundaries*.

12. Suro and Singer, "Changing Patterns of Latino Growth in Metropolitan America," 196, 197; Frey, "Melting Pot Suburbs," in 174, 175, 186, 199.

13. The restoration included the installation of vivid stained-glass images portraying the historic evolution of the community, including the struggles of workers and clergy, as well as the specter of demolition (represented ominously by a wrecking ball).

14. Paral, "Suburban Immigrant Characteristics," 1–3; Katz and Lang, "Introduction," 10, 11; Logan, "Ethnic Diversity Grows, Neighborhood Integration Lags," 248.

15. Taylor, *A Spanish-Mexican Peasant Community*, 213, 280.

16. Montoya, *La experiencia potosina en Chicago*, 21, 27. On transnationalism, see Schiller, Basch, and Blanc-Szanton, "Transnationalism."

17. Jesús Escalante and Carlos Hernández-Zapata, quoted in Montoya, *La experiencia potosina en Chicago*, 64, 65.

18. ACOPIL, "Segunda semana potosina en Chicago," pamphlet (Chicago: Asociación de Clubes y Organizaciones Potosinas en Illinois, 2000); Montoya, *La experiencia potosina en Chicago*, 21.

19. Real names were withheld to assure the respondents' privacy; the author conducted the interviews in Chicago in the autumn of 2000.

20. On nonreligious migrant networks, see Goldring, "The Mexican State and Transmigrant Organizations."

21. Paral, "Suburban Immigrant Characteristics," 1–3; Karen Brandon, "Many Migrants Harvest Jobs Manicuring Suburban Lawns," *Chicago Tribune*, July 3, 1992, 11; Dan Mihalopoulos, "Busy Store Links Elgin, Mexico," *Chicago Tribune*, March 1, 2000, 1; Gary Moore, "Waukegan's Little Sisters: Two Mexican Towns Share a Growing Kinship with the Big Destination Up North," *Chicago Tribune*, January 31, 1999, 1.

22. Dolan, *In Search of an American Catholicism*, 179.

23. See Institute for Latino Studies, University of Notre Dame, *Bordering the Mainstream*.

24. Hirsch, *Making the Second Ghetto*, 53, 86, 127, 195.

25. U.S. District Court, Northern District of Illinois, Eastern Division, *Summons against Town of Cicero and Henry J. Klosak, President of Cicero, and the Cicero Housing Authority; USA vs. Town of Cicero, Henry J. Klosak, and the Cicero Housing Authority*, January 14, 1983; *USA v. Town of Cicero, Illinois*, and *Leadership Council for Metropolitan Open Communities v. Town of Cicero Illinois*, Settlement Agreement and Order, May 13, 1996.

26. Office of Hispanic Ministry, Archdiocese of Chicago, "Estimates of Attendance Counts for October 2000," typescript, March 27, 2001.

27. This section is based on a recorded interview conducted at St. Mary of Celle Church in March 2003. The following year, Father Prendergast was rotated out of the parish.

28. For background on the Scalabrini Fathers, see D'Agostino, "The Scalabrini Fathers, the Italian Emigrant Church, and Ethnic Nationalism in America."

29. Melrose Park, *Centennial Celebration, 1882–1982: One Hundred Years of Progress*, 67, 69; Orsi, *The Madonna of 115th Street*, 230.

30. John Cardinal Cody, archbishop of Chicago, to Rev. Lawrence Cozzi, C.S., rector, Sacred Heart Seminary, Stone Park, Illinois, November 15, 1974, Archives of the Missionary Fathers of St. Charles, Western Region, Oak Park, Illinois (SA). The Cubans themselves later built a shrine at the back of the church where residents from throughout the suburbs attended a special yearly mass during the 1970s.

31. "Meeting with Father Pedro Rodriguez re: Masses in Spanish in Western Suburbs, Pastoral Center," April 30, 1985, SA. See also Very Rev. Peter Sordi, C.S.,

and the Confreres of Our Lady of Mt. Carmel Church, "Summary of the Meeting of January 10, 1986," and Fr. Olmes Milani, C.S., "Apostolate for the Latinos from the Our Lady of Mount Carmel Church in Melrose Park," September 1985, SA.

32. Koenig, *Caritas Christi Urget Nos,* 2:1022. See also Anne Keegan, "Shock in Pilsen Parish Felt in the Suburbs Too," *Chicago Tribune,* February 13, 1990, 11; Bill Cunniff, "Museum Houses Memories, Artifacts from the 1950s," *Chicago Sun-Times,* August 2, 2002, 14; Melita M. Garza, "Immigrants Make Their Mark on Chicago and Suburbs," *Chicago Tribune,* October 12, 1995, 11.

33. Our Lady of Mt. Carmel Parish Report, presented to the Provincial Consulting Committee, March 2, 1992; "Report of the Consulting Committee and Proposals of the Provincial Administration," Assembly 1992, Province of Saint John the Baptist, SA; P. Pietro Corbellini, "Relazione summaria annuale del Centro per i Latino-Americani," September 16, 1974, Latino Center File, Stone Park, SA.

34. Ciallela, "From Italian National Parish to Multicultural Community," 128, 288; Rev. Lawrence Cozzi, C.S., rector, Sacred Heart Seminary, Stone Park, Illinois, to Very Rev. Umberto Rizzi, C.S., Our Lady of Mt. Carmel Church, Melrose Park, Illinois, April 7, 1975, SA; "Italian Cultural Center," *Chicago Catholic,* January 25, 1980, 11.

35. Charles Leroux and Ron Grossman, "Suburban Dream Has New Followers," *Chicago Tribune,* December 2, 2001.

36. Palmer, "Building Ethnic Communities in a Small City," 138.

37. Ibid., 146, 147.

38. Koenig, ed., *A History of the Parishes of the Archdiocese of Chicago,* 151. See also Fishman, *Bourgeois Utopias;* Garreau, *Edge City;* and Johnson, *Chicago Metropolis 2020.*

39. Teresa Puente, "A New Migration," *Chicago Tribune,* August 16, 1998, 1; Lowell Livezey and Mark Bouman, "Religious Geography," in Grossman, Keating, and Rieff, eds., *The Encyclopedia of Chicago,* 696.

40. For the Chicago urban counterpart, see Dahm, *Parish Ministry in a Hispanic Community.*

41. On the suburban Mexican-American landscape in the Southwest, see Herzog, *From Aztec to High Tech,* and Straughan and Hondagneu-Sotelo, "From Immigrants in the City, to Immigrant City."

42. Dan Mihalopoulos, "Church Is *Mision* Accomplished: Hispanics in the Suburbs Are Flocking to a Palatine House of Worship," *Chicago Tribune,* February 23, 2000, 1.

43. Melissa Wahl, "Banco Popular Just That," *Chicago Tribune,* June 24, 1999, 1.

44. Cathleen Falsani, "Discrimination in the Church?" *Chicago Sun-Times,* February 5, 2001, 6.

45. Amy Carr, "Archdiocese Trying to Reach Out to Growing Hispanic Community," *Daily Herald* (Arlington Heights), April 10, 1997, 1, 9.

46. Dahm, *Parish Ministry in a Hispanic Community,* ix, 259, 277.

47. McMahon, *What Parish Are You From?* 189.

Chapter 7. New Urban Opportunities

1. See, for example, Elizondo's discussion of his upbringing as well as his pastoral work in San Antonio in *A God of Incredible Surprises.*

2. Archdiocese of San Antonio, "Proposal for Commission on Mexican-American Affairs," revised April 5, 1971, Box 43, Joe J. Bernal Papers; Russell C. Smyle, business manager, Archdiocese of San Antonio, to Les Dunbar, executive director, Field Foundation, New York, May 5, 1977, Box 144, Field Foundation, in Center for American History, University of Texas, Austin.

3. Elizondo, *A God of Incredible Surprises,* 127, 135, 146–149.

4. See John J. Shaughnessy, "Offering Respect: Theologian Emphasizes Acceptance of Differences," *Indianapolis Star,* May 15, 2004, F3.

5. Elizondo, *The Future Is Mestizo,* 58.

6. Elizondo, "Hispanic Theology and Popular Piety," 178.

7. Elizondo, *"Mestizaje* as a Locus of Theological Reflection," 166, 167.

8. A. Perez, "The History of Hispanic Liturgy since 1965," 385. See also Pedraza, "Pope John Paul II's Visit and the Process of Democratic Transition in Cuba."

9. Romero, "Charism and Power," 150, 154. See also Ramirez, "The Hispanic Peoples of the United States and the Church from 1965 to 1985."

10. Father Ralph Ruiz, provincial chairman, PADRES, San Antonio, to Most Rev. Francis J. Furey, chairman, Committee on Priestly Formation, San Antonio, October 9, 1969, PADRES File, 1967–1977, AASA.

11. Ibid.

12. "PADRES Formed: 'La Raza on Move,' Casso Declares," ca. February 5, 1970, Box 43, Bernal Papers.

13. Father Henry Casso, Holy Family, press release, San Antonio. October 9, 1969, Social Problems, PADRES, 1967–1977, AASA; Sandoval, *On the Move,* 102. See also Sandoval, "The Church and el Movimiento"; and Matovina, "Representation and the Reconstruction of Power."

14. Medina, "Las Hermanas," 170, 271.

15. See the seminal work by Gutiérrez, *A Theology of Liberation.*

16. Rev. Virgilio Elizondo, president, Mexican American Cultural Center, "Report of Activities September 1971 to September 1972, Presented to the Texas Catholic Conference," Austin, September 25, 1972, Julian Samora Papers, Benson Latin American Library, University of Texas, Austin.

17. Elizondo, "Hispanic Theology and Popular Piety," 280.

18. Virgilio P. Elizondo, president, Mexican American Cultural Center, "Dear Friend," June 1, 1982, Mexican American Cultural Center File, AASA.

19. García, "La iglesia desde el Concilio Vaticano II y Medellín," 461.

20. Sandoval, *On the Move,* 79–83.

21. A. Perez, "The History of Hispanic Liturgy since 1965," 395.

22. See Skerry, *Mexican Americans.*

23. Johnson, Cheatwood, and Bradshaw, "The Landscape of Death," 114.

24. E. D. Yoes Jr., "COPS Comes to San Antonio," *Progressive*, May 1977, 33–36, Box 144, Field Foundation. On Church and community, see also Fitzpatrick, "The Church and Social Issues."

25. Jordan McMorrough, "Bienvenido, Archbishop-Designate José H. Gomez!" *Today's Catholic* (San Antonio), January 21, 2005.

26. Diocese of Brooklyn, *Diocese of Immigrants*, 123.

27. Ibid., 124.

28. Vidal, "Citizens Yet Strangers," 111.

29. Sexton, *Spanish Harlem*, 71, 74, 78.

30. Vidal, "Citizens Yet Strangers," 143. See also Juan Gonzalez, *Harvest of Empire*.

31. Vidal, "Citizens Yet Strangers," 107. See also Diaz-Stevens, "Analyzing Popular Religiosity for Socio-religious Meaning," and Vidal, "Popular Religion among the Hispanics in the General Area of Newark."

32. Ashley, "The Stations of the Cross," 341, 360, 362. See also Appleby, "Public Catholicism."

33. Vidal, "Citizens Yet Strangers," 108. See also Deck, "The Challenge of Evangelical/Pentecostal Christianity to Hispanic Catholicism"; Warner, "Approaching Religious Diversity"; and Casanova, *Public Religions in the Modern World*.

34. Diaz-Stevens, "From Puerto Rican to Hispanic," 39.

35. Fitzpatrick, *The Stranger Is Our Own*, 205–208.

36. Vidal, "Popular Religion among the Hispanics in the General Area of Newark," 254.

37. Vidal, "Citizens Yet Strangers," 87.

38. A. Perez, "The History of Hispanic Liturgy since 1965," 386.

39. Quoted in Petroamerica Pagan de Colon, "Migration Trends," address to the First Annual Conference of Education of New Yorkers of Puerto Rican Origin, Hunter College, May 9, 1959, Welfare Council of New York, Julian Samora Papers. Benson Latin American Collection, University of Texas, Austin.

40. Minutes of meeting of the Legal Committee of the Subcommittee on Housing, Mayor's Committee on Puerto Rican Affairs in New York City, October 24, 1951, Puerto Rican Problems in NYC, Vincent Impelliteri file, New York City Municipal Archives and Records Center; Caro, *The Powerbroker*, 416. See also Schwartz, *The New York Approach*.

41. Kantrowitz, *Ethnic and Racial Segregation in the New York Metropolis*, 34, 88. 112. See also Duany, "La religiosidad popular en Puerto Rico"; Perez y Mena, *Speaking with the Dead*; and Orsi, "Introduction: Crossing the City Line."

42. Rivera-Batiz and Santiago, *Puerto Ricans in the United States*, 102–105; Amy Waldman, "Rubble to Rebirth: Tales of the Bronx," *New York Times*, April 7, 1999, E1.

43. E. Gonzalez, *The Bronx*, 132, 144; Jonnes, *We're Still Here*, 169, 170, 185. See also Ultan and Hermalyn, *The Bronx*, and Ultan and Unger, *Bronx Accent*.

44. Trumino, "The Northwest Bronx Community and Clergy Coalition," 36, 43, 47.

45. Bronx Museum of the Arts, *Devastation/Resurrection*, 94; Rooney, *Organizing the South Bronx*, 69, 200. See also O'Connor and Koch, *His Eminence and Hizzoner*, and Pantoja, "Religious Diversity and Ethnicity among Latinos."

46. Trumino, "The Northwest Bronx Community and Clergy Coalition," 291, 318. See also Hannon, "Saints and Patriots."

47. Diocese of Brooklyn, *Diocese of Immigrants*, 167.

48. Fitzpatrick, *The Stranger Is Our Own*, 60.

49. Ibid., 126.

50. Bayor, "The Neighborhood Invasion Pattern," 34.

51. Diaz-Stevens, Oxcart Catholicism on Fifth Avenue, 193–194.

52. Goris, "Dominican Immigrants," 42.

53. Ibid., 43. See also Goris, "Rites for a Rising Nationalism."

54. Levitt, "Local-Level Global Religion," 2–4, 11, 12.

55. Ibid., 5. See also Levitt, "The Ties That Change."

56. Dolan, "Conclusion," 447–450.

57. E. Gonzalez, *The Bronx*, 24.

58. Moquin and Richards, *Assumptionists in the United States*, 41, 66.

59. For recent Mexican immigration to New York City, see R. Smith, "Los Ausentes Siempre Presentes."

60. Ibid., 20, 63–67.

61. Daniel J. Wakin, "New York, Prime Conversion Ground," *New York Times*, July 11, 2004, 29. See also www.tepeyac.org (Asociación Tepeyac de Nueva York website) and R. Smith, "Mexicans in New York."

62. Smith, "'Los Ausentes Siempre Presentes,'" 100–102. See also R. Smith, "Transnational Localities."

63. "La antorcha guadalupana hacia NY, salió de Buena Vista," *El Diario/La Prensa* (New York), October 16, 2004, 12. See also Vasquez and Marquardt, *Globalizing the Sacred*.

64. Foner, "What's New about Transnationalism?" 368–370.

65. Daniel J. Wakin, "Latino Church Greets Its New Home with a Procession of the Faithful," *New York Times*, April 14, 2003, F1.

66. Mahler, "Tres Veces Mojados," 41, 42.

67. Ibid., 283, 347; Mahler, "Suburban Transnational Migrants," 178. See also Solis, "Immigration Status and Identity."

68. Foner, "What's New about Transnationalism?" 49. See also Goldring, "The Mexican State and Transmigrant Organizations."

69. Ricourt and Danta, *Hispanas de Queens*, 7, 92.

70. Goizueta, *Caminemos con Jesus*, 118. See also Espinosa, Elizondo, and Miranda, eds., *Latino Religious and Civic Activism in the United States*.

Chapter 8. Globalization and the New Immigrant Church

1. See, for example, Mohl, "Globalization, Latinization, and the Nuevo New South."

2. Vasquez and Marquardt, *Globalizing the Sacred*, 23, 24, 33.

3. Sanneh, *Whose Religion Is Christianity?* 22.

4. Perez Vilariño and Sequeiros Tizon, "The Demographic Transition of the Catholic Priesthood and the End of Clericalism in Spain," 25–28. See also Payne, *Spain's First Democracy;* Payne, *Spanish Catholicism;* Delpech, *The Oppression of Protestants in Spain;* and Mackay, *The Other Spanish Christ.*

5. Vidal, "Popular Religion among the Hispanics in the General Area of Newark," 344.

6. Peterson and Vasquez, "The New Evangelization in Latin American Perspective," 3. See also Ebaugh, "Vatican II and the Reconceptualization of the Church"; MacEoin and Riley, *Puebla;* and Chestnut, "A Preferential Option for the Spirit."

7. Freixedo, *Mi iglesia duerme*, 262.

8. Ibid., 197.

9. Chaunu, *The Reformation*, 276. See also Lynch, *Spain, 1516–1598.*

10. Stevens-Arroyo, "The Evolution of Marian Devotionalism within Christianity and the Ibero-Mediterrean Polity," 54–57, 59.

11. Dolan, "Conclusion," 452, 453. See also Dolan, *The Immigrant Church.*

12. McNally, "The Council of Trent, the Spiritual Exercises, and the Catholic Reform," 62.

13. Stevens-Arroyo, "The Evolution of Marian Devotionalism within Christianity and the Ibero-Mediterrean Polity," 69.

14. Ibid., 52.

15. Deck, "The Challenge of Evangelical/Pentecostal Christianity to Hispanic Catholicism," 425.

16. McNally, "The Council of Trent, the Spiritual Exercises, and the Catholic Reform," 53.

17. Maldonado, *Crossing Guadalupe Street*, 171.

18. See pt. 2, "Genesis of the Hispano Church," in Stevens-Arroyo, ed., *Prophets Denied Honor,* 176.

19. See Pantoja, "Religious Diversity and Ethnicity among Latinos."

20. See Mosqueda, *Chicanos, Catholicism, and Political Ideology;* Yinger, *Cesar Chavez;* Ferris and Sandoval, *The Fight in the Fields;* and Matthiessen, *Sal Si Puedes.*

21. Diaz-Stevens, "Latinas and the Church"; Cadena, "Chicano Clergy and the Emergence of Liberation Theology," 107. See also Abalos, *Latinos in the United States;* Davalos, "The Real Way of Praying"; and Tabares, "Pastoral Care of Catholic South Americans Living in the United States."

22. Hall, *Mary, Mother and Warrior,* 275, 279; Durand and Massey, *Miracles on the Border,* 64–66.

23. Diaz-Stevens, "Latinas and the Church." See also Leon, "Religious Movement in the United States–Mexico Borderlands: Toward a Theory of Chicana/o Religious Poetics," and his *La Llorona's Children's Children.*

24. See Justo Gonzalez, "Latino/a Theology." See also Isasi-Diaz, *En la Lucha / In the Struggle;* Menes, "A Brief Overview of the Cultural and Religious *Mestizaje*"; and Anzaldua, *Borderlands / La Frontera.*

25. Dahm, *Parish Ministry in a Hispanic Community,* 69, 77, 174.

26. Medina, "Las Hermanas," 117.

27. See Espin, "Tradition and Popular Religion," and National Conference of Catholic Bishops, "Called to Global Solidarity."

28. See also Mahler's *Salvadorians in Suburbia* and *American Dreaming,* and Miller, "Religion in Los Angeles."

29. Dahm, *Parish Ministry in a Hispanic Community,* 116. See also Deck, *The Second Wave,* and Sandoval, "Hispanic Immigrants and the Church."

30. See R. Smith, "Los Ausentes Siempre Presentes," and Fletcher, *La Casa de Mis Sueños.*

31. Warner, "Approaching Religious Diversity," 204. See also Wuthnow, *Christianity in the Twenty-first Century.*

32. Peterson, Vasquez, and Williams, "Introduction," 17.

33. Ibid., 214.

34. Vasquez, "Central and South American Religious Communities," 86.

35. Vasquez and Marquardt, *Globalizing the Sacred,* 9.

36. See Coleman, *The Globalisation of Charismatic Christianity;* B. Smith, *Religious Politics in Latin America;* Freston, *Evangelicals and Politics in Asia, Africa, and Latin America;* Gill, *Rendering unto Caesar;* and Brusco, *The Reformation of Machismo.*

37. Caraballo Ireland, "The Role of the Pentecostal Church as a Service Provider in the Puerto Rican Community, Boston, Massachusetts," 135, 139.

38. Paterson and Vasquez, "Upwards, Never Down," 188–191.

39. "Declaration of the Bishops of Puerto Rico on the [Catholic] Pentecostal Movement," translated from *El Imparcial,* June 15, 1972, in McDonnell, *Charismatic Renewal and the Churches,* 121.

40. See Sullivan, "St. Catherine's Catholic Church."

41. Paterson and Vasquez, "Upwards, Never Down," 199, 200.

42. Vasquez and Marquardt, *Globalizing the Sacred,* 221.

43. Berryman, *Religion in the Megacity,* 144.

44. Thumma, "Exploring the Megachurch Phenomena."

45. Vasquez, "Central and South American Religious Communities," 91. See also Jenkins, *The Next Christendom,* and Espinosa, "The Impact of Pluralism on Trends in Latin American and U.S. Latino Religions and Society."

46. Vasquez, "Central and South American Religious Communities," 101. See also Aguilar Zinser, "Repatriation of Guatemalan Refugees in Mexico."

47. Golden and McConnell, *Sanctuary*, 18, 44. See also Straughan and Hon-dagneu-Sotelo, "From Immigrants in the City to Immigrant City."

48. Hamilton and Chincilla, *Seeking Community in a Global City*, 145.

49. Davis, "Challenges to the Pastoral Care of Central Americans in the United States," 26–28.

50. Fernando Alanís Enciso, "Inmigración ilegal de centroamericanos: El caso de la Iglesia Católica y las autoridades migratorias en Nuevo Laredo, Tamaulipas," paper presented at the annual meeting of CEHILA-U.S.A., Chicago, 1995.

51. Sommers, "Inventing Latinismo," 38, 39, 42.

52. Cadaval, *Creating a Latino Identity in the Nation's Capital*, 55.

53. See Davis, *City of Quartz*.

54. Hamilton and Chincilla, *Seeking Community in a Global City*, 48.

55. Wellmeier, "Santa Eulalia's People in Exile," 100–105, 113, 114. See also Warner, "Immigration and Religious Communities in the United States."

56. Odem, "Our Lady of Guadalupe in the New South," 26, 33, 45. See also Mohl, "The Transformation of the Late-Twentieth-Century South."

57. Vasquez and Marquardt, *Globalizing the Sacred*, 224.

58. Dolan, *In Search of an American Catholicism*, 131. See also Warner, "Approaching Religious Diversity," and Miller, "Religion in Los Angeles," in *From Chicago to L.A.*

Epilogue. Latino Religious Tradition as Metaphor

1. Espin, "Popular Catholicism among Latinos," 312, 314, 321; Espin, "Tradition and Popular Religion"; Kapitzke, *Religion, Power, and Politics in Colonial St. Augustine*, 132–133.

2. Wilson, *The Myth of Santa Fe*, 25, 163. See also Hall, *Mary, Mother and Warrior*; Turner, *Dramas, Fields, and Metaphors*; Historic Santa Fe Foundation, *Old Santa Fe Today*; and Ribero-Ortega, "La Guadalupana and la Conquistadora in the Catholic History of New Mexico."

3. Dahm, *Parish Ministry in a Hispanic Community*, 196–199. See Schiller and Fouron, *Georges Woke Up Laughing*.

4. Vidal, "Popular Religion among the Hispanics in the General Area of Newark," 257.

5. See Pantoja, "Religious Diversity and Ethnicity among Latinos."

6. Binder and Reimers, *All the Nations under Heaven*, 149; Vidal, "Towards an Understanding of Synthesis in Iberian and Hispanic American Popular Religiosity," 72, 87–88.

7. Vecsey, "Pueblo Indian Catholicism," 29.

8. Bremer, *Blessed with Tourists*, 132.

9. Ibid., 135.

10. Ibid., 141.

11. McMurtry, *In a Narrow Grave*, 44.

12. Stevens-Arroyo, "Introduction," 28.

13. Charles, "Transnationalism in the Construct of Haitian Migrants' Racial Categories of Identity in New York City," 313, 316. See also Orsi, "The Religious Boundaries of an In-Between People.".

14. Moller and Wilson, "Images of Latino Philadelphia," 393. See also Vazquez, "The Development of Pan-Latino Philadelphia, 1892–1945."

15. Kirk, *Between God and the Party*, 95.

16. See Soja, *Postmetropolis*, and Hise, *Magnetic Los Angeles*.

17. Logan, Alba, and Zhang, "Immigrant Enclaves and Ethnic Communities in New York and Los Angeles," 311, 319, 321. See also Alba and Nee, *Remaking the American Mainstream*, and Logan, "Still a Global City."

18. For a different perspective on another suburbanizing religious minority, Orthodox Jews, see Etan Diamond, *And I Will Dwell in Their Midst*, and Etan Diamond, "The Kosher Lifestyle."

19. McGreevy, "Catholicism in the United States and the Problem of Diversity," 200. See also McGreevy, *Catholicism and American Freedom*.

20. Wuthnow, *Christianity in the Twenty-first Century*, 47, 50–54.

21. Warner, "Work in Progress toward a New Paradigm for the Sociological Study of Religion in the United States," 1058 1061, 1076. See also Sanneh, "Conclusion"; Justo Gonzalez, "Reinventing Dogmatics"; and McNally, "The Universal in the Particular."

Bibliography

Archival Sources

Archives of the Archdiocese of San Antonio
Archives of the Chicago Archdiocese
Archives of the Diocese of Fort Wayne–South Bend, Indiana
Balch Institute for Ethnic Studies, Philadelphia
Catholic Church Extension Society Papers, Loyola University of Chicago
Chicago Historical Society
Claretian Missionary Fathers Archive, Oak Park, Illinois
Daughters of the Republic of Texas Library, San Antonio
Hunter College of the City University of New York, Center for Puerto Rican Studies Library
Robert E. Lucey Papers, University of Notre Dame, Hesburgh Library
Redemptorist Archives of the Vice-Province of New Orleans, New Orleans
Redemptorist Fathers Archives, Bay Ridge, Brooklyn, New York
Scalabrinian Archives, Western Branch of the Missionaries of St. Charles, Oak Park, Illinois
Spanish Book, New York City Municipal Archives and Records Center
Union Theological Seminary
University of California, Berkeley, Bancroft Library
University of Illinois at Chicago
University of Miami, Reichter Library
University of Texas, Austin, Benson Latin American Library
University of Texas, Austin, Center for American History
University of Texas at San Antonio

Secondary Sources

Abalos, David T. *Latinos in the United States: The Sacred and the Political.* Notre Dame, Ind.: University of Notre Dame Press, 1986.

Abramson, Harold J. "Ethnic Diversity within Catholicism: A Comparative Analysis of Contemporary and Historical Religion." *Journal of Social History* 4 (Summer 1971): 359–388.

Adessa, Domenick J. "Refugee Cuban Children: The Role of the Catholic Welfare Bureau of the Diocese of Miami, Florida, in Receiving, Caring for, and Placing Unaccompanied Cuban Refugee Children, 1960–1963." Master's thesis, Fordham University School of Social Service, 1964.

Aguilar Zinser, Adolfo. "Repatriation of Guatemalan Refugees in Mexico: Conditions and Prospects." In *Repatriation under Conflict in Central America.* Edited by Mary Ann Larkin, Frederick C. Cuny, and Barry N. Stein. Washington, D.C.: Georgetown University, Center for Immigration Policy and Refugee Assistance, 1991.

Alanís Enciso, Fernando S. "Los extranjeros en Mexico, la inmigración, y el gobierno: Tolerancia o intolerancia religiosa, 1821–1830." *Historia Mexicana* 45
  (January–March 1996): 539–566.
————. "Inmigración ilegal de centroamericanos: El caso de la Iglesia Católica y
  las autoridades migratorias en Nuevo Laredo, Tamaulipas." Paper presented
  at the annual meeting of Comisión para el Estudio de Historia de la Iglesia en
  América Latina y el Caribe (CEHILA-U.S.A.), Chicago, April 1995.
Alba, Richard, and Victor Nee. *Remaking the American Mainstream: Assimilation
  and Contemporary Immigration*. Cambridge, Mass.: Harvard University Press,
  2003.
Albion, Robert G. *The Rise of New York Port, 1815–1860*. New York: Charles Scribner's Sons, 1939.
Alegría, Ricardo E. *La fiesta de Santiago Apóstol en Loiza Aldea*. San Juan, P.R.: Col-
  ección de Estudios Puertorriqueños, 1954.
Alfonso, Pablo M. *Cuba, Castro, y los católicos: Del humanismo revolucionario al marx-
  ismo totalitario*. Miami: Ediciones Hispamerican Books, 1985.
Almaraz, Felix D., Jr. *The San Antonio Missions and Their System of Land Tenure*. Aus-
  tin: University of Texas Press, 1989.
Alonso, Maria Mercedes. *Muñoz Marin vs. the Bishops: An Approach to Church and
  State*. Hato Rey, P.R.: Publicaciones Puertorriqueñas, 1998.
Alvear Acevedo, Carlos. "La iglesia de Mexico en el período 1900–1962." In *His-
  toria general de la iglesia en América Latina*, vol. 5, *Mexico*. Edited by Enrique
  D. Dussel. Salamanca: Comisión para el Estudio de Historia de la Iglesia en
  América Latina y el Caribe, 1984.
Andreu Iglesias, Cesar, ed. *Memoirs of Bernardo Vega: A Contribution to the History of
  the Puerto Rican Community in New York*. New York: Monthly Review, 1984.
Anzaldua, Gloria. *Borderlands / La Frontera: The New Mestiza*. San Francisco: Aunt
  Lute Books, 1987.
Appleby, R. Scott. "Public Catholicism." In *Religion and American Cultures: An En-
  cyclopedia of Traditions, Diversity, and Popular Expressions*, vol. 1. Edited by Gary
  Laderman and Luis Leon. Santa Barbara, Calif.: ABC CLIO, 2003.
Archdiocese of San Antonio. *Archdiocese of San Antonio, 1874–1974*. San Antonio,
  Tex.: Archdiocese of San Antonio, 1974.
Arreola, Daniel D. *Tejano South Texas: A Mexican American Cultural Province*. Aus-
  tin: University of Texas Press, 2002.
Ashley, Wayne. "The Stations of the Cross: Christ, Politics, and Processions on
  New York City's Lower East Side." In *Gods of the City: Religion and the American
  Urban Landscape*. Edited by Robert A. Orsi. Bloomington: Indiana University
  Press, 1999.
Augelli, John P. "San Lorenzo, a Case Study of Recent Migrations in Interior
  Puerto Rico" (1952). In *Portrait of a Society: Readings on Puerto Rican Sociology*.
  Edited by Eugenio Fernandez Mendez. Rio Piedras: University of Puerto Rico
  Press, 1972.

Avalos, Hector, ed. *Introduction to the U.S. Latina and Latino Religious Experience.* Boston: Brill Academic Publishers, 2004.

Badillo, David A. "The Catholic Church and the Making of Mexican-American Parish Communities in the Midwest." In *Mexican Americans and the Catholic Church, 1900–1965.* Edited by Jay P. Dolan and Gilberto M. Hinojosa. Notre Dame, Ind.: University of Notre Dame Press, 1994.

———. "Catholicism and the Search for Nationhood in Miami's Cuban Community." *U.S. Catholic Historian* 20 (Fall 2002): 75–90.

———. "Incorporating Reform and Religion: Americanization and Mexican Immigrants in Chicago." In *Pots of Promise: Mexicans, Reformers, and the Hull-House Kilns, Chicago, 1920–1940.* Edited by Cheryl R. Ganz and Margaret Strobel. Urbana: University of Illinois Press, 2003.

———. "Titi Yeya's Memories: A Matriarch of the Puerto Rican Migration." In *Race and Ethnicity in New York City.* Edited by Jerome Krase and Ray Hutchison. Special issue of *Research in Urban Sociology* 7 (2004): 137–158.

Baralt, Guillermo A. *La Buena Vista, 1833–1904: Estancia de frutos menores, fábrica de harinas, y hacienda cafetelera.* San Juan, P.R.: Fideicomiso de Conservación de Puerto Rico, 1988.

Barnet, Miguel. *Afro-Cuban Religions.* Princeton, N.J.: Markus Wiener, 2001.

Bartholomew, Harland, and Associates. *A Comprehensive City Plan, San Antonio, Texas: 1933 Master Plan, City of San Antonio.* St. Louis: Harland Bartholomew and Associates, 1933.

Bascom, William. *The Yoruba of Southwestern Nigeria.* New York: Holt, Rinehart and Winston, 1969.

Bayor, Ronald H. "The Neighborhood Invasion Pattern." In *Neighborhoods in Urban America.* Edited by Ronald H. Bayor. Port Washington, N.Y.: Kennikat, 1982.

———. *Neighbors in Conflict: The Irish, Germans, Jews, and Italians of New York City, 1929–1941.* Baltimore: Johns Hopkins University Press, 1978.

Bazant, Jan. *Alienation of Church Wealth in Mexico: Social and Economic Aspects of the Liberal Revolution, 1856–1875.* London: Cambridge University Press, 1971.

Beezley, William H. "Home Altars: Private Reflections of Public Life." In *Home Altars of Mexico.* Edited by Ramon A. Gutierrez. Albuquerque: University of New Mexico Press, 1997.

Befiglio, Valentine J. "Italians in Small Town and Rural Texas." In *Italian Immigrants in Rural and Small Town America.* Edited by Rudolph J. Vecoli. Staten Island, N.Y.: American Italian Historical Association, 1987.

Benavides, Gustavo. "Resistance and Accommodation in Latin American Popular Religiosity." In *An Enduring Flame: Studies on Latino Popular Religiosity.* Edited by Anthony M. Stevens-Arroyo and Ana Maria Diaz-Stevens. New York: Bildner Center for Western Hemisphere Studies, 1994.

Berger, Peter L. "Reflections on the Sociology of Religion Today." *Sociology of Religion* 62 (Winter 2001): 443–454.

———. *The Sacred Canopy: Elements of a Sociological Theory of Religion.* Garden City, N.Y.: Anchor Books, 1967.

Berryman, Phillip. *Religion in the Megacity: Catholic and Protestant Portraits from Latin America.* Maryknoll, N.Y.: Orbis Books, 1996.

Betances, Samuel. "The Prejudice of Having No Prejudice in Puerto Rico, Part 2." *The Rican* 2 (Spring 1973): 22–31.

Betto, Frei, ed. *Fidel and Religion: Castro Talks on Revolution and Religion with Frei Betto.* New York: Simon and Schuster, 1987.

Binder, Frederick M., and David M. Reimers. *All the Nations under Heaven: An Ethnic and Racial History of New York City.* New York: Columbia University Press, 1995.

Blackwelder, Julia K. *Women of the Depression: Caste and Culture in San Antonio, 1929–1939.* College Station: Texas A&M University Press, 1984.

Borland, Katherine. "Folklife of Miami's Nicaraguan Communities." In "Nicaraguan Folklife in Miami." Edited by Brent Cantrell. Occasional Papers 2, Historical Association of Southern Florida. Miami: Historical Museum of Southern Florida Folklife Program, 1993.

Boswell, Thomas D., and James R. Curtis. *The Cuban-American Experience: Culture, Images, and Perspectives.* Totowa, N.J.: Rowman and Allanheld, 1983.

Brading, D. A. *Mexican Phoenix: Our Lady of Guadalupe, Image and Tradition across Five Centuries.* Cambridge: Cambridge University Press, 2001.

Bram, Joseph. "Spirits, Mediums, and Believers in Contemporary Puerto Rico" (1958). In *Portrait of a Society: Readings on Puerto Rican Sociology.* Edited by Eugenio Fernandez Mendez. Rio Piedras: University of Puerto Rico Press, 1972.

Bremer, Thomas S. *Blessed with Tourists: The Borderlands of Religion and Tourism in San Antonio.* Chapel Hill: University of North Carolina Press, 2004.

Bronder, Saul E. *Social Justice and Church Authority: The Public Life of Archbishop Robert E. Lucey.* Philadelphia: Temple University Press, 1982.

Bronx Museum of the Arts. *Devastation/Resurrection: The South Bronx.* Bronx, N.Y.: Bronx Museum of the Arts, 1979.

Brooks, Philip C. *Diplomacy and the Borderlands: The Adams-Onis Treaty of 1819.* Berkeley: University of California Press, 1939.

Brown, Peter. *The Rise of Western Christendom: Triumph and Diversity, A.D. 200–1000.* Oxford: Blackwell, 1996.

Brown, Peter. *The World of Late Antiquity, A.D. 150–750.* London: Thames and Hudson, 1971.

Brusco, Elizabeth E. *The Reformation of Machismo: Evangelical Conversion and Gender in Colombia.* Austin: University of Texas Press, 1995.

Burns, Jeffrey M. "The Mexican Catholic Community in California." In *Mexican Americans and the Catholic Church, 1900–1965.* Edited by Jay P. Dolan and Gilberto M. Hinojosa. Notre Dame, Ind.: University of Notre Dame Press, 1994.

Byer, Glen C. J. "The Constitution on the Sacred Liturgy and the New Millennium." *Liturgical Ministry* 8 (Fall 1999): 175–182.

Cadaval, Olivia. *Creating a Latino Identity in the Nation's Capital: The Latino Festival.* New York: Garland, 1998.

Cadena, Gilbert R. "Chicano Clergy and the Emergence of Liberation Theology." *Hispanic Journal of Behavioral Sciences* 11 (May 1989): 107–121.

Callahan, William J. *Church, Politics, and Society in Spain, 1750–1874.* Cambridge, Mass.: Harvard University Press, 1984.

Caplow, Theodore, Sheldon Stryker, and Samuel E. Wallace. *The Urban Ambience: A Study of San Juan, Puerto Rico.* Totowa, N.J.: Bedminster, 1964.

Caraballo Ireland, Elba R. "The Role of the Pentecostal Church as a Service Provider in the Puerto Rican Community, Boston, Massachusetts: A Case Study." Ph.D. dissertation, Brandeis University, 1990.

Caro, Robert A. *The Powerbroker: Robert Moses and the Fall of New York.* New York: Vintage Books, 1974.

Caro Costas, Aida R. "The Organization of an Institutional and Social Life." In *Puerto Rico: A Political and Cultural History.* Edited by Arturo Morales Carrión. New York: W. W. Norton, 1983.

Carrasco, David. *Daily Life of the Aztecs: People of the Sun and Earth.* Westport, Conn.: Greenwood, 1998.

Carroll, Henry K. *Report on the Island of Porto Rico.* 1899; reprint New York: Arno, 1975.

Casanova, Jose. *Public Religions in the Modern World.* Chicago: University of Chicago Press, 1994.

———. "Religion, the New Millennium, and Globalization." *Sociology of Religion* 62 (Winter 2001): 415–441.

Casanovas, Joan. *Bread or Bullets! Urban Labor and Spanish Colonialism in Cuba, 1850–1898.* Pittsburgh: University of Pittsburgh Press, 1998.

Castaneda, Jorge. *Utopia Unarmed: The Latin American Left after the Cold War.* New York: Alfred A. Knopf, 1993.

Castellanos, Jorge, and Isabel Castellanos. *Cultura Afrocubana*, vol. 3, *Las Religiones y las Lenguas.* Miami: Ediciones Universal, 1992.

Chappelle, Angela Marie. "Local Welfare Work of Religious Organizations in San Antonio, Texas." Master's thesis, University of Texas, 1939.

Charles, Carolle. "Transnationalism in the Construct of Haitian Migrants' Racial Categories of Identity in New York City." In *Towards a Transnational Perspective on Migration: Race, Class, Ethnicity, and Nationalism Reconsidered.* Edited by Nina Glick Schiller, Linda Basch, and Cristina Blanc-Szanton. *Annals of the New York Academy of Sciences* 645 (July 1992).

Chaunu, Pierre. *The Reformation.* New York: St. Martin's, 1990.

Chavez, Angélico. *Our Lady of the Conquest.* Santa Fe: Historical Society of New Mexico, 1948.

Chenault, Lawrence R. *The Puerto Rican Migrant in New York City.* New York: Columbia University Press, 1970, 1938.

Chestnut, R. Andrew. "A Preferential Option for the Spirit: The Catholic Charismatic Renewal in Latin America's New Religious Economy." *Latin American Politics and Society* 45 (2003): 55–84.

Christian, William A., Jr. *Apparitions in Late Medieval and Renaissance Spain.* Princeton, N.J.: Princeton University Press, 1981.

———. *Local Religion in Sixteenth-Century Spain.* Princeton, N.J.: Princeton University Press, 1981.

———. "Spain in Latino Religiosity." In *El Cuerpo de Cristo: The Hispanic Presence in the U.S. Catholic Church.* Edited by Peter Casarella and Raul Gomez. New York: Crossroad, 1998.

———. *Visionaries: The Spanish Republic and the Reign of Christ.* Berkeley: University of California Press, 1996.

Ciallela, Pietro C. "From Italian National Parish to Multicultural Community: The Expanding Scalabrinian Mission in the Chicago Area, 1960–1980." Master's thesis, Catholic Theological Union at Chicago, 2002.

Clark, Juan. *Religious Repression in Cuba.* Coral Gables, Fla.: North-South Center, 1985.

Clark, Juan, Angel De Fana, and Amaya Sanchez. *Human Rights in Cuba: An Experiential Perspective.* Miami, SAETA Ediciones, 1991.

Clark, Juan, et al. *The 1980 Mariel Exodus: An Assessment and Prospect.* Washington, D.C.: Council for Inter-American Security, 1981.

Clark, Victor S. *Porto Rico and Its Problems.* Washington, D.C.: Brookings Institution, 1930.

———. "Mexican Labor in the United States" (1908). In *Mexican Labor in the United States.* Edited by Carlos E. Cortes. New York: Arno, 1974.

Clinchy, Everett R. *Equality of Opportunity for Latin-Americans in Texas: A Study of the Economic, Social, and Educational Discrimination against Latin-Americans in Texas and of the Effect of the State Government on Their Behalf.* 1954; reprint New York: Arno, 1976.

Cohalan, Florence D. *A Popular History of the Archdiocese of New York.* Yonkers, N.Y.: United States Historical Society, 1983.

Coleman, Simon. *The Globalisation of Charismatic Christianity: Spreading the Gospel of Prosperity.* Cambridge: Cambridge University Press, 2000.

Collins, Roger. *Early Medieval Spain: Unity in Diversity, 400–1000.* New York: St. Martin's, 1983.

Colman, Barry J., ed. *Readings in Church History.* Westminster, Md.: Newman, 1965.

Conzen, Kathleen Neils. "The Place of Religion in Urban and Community Studies." *Religion and American Culture* 6 (Summer 1996): 108–114.

Cooney, John. *The American Pope: The Life and Times of Francis Cardinal Spellman.* New York: Times Books, 1984.

Cotto-Thorner, Guillermo. *Trópico en Manhattan.* 1951; reprint San Juan, P.R.: Editorial Cordillera, 1967.

Covello, Leonard. *The Social Background of the Italo-American School Child: A Study of the Southern Italian Family Mores and Their Effect on the School Situation in Italy and America.* Totowa, N.J.: Rowman and Littlefield, 1967.

Crahan, Margaret E. "Salvation through Christ or Marx: Religion in Revolutionary Cuba." *Journal of Inter-American Studies and World Affairs* 21 (February 1979): 157–184.

Crook, Carland E. "San Antonio, Texas, 1846–1861." Master's thesis, Rice University, 1964.

Cros Sandoval, Mercedes. "Afro-Cuban Religion in Perspective." In *Enigmatic Powers: Syncretism with African and Indigenous Peoples' Religions among Latinos.* Edited by Anthony M. Stevens-Arroyo and Andres I. Perez y Mena. New York: Bildner Center for Western Hemisphere Studies, 1995.

Crow, John A. *Mexico Today.* New York: Harper and Brothers, 1957.

Cruz, Arturo J., and Jaime Suchlicki. *The Impact of Nicaraguans in Miami.* Coral Gables, Fla.: Institute of Interamerican Studies, University of Miami, 1990.

D'Agostino, Peter R. *Rome in America: Transnational Catholic Ideology from the Risorgimento to Fascism.* Chapel Hill: University of North Carolina Press, 2004.

———. "The Scalabrini Fathers, the Italian Emigrant Church, and Ethnic Nationalism in America." *Religion and American Culture* 7 (Winter 1997): 121–159.

Dahm, Charles W. *Parish Ministry in a Hispanic Community.* New York: Paulist, 2004.

Davalos, Karen Mary. "'The Real Way of Praying': The Via Crucis, *Mexicano* Sacred Space, and the Architecture of Domination." In *Horizons of the Sacred: Mexican Traditions in U.S. Catholicism.* Edited by Timothy Matovina and Gary Riebe-Estrella. Ithaca, N.Y.: Cornell University Press, 2002.

Davis, Kenneth G. "Challenges to the Pastoral Care of Central Americans in the United States." In *Bridging Boundaries: The Pastoral Care of U.S. Hispanics.* Edited by Kenneth G. Davis and Yolanda Tarango. Scranton, Pa.: University of Scranton Press, 1999.

———. "The Hispanic Shift: Continuity Rather than Conversion?" In *Bridging Boundaries: The Pastoral Care of U.S. Hispanics.* Edited by Kenneth G. Davis and Yolanda Tarango. Scranton, Pa.: University of Scranton Press, 1999.

Davis, Mike. *City of Quartz: Excavating the Future in Los Angeles.* London: Verso, 1990.

Deck, Allan Figueroa. "The Challenge of Evangelical/Pentecostal Christianity to Hispanic Catholicism." In *Hispanic Catholic Culture in the U.S.: Issues and Concerns.* Edited by Jay P. Dolan and Allan Figueroa Deck. Notre Dame, Ind.: University of Notre Dame Press, 1994.

———. "Introduction." In *Frontiers of Hispanic Theology in the United States.* Edited by Allan Figueroa Deck. Maryknoll, N.Y.: Orbis Books, 1992.

———. *The Second Wave: Hispanic Ministry and the Evangelization of Cultures.* New York: Paulist, 1989.

De Hostos, Adolfo, ed. *Diccionario histórico bibliográfico comentado de Puerto Rico.* Barcelona: Industrias Gráficas Manuel Pareja, 1975.

De Las Casas, Bartolomé. *Bartolomé de Las Casas: A Selection of His Writings*. Edited by George Sanderlin. New York: Alfred A. Knopf, 1971.

De la Torre, Miguel. *La Lucha for Cuba: Religion and Politics on the Streets of Miami*. Berkeley: University of California Press, 2003.

———. *The Quest for the Cuban Christ: A Historical Search*. Gainesville: University Press of Florida, 2002.

De Leon, Arnoldo. *The Tejano Community, 1836–1900*. Albuquerque: University of New Mexico Press, 1982.

———. *They Called Them Greasers: Anglo Attitudes toward Mexicans in Texas, 1821–1900*. Austin: University of Texas Press, 1983.

De los Angeles Torres, Maria. *The Lost Apple: Operation Pedro Pan, Cuban Children in the U.S., and the Promise of a Better Future*. Boston: Beacon, 2003.

Delpech, Jacques. *The Oppression of Protestants in Spain*. London: Lutterworth, 1956.

De Luna, Anita. *Faith Formation and Popular Religion: Lessons from the Tejano Experience*. Lanham, Md.: Rowman and Littlefield, 2002.

Dewart, Leslie. *Christianity and Revolution: The Lesson of Cuba*. New York: Herder and Herder, 1963.

Diamond, Etan. *And I Will Dwell in Their Midst: Orthodox Jews in Suburbia*. Chapel Hill: University of North Carolina Press, 2000.

———. "The Kosher Lifestyle: Religious Consumerism and Suburban Orthodox Jews." *Journal of Urban History* 28 (May 2002): 488–505.

Diaz, Miguel H. "Díme con Quien Andas y Te Diré Quien Eres: We Walk with Our Lady of Charity." In *From the Heart of Our People: Latino/a Explorations in Catholic Systematic Theology*. Edited by Orlando O. Espin and Miguel H. Diaz. Maryknoll, N.Y.: Orbis Books, 1999.

Diaz-Stevens, Ana Maria. "Analyzing Popular Religiosity for Socio-religious Meaning." In *An Enduring Flame: Studies on Latino Popular Religiosity*. Edited by Anthony M. Stevens-Arroyo and Ana Maria Diaz-Stevens. New York: Bildner Center for Western Hemisphere Studies, 1994.

———. "Aspects of the Puerto Rican Religious Experience: A Sociohistorical Overview." In *Latinos in New York: Communities in Transition*. Edited by Gabriel Haslip-Viera and Sherrie L. Baver. Notre Dame, Ind.: University of Notre Dame Press, 1996.

———. "From Puerto Rican to Hispanic: The Politics of the Fiestas Patronales in New York." *Latino Studies Journal* 1 (January 1990): 28–47.

———. "Latinas and the Church." In *Hispanic Catholic Culture in the U.S.: Issues and Concerns*. Edited by Jay P. Dolan and Allan Figueroa Deck. Notre Dame, Ind.: University of Notre Dame Press, 1994.

———. "Missionizing the Missionaries: Religious Congregations of Women in Puerto Rico, 1910–1960." *U.S. Catholic Historian* 21 (Winter 2003): 33–51.

———. *Oxcart Catholicism on Fifth Avenue: The Impact of the Puerto Rican Migration upon the Archdiocese of New York*. Notre Dame, Ind.: University of Notre Dame Press, 1993.

————. "The Saving Grace: The Matriarchal Core of Latino Catholicism." *Latino Studies Journal* 4 (September 1993): 60–78.

Diaz-Stevens, Ana Maria, and Anthony M. Stevens-Arroyo. *Recognizing the Latino Resurgence in U.S. Religion: The Emmaus Paradigm.* Boulder, Colo.: Westview, 1998.

Dietz, James L. *Economic History of Puerto Rico: Institutional Change and Capitalist Development.* Princeton, N.J.: Princeton University Press, 1986.

Diocese of Brooklyn. *Diocese of Immigrants: The Brooklyn Catholic Experience, 1853–2003.* Strasbourg, France: Editions du Signe, 2004.

Dohen, Dorothy Marie. "The Background of Consensual Union in Puerto Rico." Master's thesis, Fordham University, 1959.

Dolan, Jay P. *The American Catholic Experience: A History From Colonial Times to the Present.* Notre Dame, Ind.: University of Notre Dame Press, 1992.

————. "Conclusion" In *Hispanic Catholic Culture in the U.S.: Issues and Concerns.* Edited by Jay P. Dolan and Allan Figueroa Deck. Notre Dame, Ind.: University of Notre Dame Press, 1994.

————. *The Immigrant Church: New York's Irish and German Catholics.* Baltimore: Johns Hopkins University Press, 1977.

————. *In Search of an American Catholicism: A History of Religion and Culture in Tension.* New York: Oxford University Press, 2002.

Downs, Fane. "The History of Mexicans in Texas, 1820–1845." Ph.D. dissertation, Texas Tech University, 1970.

Duany, Jorge. "La religiosidad popular en Puerto Rico: Reseña de la literatura desde la perspectiva antropológica." In *Vírgenes, magos, y escapularios: Imaginería, etnicidad, y religiosidad popular en Puerto Rico.* Edited by Angel G. Quintero Rivera. San Juan, P.R.: Fundación Puertorriqueña de las Humanidades, 1998.

Dulles, John W. F. *Yesterday in Mexico: A Chronicle of the Revolution, 1919–1936.* Austin: University of Texas Press, 1961.

Dunnington, Jacqueline O. *Guadalupe: Our Lady of New Mexico.* Santa Fe: Museum of New Mexico Press, 1999.

Durand, Jorge, and Douglas S. Massey. *Miracles on the Border: Retablos of Mexican Migrants to the United States.* Tucson: University of Arizona Press, 1995.

Dussel, Enrique D., ed. *Historia general de la iglesia en América Latina,* vol. 1, *Introducción general.* Salamanca: Comisión para el Estudio de Historia de la Iglesia en América Latina y el Caribe, 1983.

————. *History and the Theology of Liberation: A Latin American Perspective.* Maryknoll, N.Y.: Orbis Books, 1976.

Dyrud, Keith P., Michael Novak, and Rudolph J. Vecoli, eds. *The Other Catholics.* New York: Arno, 1978.

Ebaugh, Helen R. "Vatican II and the Reconceptualization of the Church." In *Vatican II and U.S. Catholicism: Twenty-five Years Later.* Edited by Helen R. Ebaugh. Greenwich, Conn..: JAI, 1991.

Ebaugh, Helen R., and Janet S. Chafetz, eds. *Religion and the New Immigrants:*

Continuities and Adaptations in Immigrant Congregations. Walnut Creek, Calif.: Altamira, 2000.

Eiras Roel, Antonio, and Ofelín Rey Castelao. *Los gallegos y América.* Madrid: Editorial Mapfre, 1992.

Elizondo, Virgilio. *The Future Is Mestizo: Life Where Cultures Meet.* Bloomington, Ind.: Meyer-Stone Books, 1988.

———. *Galilean Journey: The Mexican-American Promise.* Maryknoll, N.Y.: Orbis Books, 1983.

———. *A God of Incredible Surprises: Jesus of Galilee.* Lanham, Md.: Rowman and Littlefield, 2003.

———. *Guadalupe: Mother of the New Creation.* Maryknoll, N.Y.: Orbis Books, 1997.

———. "Hispanic Theology and Popular Piety: From Interreligious Encounter to a New Ecumenism" (1993). In *Beyond Borders: Writings of Virgilio Elizondo and Friends.* Edited by Timothy M. Matovina. Maryknoll, N.Y.: Orbis Books, 2000.

———. "*Mestizaje* as a Locus of Theological Reflection" (1983). In *Beyond Borders: Writings of Virgilio Elizondo and Friends.* Edited by Timothy M. Matovina. Maryknoll, N.Y.: Orbis Books, 2000.

Ernst, Robert. *Immigrant Life in New York City, 1825–1863.* Syracuse: Syracuse University Press, 1994, 1949.

Espin, Orlando O. "Popular Catholicism among Latinos." In *Hispanic Catholic Culture in the U.S.: Issues and Concerns.* Edited by Jay P. Dolan and Allan Figueroa Deck. Notre Dame, Ind.: University of Notre Dame Press, 1994.

Espin, Orlando O. "Tradition and Popular Religion: An Understanding of the *Sensus Fidelium.*" In *Old Masks, New Faces: Religion and Latino Identities.* Edited by Anthony M. Stevens-Arroyo and Gilbert R. Cadena. New York: Bildner Center for Western Hemisphere Studies, 1995.

Espinosa, Gaston. "*El Azteca:* Francisco Olazábal and Latino Pentecostal Charisma, Power, and Faith in the Borderlands." *Journal of the American Academy of Religion* 67 (September 1999): 597–616.

———. "Borderland Religion: Los Angeles and the Origins of the Latino Pentecostal Movement in the U.S., Mexico, and Puerto Rico, 1900–1945." Ph.D. dissertation, University of California, Santa Barbara, 1999.

———. "The Impact of Pluralism on Trends in Latin American and U.S. Latino Religions and Society." In *Perspectivas.* Edited by Renata Furst-Lambert. Princeton, N.J.: Hispanic Theological Initiative Occasional Paper Series, 2003.

Espinosa, Gaston, Virgilio Elizondo, and Jesse Miranda, eds. *Latino Religious and Civic Activism in the United States.* New York: Oxford University Press, 2005.

Estades, Rosa. "Symbolic Unity: The Puerto Rican Day Parade." In *The Puerto Rican Struggle: Essays on Survival in the U.S.* Edited by Clara E. Rodriguez, Virginia Sanchez Korrol, and Jose Oscar Alers. New York: Puerto Rican Migration Research Consortium, 1980.

Estévez, Felipe J. "La contribución social del Padre Varela en los Estados Unidos." In *El Padre Varela: Pensador, sacerdote, patriota.* Edited by Roberto Esquenazi-Mayo. Washington, D.C.: Georgetown University Press, 1990.

Fehrenbach, T. R. *The San Antonio Story: A Pictorial and Entertaining Commentary on the Growth and Development of San Antonio, Texas.* Tulsa: Continental Heritage, 1978.

Fernandez-Armesto, Felipe, and Derek Wilson. *Reformations: A Radical Interpretation of Christianity and the World, 1500–2000.* New York: Scribner, 1996.

Ferree, William, Ivan Illich, and Joseph P. Fitzpatrick, eds. *Spiritual Care of Puerto Rican Migrants.* 1955; reprint New York: Arno, 1980.

Ferris, Susan, and Ricardo Sandoval. *The Fight in the Fields: Cesar Chavez and the Farmworkers Movement.* New York: Harcourt Brace, 1997.

Finks, David. *The Radical Vision of Saul Alinsky.* New York: Paulist, 1984.

Fishman, Robert. *Bourgeois Utopias: The Rise and Fall of Suburbia.* New York: Basic Books, 1987.

Fitzpatrick, Joseph P. "The Church and Social Issues: Institutional Commitments." In *Vatican II and U.S. Catholicism: Twenty-five Years Later.* Edited by Helen R. Ebaugh. Greenwich, Conn.: JAI, 1991.

———. "The Dilemma of Social Research and Social Policy: The Puerto Rican Case, 1953–1993." In *Old Masks, New Faces: Religion and Latino Identities.* Edited by Anthony M. Stevens-Arroyo and Gilbert R. Cadena. New York: Bildner Center for Western Hemisphere Studies, 1995.

———. *Puerto Rican Americans: The Meaning of Migration to the Mainland.* 1971; reprint Englewood Cliffs, N.J.: Prentice-Hall, 1987.

———. *The Stranger Is Our Own: Reflections on the Journey of Puerto Rican Migrants.* Kansas City, Mo.: Sheed and Ward, 1996.

Fletcher, Peri L. *La Casa de Mis Sueños: Dreams of Home in a Transnational Mexican Community.* Boulder, Colo.: Westview, 1999.

Fletcher, Richard. *Moorish Spain.* New York: Henry Holt, 1992.

Flores, Richard R. "Para el Niño Dios: Sociability and Commemorative Sentiment in Popular Religious Practice." In *An Enduring Flame: Studies on Latino Popular Religiosity.* Edited by Anthony M. Stevens-Arroyo and Ana Maria Diaz-Stevens. New York: Bildner Center for Western Hemisphere Studies, 1994.

———. "'Los Pastores': Performance, Poetics, and Politics in Folk Drama." Ph.D. dissertation, University of Texas, Austin, 1989.

Foner, Nancy. "What's New about Transnationalism? New York Immigrants Today and at the Turn of the Century." *Diaspora* 6 (Winter 1997): 355–375.

Francis, Mark R. "The Hispanic Liturgical Year: The People's Calendar." *Liturgical Ministry* 7 (Summer 1998): 97–107.

Freixedo, Salvador. *Mi iglesia duerme.* Mexico City: Editorial Posada, 1969.

Freston, Paul. *Evangelicals and Politics in Asia, Africa, and Latin America.* Cambridge: Cambridge University Press, 2001.

Frey, William H. "Melting Pot Suburbs: A Study of Suburban Diversity." In *Redefining*

Urban and Suburban America: Evidence from Census 2000. Edited by Bruce Katz and Robert E. Lang. Washington, D.C.: Brookings Institution Press, 2003.

Gaffey, James P. *Francis Clement Kelley and the American Catholic Dream*, vol. 1. Bensenville, Ill.: Heritage Foundation, 1980.

Gamm, Gerald. *Urban Exodus: Why the Jews Left Boston and the Catholics Stayed.* Cambridge, Mass.: Harvard University Press, 1999.

Gannon, Robert I. *Up to the Present: The Story of Fordham.* Garden City, N.Y.: Doubleday, 1967.

García, Jesús. "La iglesia desde el Concilio Vaticano II y Medellín." In *Historia general de la iglesia en América Latina*, vol. 5, *Mexico*. Edited by Enrique D. Dussel. Salamanca: Comisión para el Estudio de Historia de la Iglesia en América Latina y el Caribe, 1984.

Garcia, Maria Cristina. "Adapting to Exile: Cuban Women in the United States, 1959–1973." *Latino Studies Journal* 2 (May 1991): 17–33.

———. *Havana USA: Cuban Exiles and Cuban Americans in South Florida, 1959–1994.* Berkeley: University of California Press, 1996.

Garcia, Richard A. *Rise of the Mexican American Middle Class: San Antonio, 1929–1941.* College Station: Texas A&M University Press, 1991.

Garreau, Joel. *Edge City: Life on the New Frontier.* New York: Doubleday, 1991.

Gibson, Charles. *The Aztecs under Spanish Rule: A History of the Indians of the Valley of Mexico, 1519–1810.* Stanford: Stanford University Press, 1964.

Gilfoyle, Timothy J. "White Cities, Linguistic Turns, and Disneylands: The New Paradigms of Urban History." *Reviews in American History* 26 (1998): 175–204.

Gill, Anthony. *Rendering unto Caesar: The Catholic Church and the State in Latin America.* Chicago: University of Chicago Press, 1998.

Glazer, Nathan, and Daniel P. Moynihan. *Beyond the Melting Pot: The Negroes, Puerto Ricans, Jews, Italians, and Irish of New York City.* 2nd ed. Cambridge, Mass.: Massachusetts Institute of Technology Press, 1970.

Goizueta, Roberto S. *Caminemos con Jesus: Toward a Hispanic/Latino Theology of Accompaniment.* Maryknoll, N.Y.: Orbis Books, 1995.

Golden, Renny, and Michael McConnell. *Sanctuary: The New Underground Railroad.* Maryknoll, N.Y.: Orbis Books, 1986.

Goldring, Luin. "The Mexican State and Transmigrant Organizations: Negotiating the Boundaries of Membership and Participation." *Latin American Research Review* 37 (2002): 55–99.

Gomez Treto, Raul. *The Church and Socialism in Cuba.* Maryknoll, N.Y.: Orbis Books, 1988.

Gonzalez, Adele J. "Pastoral Care of 'los Marielitos.'" In *Bridging Boundaries: The Pastoral Care of U.S. Hispanics.* Edited by Kenneth G. Davis and Yolanda Tarango. Scranton, Pa.: University of Scranton Press, 1999.

Gonzalez, Evelyn. *The Bronx.* New York: Columbia University Press, 2004.

Gonzalez, Juan. *Harvest of Empire: A History of Latinos in America.* New York: Penguin Books, 2000.

Gonzalez, Justo L. "Characteristics of Latino Protestant Theology." In *Hispanic Christianity within Mainline Protestant Traditions: A Bibliography*. Edited by Paul Barton and David Maldonado Jr. Decatur, Ga.: Asociación para la Educación Teológica Hispana, 1998.

———. "In Quest of a Protestant Hispanic Ecclesiology." In *Teología en Conjunto: A Collaborative Hispanic Protestant Theology*. Edited by Jose David Rodriguez and Loida I. Martell-Otero. Louisville, Ky.: Westminster John Knox, 1997.

———. "Latino/a Theology." In *Handbook of U.S. Theologies of Liberation*. Edited by Miguel A. De la Torre. St. Louis: Chalice, 2004.

———. "Postscript: Hanging on an Empty Cross—The Hispanic Mainline Experience." In *Protestantes / Protestants: Hispanic Christianity within Mainline Traditions*. Edited by David Maldonado Jr. Nashville: Abingdon, 1999.

———. "Reinventing Dogmatics: A Footnote from a Reinvented Protestant." In *From the Heart of Our People: Latino/a Explorations in Catholic Systematic Theology*. Edited by Orlando O. Espin and Miguel H. Diaz. Maryknoll, N.Y.: Orbis Books, 1999.

Gonzalez-Pando, Miguel. *The Cuban Americans*. Westport, Conn.: Greenwood, 1998.

Goris, Anneris. "Dominican Immigrants: Social and Religious Context." In *Bridging Boundaries: The Pastoral Care of U.S. Hispanics*. Edited by Kenneth G. Davis and Yolanda Tarango. Scranton, Pa.: University of Scranton Press, 1999.

———. "Rites for a Rising Nationalism: Religious Meaning and Dominican Community Identity in New York City." In *Old Masks, New Faces: Religion and Latino Identities*. Edited by Anthony M. Stevens-Arroyo and Gilbert R. Cadena. New York: Bildner Center for Western Hemisphere Studies, 1995.

Grebler, Leo, Joan W. Moore, and Ralph C. Guzman. *The Mexican-American People: The Nation's Second Largest Minority*. New York: Free Press, 1970.

Greene, Graham. *Another Mexico*. New York: Viking, 1939.

Greene, Richard P. "Chicago's New Immigrants, Indigenous Poor, and Edge Cities." *Annals of the American Academy of Political and Social Science* 551 (May 1997): 178–190.

Gremillion, Joseph, and Jim Castelli. *The Emerging Parish: The Notre Dame Study of Catholic Life since Vatican II*. San Francisco: Harper and Row, 1987.

Grenier, Guillermo J., and Lisandro Perez. *The Legacy of Exile: Cubans in the United States*. Boston: Allyn and Bacon, 2003.

Griffin, Charles C. *The United States and the Disruption of the Spanish Empire, 1810–1822: A Study of the Relations of the United States with Spain and with the Rebel Spanish Colonies*. New York: Octagon Books, 1968.

Grimes, Kimberly M. *Crossing Borders: Changing Social Identities in Southern Mexico*. Tucson: University of Arizona Press, 1998.

Grimes, Ronald L. *Symbol and Conquest: Public Ritual and Drama in Santa Fe, New Mexico*. Ithaca, N.Y.: Cornell University Press, 1976.

Grossman, James R., Ann Durkin Keating, and Janice L. Rieff, eds. *The Encyclopedia of Chicago*. Chicago: University of Chicago Press, 2004.

Guerrero, Andres G. *A Chicano Theology*. Maryknoll, N.Y.: Orbis Books, 1987.

Gutiérrez, Gustavo. *Las Casas: In Search of the Poor of Jesus Christ*. Maryknoll, N.Y.: Orbis Books, 1993.

———. *A Theology of Liberation: History, Politics, and Salvation*. Maryknoll, N.Y.: Orbis Books, 1973.

Gutierrez, Ramon A. "El Santuario de Chimayo: A Syncretic Shrine in New Mexico." In *Feasts and Celebrations in North American Ethnic Communities*. Edited by Ramon A. Gutierrez and Genevieve Fabre. Albuquerque: University of New Mexico Press, 1995.

———. *When Jesus Came the Corn Mothers Went Away: Marriage, Sexuality, and Power in New Mexico, 1500–1846*. Stanford, Calif.: Stanford University Press, 1991.

Hageman, Alice L., and Philip E. Wheaton, eds. *Religion in Cuba Today: A New Church in a New Society*. New York: Association, 1971.

Hall, Linda B. *Mary, Mother and Warrior: The Virgin in Spain and the Americas*. Austin: University of Texas Press, 2004.

Hamilton, Nora, and Norma Stoltz Chincilla. *Seeking Community in a Global City: Guatemalans and Salvadorans in Los Angeles*. Philadelphia: Temple University Press, 2001.

Haney, Patrick J., and Walt Vanderbush. "The Role of Ethnic Interest Groups in U.S. Foreign Policy: The Case of the Cuban American National Foundation." *International Studies Quarterly* 43 (1999): 341–361.

Hannon, Jane Colleen. "Saints and Patriots: Catholicism in the Bronx, 1920–1940." Ph.D. dissertation, University of Notre Dame, 2000.

Hasdorff, James C. "The *Southern Messenger* and the Mexican Church-State Controversy, 1917–1941." *Journal of Texas Catholic History and Culture* 5 (1994): 25–46.

Hennesey, James J. *American Catholics: A History of the Roman Catholic Community in the United States*. New York: Oxford University Press, 1981.

Herrera, Maria Cristina. "The Cuban Ecclesial Enclave in Miami: A Critical Profile." *U.S. Catholic Historian* 9 (Spring 1990): 209–221.

Hernandez, Jose M. "The ACU: Transplanting a Cuban Lay Organization to the United States." *U.S. Catholic Historian* 21 (Winter 2003): 99–114.

Hernández Madrid, Miguel J. "Migrantes y conversos religiosos: Cambios de identidad cultural en el noroeste de Michoacán." In *Fronteras Fragmentadas*. Edited by Gail Mummert. Zamora, Mexico: Colegio de Michoacán, 1999.

Herzog, Lawrence A. *From Aztec to High Tech: Architecture and Landscape across the Mexico-United States Border*. Baltimore: Johns Hopkins University Press, 1999.

Hinojosa, Gilberto M. "Mexican-American Faith Communities in Texas and the Southwest." In *Mexican Americans and the Catholic Church, 1900–1965*. Edited by Jay P. Dolan and Gilberto M. Hinojosa. Notre Dame, Ind.: University of Notre Dame Press, 1994.

Hirsch, Arnold. *Making the Second Ghetto: Race and Housing in Chicago, 1940–1960*. Cambridge: Cambridge University Press, 1983.

Historic Santa Fe Foundation. *Old Santa Fe Today.* Albuquerque: University of New Mexico Press, 1982.

History Task Force, Centro de Estudios Puertorriqueños. *Labor Migration under Capitalism: The Puerto Rican Experience.* New York: Monthly Review, 1979.

Howard, Philip A. *Changing History: Afro-Cuban Cabildos and Societies of Color in the Nineteenth Century.* Baton Rouge: Louisiana State University Press, 1998.

Hurtig, Janise D. "Hispanic Immigrant Churches and the Construction of Identity." In *Public Religion and Urban Transformation: Faith in the City.* Edited by Lowell W. Livezey. New York: New York University Press, 2000.

Institute for Latino Studies, University of Notre Dame. *Bordering the Mainstream: A Needs Assessment of Latinos in Berwyn and Cicero, Illinois.* Notre Dame, Ind.: Institute for Latino Studies, 2002.

Instituto Cubano de Cooperación y Solidaridad en Venezuela (ICOSOCV). *El presidio político en Cuba comunista: Testimonio.* Caracas: ICOSOCV Ediciones, 1982.

Isasi-Diaz, Ada Maria. *En la Lucha / In the Struggle: Elaborating a Mujerista Theology.* Minneapolis: Fortress, 2004.

James, Winston. *Holding Aloft the Banner of Ethiopia: Caribbean Radicalism in Early Twentieth-Century America.* London: Verso, 1998.

Jenkins, Philip. *The Next Christendom: The Coming of Global Christianity.* New York: Oxford University Press, 2002.

Jimenez de Wagenheim, Olga. *Puerto Rico: An Interpretive History from Pre-Columbian Times to 1900.* Princeton, N.J.: Marcus Weiner, 1998.

Johnson, Charles T. "Edgewood: A History of a San Antonio Suburb, 1870–1959." Master's thesis, Trinity University, 1960.

Johnson, David N. "Exiles and Intrigue: Francisco I. Madero and the Mexican Revolutionary Junta in San Antonio, 1910–1911." Master's thesis, Trinity University, 1975.

Johnson, David R., Derral Cheatwood, and Benjamin Bradshaw. "The Landscape of Death: Homicide as a Health Problem." In *On the Border: The Environmental History of San Antonio.* Edited by Char Miller. Pittsburgh: University of Pittsburgh Press, 2001.

Johnson, Elmer W. *Chicago Metropolis 2020: Preparing Metropolitan Chicago for the Twenty-first Century.* Executive summary. Chicago: Commercial Club of Chicago, 1998.

Jones, Anita E. "Conditions Surrounding Mexicans in Chicago." Ph.D. dissertation, University of Chicago, 1928.

Jonnes, Jill. *We're Still Here: The Rise, Fall, and Resurrection of the South Bronx.* Boston: Atlantic Monthly, 1986.

Jordan, Winthrop D. *White over Black: American Attitudes toward the Negro, 1550–1812.* Baltimore: Penguin Books, 1969.

Julian de Nieves, Elisa. *The Catholic Church in Colonial Puerto Rico, 1898–1964.* Rio Piedras, P.R.: Editorial Edil, 1982.

Kandell, Jonathan. *La Capital: The Biography of Mexico City*. New York: Random House, 1988.

Kane, Paula M. *Separatism and Subculture: Boston Catholicism, 1900–1920*. Chapel Hill: University of North Carolina Press, 1994.

Kantowicz, Edward R. "The American Catholic Church Comes of Age." In *Modern American Catholicism, 1900–1965: Selected Historical Essays*. Edited by Edward R. Kantowicz. New York: Garland, 1988.

Kantrowitz, Nathan. *Ethnic and Racial Segregation in the New York Metropolis: Residential Patterns among White Ethnic Groups, Blacks, and Puerto Ricans*. New York: Praeger, 1973.

Kapitzke, Robert L. *Religion, Power, and Politics in Colonial St. Augustine*. Gainesville: University Press of Florida, 2001.

Katz, Bruce, and Robert E. Lang. "Introduction." In *Redefining Urban and Suburban America: Evidence from Census 2000*. Edited by Bruce Katz and Robert E. Lang. Washington, D.C.: Brookings Institution Press, 2003.

Kelley, Francis C. *The Bishop Jots It Down: An Autobiographical Strain on Memories*. New York: Harper and Brothers, 1939.

———. *The Book of Red and Yellow: Being a Story of Blood and a Yellow Streak*. Chicago: Catholic Church Extension Society, 1915.

———. *The Story of Extension*. Chicago: Extension Press, 1922.

Kelliher, Thomas G., Jr. "Hispanic Catholics and the Archdiocese of Chicago, 1923–1970." Ph.D. dissertation, University of Notre Dame, 1996.

———. "Mexican Catholics and Chicago's Parishes, 1955–1976." Cushwa Center for the Study of American Catholicism (Notre Dame, Ind.), Working Paper Series 25, no. 1 (Spring 1993).

Kerr, Louise Año Nuevo. "The Chicano Experience in Chicago, 1920–1970." Ph.D. dissertation, University of Illinois, Chicago Circle, 1976.

Kirk, John M. *Between God and the Party: Religion and Politics in Revolutionary Cuba*. Tampa: University of South Florida Press, 1989.

———. "From Counterrevolution to *Modus Vivendi*: The Church in Cuba, 1959–84." In *Cuba: Twenty-five Years of Revolution, 1959–1984*. Edited by Sandor Halebsky and John M. Kirk. New York: Praeger, 1985.

Koenig, Harry C. *Caritas Christi Urget Nos: A History of the Offices, Agencies, and Institutions of the Archdiocese of Chicago*, vol. 2. Chicago: Catholic Archdiocese of Chicago, 1981.

———, ed. *A History of the Parishes of the Archdiocese of Chicago*, vol. 2. Chicago: Catholic Archdiocese of Chicago, 1980.

Krase, Jerome. "Italian American Urban Landscapes: Images of Social and Cultural Capital." *Italian Americana* 21 (Winter 2003): 17–44.

Lampe, Armando. "Las iglesias a la hora de la revolución cubana." In *Historia general de la iglesia en América Latina*, vol. 4, *Caribe*. Edited by Enrique D. Dussel. Salamanca: Comisión para el Estudio de Historia de la Iglesia en América Latina y el Caribe, 1983.

Lang, Robert E. *Edgeless Cities: Exploring the Elusive Metropolis.* Washington, D.C.: Brookings Institution Press, 2003.

Leal, Luis. "*La Conquistadora* as History and Fictitious Autobiography." In *Fray Angelico Chavez: Poet, Priest, and Artist.* Edited by Ellen McCracken. Albuquerque: University of New Mexico Press, 2000.

Leeder, Elaine. *The Gentle General: Rose Pesotta, Anarchist and Labor Organizer.* Albany: State University of New York Press, 1993.

Lennon, John J. *A Comparative Study of the Patterns of Acculturation of Selected Puerto Rican Protestant and Roman Catholic Families in an Urban Metropolitan Area.* San Francisco: R&E Research Associates, 1975.

Leon, Luis D. *La Llorona's Children's Children: Religion, Life, and Death in the U.S.-Mexican Borderlands.* Berkeley: University of California Press, 2004.

———. "Religious Movement in the United States–Mexico Borderlands: Toward a Theory of Chicana/o Religious Poetics." Ph.D. dissertation, University of California, Santa Barbara, 1997.

Lernoux, Peggy. *People of God: The Struggle for World Catholicism.* New York: Penguin Books, 1989.

Levitt, Peggy. "Local-Level Global Religion: The Case of U.S.-Dominican Migration." *Journal for the Scientific Study of Religion* 37 (March 1998): 74–89.

———. "The Ties That Change: Relations to the Ancestral Home over the Life Cycle." In *The Changing Face of Home: The Transnational Lives of the Second Generation.* Edited by Peggy Levitt and Mary C. Waters. New York: Russell Sage Foundation, 2002.

Lewis, Gordon K. *Main Currents in Caribbean Thought: The Historical Evolution of Caribbean Society in Its Ideological Aspects, 1492–1900.* Baltimore: Johns Hopkins University Press, 1983.

———. *Puerto Rico: Freedom and Power in the Caribbean.* New York: Monthly Review, 1963.

Liptak, Dolores. "The Incorporation of Immigrants into the American Catholic Community, 1790–1990." In *Today's Immigrants and Refugees: A Christian Understanding.* Edited by Office of Pastoral Care of Migrants and Refugees, Bishops' Committee on Migration, National Conference of Catholic Bishops. Washington, D.C.: United States Catholic Conference, 1988.

Logan, John R. "Ethnic Diversity Grows, Neighborhood Integration Lags." In *Redefining Urban and Suburban America: Evidence from Census 2000.* Edited by Bruce Katz and Robert E. Lang. Washington, D.C.: Brookings Institution Press, 2003.

———. "Still a Global City: The Racial and Ethnic Segmentation of New York." In *Globalizing Cities: A New Spatial Order?* Edited by Peter Marcuse and Ronald van Kempen. Oxford: Blackwell, 2000.

Logan, John R., Richard D. Alba, and Wenquan Zhang. "Immigrant Enclaves and Ethnic Communities in New York and Los Angeles." *American Journal of Sociology* 67 (April 2002): 299–322.

Lugo-Silva, Enrique. *The Tugwell Administration in Puerto Rico, 1941–1946.* Rio Piedras, P.R.: Editorial Cultura, 1955.

Luis, William. *Culture and Customs of Cuba.* Westport, Conn.: Greenwood, 2001.

Lynch, John. *Spain, 1516–1598.* Oxford: Blackwell, 1992.

MacEoin, Gary, and Nivita Riley. *Puebla: A Church Being Born.* New York: Paulist, 1980.

Mackay, John A. *The Other Spanish Christ: A Study in the Spiritual History of Spain and South America.* New York: Macmillan, 1933.

Mackey, William F., and Von N. Beebe. *Bilingual Schooling and the Miami Experience.* Coral Gables, Fla.: University of Miami, Institute of Interamerican Studies, 1990.

MacLachlan, Colin M., and William H. Beezley. *El Gran Pueblo: A History of Greater Mexico.* Englewood Cliffs, N.J.: Prentice-Hall, 1994.

Martí, José. *The America of José Martí: Selected Writings of José Martí Translated from the Spanish.* Edited by Juan de Onís. New York: Funk and Wagnalls, 1968.

Mahler, Sarah J. *American Dreaming: Immigrant Life on the Margins.* Princeton, N.J.: Princeton University Press, 1995.

———. *Salvadorans in Suburbia: Symbiosis and Conflict.* Boston: Allyn and Bacon, 1995.

———. "Suburban Transnational Migrants: Long Island's Salvadorans." In *Migration, Transnationalization, and Race in a Changing New York.* Edited by Hector R. Cordero-Guzman, Robert C. Smith, and Ramon Grosfoguel. Philadelphia: Temple University Press, 2001.

———. "Tres Veces Mojados: Undocumented Central and South American Migration to Suburban Long Island." Ph.D. dissertation, Columbia University, 1992.

Maldonado, A. W. *Teodoro Moscoso and Puerto Rico's Operation Bootstrap.* Gainesville: University of Florida Press, 1997.

Maldonado, David, Jr. *Crossing Guadalupe Street: Growing Up Hispanic and Protestant.* Albuquerque: University of New Mexico Press, 2001.

Manning, William R. *Early Diplomatic Relations between the United States and Mexico.* Baltimore: Johns Hopkins University Press, 1916.

Martinez-Alier, Verena. *Marriage, Class, and Colour in Nineteenth-Century Cuba: A Study of Racial Attitudes and Sexual Values in a Slave Society.* London: Cambridge University Press, 1974.

Martinez-Fernandez, Luis. *Protestantism and Political Conflict in the Nineteenth-Century Hispanic Caribbean.* New Brunswick, N.J.: Rutgers University Press, 2002.

Martino, John. *I Was Castro's Prisoner: An American Tells His Story.* New York: Devin-Adair, 1963.

Marquez, Benjamin. *LULAC: The Evolution of a Mexican American Political Organization.* Austin: University of Texas Press, 1993.

Masud Piloto, Felix. *With Open Arms: Cuban Migration to the United States.* Totowa, N.J.: Rowman and Littlefield, 1988.

Matovina, Timothy M., ed. *Beyond Borders: Writings of Virgilio Elizondo and Friends.* Maryknoll, N.Y.: Orbis Books, 2000.

———. "Companion in Exile: Guadalupan Devotion at San Fernando Cathedral, San Antonio, Texas, 1900–1940." In *Horizons of the Sacred: Mexican Traditions in U.S. Catholicism.* Edited by Timothy M. Matovina and Gary Riebe-Estrella. Ithaca, N.Y.: Cornell University Press, 2002.

———. "Our Lady of Guadalupe Celebrations in San Antonio, Texas, 1840–41." *Journal of Hispanic/Latino Theology* 1 (November 1993): 77–96.

———. "Our Lady of Guadalupe: Patroness of America," *America,* December 8, 2003, 8–12.

———. "Representation and the Reconstruction of Power: The Rise of PADRES and Las Hermanas." In *What's Left? Liberal American Catholics.* Edited by Mary Jo Weaver. Bloomington: Indiana University Press, 1999.

———. "Sacred Place and Collective Memory: San Fernando Cathedral, San Antonio, Texas." *U.S. Catholic Historian* 15 (Winter 1997): 33–50.

———. "Tejano Lay Initiatives in Worship, 1830–1860." Cushwa Center for the Study of American Catholicism (Notre Dame, Ind.), Working Paper Series 25 (Fall 1993).

———. *Tejano Religion and Ethnicity: San Antonio, 1821–1860.* Austin: University of Texas Press, 1995.

Matovina, Timothy M., and Gerald E. Poyo, eds. *Presente! U.S. Latino Catholics from Colonial Origins to the Present.* Maryknoll, N.Y.: Orbis Books, 2000.

Matovina, Timothy M., and Gary Riebe-Estrella, eds. *Horizons of the Sacred: Mexican Traditions in U.S. Catholicism.* Ithaca, N.Y.: Cornell University Press, 2002.

Matthiessen, Peter. *Sal Si Puedes: Cesar Chavez and the New American Revolution.* New York: Random House, 1969.

McCarthy, Malachy R. "Which Christ Came to Chicago? Catholic and Protestant Programs to Evangelize, Socialize, and Americanize the Mexican Immigrant, 1900–1940." Ph.D. dissertation, Loyola University of Chicago, 2002.

McCormick, Theodore E. "Puerto Rico and the Lay Apostolate." In *The Lay Apostolate in Latin America Today.* Edited by Margaret Bates. Washington, D.C.: Catholic University of America Press, 1960.

McDonnell, Kilian. *Charismatic Renewal and the Churches.* New York: Seabury, 1976.

McGreevy, John T. *Catholicism and American Freedom: A History.* New York: W. W. Norton, 2003.

———. "Catholicism in the United States and the Problem of Diversity: The View from History." In *What's Left? Liberal American Catholics.* Edited by Mary Jo Weaver. Bloomington: Indiana University Press, 1999.

———. *Parish Boundaries: The Catholic Encounter with Race in the Twentieth-Century Urban North.* Chicago: University of Chicago Press, 1996.

McKay, Claude. *Harlem: Negro Metropolis.* New York: E. P. Dutton, 1940.

McMahon, Eileen M. *What Parish Are You From? A Chicago Irish Community and Race Relations.* Lexington, Ky.: University Press of Chicago, 1995.

McMurtry, Larry. *In a Narrow Grave: Essays on Texas*. New York: Simon and Schuster, 1968.

McNally, Michael J. *Catholicism in South Florida, 1868–1968*. Gainesville: University of Florida Press, 1982.

———. "Presence and Persistence: Catholicism among Latinos in Tampa's Ybor City, 1885–1985." *U.S. Catholic Historian* 14 (Spring 1996): 73–91.

———. "The Universal in the Particular: The New Regional History and Catholicism in the United States." *U.S. Catholic Historian* 18 (Summer 2000): 1–10.

McNally, Robert E. "The Council of Trent, the Spiritual Exercises, and the Catholic Reform." *Church History* 34 (March 1965): 36–56.

McWilliams, Carey. *North from Mexico: The Spanish-Speaking People of the United States*. New York: Praeger, 1948.

Mecham, J. Lloyd. *Church and State in Latin America: A Study in Politico-ecclesiastical Relations*. Chapel Hill: University of North Carolina Press, 1966.

Medina, Lara. "Las Hermanas: Chicana/Latina Religious-Political Activism, 1971–1997." Ph.D. dissertation, Claremont Graduate University, 1998.

Medina, Lara, and Gilbert R. Cadena. "Dias de los Muertos: Public Ritual, Community Renewal, and Popular Religion in Los Angeles." *In Horizons of the Sacred: Mexican Traditions in U.S. Catholicism*. Edited by Timothy M. Matovina and Gary Riebe-Estrella. Ithaca, N.Y.: Cornell University Press, 2002.

Melrose Park. *Centennial Celebration, 1882–1982: One Hundred Years of Progress*. Melrose Park, Ill.: Village of Melrose Park, 1982.

Mencke, John G. *Mulattoes and Race Mixture: American Attitudes and Images, 1865–1918*. Ann Arbor, Mich.: UMI Research Press, 1979.

Menes, Orlando R. "A Brief Overview of the Cultural and Religious *Mestizaje*." In *Renaming Ecstasy: Latino Writings on the Sacred*. Edited by Orlando R. Menes. Tempe, Arizona: Bilingual, 2004.

Meier, August, and Elliott Rudwick. "The Origins of Nonviolent Direct Action in Afro-American Protest: A Note on Historical Discontinuities." In *Along the Color Line: Explorations in the Black Experience*. Edited by August Meier and Elliott Rudwick. Urbana: University of Illinois Press, 1976.

Menocal, Maria Rosa. *The Ornament of the World: How Muslims, Jews, and Christians Created a Culture of Tolerance in Medieval Spain*. Boston: Little, Brown, 2002.

Meyer, Jean A. *The Cristero Rebellion: The Mexican People between Church and State, 1926- 1929*. Cambridge: Cambridge University Press, 1976.

Miller, Donald E. "Religion in Los Angeles: Patterns of Spiritual Practice in a Postmodern City." In *From Chicago to L.A.: Making Sense of Urban Theory*. Edited by Michael J. Dear. Thousand Oaks, Calif.: Sage, 2002.

Mohl, Raymond A. "Globalization, Latinization, and the Nuevo New South." *Journal of American Ethnic History* 22 (Summer 2003): 31–66.

———. "The Transformation of the Late-Twentieth-Century South." *Florida Historical Quarterly* 76 (Winter 1998): 326–337.

Moller, Maria, and Kathryn E. Wilson. "Images of Latino Philadelphia: An Essay in Photographs." *Pennsylvania Magazine of History and Biography* 128 (October 2004): 385–398.

Montejano, David. *Anglos and Mexicans in the Making of Texas, 1836–1986.* Austin: University of Texas Press, 1987.

Montejano y Aguinaga, Rafael. *El clero y la independencia en San Luis Potosí.* San Luis Potosí, Mexico: Academia de Historia Potosina, 1971.

Montoya, Ramón Alejandro. *La experiencia potosina en Chicago.* San Luis Potosí, Mexico: Colegio de San Luis, 1997.

Moore, Carlos. "Afro-Cubans and the Communist Revolution." In *African Presence in the Americas.* Edited by Carlos Moore, Tanya R. Sanders, and Shawna Moore. Trenton, N.J.: Africa World, 1995.

Moore, Donald T. "American Religious Influence in Puerto Rico in the Twentieth Century." Working Paper 84, Inter American University of Puerto Rico (November 1998).

Morales-Carrion, Arturo. *Puerto Rico and the Non Hispanic Caribbean: A Study in the Decline of Spanish Exclusivism.* Rio Piedras: University of Puerto Rico, 1952.

Morris, Charles S. *American Catholic: The Saints and Sinners Who Built America's Most Powerful Church.* New York: Times Books, 1997.

Morrisey, Pat, ed. *Miami's Neighborhoods.* Miami: Miami News, 1982.

Mosqueda, Lawrence J. *Chicanos, Catholicism, and Political Ideology.* Lanham, Md.: University Press of America, 1986.

Moquin, Henry, and Richard Richards. *Assumptionists in the United States.* Worchester, Mass.: Assumption Communications, 1994.

Naisson, Mark. *Communists in Harlem during the Depression.* Urbana: University of Illinois Press, 1983.

Narrett, David E. "A Choice of Destiny: Immigration Policy, Slavery, and the Annexation of Texas." *Southwestern Historical Quarterly* 100 (January 1997): 271–304.

National Conference of Catholic Bishops. *Called to Global Solidarity: International Challenges for U.S. Parishes.* Washington, D.C.: United States Catholic Conference, 1997.

Neary, Timothy B. "Black-Belt Catholic Space: African-American Parishes in Interwar Chicago." *U.S. Catholic Historian* 18 (Fall 2000): 76–91.

Nebel, Richard. *Santa María Tonantzín Virgen de Guadalupe: Continuidad y transformación religiosa en Mexico.* Mexico City: Fondo de Cultura Económica, 1992.

Nirenberg, David. *Communities of Violence: Persecution of Minorities in the Middle Ages.* Princeton, N.J.: Princeton University Press, 1996.

———. "Conversion, Sex, and Segregation: Jews and Christians in Medieval Spain." *American Historical Review* 107 (October 2002): 1065–1093.

O'Brien, David. *Public Catholicism.* New York: Macmillan, 1989.

O'Connor, John Cardinal, and Edward I. Koch. *His Eminence and Hizzoner: A Candid Exchange.* New York: William Morrow, 1989.

Odem, Mary E. "Our Lady of Guadalupe in the New South: Latino Immigrants and the Politics of Integration in the Catholic Church." *Journal of American Ethnic History* 24 (Fall 2004): 26–57.

Orsi, Robert A. "Introduction: Crossing the City Line." In *Gods of the City: Religion and the American Urban Landscape.* Edited by Robert A. Orsi. Bloomington: Indiana University Press, 1999.

———. *The Madonna on 115th Street: Faith and Community in Italian Harlem, 1880–1950.* New Haven, Conn.: Yale University Press, 1985.

———. "The Religious Boundaries of an In-Between People: Street *Feste* and the Problem of the Dark-Skinned Other in Italian Harlem, 1920–1990." *American Quarterly* 44 (September 1992): 313–347.

———. *Thank You, St. Jude: Women's Devotion to the Patron Saint of Hopeless Causes.* New Haven, Conn.: Yale University Press, 1996.

Palmer, Susan L. "Building Ethnic Communities in a Small City: Romanians and Mexicans in Aurora, Illinois, 1900–1940." Ph.D. dissertation, Northern Illinois University, 1986.

Pantoja, Segundo S. "Religious Diversity and Ethnicity among Latinos." In *New York Glory: Religions in the City.* Edited by Tony Carnes and Anna Karpathakis. New York: New York University Press, 2001.

Paral, Rob. "Suburban Immigrant Characteristics: Assessments of Key Characteristics and Needs." Chicago: Fund for Immigrants and Refugees, 2000.

Pedraza, Silvia. "Pope John Paul II's Visit and the Process of Democratic Transition in Cuba." In *Papal Overtures in a Cuban Key: The Pope's Visit and Civic Space for Cuban Religion.* Edited by Anthony M. Stevens-Arroyo. Scranton, Pa.: University of Scranton Press, 2003.

Pedraza, Teresita. "'This Too Shall Pass': The Resistance and Endurance of Religion in Cuba." *Cuban Studies* 28 (1998): 16–39.

Perez, Arturo J. *Popular Catholicism: A Hispanic Perspective.* Washington, D.C.: Pastoral, 1988.

———. "The History of Hispanic Liturgy since 1965." In *Hispanic Catholic Culture in the U.S.: Issues and Concerns.* Edited by Jay P. Dolan and Allan Figueroa Deck. Notre Dame, Ind.: University of Notre Dame Press, 1994.

Perez, Gina M. "The Near Northwest Side Story: Gender, Migration, and Everyday Life in Chicago and San Sebastian, Puerto Rico." Ph.D. dissertation, Northwestern University, 2000.

Perez, Lisandro. "Cuban Catholics in the United States." In *Puerto Rican and Cuban Catholics in the U.S., 1900–1965.* Edited by Jay P. Dolan and Jaime R. Vidal. Notre Dame, Ind.: University of Notre Dame Press, 1994.

Perez Firmat, Gustavo. *Life on the Hyphen: The Cuban-American Way.* Austin: University of Texas Press, 1994.

———. *Next Year in Cuba: A Cubano's Coming-of-Age in America.* New York: Anchor Books, 1995.

Perez Vilariño, Jose, and Jose L. Sequeiros Tizon. "The Demographic Transition of the Catholic Priesthood and the End of Clericalism in Spain." *Sociology of Religion* 59 (Spring 1998): 25–35.

Perez y Mena, Andres I. *Speaking with the Dead: Development of Afro-Latin Religion among Puerto Ricans in the United States.* New York: AMS Press, 1991.

Peterson, Anna L., and Manuel A. Vasquez. "The New Evangelization in Latin American Perspective." *Cross Currents* 48 (Fall 1998): 311–329.

———. "'Upwards, Never Down': The Catholic Charismatic Renewal in Transnational Perspective." In *Christianity, Social Change, and Globalization in the Americas.* Edited by Anna L. Peterson, Manuel A. Vasquez, and Philip Williams. New Brunswick, N.J.: Rutgers University Press, 2001.

Peterson, Anna L., Manuel A.Vasquez, and Philip Williams. "The Global and the Local." In *Christianity, Social Change, and Globalization in the Americas.* Edited by Anna L. Peterson, Manuel A. Vasquez, and Philip Williams. New Brunswick, N.J.: Rutgers University Press, 2001.

———. "Introduction: Christianity and Social Change in the Shadow of Globalization." In *Christianity, Social Change, and Globalization in the Americas.* Edited by Anna L. Peterson, Manuel A. Vasquez, and Philip Williams. New Brunswick, N.J.: Rutgers University Press, 2001).

Philpott, Thomas L. *The Slum and the Ghetto: Neighborhood Deterioration and Middle-Class Reform, Chicago, 1880–1930.* New York: Oxford University Press, 1978.

Picó, Fernando. *Libertad y servidumbre en el Puerto Rico del siglo XIX: Los jornaleros utuadeños en vísperas del auge del café.* Río Piedras, P.R.: Ediciones Huracán, 1979.

Pike, Ruth. *Linajudos and Conversos in Seville: Greed and Prejudice in Sixteenth and Seventeenth Century Spain.* New York: Peter Lang, 2000.

Poole, Stafford. "Iberian Catholicism Comes to the Americas." In *Christianity Comes to the Americas, 1492–1776.* Edited by Charles H. Lippy, Robert Choquette, and Stafford Poole. New York: Paragon House, 1992.

———. *Our Lady of Guadalupe: The Origins and Sources of a Mexican National Symbol, 1531–1797.* Tucson: University of Arizona Press, 1996.

———. "The Woman of the Apocalypse." In *The Church in Colonial Latin America.* Edited by John F. Schwaller. Wilmington, Del.: Scholarly Resources, 2000.

Portes, Alejandro, and Alex Stepick. *City on the Edge: The Transformation of Miami.* Berkeley: University of California Press, 1993.

Portes Gil, Emilio. *The Conflict between the Civil Power and the Clergy.* Mexico City: n.p., 1934.

Powell, Philip W. *Tree of Hate: Propaganda and Prejudices Affecting United States Relations with the Hispanic World.* New York: Basic Books, 1971.

Poyo, Gerald E. "The Cuban Experience in the United States, 1865–1940: Migration, Community, and Identity." *Cuban Studies* 21 (1991): 19–36.

———. "Immigrants and Integration in Late Eighteenth-Century Bexar." In *Tejano Origins in Eighteenth-Century San Antonio.* Edited by Gerald E. Poyo and Gilberto M. Hinojosa. Austin: University of Texas Press, 1991.

————. "Integration without Assimilation: Cuban Catholics in Miami, 1960–1980." *U.S. Catholic Historian* 20 (Fall 2002): 91–109.

————. *"With All, and for the Good of All": The Emergence of Popular Nationalism in the Cuban Communities of the United States, 1848–1898.* Durham, N.C.: Duke University Press, 1989.

Privett, Steven A. *The U.S. Catholic Church and Its Hispanic Members: The Pastoral Vision of Archbishop Robert E. Lucey.* San Antonio, Tex.: Trinity University Press, 1988.

Puerto Rico Bureau of Labor. *Report on the Housing Conditions of Laborers in Porto Rico.* San Juan, P.R.: Bureau of Supplies, Printing, and Transportation, 1914.

Puerto Rico Reconstruction Administration. *Census of Puerto Rico: 1935; Population and Agriculture.* Washington, D.C.: Government Printing Office, 1938.

Pulido, Alberto L. "Sacred Expressions of the Popular: An Examination of los Hermanos Penitentes of New Mexico and los Hermanos Cheos of Puerto Rico." *Centro: Journal of the Center for Puerto Rican Studies* 11 (Spring 2000): 56–69.

Quezada, Juan A. "Father Carmelo Tranchese, S.J.: A Pioneer Social Worker in San Antonio, Texas, 1932–1953." Master's thesis, St. Mary's University, 1972.

Quirk, Robert E. *The Mexican Revolution and the Catholic Church, 1910–1929.* Bloomington: Indiana University Press, 1973.

Ralph, James R., Jr. *Northern Protest: Martin Luther King Jr., Chicago, and the Civil Rights Movement.* Cambridge, Mass.: Harvard University Press, 1993.

Ramirez, Daniel. "Borderlands Praxis: The Immigrant Experience in Latino Pentecostal Churches," *Journal of the American Academy of Religion* 67 (September 1999): 573-596.

Ramirez, Ricardo. "The Hispanic Peoples of the United States and the Church from 1965 to 1985." *U.S. Catholic Historian* 9 (Spring 1990): 165–177.

Ramirez Calzadilla, Jorge. "Religion in the Work of Fernando Ortiz." In *Cuban Counterpoints: The Legacy of Fernando Ortiz.* Edited by Mauricio A. Font and Alfonso W. Quiroz. Lanham, Md.: Lexington Books, 2005.

Ramos Mattei, Andrés A. *Betances en el Ciclo Revolucionario Antillano, 1867–1875.* San Juan, P.R.: Instituto de Cultura Puertorriqueña, 1987.

Reich, Julie M., Michael A. Stegman, and Nancy W. Stegman. *Relocating the Dispossessed Elderly: A Study of Mexican-Americans.* Philadelphia: University of Pennsylvania Institute for Environmental Studies, 1966.

Reich, Peter L. *Mexico's Hidden Revolution: The Catholic Church in Law and Politics since 1929.* Notre Dame, Ind.: University of Notre Dame Press, 1995.

Reilly, Bernard F. *The Contest of Christian and Muslim Spain, 1031–1157.* Cambridge, Mass.: Blackwell, 1992.

Reps, John W. *Cities of the American West: A History of Frontier Urban Planning.* Princeton, N.J.: Princeton University Press, 1979.

————. *The Forgotten Frontier: Urban Planning in the American West before 1890.* Columbia: University of Missouri Press,1981.

Reuter, Frank T. *Catholic Influence on American Colonial Policies, 1898–1904.* Austin: University of Texas, 1967.

Ribero-Ortega, Pedro. "La Guadalupana and la Conquistadora in the Catholic History of New Mexico." In *Seeds of Struggle / Harvest of Faith: The History of the Catholic Church in New Mexico*. Edited by Thomas J. Steele, Paul Rhetts, and Barbe Awalt. Albuquerque: LPD Press, 1998.

Ricard, Robert. *The Spiritual Conquest of Mexico: An Essay on the Apostolate and the Evangelizing Methods of the Mendicant Orders in New Spain, 1523–1572*. French original 1933. Berkeley: University of California Press, 1966.

Ricourt, Milagros, and Ruby Danta. *Hispanas de Queens: Latino Panethnicity in a New York City Neighborhood*. Ithaca, N.Y.: Cornell University Press, 2003.

Rieff, David. *The Exile: Cuba in the Heart of Miami*. New York: Simon and Schuster, 1993.

Rivera, Luis N. *A Violent Evangelism: The Political and Religious Conquest of the Americas*. Louisville, Ky.: Westminster John Knox, 1992.

Rivera-Batiz, Francisco, and Carlos Santiago. *Puerto Ricans in the United States: A Changing Reality*. Washington, D.C.: National Puerto Rican Coalition, 1994.

Rivera-Pagan, Luis N. "Formation of a Hispanic Theology." In *Hidden Stories: Unveiling the History of the Latino Church*. Edited by Daniel R. Rodriguez-Diaz and David Cortes-Fuentes. Decatur, Ga.: Asociación para la Educación Teológica Hispana, 1994.

Rodriguez, Clara E. *Puerto Ricans: Born in the U.S.A.* Boulder, Colo.: Westview, 1991.

Rogler, Charles C. *Comerio: A Study of a Puerto Rican Town*. Lawrence: University of Kansas, 1940.

Roman, Richard. "Church-State Relations and the Mexican Constitutional Congress, 1916–1917." *Journal of Church and State* 20 (Winter 1978): 73–80.

Romero, Juan. "Charism and Power: An Essay on the History of PADRES." *U.S. Catholic Historian* 9 (Spring 1990): 147–163.

———. *Reluctant Dawn: Historia del Padre A. J. Martinez, Cura de Taos*. San Antonio: Mexican American Cultural Center, 1976.

Rooney, Jim. *Organizing the South Bronx*. Albany: State University of New York Press, 1995.

Rybolt, John E. "Parish Apostolate: New Opportunities in the Local Church." In *The American Vincentians: A Popular History of the Congregation of the Mission in the United States*. Edited by John E. Rybolt. Brooklyn, N.Y.: New City, 1988.

Salisbury, Joyce E. *Iberian Popular Religion, 600 B.C. to 700 A.D.* New York: Edwin Mellen, 1985.

Sanchez, Jose M. *Anticlericalism: A Brief History*. Notre Dame, Ind.: University of Notre Dame Press, 1972.

———. *The Spanish Civil War as a Religious Tragedy*. Notre Dame, Ind.: University of Notre Dame Press, 1987.

Sanchez Korrol, Virginia. *From Colonia to Community: The History of the Puerto Ricans in New York City, 1917–1948*. Berkeley: University of California Press, 1983.

Sandoval, Moises. "The Church and el Movimiento." In *Fronteras: A History of the Latin American Church in the USA since 1513*. Edited by Moises Sandoval. San Antonio, Tex.: Mexican American Cultural Center, 1983.

———. *On the Move: A History of the Hispanic Church in the United States*. Maryknoll, N.Y.: Orbis Books., 1990.

Sanneh, Lamin. "Conclusion: The Current Transformation of Christianity." In *The Changing Face of Christianity: Africa, the West, and the World*. Edited by Lamin Sanneh and Joel A. Carpenter. New York: Oxford University Press, 2005.

———. *Encountering the West: Christianity and Global Cultural Process—The African Dimension*. Maryknoll, N.Y.: Orbis Books, 1993.

———. *Translating the Message: The Missionary Impact on Culture*. Maryknoll, N.Y.: Orbis Books, 1997.

———. *West African Christianity: The Religious Impact*. Maryknoll, N.Y.: Orbis Books, 1983.

Santaella Rivera, Estéban. *Historia de los hermanos cheos: Recopilación de escritos y relatos*. Santo Domingo, D.R.: Editora Alfa y Omega, 1979.

Schiller, Nina Glick. "Transmigrants and Nation-States: Something Old and Something New in the U.S. Immigrant Experience." In *The Handbook of International Migration: The American Experience*. Edited by Charles Hirschman, Philip Kasinitz, and Josh DeWind. New York: Russell Sage Foundation, 1999.

Schiller, Nina Glick, Linda Basch, and Cristina Blanc-Szanton. "Transnationalism: A New Analytic Framework for Understanding Migration." In *Towards a Transnational Perspective on Migration: Race, Class, Ethnicity, and Nationalism Reconsidered*. Edited by Nina Glick Schiller, Linda Basch, and Cristina Blanc-Szanton. *Annals of the New York Academy of Sciences* 645 (July 1992).

Schiller, Nina Glick, and Georges Eugene Fouron. *Georges Woke Up Laughing: Long-Distance Nationalism and the Search for Home*. Durham, N.C.: Duke University Press, 2001.

Schlarman, Joseph H. *Mexico, a Land of Volcanoes: From Cortes to Aleman*. Milwaukee: Bruce, 1950.

Schwartz, Joel. *The New York Approach: Robert Moses, Urban Liberals, and Redevelopment of the Inner City*. Columbus: Ohio State University Press, 1993.

Schwartz, Stuart B. "The Hurricane of San Ciriaco: Disaster, Politics, and Society in Puerto Rico, 1899–1901." *Hispanic American Historical Review* 72 (1992): 303–334.

Sciorra, Joseph. "'We Go Where the Italians Live': Religious Processions as Ethnic and Territorial Markers in a Multi-ethnic Brooklyn Neighborhood." In *Gods of the City: Religion and the American Urban Landscape*. Edited by Robert A. Orsi. Bloomington: Indiana University Press, 1999.

Seda Bonilla, Eduardo. *Los derechos civiles en la cultura puertorriqueña*. Río Piedras, P.R.: Editorial Universitaria, 1963.

Sedaño, Alicia Olivera. *Aspectos del conflicto religioso de 1926 a 1929: Sus antecedentes y consecuencias*. Mexico City: Instituto Nacional de Antropología e Historia, 1966.

Segre, Roberto, Mario Coyula, and Joseph L. Scarpaci. *Havana: Two Faces of the Antillean Metropolis.* New York: John Wiley and Sons, 1997.

Sexton, Patricia C. *Spanish Harlem: An Anatomy of Poverty.* New York: Harper and Row, 1965.

Shapiro, Harold A. "The Pecan Shellers of San Antonio, Texas." *Southwestern Social Science Quarterly* 32 (March 1952): 229–244.

Shea, John G. *History of the Catholic Church in the United States,* vol. 3. New York: John G. Shea, 1890.

Sheerin, John B. "American Catholics and Ecumenism." In *Contemporary Catholicism in the United States.* Edited by Philip Gleason. Notre Dame, Ind.: University of Notre Dame Press, 1969.

Silva Gotay, Samuel. "Historia social de las iglesias en Puerto Rico." In *Historia general de la iglesia en América Latina,* vol. 4, *Caribe.* Edited by Enrique D. Dussel. Salamanca: Comisión para el Estudio de Historia de la Iglesia en América Latina y el Caribe, 1983.

———. "The Ideological Dimensions of Popular Religiosity and Cultural Identity in Puerto Rico." In *An Enduring Flame: Studies on Latino Popular Religiosity.* Edited by Anthony M. Stevens-Arroyo and Ana Maria Diaz-Stevens. New York: Bildner Center for Western Hemisphere Studies, 1994.

Simons, Helen, and Cathryn A. Hoyt. *Hispanic Texas: A Historical Guide.* Austin: University of Texas Press, 1992.

Skerrett, Ellen. "The Irish Parish in Chicago, 1880–1930." Notre Dame Working Paper Series 9, no. 2 (Spring 1981).

Skerry, Peter. *Mexican Americans: The Ambivalent Minority.* New York: Free Press, 1993.

Smith, Brian H. *Religious Politics in Latin America: Pentecostal vs. Catholic.* Notre Dame, Ind.: University of Notre Dame Press, 1998.

Smith, Robert C. "'Los Ausentes Siempre Presentes': The Imagining, Making, and Politics of a Transnational Community between Ticuani, Puebla, Mexico, and New York City." Ph.D. dissertation, Columbia University, 1995.

———. "Mexicans in New York: Memberships and Incorporation in a New Immigrant Community." In *Latinos in New York: Communities in Transition.* Edited by Gabriel Haslip-Viera and Sherrie L. Baver. Notre Dame, Ind.: University of Notre Dame Press, 1996.

———. "Transnational Localities: Community, Technology, and the Politics of Membership within the Context of Mexico and U.S. Migration." In *Transnationalism from Below.* Edited by Michael P. Smith and Luis Eduardo Guarnizo. New Brunswick, N.J.: Transaction, 1998.

Soja, Edward. *Postmetropolis: Critical Studies of Cities and Regions.* Oxford: Blackwell, 2000.

Solis, Jocelyn. "Immigration Status and Identity: Undocumented Mexicans in New York." In *Mambo Montage: The Latinization of New York.* Edited by Lao-Agustin Montes and Arlene Davila. New York: Columbia University Press, 2001.

Sommers, Laurie Kay. "Inventing Latinismo: The Creation of 'Hispanic' Panethnicity in the United States." *Journal of American Folklore* 104 (1991): 32–53.

―――. "Musical Traditions of Miami's New Managua." In "Nicaraguan Folklife in Miami." Edited by Brent Cantrell. Occasional Papers 2, Historical Association of Southern Florida. Miami: Historical Museum of Southern Florida Folklife Program, 1993.

Stepick, Alex, and Carol Dutton Stepick. "Power and Identity: Miami Cubans." In *Latinos: Remaking America*. Edited by Marcelo M. Suarez-Orozco and Mariela M. Paez. Berkeley: University of California Press, 2002.

Stevens-Arroyo, Anthony M. "The Catholic Ethos as Politics: The Puerto Rican Nationalists." In *Twentieth-Century World Religious Movements in Neo-Weberian Perspective*. Edited by William H. Swatos Jr. Lewiston, N.Y.: Edwin Mellen, 1992.

―――. "Catholicism as Civilization: Contemporary Reflections on the Political Philosophy of Pedro Albizu Campos." Working Paper 50, Inter American University of Puerto Rico, 1992.

―――. "The Emergence of a Social Identity among Latino Catholics: An Appraisal." In *Hispanic Catholic Culture in the U.S.: Issues and Concerns*. Edited by Jay P. Dolan and Allan Figueroa Deck. Notre Dame, Ind.: University of Notre Dame Press, 1994.

―――. "The Evolution of Marian Devotionalism within Christianity and the Ibero-Mediterrean Polity." *Journal for the Scientific Study of Religion* 37 (March 1998): 50–73.

―――. "The Inter-Atlantic Paradigm: The Failure of Spanish Medieval Colonization of the Canary and Caribbean Islands." *Comparative Studies in Society and History* 35 (July 1993): 515–543.

―――. "Introduction." In *An Enduring Flame: Studies on Latino Popular Religiosity*. Edited by Anthony M. Stevens-Arroyo and Ana Maria Diaz-Stevens. New York: Bildner Center for Western Hemisphere Studies, 1994.

―――. "Jaime Balmes Redux: Catholicism as Civilization in the Political Philosophy of Pedro Albizu Campos." In *Bridging the Atlantic: Toward a Reassessment of Iberian and Latin American Cultural Ties*. Edited by Marina Perez de Mendiola. Albany: State University of New York Press, 1996.

―――, ed. *Papal Overtures in a Cuban Key: The Pope's Visit and Civic Space for Cuban Religion*. Scranton, Pa.: University of Scranton Press, 2003.

―――, ed. *Prophets Denied Honor: An Anthology of the Hispanic Church in the United States*. Maryknoll, N.Y.: Orbis Books, 1980.

Stevens-Arroyo, Anthony M., and Ana Maria Diaz-Stevens. "Religious Faith and Institutions in the Forging of Latino Identities." In *Handbook of Hispanic Cultures in the United States*, vol. 4. Edited by Felix M. Padilla. Houston: Arte Público, 1994.

Steward, Julian, et al. *The People of Puerto Rico*. Urbana: University of Illinois Press, 1956.

Stewart, Kenneth L., and Arnoldo De Leon. *Not Room Enough: Mexicans, Anglos, and Socio- economic Change in Texas, 1850–1900*. Albuquerque: University of New Mexico Press, 1993.

Straughan, Jerome, and Pierrette Hondagneu-Sotelo. "From Immigrants in the City to Immigrant City." In *From Chicago to L.A.: Making Sense of Urban Theory*. Edited by Michael J. Dear. Thousand Oaks, Calif.: Sage, 2002.

Strong, Miriam. "Refugees from Castro's Cuba—Of Fish and Freedom: An Historical Account of the Cuban Refugees Received and Relieved by His Excellency, Bishop Coleman F. Carroll, In the Catholic Diocese of Miami, Florida, 1959 to 1964." Master's thesis, Fordham University School of Social Service, 1964.

Sullivan, Kathleen. "St. Catherine's Catholic Church: One Church, Parallel Congregations." In *Religion and the New Immigrants: Continuities and Adaptations in Immigrant Congregations*. Edited by Helen R. Ebaugh and Janet S. Chafetz. Walnut Creek, Calif.: Altamira, 2000.

Suro, Robert, and Audrey Singer. "Changing Patterns of Latino Growth in Metropolitan America." In *Redefining Urban and Suburban America: Evidence from Census 2000*. Edited by Bruce Katz and Robert E. Lang. Washington, D.C.: Brookings Institution Press, 2003.

Sweetser, Thomas P., and Carol W. Holden. *Leadership in a Successful Parish*. San Francisco: Harper and Row, 1987.

Sylvest, Edwin E., Jr. *Nuestra Señora de Guadalupe: Mother of God, Mother of the Americas*. Dallas: Bridwell Library, Southern Methodist University, 1992.

Tabares, Fanny. "Pastoral Care of Catholic South Americans Living in the United States." In *Bridging Boundaries: The Pastoral Care of U.S. Hispanics*. Edited by Kenneth G. Davis and Yolanda Tarango. Scranton, Pa.: University of Scranton Press, 1999.

Taylor, Paul S. *A Spanish-Mexican Peasant Community: Arandas in Jalisco, Mexico*. Berkeley: University of California Press, 1933.

Thumma, Scott. "Exploring the Megachurch Phenomena: Their Characteristics and Cultural Context." Available at http://hirr.hartsem.edu/bookshelf/thumma_article2.html (Hartford Seminary).

Tijerina, Andres. *Tejano Empire: Life on the South Texas Ranchos*. College Station: Texas A&M University Press, 1998.

Tomasi, Silvano M. "The Pastoral Care of Newcomers Today: Practices and Models of the Catholic Church in the United States." In *Today's Immigrants and Refugees: A Christian Understanding*. Edited by Office of Pastoral Care of Migrants and Refugees, Bishops' Committee on Migration, National Conference of Catholic Bishops. Washington, D.C.: United States Catholic Conference, 1988.

Toynbee, Arnold. *An Historian's Approach to Religion*. London: Oxford University Press, 1956.

Trias Monge, Jose. *Puerto Rico: The Trials of the Oldest Colony in the World*. New Haven, Conn.: Yale University Press, 1997.

Triay, Victor A. *Fleeing Castro: Operation Pedro Pan and the Cuban Children's Program*. Gainesville: University Press of Florida, 1998.

Trumino, Joseph A. "The Northwest Bronx Community and Clergy Coalition: A Neighborhood Organization and Its Membership in Conflict and Struggle." Ph.D. dissertation, City University of New York, 1991.

Turner, Victor. *Dramas, Fields, and Metaphors: Symbolic Action in Human Society*. Ithaca, N.Y.: Cornell University Press, 1974.

Turner, Victor, and Edith Turner. *Image and Pilgrimage in Christian Culture: Anthropological Perspectives*. New York: Columbia University Press, 1978.

Tweed, Thomas A. "Diasporic Nationalism and Urban Landscape: Cuban Immigrants at a Catholic Shrine in Miami." In *Gods of the City: Religion and the American Urban Landscape*. Edited by Robert A. Orsi. Bloomington: Indiana University Press, 1999.

———. *Our Lady of the Exile: Diasporic Religion at a Cuban Catholic Shrine in Miami*. New York: Oxford University Press, 1997.

Ultan, Lloyd, and Gary Hermalyn. *The Bronx: It Was Only Yesterday, 1935–1965*. Bronx, N.Y.: Bronx County Historical Society, 1992.

Ultan, Lloyd, and Barbara Unger. *Bronx Accent: A Literary and Pictorial History of the Borough*. New Brunswick, N.J.: Rutgers University Press, 2000.

University of Miami. *The Cuban Immigration, 1959–1966, and Its Impact on Miami-Dade County, Florida*. Coral Gables, Fla.: Research Institute for Cuba and the Caribbean, University of Miami, 1967.

Valdes, Dionicio N. *Barrios Norteños: St. Paul and Midwestern Mexican Communities in the Twentieth Century*. Austin: University of Texas Press, 2000.

Valls, Jorge. *Forty Years and Twenty Days*. New York: Americas Watch Committee, 1986.

Vargas, Zaragosa. "Tejana Radical: Emma Tenayuca and the San Antonio Labor Movement during the Great Depression." *Pacific Historical Review* 66 (November 1997): 553–580.

Vasquez, Manuel A. "Central and South American Religious Communities." In *Religion and American Cultures: An Encyclopedia of Traditions, Diversity, and Popular Expressions*, vol. 1. Edited by Gary Laderman and Luis Leon. Santa Barbara, Calif.: ABC CLIO, 2003.

Vasquez, Manuel A., and Marie Friedmann Marquardt. *Globalizing the Sacred: Religion across the Americas*. New Brunswick, N.J.: Rutgers University Press, 2003.

Vazquez, Victor. "The Development of Pan-Latino Philadelphia, 1892–1945." *Pennsylvania Magazine of History and Biography* 128 (October 2004): 367–384.

Vecoli, Rudolph J. "Prelates and Peasants: Italian Immigrants and the Catholic Church." *Journal of Social History* 2 (Spring 1969): 217–268.

Vecsey, Christopher. "Pueblo Indian Catholicism: The Isleta Case." Cushwa Center for the Study of American Catholicism (Notre Dame, Ind.), Working Paper Series 28, Fall 1996.

Veliz, Claudio. *The Centralist Tradition of Latin America.* Princeton, N.J.: Princeton University Press, 1980.

Vidal, Jaime R. "Citizens Yet Strangers: The Puerto Rican Experience." In *Puerto Rican and Cuban Catholics in the U.S., 1900–1965.* Edited by Jay P. Dolan and Jaime R. Vidal. Notre Dame, Ind.: University of Notre Dame Press, 1994.

———. "Popular Religion among the Hispanics in the General Area of Newark." In *Presencia Nueva, Knowledge for Service and Hope: A Study of Hispanics in the Archdiocese of Newark.* Edited by the Archdiocese of Newark. Newark, N.J.: Archdiocese of Newark, 1988.

———. "Towards an Understanding of Synthesis in Iberian and Hispanic American Popular Religiosity." In *An Enduring Flame: Studies on Latino Popular Religiosity.* Edited by Anthony M. Stevens-Arroyo and Ana Maria Diaz-Stevens. New York: Bildner Center for Western Hemisphere Studies, 1994.

Villafañe, Eldin. *The Liberating Spirit: Toward an Hispanic American Pentecostal Social Ethic.* Lanham, Md.: University Press of America, 1992.

Vinca, Robert H. "The American Catholic Reaction to the Persecution of the Church in Mexico, 1926–1936" (1968). In *Modern American Catholicism, 1900–1965: Selected Historical Essays.* Edited by Edward R. Kantowicz. New York: Garland, 1988.

Wakefield, Dan. *Island in the City: The World of Spanish Harlem.* Boston: Houghton Mifflin, 1959.

Walsh, Bryan O. "Cuban Refugee Children." *Journal of Inter-American Studies and World Affairs* 13 (July-October 1971): 378–415.

———. "Religion in the Cuban Diaspora: A Critical Profile." Paper delivered at the 2000 meeting of the Latin American Studies Association, Miami (March).

Ware, Caroline F. *Greenwich Village, 1920–1930: A Comment on American Civilization in the Post-war Years.* Boston: Houghton Mifflin, 1935.

Warner, R. Stephen. "Approaching Religious Diversity: Barriers, Byways, and Beginnings." *Sociology of Religion* 59 (Fall 1998): 193–215.

———. "Convergence toward the New Paradigm: A Case of Induction." In *Rational Choice Theory and Religion: Summary and Assessment.* Edited by Lawrence A. Young. New York: Routledge, 1997.

———. "Immigration and Religious Communities in the United States." In *Gatherings in Diaspora: Religious Communities and the New Immigration.* Edited by R. Stephen Warner and Judith G. Wittner. Philadelphia: Temple University Press, 1998.

———. "The Place of the Congregation in the Contemporary American Religious Configuration." In *American Congregations,* vol. 2, *New Perspectives in the Study of Congregations.* Edited by James P. Wind and James W. Lewis. Chicago: University of Chicago Press, 1994.

———. "Work in Progress toward a New Paradigm for the Sociological Study of Religion in the United States." *American Journal of Sociology* 98 (March 1993): 1044–1093.

Warren, Richard A. "Displaced 'Pan-Americans' and the Transformation of the Catholic Church in Philadelphia, 1789–1850." *Pennsylvania Magazine of History and Biography* 128 (October 2004): 343–366.

Weber, David J. *The Mexican Frontier, 1821–1846: The American Southwest under Mexico.* Albuquerque: University of New Mexico Press, 1982.

———. *The Spanish Frontier in North America.* New Haven, Conn.: Yale University Press, 1992.

Wellmeier, Nancy J. "Santa Eulalia's People in Exile: Maya Religion, Culture, and Identity in Los Angeles." In *Gatherings in Diaspora: Religious Communities and the New Immigration.* Edited by R. Stephen Warner and Judith G. Wittner. Philadelphia: Temple University Press, 1998.

Williamson, Joel. *New People: Miscegenation and Mulattoes in the United States.* New York: New York University Press, 1984.

Wilson, Chris. *The Myth of Santa Fe: Creating a Modern Regional Tradition.* Albuquerque: University of New Mexico Press, 1997.

Wright, Pearl. "Religious *Fiestas* in San Antonio." Master's thesis, St. Mary's University, 1946.

Wright, Robert E. "The Hispanic Church in Texas under Spain and Mexico." *U.S. Catholic Historian* 20 (Fall 2002): 15–33.

———. "Local Church Emergence and Mission Decline: The Historiography of the Catholic Church in the Southwest during the Spanish and Mexican Periods." *U.S. Catholic Historian* 9 (Spring 1990): 27–48.

———. "Popular Religiosity: Review of Literature." *Liturgical Ministry* 7 (Summer 1998): 141–146.

Wuthnow, Robert. *Christianity in the Twenty-first Century: Reflections on the Challenges Ahead.* New York: Oxford University Press, 1993.

Yinger, Winthrop. *Cesar Chavez: The Rhetoric of Nonviolence.* Hicksville, N.Y.: Exposition, 1975.

Zamudio, Patricia. "Huejuquillense Immigrants in Chicago: Culture, Gender, and Community in the Shaping of Consciousness." Ph.D. dissertation, Northwestern University, 1999.

Zolberg, Aristide R., Astri Suhrke, and Sergio Aguayo. *Escape from Violence: Conflict and the Refugee Crisis in the Developing World.* New York: Oxford University Press, 1989.

Index

Puebla Conference of Latin American
  Bishops (1979), 184
Pueblo Indians, 8, 205
Pueblo Revolt, 8
Puerto Rican Day Parade, 166, 168
Puerto Rican nationalism, 58–59
Puerto Ricans (ethnics/migrants), xix, xxiii,
  114–15, 182, 196, 205, 207, 210; in
  Chicago, xxi, xxii, 62, 85–91, 130–31,
  151; in Miami, 99; in New York City,
  xx, xxii, 14, 52–65, 73, 76–83, 154–55,
  165–73, 179, 207
Puerto Rico, xiv, xxi, xxii, 3, 5, 13, 14, 17–21,
  26, 45–52, 53–56, 58–65, 73–76, 78, 79,
  81–83, 86, 93, 96, 100, 150, 195, 204

quinceañeras, xviii, 134, 144, 188, 204

Ramírez Calzadilla, Jorge, 93
Redemptorists, 34, 35, 41, 47–49, 51, 79,
  83, 88
religious orders, Catholic. *See* Augustinians;
  Capuchins; Claretians; Franciscans;
  Jesuits; Redemptorists; Scalabrinians;
  Vincentians
rezadoras, 188, 189
Ricourt, Milagros, 180
Rivera, Aurelia, 60–64
Rodriguez, Edmundo, 160, 163
Rodríguez Medina, José, 46
Román, Agustín, 104, 105, 112
Romero, Oscar, 180, 197
Rosas, Carlos, 162, 163
Ruiz, Ralph, 159
Ruiz y Flores, Leopoldo, 29, 32

Sacerdotes Hispanos, 159
Sacred Heart Church (Melrose Park), 142
St. Anthony of Padua Church (Cicero), 137
St. Augustine, Florida, 5, 203
St. Cecilia's Church (New York), 55, 79, 80
St. Charles Borromeo Church (Melrose
  Park), 143–46
St. Francis of Assisi Church (Chicago),
  122–24, 128
St. James, 1–2
St. Jude Thaddeus, 122–23
St. Mary of Celle Church (Berwyn), 137–41
St. Patrick's Cathedral, 80, 174, 178
St. Philip Neri Seminary, 28
Salvadorans (ethnics/immigrants), 179–80,
  196, 198, 200, 202

San Antonio, Texas, xi, xviii, xx, xxi, xxii,
  8–10, 25, 29, 30, 32–42, 66, 67–73, 147,
  155–64, 181; suburban Latino parishes
  in, 70–71; urban Latino parishes in, 13,
  25–27, 29–30, 33–34, 35–37, 38–40, 41,
  163–64, 205–6
San Antonio missions, 8–10, 12, 26, 33, 34,
  161, 205–6
Sánchez, Miguel, 3
Sanchez, Roberto, 159
Sanctuary movement, 168, 198
San Fernando Cathedral, 9, 13, 29, 30, 34,
  37, 38, 43, 71, 156, 181, 206
San Fernando de Béjar, 9
San Francisco, California, Latinos in, 199
San Juan, Puerto Rico, 5, 17, 18, 47, 49, 50,
  52, 53, 61, 63–65, 73–74, 151, 184
San Juan de los Lagos (shrine), 188–89
San Lázaro, 16, 98
San Luis Potosí, immigrants from, living in
  Chicago, 124–33
Sanneh, Lamin, 183
Santa Bárbara, 16, 98
Santa Cruz de Tlaltelolco, College of, 3
Santa Fe, 8, 69, 75, 159, 203
Santería, 110, 112
Santiago de Compostela, 2
Santo Domingo, 5, 53, 174
santos de palo, xiv, 51
Sardiñas, Guillermo, 94
Scalabrini, John Baptiste, 141
Scalabrinians, 141–47
secularism, xvi, 67, 183
secularization (Spanish missions), 7, 9
Seminario San Carlos y San Ambosio, 17
Seville, 203
Shaw, John William, 26, 33, 55
Smith, Sherrill, 72, 73
social justice, Latinos and. *See* church move-
  ments; liberation theology
Somoza, Anastasio, 116, 196
Southeast Bronx Community Organization,
  171
South East Pastoral Institute, 115, 162
Southern Messenger (San Antonio), 29
Spain, xii, xiii, xviii, xx, 1–2, 4–7, 11, 14, 17,
  19, 20, 32, 43–44, 45, 53, 55, 59, 77, 99,
  183, 185
Spaniards (ethnics/immigrants), 54–55,
  57–58, 83
Spanish Civil War, 44, 59
Spanish Jews, 1, 4